D1468716

BIBLICAL AUTHORITY FOR TODAY

BIBLICAL AUTHORITY FOR TODAY

A WORLD COUNCIL OF CHURCHES SYMPOSIUM ON 'THE BIBLICAL AUTHORITY FOR THE CHURCHES' SOCIAL AND POLITICAL MESSAGE TODAY'

edited by

ALAN RICHARDSON, D.D.
Canon of Durham

W. SCHWEITZER, DR. THEOL.
Secretary in the Study Department,
World Council of Churches, Geneva

PHILADELPHIA
WESTMINSTER PRESS

First published 1951 *in Great Britain*
by SCM Press Ltd

Printed in Great Britain

CONTENTS

FOREWORD: Our Common Starting Point 7

PREFACE 9

Part One

THE AUTHORITY OF THE BIBLE

FUNDAMENTAL CONSIDERATIONS

1 Greek Orthodox *by Panayotis I. Bratsiotis, D.D., Professor of Theology, University of Athens, Greece.* 17

2 Methodist *by Clarence T. Craig, Ph.D., D.D., Dean of the Drew Theological Seminary, Drew University, Madison, N.J., U.S.A.* 30

3 Congregationalist *by Hubert Cunliffe-Jones, B.D., B.Litt., Principal of the Yorkshire United Independent College, Bradford, Great Britain.* 45

4 Baptist *by Vinjamuri E. Devadutt, M.A., B.D., Ph.D., Dean of Theology, Professor of Philosophy and History, Serampore College, Serampore, India.* 59

5 Reformed *by Barnabas Nagy, Dr. Theol., Professor of Theology, Theological Faculty, Sarospatak, Hungary.* 82

6 Lutheran *by Regin Prenter, Dr. Theol., Professor of Dogmatic Theology, University of Aarhus, Denmark.* 98

7 Anglican *by Alan Richardson, D.D., Canon of Durham, Great Britain.* 112

Part Two

BIBLICAL THEOLOGY AND ETHICS TODAY

A SURVEY OF THE WORLD POSITION

by Wolfgang Schweitzer, Dr. Theol., Secretary in the Study Department, World Council of Churches, Geneva, Switzerland. 127

Part Three

PRINCIPLES OF INTERPRETATION

1 *by C. Harold Dodd, D.D., Professor Emeritus in the University of Cambridge, Great Britain.* 157

2 *by Georges Florovsky, D.D., Professor of Systematic Theology, St. Vladimir's Orthodox Theological Seminary and Academy, New York, U.S.A.* 163

3 *by John Marsh, M.A., D.Phil., Professor of Theology, University of Nottingham, Great Britain.* 181

4 *by James Muilenburg, D.D., Professor of Theology, Union Theological Seminary, New York, U.S.A.* 198

5 *by G. Ernest Wright, D.D., Professor of Theology, McCormick Theological Seminary, Chicago, U.S.A.* 219

6 Guiding Principles for the Interpretation of the Bible, as accepted by the Ecumenical Study Conference at Wadham College, Oxford, 1949. 240

Part Four

SOME SPECIFIC APPLICATIONS

1 The Church's Responsibility for the World *by Hendrikus Berkhof, Dr. Theol., Director of the Seminar of the Dutch Reformed Church, Driebergen, The Netherlands.* 247

2 The Question of Property in the Light of the Old Testament *by Walther Eichrodt, D.D., Professor of Old Testament Theology, University of Basle, Switzerland.* 257

3 The Rule of Law *by Erik Wolf, D.D., Professor of Law, Freiburg i-B., Germany.* 275

4 Church and State in the Light of the New Testament *by Hans von Campenhausen, D.D., Professor of New Testament Theology and Church History, University of Heidelberg, Germany.* 293

5 Nation and Race *by Surjit Singh, Ph.D., Professor of Theology, Theological College, Saharanpur, India.* 310

6 Civilisation *by Stephen Neill, D.D., Bishop, Associate General Secretary of the World Council of Churches, Geneva, Switzerland.* 323

INDEXES 339

FOREWORD

OUR COMMON STARTING POINT

In this book we, as members of different Christian confessions and denominations, living in different parts of the world, have made an attempt to read and interpret Holy Scripture together. We could not have done so unless our common starting point had been the Bible, which bound us together even before we knew each other personally. In all our churches around the world, the Bible is read and its message proclaimed in preaching, in liturgy, in fellowship and in service: the message of man's salvation through Jesus Christ, our Lord.

It has always been the task of the Church to unfold the message of the Bible and to defend it against misinterpretations. This is, in fact, the root of all Christian theology. But at the same time it is the source of many divisions which exist among us. If we in the fellowship of the World Council of Churches are eager to draw nearer to one another, it is most natural that we should turn to the Bible which bears the testimony of the undivided Church of apostolic times. To look for guidance in the Word of God is, it seems to us, especially urgent in a time like ours when the Church has to face so many difficult questions in all realms of human life. Thus, we hope that our common approach to the Bible will not only bring us nearer to each other, but will also enable us to make a common witness to our faith, even in the social and political realm; it was this latter question on which we had been asked to concentrate our studies and to which we have tried to find a first tentative answer.

This book will demonstrate some of the differences which actually exist among us in our approach to the Bible and in our methods of interpreting it. We had no intention of concealing them. On the other hand, the 'Guiding Principles for the Interpretation of the Bible', which are printed on pp. 240ff., will give evidence of the degree of agreement which we have reached so far. We are aware of the tentative character of this document. Many points need still to be reconciled with one another. We hope that our symposium will be read as an invitation to study these problems further. It is not the end but rather the beginning of an ecumenical conversation and co-operation which, we hope and pray, will promote mutual understanding between Christians and a better common testimony in the world.

HENDRIKUS BERKHOF
PANAYOTIS J. BRATSIOTIS
HANS VON CAMPENHAUSEN
CLARENCE T. CRAIG
HUBERT CUNLIFFE-JONES
VINJAMURI E. DEVADUTT
C. HAROLD DODD
WALTHER EICHRODT
GEORGES FLOROVSKY
JOHN MARSH
JAMES MUILENBURG
BARNABAS NAGY
STEPHEN NEILL
REGIN PRENTER
ALAN RICHARDSON
WOLFGANG SCHWEITZER
SURJIT SINGH
ERIK WOLF
G. ERNEST WRIGHT

PREFACE

There can be no doubt that the Church today has to carry a great responsibility in public life. In an age of change and uncertainty, men outside the Church are searching in every quarter for some authoritative guidance in social and political matters: and Christian men, often those who themselves bear direct responsibility in social and political life, are asking the Church's scholars and leaders to tell them what guidance the Church can give them in the pressing problems of their everyday lives. Do the Churches possess any answers to their concrete questions? Above all, can they see their way more clearly towards the giving of an *agreed* answer—one which would not be at once contradicted by one or more of the great Christian traditions or of the dominating schools of thought within Christendom? Until the Churches can speak with something more like a united voice, men will not listen very seriously to what they say.

These are some of the questions for which the World Council of Churches tries to find adequate answers which are acceptable to all the Churches which are members of this fellowship. At the Amsterdam Assembly in 1948, Sections III and IV dealt with the problem of the present 'Disorder in Society' and with the 'International Disorder';[1] similar problems will doubtless continually be on the agenda of any World Council Assembly or other ecumenical gathering.

If the Churches desire to speak to these problems with one voice, the question is inevitably raised: What is the legitimate source of our common testimony in the world? And it is this question which has led the World Council to request its Study Department to launch an ecumenical enquiry on 'The Bible and the Church's Message to the World'. The present volume is the first major tangible result of the studies which have been

[1] See: *The Church and the Disorder of Society* and *The Church and the International Disorder* (both London, S.C.M. Press, 1948).

undertaken in this field. Like the study volumes which have been prepared for the Amsterdam Assembly, 1948, this volume shows that it is not the task of the Study Department to undertake the Churches' thinking for them (which, in fact, it cannot do), but rather to stimulate the Churches to think out their common problems together.

For some years now the Department has devoted some time and energy to the pursuit of this study. With the cessation of hostilities in 1945, it was soon apparent that no such thing as 'Christian guidance' could be given to our world in its social and political perplexities, as long as the relevance of the Bible's message could not be clearly defined. Christians, who believe that the Bible is God's Word to men, must faithfully accept the Bible as authoritative in their own personal life and conduct, and even in the social relationships of the Christian community to which they belong; but it is less obvious that the Bible is also relevant to the life of societies, nations and cultures. It cannot be claimed that there is any generally accepted *Christian answer* to this question even amongst those Christian bodies which co-operate in the World Council of Churches. Thus it seemed clear that it was the first task of the Study Department to clarify these fundamental problems on an ecumenical basis.

In the years which have followed the Second World War, the Study Department has arranged ecumenical conferences for the study of these questions: at London in 1946, at Bossey (Switzerland) in 1947, at Zetten (Holland) in 1948 and at Wadham College, Oxford, in 1949. To these conferences came many distinguished scholars from many Christian confessions and from many parts of the world. Much had been achieved, not only in the actual conferences, but also through the circulation of documents amongst scholars in widely different lands; but it was seen to be necessary, if the discussion was to be broadened as it was hoped, that the publication of such a work as this should be undertaken. Accordingly, plans were laid down, representative authors were commissioned to write or re-write their contributions, and the volume gradually took shape. It is hardly possible to convey any adequate impression of the amount of discussion, criticism and re-consideration which has gone into the making of this book. The Conference at Zetten became, to all intents and purposes, an editorial board, doing nothing but work over the contributions which were already in hand, and make arrangements for the production of such material as was still seen to be needed.

Most of the contributors to this book have themselves personally taken part in one or more of these conferences, together with a number of other distinguished scholars, whose names do not appear in our pages, but to whom all the contributors would desire to express their gratitude for much sound advice, ready encouragement and vigorous criticism. It should thus become clear that the various contributions to these pages, though standing under the name of an individual writer, are in fact the outcome of much ecumenical discussion; they may be taken to represent the author's considered opinion after he has had the opportunity of reflecting upon such advice and criticism as he may have received. It is the editors' belief that this volume is ecumenical not only in the sense that it is written by scholars of differing confessions, but also, and more significantly, in the sense that it is the fruit of a genuinely inter-confessional 'traffic in knowledge', a real sharing of the riches and insights of the several branches of the world Christian community.

A glance at the list of contributors will show that most of the main Christian traditions—with one notable exception—are represented in this volume, as indeed they were represented at the discussion out of which it arose. It is a matter for regret that the book contains no Roman Catholic contribution, especially in view of the new emphasis upon Biblical study which seems to be so marked a feature of life in that communion today; it was not the wish of the Study Department that this should be so.

Every confession looks at the Bible from the point of view of its own tradition or customary ways of interpretation. Were it not so, there would be no need for ecumenical Bible study at all. Even the 'detached' or 'disinterested' standpoint of liberal scholarship turns out, upon examination, to be but another 'tradition'. The fact is that the believing attitude of Christians towards the Bible and its message is always mediated to them by the particular Church or community from which they have received it. That is why the question about tradition, in its various forms, arises frequently in the following pages, especially in *Part I* of our volume. This first part deals with some fundamental considerations concerning the Bible's authority in social and political matters, more particularly the questions of the authority of the Bible in relation to the authority of the Church, of 'natural law', of 'general revelation', of tradition, of the *testimonium Spiritus Sancti internum*, of 'reason', and so on. It should, however, be clearly understood that behind all these discussions there is no question of an alternative (still less a rival) authority to the Bible in the Church's tradition, in 'natural law' or the like, but rather whether amidst the varying emphases of our different confessional standpoints there is to be found a common basis from which the Churches may together declare what is the message of the Bible for the world today.

At every stage of our discussion a consideration of the matters which individual scholars or particular Churches, thinking alone, are apt to take for granted—such as principles of interpretation—was found to be unavoidable; and it should readily become apparent that presuppositions of this kind are proper and necessary matters of discussion in ecumenical Bible-study work. These questions, which are treated in *Parts II* and *III* of our volume, are thus not discussed for their own sake but only in so far as they must necessarily precede any realistic consideration of the message of the Bible for the modern world.

Part II consists of a single essay surveying the present position of study in the sphere of Biblical interpretation and the application of Biblical theology to Christian ethics in different parts of the world Church at the present time. It is impossible within the limitations of time and space, and indeed of human capacity, for any one author to do justice to all the rich variety of thinking and action which is taking place upon this theme today; but it has been judged useful to include such a survey as an introduction to the following Part III and in some sense also to Part IV.

In *Part III* scholars of different confessions and theological traditions deal with the hermeneutical principles of Biblical interpretation. But this part does not only describe differences of opinion. It has been our experience—and one for which we are profoundly grateful to God—that, when an ecumenical group sits down with the Bible open before it at a specific passage, there emerges a common agreement concerning what the Holy Spirit wills to speak through *this* Scripture. When the passage has been expounded, and all have made their contributions, there arises a broad and illuminating understanding about its meaning and relevance for us today. This experience was most notably possessed by those who met at Wadham College, Oxford, in 1949, where three of the five authors of this part of the volume were present. An attempt to summarise the method we have found to be fruitful has already been published under the title 'Guiding Principles for the Interpretation of the Bible'[1]; for the convenience of our readers, it is reprinted in this volume on pp. 240ff.

Finally, in *Part IV* an attempt is made to apply the above principles and precepts to an actual consideration of some of the specific problems which confront Christians (and others) in the world today. It was, of course, impossible to do more than treat a selection of the great issues which perplex us in our age; and the essays in this part of the book should be regarded only as sketches of how the message of the Bible might be brought to bear upon our modern dilemmas rather than as fixed and final pronouncements of Christian truth in these matters.

The contributors to this volume desire to express their gratitude to all who have helped them in this undertaking with their generous information, advice and criticism. It is the prayer of all those who have taken part in this enterprise of ecumenical Bible-study that God will consecrate the fruit of their labours and will use it in the fulfilment of His promises, that the Spirit of truth will guide His disciples into all truth, and that the Lord of the Church will gather into one the children of God that are scattered abroad.

ALAN RICHARDSON
WOLFGANG SCHWEITZER

Geneva
September, 1950

[1] *Ecumenical Review*, Vol. II, No. 1, pp. 81-86, and in the pamphlet *The Bible and the Church's Message to the World*, published by the World Council's Study Department in September, 1949.

Part One

THE AUTHORITY OF THE BIBLE

Fundamental Considerations

1

AN ORTHODOX CONTRIBUTION

by

PANAYOTIS I. BRATSIOTIS

Translated from the Greek by E. Every

Note

The views here set forth correspond principally to the data of Greek Orthodox theology, and not to those of Slavonic theology or Rumanian theology, about which the author of this present study is not in a position to be well-informed, owing to his ignorance of the languages concerned. He does not, however, believe that it is likely that the rest of Orthodox theology will disagree essentially with the position formulated here.

I *Revelation—Bible—Tradition and Church*

The Bible is most intimately connected with the divine revelation which has its evidence in the Bible and constitutes the chief subject of the Bible. But the Bible ought not to be identified with that revelation, nor should inspiration be identified with revelation, as it often is. The Bible presupposes revelation, and inspiration presupposes revelation.

Revelation, regarded subjectively, is called 'Apocalypse' in the New Testament (Luke 10.21; Rom. 16.25; I Cor. 2.10; Gal. 1.16, etc.); regarded objectively it is called *Phanerosis* (John 9.13; Rom. 1.19, 3.21); it signifies the self-manifestation or self-communication of God. But revelation is not understood only in this way in Orthodox theology. Nor is it understood in an intellectualistic manner, that is, only as a communication of truths or of things known; but it is simultaneously understood as a transmission of divine life and power and especially as creative energy or release of the energies[1] of God, through which he either reveals his nature and his saving purposes for man and

[1] 'Ενέργεια.

his saving will, or transmits to him divine truths concerning his salvation. Revelation, as thus understood, presupposes the meeting of God with man and signifies in a certain way converse between them (Heb. 1.1). Hence the content of the revelation given to man through inspiration is called 'The Word of God'; its chief purpose is the salvation of man.

It is to be understood that, in speaking of revelation here, we mean the direct revelation or special revelation which is revelation in the principal sense of the word. This is the revelation *par excellence*, consisting of an extraordinary intervention of God in history, his supernatural energy, capable of being received by man only by faith, by which energy a new thing relating to man's salvation is accomplished and is given to man. The distinguishing marks of this revelation are two: (1) that it contains something creative or new, and (2) that it has in it a unity with itself and with the creation (*cosmos*).

Side by side with this revelation of God *par excellence*, the supernatural revelation, which constitutes the centre and principal subject of the Bible, the existence of indirect or *natural* revelation is recognised in Orthodox theology; this is not only testified in the Scriptures, as in Acts 14.17, 17.24; Rom. 1.20; Rom. 2.14, etc., but is also, in part, contained in the Scriptures. Neither does natural revelation render supernatural revelation superfluous nor does supernatural revelation shut out natural, but the natural demands the supernatural and the supernatural presupposes the natural revelation. The natural revelation of God, which constitutes the subject of what is called *natural theology*, is accomplished in the external cosmos and in the conscience of man on the one hand, and, on the other hand, in universal history. It is inadequate, and needs to be supplemented by supernatural revelation (Rom. 1. 20, 2.14; I Cor. 1.21). The natural revelation serves two purposes, one positive (or direct), the other negative (or indirect). Positive, inasmuch as it leads men from the creature to the Creator; and negative (or indirect), inasmuch as it shows man how inadequate is his own understanding and his own sinful nature to comprehend God and to approach him. The inadequacy of natural revelation, interwoven as it is with the inadequacy of the human spirit, which is unable especially in the sinful condition of man to absorb that revelation completely, is reflected in what is called natural theology. In the Orthodox view, Origen's apt saying concerning natural theology is applicable (*Contra Celsum*, VII, 42): 'Human nature is quite incapable of seeking God and really finding Him, without His help . . . just inasmuch as it is hardly possible for human nature to perceive God.' At any rate, Orthodox theology, following the example of the old Fathers of the Church, accepts not only the natural revelation but also the natural apprehension of God—an apprehension which is always inadequate and imperfect, even if it is not false. Yes, false, for natural revelation is often ambiguous, so that instead of leading men to God it often misleads them into idolatry.

The supernatural revelation of God, in which he is revealed in his supreme wisdom, goodness and power, and also in his holiness and righteousness, is accomplished in history, with which it is interwoven in what is called sacred history, *hiera historia*, *Heilsgeschichte*. This revelation was continuous, but also gradual and progressive, as given through the prophets in the Old Testament and crowned in all fulness in the God-Man, Jesus Christ (Heb. 1.1 *et seq.*; Col. 1.19). Indeed, through the becoming Man of the Word of God the divine revelation was made entire not only in form, but also in content, that content being, as we have said, the transmission to man of divine truth as much as the transmission of divine power and life.

But just as the absorption of natural revelation on the part of sinful and imperfect man ever was and continues to be imperfect so that it is often misunderstood and distorted, in such a manner that supernatural revelation is made necessary for man's salvation, so also the absorption of supernatural revelation has limits in this present world, and is to be completed in the end of the ages in the life beyond that of this world, when 'the servants of God shall see his face and there shall be no night there and they have no need of a candle, neither light of the sun; for the Lord God gives them light' (Rev. 22.4-5). Meanwhile, even the perfect revelation of God in Christ remains, in part, obscure and darkened to men, being perceived by faith and by divine grace working together with the spiritual powers of man: 'Now we see in a glass darkly, but then face to face' (I Cor. 13.12). Or, as S. Ambrose observes, '*umbra in lege*, *imago in Evangelio*, *veritas in coelestibus*'.

According to Orthodox theology the Church is the guardian[1] of supernatural revelation in its historical development, and the

[1] Θεματοφύλαξ.

store[1] (of supernatural revelation) is the Bible on the one hand and the apostolic tradition on the other hand; the Bible constitutes the written, and tradition the spoken, Word of God, yet both are the authoritative source of Christian teaching. The Bible is the authoritative written exposition of what God has done and does and will do for the salvation of man and for the establishment and triumph of his own kingdom. Tradition is the primitive form of the word of God, whereby the Church was founded by the Saviour and which, living from the apostles onwards in the conscience of the faithful is the conscience,[2] at once historical and religious, or the mind[3] of the whole Church. It is the imprint, without either paper or ink, upon the hearts and the conscience of the faithful, of the Gospel, as S. Irenaeus rightly observes in *Adversus Haereses*, III, 3. The Bible is an occasional (peristatic) written formulation of this spoken apostolic tradition, but in all respects made according to the providential divine will. Neither does tradition make the Bible superfluous nor does the Bible make tradition superfluous, but these both mutually supplement and interpret one another.

The Church, the Bible, and the tradition are and remain in an inseparable unity in the Orthodox Church. For this reason sayings of distinguished Protestant theologians of our epoch, like that of Emil Brunner, '*Ohne Kirche keine Bibel*', are heard with satisfaction in Orthodox theological circles, just as with the same satisfaction are heard in those circles the contemporary Protestant contentions in favour of tradition, which as time goes on are more and more numerous. (*Vide* the latest study by Professor Dahl of Oslo, entitled *Scripture and Tradition*.)

If, from the Orthodox point of view, it is not the right way of speaking to assert that 'the Church was the mother of the Bible', it is an even less correct expression to make the opposite claim that the Bible begat the Church. Of both the Bible and tradition the Church is the birthplace,[4] guardian, authoritative witness, and also authoritative interpreter. The Bible as much as tradition was begotten in the womb of the Church. For her sake both were created and both were transmitted to her. She gives evidence about the canon of Holy Scripture, that is about the fact that the content of the books constituting it is the Word of God. In the Church these books are preserved unalloyed and in

[1] Ταμεῖον. [2] Συνείδησις. [3] Φρόνημα. [4] Κοιτίς.

her alone both the Bible and tradition are securely and authoritatively interpreted. It is, however, to be understood that, when we say in Orthodox theology that the authority of the Bible and of her twin sister tradition is testified by the Church, it is implied that they both have their source in the authority of God, whose revelation and word they both contain and from whom the Church also derives her authority.

The Bible is both expounded and supplemented by the apostolic tradition and furthermore, because it had its origin in the Church (of both Old and New Testaments) and was intended for the Church, it can be faithfully and authoritatively interpreted and understood only in the light of tradition and in the womb of the Church, wherein abides continually the divine Spirit, sent to her by Christ, 'to guide her into all truth' (John 16.13). This is clearest in relation to the Old Testament, which cannot be understood in any other way except only in the light of the revelation in Christ which is treasured in the Church, and then in the light of the divine Spirit dwelling in her.

But the Bible in general is far from being self-explanatory; it is in many of its parts hard to understand because, just as the Incarnate Word of God was hidden in the flesh and yet manifested on various occasions, so 'the Word of God in book-form'[1] is often hidden within human language, though that language may be the most perfect. Here must be applied the saying of S. Paul, that 'we have this treasure in earthen vessels' (II Cor. 4.7). To speak universally, the letter of the Bible remains dead without the divine Spirit in the Church who imparts life to all within her fold, whose testimony (*testimonium Spiritus Sancti*) can be regarded as completed only in the Church, i.e. in the extension of Christ himself, and not simply in the Bible (II Cor. 3.6).

But despite this fact, the Bible, constituting the crystallisation of the Word of God in writing and being providential even though it relates to particular occasions, occupies an important position in the Orthodox Church. For the Bible is, so to speak, the Lydian stone for the accurate ascertainment of the truth of tradition, although we take the view that it derives its validity from the Church which is 'the pillar and the ground of truth' (I Tim. 3.15) and, through the Church, from its principal cause, that is, from 'the Living God'. Moreover, according to the

[1] Ὁ ἔνβιβλος λόγος.

Orthodox conception, the sacred tradition contains nothing contrary to the Bible, with the content of which the content of the tradition essentially coincides, all the more because, as we have said, both are the product of the same divine Spirit, who dwells in the Church; for which reason both are regarded as having equal honour and equal validity in the Orthodox Church.

But the tradition which is regarded as having equal honour and equal validity with the Bible in the Orthodox Church is not only ecclesiastical tradition, but principally the apostolic tradition, which, being communicated by word of mouth from generation to generation, under the supervision of the divine Spirit, was preserved without change in the undivided Church of the first eight centuries.[1] The Greek Orthodox Church recognises no single person or single office as having final authority in doctrinal matters. It regards its whole body (ὅλον τὸ πλήρωμα) as bearers of the true apostolic tradition and as protectors of Orthodoxy, in accordance with the apt formulation in the Encyclical of the Orthodox Patriarch in 1848 (ὁ φύλαξ τῆς ὀρθοδοξίας τὸ σῶμα τῆς ἐκκλησίας, τοὐτέστιν ὁ λαὸς αὐτός ἐστιν). The hierarchy, which meets at the ecumenical councils, is the voice of the Church; the ecumenicity (the ecumenical character) of these councils, however, and the infallibility of their decisions, are to be tacitly recognised by the whole body of the Church. Moreover this Church (in spite of its respect for and loyalty (κλῆρος καὶ λαός) to tradition) regards tradition as something not merely static, but also dynamic. On the other hand it does not believe that this dynamism should ever override tradition so far as to create new dogmas, as this would be contrary to the conscience and spirit of the ancient Catholic Church. This, however, does not signify that the apostolic tradition is treated in the Orthodox Church as static, as many heterodox people think it is, for in her it is regarded as, and also it is, dynamic, being a treasure stored in the conscience of the Church, enlivened by the divine Spirit remaining in her, a treasure capable of clarification and exposition, without the alteration of its essential truth.

[1] Being obliged to formulate clearly and unambiguously here the undiluted Orthodox conception of the sacred tradition, we have to state that the Orthodox Church, regarding herself as the direct and faithful continuation of the ancient Catholic Church, unanimously rejects the 'Branch Theory' and recognises herself as the guardian of the genuine apostolic tradition.

II *Unity and structure of the Bible*

The Bible, although consisting of many different books, written by different authors in different epochs, and indeed belonging to two different worlds (that of the Old Testament and that of the New), nevertheless gathers them in one book, organically a unity, containing the most various pages, but inspired throughout, from start to finish, by the same divine Spirit, occupied with the same theme, and turning on the same central point and the same mystic magnet, the Christ. It begins with the creation of heaven and earth and ends with the appearance of the 'new heaven and new earth'. In the Old Testament, which contains the story of revelation before Christ, the revelation and salvation in Christ are foretold and prepared through the patriarchs and the prophets. In the New Testament the revelation and salvation in Christ, witnessed by the Apostles, are stored in writing. But this unity of the Bible does not signify in Orthodox theology the equality of the revelation stored in the Old Testament with that in the New Testament, which is much fuller than, and is superior to, that in the Old. The relationship between them is the relationship between preparation, fore-telling, type, and prophecy, on the one hand, and the realisation of all these on the other hand.

Where the structure of the Bible is concerned, we observe that Orthodox theology, rejecting verbal inspiration in the mechanical sense, accepts inspiration as being, on the one hand a communication of divine truths, and also on the other hand a supervision of the Holy Spirit for their right formulation, but always analogously to the particular character of each of the inspired men. Hence, as in the incarnate Word of God, so also in the Holy Scripture, which constitutes the Word of God in book-form, Orthodox theology distinguishes a divine and a human element and receives the essence of the Bible as divine, the form as human. Inspiration is chiefly centred upon the essence of the Bible, although it radiates its brightness often also on the form which is given to saving truths, even if the form is to be recognised as the sphere in which the human initiative of the inspired man moves freely. *In scripturis per hominem, more hominum, loquitur Deus* (Augustine).

In Orthodox theology different degrees of the inspiration of the Bible are distinguished; of these the highest is the degree of inspiration of the prophets and that of the apostles. The existence of different degrees of inspiration in the Bible is related to (*a*) the gradual progress of the divine revelation, (*b*) the differences of manner of out-pouring and energy of the Holy Spirit, and (*c*) the more or less abundant showing forth of the spiritual gift of inspiration, in proportion to the receptiveness of each inspired writer. Here the words of the Apostle Paul may in any case be applied: 'There is one glory of the sun and another glory of the moon and another glory of the stars, and one star differeth from another star in glory' (I Cor. 15.41).

Inter-related with the inspiration of the Bible is the power of the Bible to work internally, which results from the spiritual grace (*pneumatike charis*) residing in it; this, so called by the Church Fathers, was characterised by the seventeenth century reformers as the *testimonium Spiritus Sancti*. (See Theodoret in Migne P. G. 82,676 and Amphilochios in Migne P. G. 37, 1597). But although a sanctifying power in the Bible is recognised by these Fathers as resulting from the simple reading of the Bible and as due to the 'spiritual grace' of the Bible mentioned above, nevertheless, neither by any of them nor by the Orthodox Church is this grace regarded as the chief foundation of the authority of the Bible.

III *The authority of the Bible from the dogmatic point of view, and most of all from the ethical point of view.*

As the purpose of the divine revelation is the salvation of man, so is that of the Bible. Hence it may well be understood that the authority of the Bible refers most of all to everything in the Bible which relates to man's salvation. But salvation is not regarded in the Orthodox Church as exclusively the accomplishment of faith or of the grace of God (*sola fide* or *sola gratia*); it is rather the product of divine grace and human freedom together, or, speaking differently, a product of faith working through love (Gal. 5.6). Not only definite events in the story of divine revelation and the religious truths related to them, all of which constitute an object of faith, but also ethical principles and commandments, especially those related to the revelation of God in Christ and describing the life that is in accordance with the faith, have for their aim the salvation of man. 'Every scripture is given by inspiration of God, and is profitable for doctrine, for reproof, for correction, for instruction in righteousness' (II Tim. 3.16).

This does not mean that the Bible is a hand-book of moral teaching, but it means that the Bible contains moral teaching and particularly divine commands, of which the execution in faith and obedience is indispensable to salvation (Matt. 7.21,24, 25.35 *et seq.*; Rev. 14.13, 20.13, 22.14).

Where questions of faith and morals are concerned, the primary and dominant position as a Biblical source of divine revelation certainly belongs, in Orthodox theology, to the New Testament; the Old Testament, on account of the imperfection of the divine revelation contained in it and testified by it, is used not separately or in its own right, but in connection with the New Testament and in the light of the New Testament only. This last is the fulfilment of the Old Testament and is both the central point from which it should be studied and the measure according to which it should be studied (see Matt. 5.17-48). Hence, according to Orthodox theology, it is to be deduced that where questions of faith and morals are concerned, we can make an appeal to the light of the Old Testament, in its development, but we are not permitted to quote Old Testament passages relating to such questions indiscriminately, without placing them side by side with parallel New Testament passages. A method which is contrary to the Christocentric one, such as would be involved in an indiscriminate use of Old Testament and New Testament evidence in relation to the questions here concerned, could certainly lead to the corruption of the genuine spirit of Christian teaching, and this has repeatedly taken place in the history of Christian theology and of the Christian Church.

The moral content of the Bible has a double origin, in so far as part of it is the product of natural revelation (in the law of conscience planted in man) and another part is the product of supernatural revelation. And the material of a moral nature derived from natural revelation in the Bible is sanctified and confirmed under the light of supernatural revelation, with which natural revelation is interwoven in the Bible. The material relating to morals in the Bible has also a double form, because part of it is formulated in laws or ordinances and another part is formulated in general principles or commandments, related to the moral character or the motive of acts, or relating to an *ethos*. This later element, already adequately represented in the Old Testament and not absent even in the Mosaic law, is the dominant one and the characteristic one in the eminently moral religion of the New Testament. On the contrary, the legal character is the ruling element in Old Testament ethics; this is overcome in the ethic of the Gospel through the conceptions of spirituality, freedom and grace, which make up its character. But a third distinction ought to be made between parts of the moral content of the Bible, in that many ordinances of the Mosaic law and many moral exhortations in the Old Testament have a merely occasional and temporary character, whereas the religio-ethical principles, commandments and exhortations of the New Testament have an eternal validity, according to the predominant view, at least, in Greek theology.

In Orthodox theology, despite the admitted insufficiency of the law for the salvation of man and despite the many-sided superiority of the Gospel to the law, which has the character of a pre-education in relation to Christ (Gal. 3.24), nevertheless the antithesis between law and Gospel is not recognised to be of such a character that it prevents the use of the term 'evangelical law', used by the Church Fathers and not rejected by some Protestant theologians also, to signify the moral precepts of Christ. It is believed that this way of thinking, far removed as it is from any kind of antinomistic prejudice, in Orthodox theology, agrees with sufficient data of the New Testament. In the first place, the conception of the law is interwoven with that of the Kingdom of God; which, in any case, is not so foreign to the conception of theocracy in the widest sense of the word (that is, the sense of the sovereignty of the divine will) that the fear of theocracy prevailing among many theologians should be thus justified. Also the conception of the Covenant is not foreign to the conception of the law; the Covenant, like the law, expresses the will of God. Then comes the contrast drawn by Jesus Christ himself between the commandments which he gives and those of the Mosaic Law in the Sermon on the Mount. 'Ye have heard that it was said by them of old time . . . but I say unto you' (Matt. 5). But also the framework of the narrative (He went up into the mountain, etc., in contrast with Sinai) and all of S. Matthew's presentation of the Sermon on the Mount, this constitutional charter or Magna Carta of the Kingdom of Heaven, that is, of the ideal Christian community and not merely of the apostolic circle, conveys the impression that henceforth a new law replaces the old law (*vide* the end of the Sermon on the Mount in Matt. 7.24. Also Matt. 28.20 and Luke 17.10. But in the Fourth Gospel also reference is made to the commandments of Christ (*entolai*); John 13.34, 14.15 and 21, 15.10 and 12; *vide* I John 5.3; II John 6, etc.).

This evangelical law has the character of 'good news' and is described as 'the law of the spirit and of life in Christ' (Rom. 8.2), and as 'the law of Christ' (Gal. 6.2) and 'that perfect law, the law of liberty' (Jas. 1.25) and 'the royal law' (Jas. 2.8). It is summarised and brought to its completion in the double commandment of love of God and love of one's neighbour (Matt. 22.40; Rom. 13.10). It is inseparably connected with all the Christian virtues and is not broken up into various details by the needs of casuistry.

But the moral law of the Decalogue is not cancelled by the Gospel; it is in force all over the Christian world as a divine law and as a preliminary step to the Gospel, by which it is completed, and, side by side with the Sermon on the Mount as spoken by the Lord, it constitutes part of the catechism of the Orthodox Church. In any case the morality of the New Testament is recognised in Orthodox theology as being the completion and making whole not only of the law and general morality of the Old Testament but also of the natural moral law and of natural morality.

More especially with reference to the authority of the Bible from the point of view of political and social morality, the Orthodox way of thinking might thus be formulated in its general outlines: Although Orthodox theology may recognise that the Bible does not contain detailed ordinances claiming to regulate the civic life and social intercourse and political relationships of men and peoples, and although it may not deny that Biblical morality (especially in the Old Testament) happens to be, in part, provisional, nevertheless it believes that in its very provisional character (in the Old Testament), it still contains a definite *ethos* of eternal validity and that this *ethos* together with faith in Christ ought to inspire and govern the attitude of the Church and of each one of the faithful to matters political and social, through all the duration of the Church's earthly career, 'to prove that good and acceptable and perfect will of God' (Rom. 12.2). Reverence for human personality, social justice and love of others to the point of self-sacrifice make up the essence of this *ethos*.

Generally speaking, Orthodox theology does not imagine that we are justified in copying or in transplanting institutions from the Bible into the systems of modern states, taking them chiefly from the Old Testament (e.g. the institution of the Sabbatical Year and the Year of Jubilee, etc.) or in seeking in the Bible detailed directions or programmes for the government of political and social life, or even for the government of the personal life of each one of the faithful. But nevertheless the prevailing opinion among the Orthodox is that in the institutions of the Old Testament, in the social preaching of its prophets and in the precepts of both Testaments, in the fundamental religious and moral principles of the Old Testament, and even more in the evangelical law and the examples of the New Testament saints, and in that of the Saviour above all, we ought to discern a spirit and a mentality which are above the distinctions of period and place. This, together with the Biblical and especially the New Testament '*ethos*' already mentioned as having eternal validity, we ought to transfuse and transubstantiate into the life of the faithful and of the community in its many manifestations and relations. This life ought to be ordered in accordance with this spirit and *ethos*. Thus, for example, the Church of our time and of every time, and her true members, cannot neglect either the spirit of community inspiring the religious and social institutions of the Old Testament (Sabbath, Sabbatical Year, Year of Jubilee, etc.) or the subjugation of the absolute right of private property both in the Old Testament and in the New Testament, or the wise attitude of Christ and the Apostles to the Roman Empire and its social institutions (Matt. 22.21; Rom. 13.1 *et seq*.; I Tim. 2.2; Philem., etc.), or even the experimental attempt of the first Church to realise the ideal of a communism of love; nor can they depart from the social ideal of the Old and New Testaments, 'Let none among you be in want' (Deut. 15.4; Acts 4.34).

The 'double ethic' finds no ground for development in Orthodox theology, being unknown both in the New Testament and in the Fathers of the Church.

It is, moreover, recognised in Orthodox theology that the Bible contributes to the ascertainment and clarification of the natural law,[1] which was of old found to exist among the various peoples of the earth, in the form of various institutions (such as the family, the community, the state, etc.) and in the form of proverbs (such as the golden rule in its negative and positive forms) and which is clearly enough declared to exist in the New Testament (in Rom. 2.14; 13.1, etc.); of this some legal ordinances and precepts of the Old Testament are manifestations. But what has been said earlier about natural religions holds also here. The innate or implanted moral law and natural law do not make superfluous the supernatural law, which is the law of grace and which both presupposes and sanctifies this previously implanted law but should never on any account be identified with it. The confusion between natural law and Christian ethics has proved disastrous and the Christian ethic should remain unmixed and unalloyed in the study of Christian morals, as long as this seriously claims the title of Christian. Finally, we note the fact that natural law has not been developed in Orthodox theology.

[1] Δίκαιον.

2

A METHODIST CONTRIBUTION

by

CLARENCE TUCKER CRAIG

The clear definition of terms is an essential preliminary in any discussion, particularly where controversial issues arise. If we are to examine the authority of the Bible, we must recall the origin and nature of the books for which high claims are to be made. These 39 Hebrew and Aramaic books comprise selections from the literature, the codes of law, and the historical records of one of the important peoples of antiquity. The 27 Greek books were chosen from among the religious expressions of the early Christian Church as documents which contained the true interpretation of her faith. Both collections are subject to the historical criticism which should be applied to all records from antiquity. In interpreting these documents we must seek to arrive at the original meaning of the authors and evaluate the historical and spiritual significance in the light of the rest of human experience.

But from this objective standpoint, these documents will hardly merit the name of Bible, the Book. For Christian faith, these are not simply accounts of the religious aspect of an ancient civilisation. They are the records of the revealing and redemptive activity of God in that segment of history where he has supremely manifested himself. As such, they present his Word to men. They do not simply record the results of man's search after God in the hope that 'they might feel after him and find him' (Acts 17.27). The Bible is the story of the progressive self-disclosure of God in crucial events. Obviously this is not a judgment to be proved by the historian; it is a faith which must find vindication in other ways.

It is clear that the word 'authority' can have no bearing except within this specifically Christian frame of reference. We may find an inspiring quality in various ancient religious writings, but they have 'authority' for us only if they are far more than that. But what kind of 'authority' can be assigned to as diverse a collection of books as that which contains Genesis and Esther, James and Romans, Chronicles and the Acts of the Apostles?

I *The meaning of authority*

When we turn to the dictionary, the definitions do not help much in the question before us. One is 'Legal or rightful power exercised by a person in virtue of his office'. This might be claimed for a Pope but hardly for a book. No power exists to enforce the obligations which it lays on men, and no body exists which has the right to give definitive interpretation of what these obligations should be. The purely spiritual nature of Biblical authority carries with it an epistemological corollary which is too often forgotten. When Christians speak of the authority of the Bible they always mean in practice *as they themselves interpret* it. It is instructive to read in as firm a Biblicist as John Calvin how he distinguishes between Biblical commands which he thinks it would be absurd to obey and those which are truly valid. Where the believer reserves the right to interpret the book, the nature of authority is, to say the least, very different from any legal structure in human society.

The dictionary gives as a further definition, 'Power derived from opinion, mental or moral superiority. Claim to be believed or obeyed.' This is a usage to which we all are accustomed; we speak of an authority in the field of physics, or Latin grammar, or Hellenistic mosaics. We recognise that we must defer to the 'authority' not because there is some power to enforce his judgments, but because he knows all about this particular subject which is now known. Naturally there is nothing infallible about such an authority nor is he in any sense final. The so-called authorities of one age are inevitably superseded as knowledge in that field grows.

It is clear that we are not speaking of the authority of the Bible in this sense. We do not mean that the Biblical writers were experts for all time in all fields. Advance of knowledge has made apparent how untenable were the claims of this kind which were made by a misguided and unwise apologetic. The Bible is not our guide in the realm of natural or biological sciences; every historical statement in its pages need not be defended as infallible; the world view of the Biblical writers inevitably contained many obsolete aspects.

Since the accepted definitions of 'authority' apply so badly to the unique position which the Bible holds, it may be questioned whether it is a fruitful term to use in this connection. Probably, however, it should be retained to designate the undisputed place of the Bible in relation to Christian faith. Christianity is not a series of general truths about God and man which may be discovered anywhere. It is not a philosophy which can be presented in logical, rational propositions. It is the *story* of the redemptive activity of God culminating in Jesus Christ. That story is found in the Bible. There is no alternative source from which it may be learned. There is no way that reason by itself could come to the conclusion that 'God was in Christ reconciling the world to himself.' There is no substitute for the accounts of this event which come from those who witnessed it with eyes of faith. When faith responds to the testimony of the Bible that its witness is true, then the Bible has for that person a position for which the word 'authority' is not too strong a term. There is a compulsion which comes from faith to faith.

II *Application to the social realm*

This understanding of the authority of the Bible, however, is not what is under discussion in this volume. It deals with man's ethical response, and more particularly with his response in the realms of social and political activity. Is there a valid sense in which the word authority can be applied to the Bible here? The question is no longer what thread of God's saving activity may be traced through these 66 books that has coherence and unity. Rather, in what sense is there authoritative direction for our conduct of social and political affairs in these documents from very different and distant civilisations?

I plead for a franker recognition of the need to divide our theme into these two parts. It is true that the ethical demands of God stand behind every message of judgment and consequently are involved in the forgiveness of sins. We cannot artificially separate God's salvation from his ethical nature.

Religion and ethics can never be divorced in a truly Christian faith. But it makes all the difference in the world in which order they are placed and how they are related. If justification is not by works of law—by obedience to commandments—but by the free gift of grace received by faith, then there is dismissed for all time the idea that the Bible contains a set of social and political principles through obedience to which man can find favour with God. Rather, those who have been redeemed by God's grace are *required* to respond by a life in the Spirit which is well-pleasing to him. This will involve a corporate response in the social and political areas, for a salvation which does not eventuate in changes in these areas as well as in purely personal relations has stopped short of full realisation.

But this does not imply the same 'authority' for the *particular* responses advocated by men in Biblical times that there is for the message of God's redeeming activity. It does not mean that the social institutions of ancient Israel are to become a pattern for every subsequent society, or that the social and political reactions of the earliest Christians, conditioned by the peculiar circumstances of their time, have the same finality as the realisation that 'God so loved the world that he gave his only Son'. Until this distinction is admitted between the relation of the Bible to the message of salvation and its relation to guiding Christian activity in social affairs, the issues before us will remain muddled and obscure.

Those who deal with abstract ideas are in danger of imagining that we can begin by setting up 'principles' and then proceed to 'apply' these to concrete, individual cases. It is rare that the Bible deals with abstract principles; here we meet rather with concrete, individual cases. Statements of principle are usually our own generalisations, and it is amazing how differently they are stated when interpreters from widely different backgrounds draw conclusions from the same Biblical data. It is futile to discuss *in vacuo* the degree of 'authority' which the Bible has in social and political questions apart from the specific instances. Nor should we be forgetful of the long history of the use of the Bible to defend ethical standards advantageous to powerful, dominant groups. Every American recalls with deep humiliation the defence of human slavery on Biblical grounds which good men in their blindness perpetrated. Yet, when we discuss the question of

Biblical authority, we must remember that slavery has the sanction of plenty of Biblical texts. In the light of this, it sounds strange to us when some European theologians today defend the patriarchal conception of the family as Biblical and therefore part of the permanent divine order.

On the one hand the Bible approves the extermination of the enemies of the people of God; on the other, it calls for absolute non-retaliation in the face of wrong (Matt. 5.39ff). Which am I expected to follow if I accept the authority of the Bible? On some pages we are told that riches are a sign of God's blessing and Christians have sought to prove their calling by seeking this sign of divine favour. On other pages we read that it is the poor who inherit the kingdom of God; and the rich can enter only by a miracle (Luke 6.20; Mark 10.25). To take interest is strictly forbidden; we should rather 'lend, expecting nothing in return' (Luke 6.35). Surely the simple Christian may be pardoned if he is perplexed in trying to use so apparently contradictory a book as his 'authority' in social and political matters.

III *Christocentric authority*

The dilemma presented by the variety of ethical standards within the Bible has led many to attempt a Christocentric solution rather than a Bibliocentric. In the form which is most often met in the U.S.A., authority is claimed for Christ alone, and a lesser position is assigned to the rest of the Bible. This was a natural concomitant of the 'life of Jesus theology', so popular a generation ago. But the approach is filled with grave historical difficulties. Can we be sure that a particular word is genuine and not shaped by the early Church? Were not the ethical teachings of Jesus influenced by the expectation of the imminent end of the age? Are they applicable in our time without making allowance for this? Can we disregard the fact that at no time did the early Church confine its ethical teaching to a repetition of the teaching of Jesus? The minute we appeal to the 'mind of Christ' we are really retreating to a realm of uncontrollable subjectivity—what *we* believe Jesus would have thought about a particular issue.

Another type of Christocentric approach is also advocated today. Its adherents insist upon the essential unity of the Bible and that we should find our 'authority' in the whole Bible. But since Christ is the centre, we should begin with him and go out from that point to an understanding of the Biblical revelation. I would agree that it is sound hermeneutical procedure to begin with Jesus Christ, but it is difficult to see how some other parts of the Bible can any longer be authoritative for us when that is the case. They may still have significance in their historical setting, but they can hardly be normative for us. For instance, if the law of God is what Jesus enunciated, that there should be no divorce at all (Mark 10.5-9), what is to be gained by going back to Deut. 24.1 to 'interpret' this in the light of Christ? If the Word of God allows no retaliation whatsoever (Matt. 5.38), what authority can the *lex talionis* have for a Christian (Ex. 21.24)? Can we interpret it in terms of Christ and say that we really should practice the Old Testament law rather than the clear words of our Lord?

But in any case, this procedure involves a highly selective treatment of the Bible and one dependent at every stage upon the opinions of the interpreter. I do not criticise this, because it is inevitable; I criticise rather the mis-use of the word 'authority'. In its place I would use 'source of guidance'. All parts of the Bible will serve this purpose in some degree. Even the dire results from the sins of men offer negative guidance. In the rich treasure house of Biblical instruction are insights into the will of God whose value has been proved again and again. The Christian consciousness must be trusted to sift the valid from the obsolete, the wheat from the chaff. The same book which contains the prohibition against boiling a kid in its mother's milk also enjoins the returning of a strayed animal to your enemy (Ex. 34.26, 23.4). There can be no infallibility in selection. Salvation guarantees no escape from errors of ethical judgment. The Bible contains no authority which will save men from such mistakes or from the need to make experiments. Once we rid ourselves of the fallacious expectation that there can be a final written authority in regard to social and political questions we will find invaluable sources of guidance to which no limits may safely be put.

IV *Other sources of guidance*

Our guidance from the Bible may be clarified if we compare and contrast it with other sources of guidance. Authority rests ultimately in the will of God. In the discovery of his will, Scripture will hold a central place, but not an exclusive one, for the Spirit of God speaks to us through other channels as well. Three of these should be examined briefly.

A. Much attention has been given to the idea of *natural law*. Originally a Stoic conception, it was incorporated into Christian thinking especially by the scholastic theologians. Because it appeared to present a separate source of moral insight in comparison with the Bible, the validity of natural law has been sharply contested by some Christian interpreters for whom *sola scriptura* has been the true slogan.

I find the debate on this subject perplexing, for it seems to me that a false contrast is set up; conceptions are treated as if they were opposites when in fact they are drawn from quite different realms. Belief in natural law is not an alternative to dependence upon revelation; it stands opposed to a positivistic interpretation of law. It holds that right and wrong are inherent in reality and not simply an arbitrary decision of men. Law reflects the nature of the cosmos and is not merely the enforcement of the will of one group over another. The sympathies of many of us are on the side of natural law despite the extreme difficulty of defining what it is in detail, for we feel that the positivistic view is destructive of the moral values in which we believe. At the same time, we are quite willing to turn this debate over to the juristic specialists, for we know that we are not restricted to this alternative. Believing in God as the ultimate source of ethical duty, we do not depend on the vagueness of natural law. Rather, we seek the will of God and that is always specific, the duty of a particular man in a special situation at a given time.

The Bible knows the law of God, but this is not a fixed revelation of a morality entirely different from the experience which men have built up. Under *Torah* the Jews included instruction of all types, ritual laws and moral laws and various civil statutes. Many of these commandments are recognised today to be aspects of Israel's institutions which have no permanent validity. Yet, for the devout Jew all of *Torah* was the will of God and no part could be disobeyed without rebellion against him. When Paul struggled with the Judaizers for a law-free gospel, he was not discussing law in the sense of God's ethical commandments but the whole structure of *Torah* as affording the approved avenue to salvation. That is the primary form under which the antithesis of law and gospel is discussed in the New Testament. At the same time it is recognised that the law of God is written in the hearts of all men so that they stand condemned when they disobey it (Rom. 2.15). Quite apart from any revelation in the Old Testament, genuine knowledge of the will of God was available. That is the testimony of the New Testament itself. Therefore to claim that the Bible is the *sole* source of ethical guidance involves nothing less than a denial of its own testimony.

In place of a discussion of natural law I would urge the necessity to examine the ethical experience of the race outside the specifically Jewish-Christian tradition. We know how much the Fathers drew from Stoic and Platonic and Aristotelian ethical writings. Christian teachers were not always as selective as they might have been. Sometimes we feel that they give us more of Aristotle than of Christ, just as in Protestant moralists it is often easier to trace the influence of Kant or Bentham or John Dewey than that of the Master. Nevertheless, our solution of social issues may often be aided by contributions from the thinking of these and of others. 'All things are yours', said the apostle of old (I Cor. 3.21). A Church which today covers the world cannot close its eyes to values in the ethical experience of cultures other than the Graeco-Roman and the European. For the Bible itself insists that God has not 'left himself without witness' (Acts 14.17). Peril lies in supposing that these sources of guidance stand on the same level with those which are more closely related to the central revelation. The believer has a focus of loyalty: 'you belong to Christ' (I Cor. 3.23).

B. Another source of guidance is to be found in the 'tradition' of the Church. This idea is interpreted in two different ways. Some have held that the Church preserved an unwritten tradition which had apostolic authority comparable to the canonical books assigned to the apostles and their pupils. But the exact content of that 'tradition' is, to say the least, unclear, and when we see the type of material which appeared in the later so-called apocryphal gospels, it seems highly unlikely that any considerable body of tradition was transmitted. The contention, however, should serve as a reminder that all of the books of the New Testament were written within the Church and it was the Church which selected those twenty-seven books as the ones which had unique authority. It was not the New Testament which authorised the Church but the Church which authorised the

New Testament as containing a sufficient guide to faith and action.

In the life of *all* branches of the Christian Church, 'traditions' have developed which possess a high degree of authority. With some, the separate standing of tradition alongside of Scripture is frankly recognised. It is accepted that new occasions teach new duties, and the later teaching of the Church should have binding obligation upon members as well as the letter of Scripture. The average individual needs guidance from the collective experience of the Church if he is to make wise decisions in such complicated areas as the social and political questions of his time. Other groups do not frankly admit the authoritative character of their particular traditions. They prefer to *claim* that Scripture is the only guide, but when a discussion of this contains ten quotations from Calvin or Luther or some other Father to one from the Bible, it is at best only a formal denial. The difference is the same as that between the theory of the school of Hillel and that of Shammai concerning the oral law of the Jews. For one school, the oral law was authoritative in its own right; for the other, it was derived by tortuous exegesis from Scripture. But tradition had authority for both groups, and so is it today.

It is less important to use the word 'tradition' or agree on a statement of its rightful position than to recognise that the contemporary Church is always a source of guidance in the areas we are considering. Of course the Church of any time may be corrupted in its vision and judgment and conformed to the world instead of being an instrument of true witness and of transformation. The Church of every age stands under the judgment of the written Word which comes to us from the past. But in the interpretation of valid standards, the Church never can and never should disregard the accumulated experience of the continuous fellowship of believers. In the consideration of no social problem can we attempt to leap directly from the Bible to the modern world, disregarding the long and fruitful grappling with these problems. It is a short-sighted contemporaneity which imagines that we are the first to be genuinely concerned with social responsibility. Church history will not afford 'solutions' any more than the Bible will directly, but it will offer 'guidance' for all who retain the inquiring spirit.

C. A third source of guidance is the *internal witness of the Holy Spirit*. Since God is our ultimate authority it might appear false to include the Holy Spirit as simply one of the channels of guidance. But the emphasis is to be laid on 'the internal witness'. If we find the will of God through tradition, it is because the Holy Spirit has guided the Church. The Spirit is as absolute as God, but the witness within me is limited by my human frailties so that this provides only one of the sources of guidance.

Like tradition, the internal witness has two distinct aspects. First of all, apart from the guidance of the Spirit we cannot expect to understand Scripture aright. There is a sense in which God is his own interpreter. 'When the Spirit of truth comes, he will guide you into all the truth' (John 16.13). The Evangelist was not thinking in this connection of entirely new truth, but of that revelation which was *the* truth. Let us not belittle this Christian conviction on the ground that sincere interpreters have differed so widely in their understanding of Scripture. Nor may we dismiss those who disagree with us with the smug taunt that evidently they are not guided by the Spirit. Instead, we need to recognise frankly that guidance by the Spirit does not insure infallibility. Mistaken exegesis does not mean that the witness of the Spirit is entirely absent. On the other hand, Scripture cannot guide men to the will of God unless his living Spirit directs those who search for the way their paths should take. When some people speak of Scripture applying directly to their situation, what they usually mean is the witness of the Spirit.

It is upon the other aspect of the guidance of the Spirit that I would dwell at greater length, the guidance of the living God in the midst of the ethical dilemmas of our own day. God is not dead; when we refer to the Old and New Testaments we do not mean that he has passed away and can no longer speak directly. Of course, there are perils in taking seriously the belief that there is truly a living God. Fanatics and fools are often more ready to claim his guidance than saints and scientists. But even though Hananiah was a false prophet that did not keep Jeremiah from being a true prophet (Jer. 28). The guidance which individuals claim must always be socially evaluated. No one who pretends to believe in the New Testament can overlook the expectation of leadership by the Holy Spirit. According to the central message of the Bible, we do not live by following some law, even a new law of Christ. The Christian's life is that which is brought forth by the Spirit. The climax of Romans is not a doctrine of justification but of life in the Spirit (Rom. 8). The guidance of the Spirit cannot be confined to questions of purely individual conduct; it includes social responsibilities as well.

The guidance of the Spirit of the living God cannot be confined to extemporaneous judgments. It involves the accumulation of facts which bear on our social dilemmas, without which we cannot make intelligent ethical decisions. After we have extracted social principles and ideals from the Bible, we cannot apply these to our contemporary situation except as we utilise dependable and accurate information. If the Spirit of truth guides the assembling of this data and there is no warping of evidence to fit our prejudices and traditional predilections, we may be sure that it is the Holy Spirit which has been assisting, even though unrecognised by the veiled perception of the investigator. Facts do not in themselves provide Christian decisions, but the latter cannot be made adequately without knowledge of the issues.

Every one of the points we have enumerated should have much fuller development, but enough has been written to outline the varied sources of guidance which must enter into Christian decisions in the social and political realms. They are by no means equally relevant in any given situation. But the moral experience outside the Bible cannot be ignored, the later traditions of the Church must be given due consideration, and the contemporary guidance by the Spirit is indispensable. The Bible is intimately related to all three. Teaching that clearly contradicts central Biblical positions can hardly be accepted as Christian. The desire to relate what is drawn from elsewhere to the nearest suggestion found in the Bible will be strong. But it is a very dubious procedure to claim that a point of view is actually derived from the Bible when for centuries readers had not been aware of the insight. In such a case, the influence which led us to find it in the Bible is our actual source of guidance. Sometimes it may prove to be the more correct exegesis. At other times it is simply *eisegesis*, reading into the Bible the ideas which we have received from elsewhere and then receiving them back with the authority with which we have come to surround the Book.

V *Special problems for Biblical authority*

It is fruitless to attempt to rank in any hierarchy these various sources of guidance because all are necessary. And yet most of us agree that the Bible is so central that we are fully justified in concentrating on this particular source of guidance. The remainder of this paper will be devoted to a few of the problems which arise in attempting to use its resources.

A. The phrase is sometimes used of the 'situation-conditioned' elements in Biblical teaching. One may appropriately ask if there is any other kind of teaching to be found. Is not the Word of God always to a particular situation? There may be passages where some of us doubt that Scripture records what was actually a Word of God for that particular situation. I, for one, do not believe that God really sent a lying spirit to deceive men in an important international crisis (I Kings 22.23). But in most cases that is not the problem which faces us. It is the radical difference between the Biblical situation and our own. How can one properly make allowance for these differences?

In purely personal relationships the differences are not so great. To honour your father and mother may call for other specific actions than in ancient Israel, but these differences are not comparable to those in social and political areas. The political course which the prophet Isaiah demanded of Israel as the will of God may have been correct for her situation as a tiny pawn amid the world Empires of her day. But the situation of Great Britain, the United States of America, and other powers is very different. How may the directives for simple agricultural communities be used to solve the problems of a complex industrial society? I have little patience with the type of oratory which pretends that Amos or Jesus was speaking to a situation just like our own. It is usually associated with the idea that the Bible presents a series of models to be imitated rather than the story of God's redeeming activity in unique events.

There is no rule-of-thumb principle to guide us in dealing with this difficult problem. Each author who discusses a particular social issue must deal with the mass of Biblical data bearing on that question, every part of which is situation-conditioned. That does not mean that the teaching is entirely irrelevant or obsolete. It does mean that there is never a one to one correspondence in situation. Allowance for this calls for a delicate exercise of judgment in which we need patience with each other in our differences of opinion.

B. A particular aspect of this problem lies in the eschatological conditioning of much Biblical teaching, especially within the New Testament. It may be stated in another form as the problem of the doctrine of the 'two ages'. This seems to be especially pertinent among those whose 'tradition' includes Luther's doctrine of the two kingdoms. Unquestionably the Jewish belief in this age and the age to come is given a radically new interpretation in the New Testament. There is constant tension between a realised redemption in Christ and a hope of the future consummation of the divine reign. Though the old world has not yet passed away, the believer already lives in a real sense in the age to come, for he possesses the guarantee of the Spirit.

There is a sense in which this is true of believers in all ages. 'We are God's children now; it does not yet appear what we shall be' (I John 3.2). Yet there is a marked difference in our situation which must not be ignored. In the New Testament, while the differences between male and female, bond and free remained, in Christ they are completely abolished (Gal. 3.28). But this situation of tension had but a short time to last; the Lord was coming soon to complete the overthrow of the powers of evil, and the new age would supersede the old. The explanation of the author of II Peter that in God's time 'soon' may be 1,000 years (3.8) cannot obliterate the fact that the ethical injunctions of the New Testament were given on a quite different basis than this desperate attempt to save the traditional belief. Those who expected to be alive at his coming could write to slaves that they should stay as they were for the few years that remained (I Cor. 7.21-24; 15.51). Even with the author of James the burning sense of social justice could be content to advise the exploited to wait patiently for the coming of the Lord (5.1-8). It is otherwise if the consummation of the new age is at an indefinite future. Nineteen hundred years have passed, and there is not a syllable in the Bible to give any warrant that 190,000 more may not pass before any final judgment. True, we know not the day or the hour, and must always be ready to face our Maker. But to make a social and political programme in the expectation that what has not happened in 1,900 years will surely happen in our time is criminal dereliction of Christian responsibility.

What are the consequences for the social and political thinking of the Church? They are tremendously far-reaching. The social and political teaching of the New Testament is entirely within the frame-work of the expectation of the imminent end of the age. There is no thought of building a more Christian social order or of Christian obligations in the use of political power. The Christians comprised a truly revolutionary society, but it was a revolution to be inaugurated by God and his angels, not by social policies which they should join in implementing. In the light of this fact, does not this whole area of duty need to be re-thought in terms of the altered time perspective of the Church? Some say, No. They believe that the Church always stands between the ages. Though this period has extended longer than was anticipated in the apostolic age, the Church still has no obligation to work for the transformation of social institutions. Its sole task is to call men to their true citizenship in the age to come. Absorption in social tasks of the present age only diverts from the real objective.

This is a point of view in which many of us cannot concur. We do not agree on the extent to which the eschatological perspective is still valid. But we do agree that whether the end of the age is near or indefinitely delayed, we face the obligation to seek to remove social injustice and to build institutions more in harmony with the will of God. Utopia cannot be built among sinful men and women, but there is nothing in the Bible which forbids us to strive with all intelligence and good will for a more Christian social order. But in such an undertaking the blueprints cannot be expected in a New Testament where the doctrine of the two ages was inevitably held in a very different way.

C. The last problem is one which has already been noted, the apparent disunity in the testimony of the Bible. A good case can be made for the unitary message of the Bible at many points. Justice and love are intertwining themes which may be traced in various blends from Genesis to Revelation because the Bible contains the story of the activity of one God. But the social obligations of men are set in quite different perspectives in Israel's theocracy and in Christian communities facing Roman persecution.

The author of I Peter enjoined subjection to the emperor and his governors as the will of God, despite the fact that a fiery ordeal had come upon his readers and they were called upon to suffer as Christians (2.13f.; 4.11f.). The Revelation of John seems to identify the ruling political power so intimately with the

Beast that it was a phase of Antichrist. If these writings come from near the same time, as many believe, a perplexing antithesis is presented. There appear to be elements of truth in both reactions to the political situation of that time, indicating how puzzling the crisis was to first century Christians as it likewise is to us. 'If the bugle gives an indistinct sound, who will get ready for battle?' (I Cor. 14.8). But it is far better to admit the obscurities in our sources of guidance than to claim the possession of a clear-cut direction which we must first of all seek from all the resources at our command.

If the Bible is used by a Spirit-filled inquirer, in the light of the best traditions of the Church, the moral experience of the race, and an accurate knowledge of the contemporary situation, it will prove an invaluable source of guidance in dealing with our social and political problems. The difficulties which we have endeavoured to face frankly only present a more earnest challenge to listen intently for God's Word. There is no uncertainty about our need to do his righteous will. And we steadfastly believe that he who seeks will find.

3

A CONGREGATIONALIST CONTRIBUTION

by

HUBERT CUNLIFFE-JONES

We must always interpret the authority of the Bible in terms of the principle *Christus Rex et Dominus Scripturae*. Christians are not interested in the authority of the Bible as a self-contained entity, but as a means by which they may know in the present the Lordship of the living Jesus Christ.

We must, to begin with, make a distinction between the Word of God in Scripture and the present Word of God in any actual situation. What the Bible does for us is to declare the meaning of the Gospel, and we hear the Word of God in the Bible when the claim and mercy of God in the Gospel becomes a reality for us. But the total Word of God in any actual situation is not simply the Word of God in Scripture, but is the Word of God in Scripture taking up into itself the claim and mercy of God as expressed in the contemporary experience of living. The claim of God is upon us in the pressure of events upon us day by day. The meaning of the Word of God is not to be discerned from these contemporary events in themselves, but the discipline and privilege of these events is part of the present Word of God to us.

In both the Word of God in Scripture and the present Word of God there is a twofold element. In the Word of God in Scripture there is the evangelical message of the Christ, but there is also the contemporary idiom of thought and transmission of thought which needs translation into the idiom of our own times. In the present Word of God, if we take seriously the fact that the claim of God is upon us in the experience of living, we must be careful not to endanger the centrality of the other element—the Word of God in Scripture. We need the Word of God in Scripture if we are to interpret the claim of God upon us in the experience of living, just as we need an actual reverence for the claim of God upon us in the experience of living, if we are to interpret the Word of God in Scripture.

Within the one Word of God in Scripture, there is an interdependence between the revelation of Christ and the revelation of the creation. The revelation of the creation is secondary and derivative, but the revelation of the Christ also presupposes it. If we ask, What is the ultimate ground of our confidence that the world is the creation of God and therefore good, we can find the answer only in faith in Jesus Christ as Saviour and Lord. Now, confidence that the world is the creation of God is historically derivative from the Covenant of God with Israel—it is from the pattern of the historical Covenant that the pattern of God's Covenant with his creation is discerned (cf. C. H. Dodd, 'Natural Law in the Bible,' *Theology*, May-June, 1946). On the other hand, it is against the background of God as the Creator that Jesus Christ, clothed with his Gospel, is presented for our acceptance. It is in the setting of the revelation of God in the natural order that Jesus makes his claim upon us as the Christ. Yet this revelation of God in the natural order, though it has its necessary part in Scripture, is never made the main emphasis, and is incidental to the revelation of the Christ.

Dr. C. H. Dodd has said that 'In Christ, man is confronted with that Word, Wisdom or Law which is the law of His creation, the same which was partially disclosed to Israel in the Torah, and is known in some measure to all mankind, through conscience and reason, as the Law of Nature'. This means that the only natural law there is is the natural law of the Living God who has revealed himself in Jesus Christ. As we use the term, we mean the apprehension of some aspect of the natural law of God which can be shared in by Christian and non-Christian alike. (There can be conceptions of the natural law, rooted in anti-Christian faiths, which so deny the true natural law that they can only be opposed.)

The simplest forms of the natural law are first, the genuine standards of moral conduct which non-Christians possess. 'For if ye love them that love you, what reward have ye? do not even the publicans the same? And if ye salute your brethren only, what do ye more than others? Do not even the Gentiles the same?' (Matt. 5.46-47). Secondly, the right of non-Christians to criticise the actions of Christians if they should in fact fall below the commonly acknowledged standards of goodness. 'Have your behaviour seemly among the Gentiles, that, wherein they speak against you as evil doers, they may by your good works, which they behold, glorify God in the day of visitation' (I Pet. 2.12).

This knowledge of the natural law comes to non-Christians in two ways—one constitutive, the other historical. The distinction between these two ways does not imply that either in theory or in practice they can be clearly demarked. Man has a constitutive knowledge of the law of God because he has been created in the image of God and cannot divest himself of the implications—positive or negative—of that fact. But the constitutive knowledge of man that he is under obligation to the law of God comes to awareness differently in different historical epochs, and any approximation in the general community to a true apprehension of the Christian understanding of the natural law of God is due to the historical fact of long-continued Christian faith and witness. This means that the appeal to the natural law, while of the greatest practical importance, is, in principle, unstable and ambiguous. It is, indeed, only within the Gospel that the natural law is without distortion the natural law of God.

For the natural law does not imply a simple appeal to a factual condition—that may be included, but there is the implication that what is appealed to as an existing fact has the right to be considered as a norm. Its truth can only be ascertained by an act of decision. The natural law is, of course, objective to the spirit of man, but is not materially objective so that it can be definitely ascertained, apart from the mental activities of recognition and assent. Man is not bound by the natural law to something which his mind does not acknowledge as binding.

The issue here is the relation between obedience and freedom. Man has freedom only in a determinate obedience, a real conformity to the nature of his existence as a creature. Without that obedience he is both distorted and unfree. Yet this obedience must be understood not as limiting freedom and as demanding conformity to the sluggish inertia of nature, but rather as releasing freedom and giving man the right to shape the powers of nature into new and distinctive forms. (Biblically the Christian interpretation of the Book of Deuteronomy is of the first importance on this point. Here is the unity of obedience and love which is the ground plan for the Gospel. Obedience is rightly to a particular loyalty. But the obedience specified is too rigidly conceived, and thus is the preparation not only for the fulfilment in Jesus Christ our Lord, but also for the denial of his Messiahship.)

It is in relation to obedience and freedom that the function of natural science is to be understood. Science not only has the power (*dynamis*) of investigating natural processes and recombining them so as to give man greater control over natural forces, but it has the right (*exousia*) to do so because the labour and suffering which the ordinary flow of nature imposes upon human beings are a heavy burden upon mankind and may be considered part of that kingdom of Satan from which our Lord declared (Luke 13.16) that it was his mission to release men. But it is possible for science not only to release men from the hindrances to the liberty of the children of God, but also to put into the hands of men terrifying powers of destruction, to facilitate the erosion of the resources of nature, and to help to destroy the foundations of human culture.

It is clear that the discipline of science can neither be rejected nor treated as an autonomous good. The truth of science must be taken up in the perspective of the Gospel as part of that total Word of God to us in the existing situation. But it is not easy to prescribe in advance what that means, except where fundamental Christian conviction is clearly outraged. Because the natural law of God is not a simple fact of reference but implies decision, in many cases it is only possible to decide by trial and error where the use of science infringes the natural order, and where it does not: the danger, of course, is that irreparable harm will be done before an evil use of science can be stopped. However, the discipline of science as a gift of God must be honoured, though the ambiguity of science must be taken seriously.

What has been said of science applies to all those factors which enter into the conduct of men in the twentieth century, Christian or non-Christian. Not all the factors which determine the conduct of Christians are due to specifically Christian sources. In what way are these factors taken up into the decisions of Christian action?

In answering this, we must begin by affirming that Jesus Christ is both the Alpha and the Omega of the universe. He is the Lord of the world, and his reign, though in part hidden, is real. He and he alone is the One Word of God. All that is part of the truth of God has its being within the truth of Christ. So that, in principle, the Christian starts his thinking about human actions from the living and reigning Christ. But Christ is also the Omega of human action not only in the sense that the Christian having begun with Christ looks forward to the triumph of his Kingdom; but also in the sense that any goodness in human action, however little it may owe historically to Christian sources, ultimately finds its fulfilment in Christ. There is a sense in which we do not start with Christ, but find in him the goal of our action.

There may well be general agreement that pragmatically the Christian is forced to come to terms with this latter attitude of mind. In the life of the world we cannot start with an agreed assumption of the authority of Christ. We must, though ourselves acknowledging the Lordship of Christ, work with those for whom Christianity is merely an episode in history. So we begin with assumptions common to Christian and non-Christian and hope to relate them sometime to Christ. Pragmatically this is necessary. But does it rest on a common basis of thinking? Or ought the Christian to start all his thinking from a Christological basis?

I affirm that there can be actually a common, though precarious, basis of thinking. The thinking which sees in Christ the Omega of the world's striving is, no doubt, in danger of (*a*) forgetting its own Christological assumptions and (*b*) giving a greater weight to common human thinking than in time of crisis it can bear. Yet happily, we are not always compelled in human living to think and to act purely in terms of ultimate assumptions. On the relative plane on which so much of our social and political actions take place, there is an area of common thinking for which Christ is the goal and the consummation instead of being the starting-point. It matters greatly that Christian thinkers should hold together both types of thinking and acknowledge Christ both as Alpha and Omega.

Man has a double relationship to the natural law whose demands he both can and cannot fulfil. It embodies the claim of God for righteousness in a form in which the general body of the community may be expected to obey it. The higher the moral demands which can be made in the form of law, the more important it is that these should actually be obeyed. Under no circumstances must the Gospel be used as a screen for pessimism about standards which are actually within the control of man. 'The rule of law' is to be honoured in human life because it means a high standard of that law which the general community can, as a matter of fact, fulfil.

Here let it be said that law for the Christian—whether as legal code or the manners and morals of a community which cannot be written into a legal code—is much wider than anything specifically Christian. We see in the Old Testament (e.g. in Amos 1-2) the interrelation between the revealed law and the common law of humanity. The function of the revealed law is to cleanse and brighten the meaning of that law which should be acknowledged by all men everywhere, whatever their sinful blindness. In the general human understanding of the meaning of law, to which the Christian as well as other human beings is subject, various elements mingle which do not all derive from distinctively Christian sources. In principle, whatever is true in all these sources serves as a guide and discipline for human action within the sphere of the Lordship of Christ, and is not incompatible with that Lordship.

Five influences may be distinguished: (1) the classical tradition which has moulded many of the best standards of European culture; (2) the Christian tradition which has not only had a deeply shaping influence upon Europe, but which has through the expansion of the nineteenth and twentieth centuries revealed itself as a world factor; (3) non-European religious traditions which shape the habits of masses of mankind and whose assertions as to the meaning of law cannot wholly be discredited; (4) the scientific tradition which is a new discipline of the powers and faculties of mankind, bringing its own standards and shaping its own outlook; (5) heretical Christian and atheistic traditions which have, as in for example the Renaissance, the Enlightenment, Marxism, etc., often given expression to a perception of standards to which the Church has been blind, but which are none the less genuine standards which enrich human life.

All these elements of law are potentially incompatible, and the present confusion in social and political standards reflects the fact that no unity has been reached which blends these traditions into a common basis for corporate society. But the law of God with which the Christian has to reckon in his social and political action, includes within itself all these factors.

The Christian tradition has been included as one of the elements which rightly form part of the natural law as it confronts all men. The transforming power of the Gospel is at work in the sphere of natural law. The characteristic Hebrew-Christian understanding of law is not the punishment of the guilty, or a careful balance of impartiality, but the active succouring of the innocent and helpless. Without destroying its character as law, the life of the Church in the midst of the world has worked to put into the content of law attitudes which have their justification and demand in the Gospel. The common law, to which all men of every religion and race are subject, only fulfils its intrinsic purpose when it is deeply influenced by the Gospel of Christ.

The natural law of God, as men have understood it, is modified by the presence of Christ in the world. Law is modified, however, in two ways. Firstly, the positive direction, to allow the common life of humanity to be governed by standards and habits and sympathies whose ultimate justification is the Gospel of Christ. It can also be modified in a negative direction when the hostility to Christ is written into the law and social standards of mankind, making the life of a community more anti-Christian than if Christ had never come. This, however, results not merely in a rejection of the Gospel, but in the perversion and defilement of the standards which even unregenerate humanity can keep. In such a situation the Church must make plain its separation from the world by appealing from the debased law of man to the Gospel and Law of Christ.

But, whenever it is the duty of the Church to emphasise its separation from the world, two conditions must be observed. Firstly, the separation from the world must be practical and not simply abstract. There is no point in making a fuss about our withdrawal from a complex social process in which we have been given no opportunity for effective participation. Secondly, in its separation from the world the Church must nourish the seeds of a genuine culture and a true law by which the life of all mankind, non-Christians as well as Christians, can be quickened.

Here, perhaps is the place to consider the question of the relation of the natural law to the grace of God by which the Christian lives. Does the Christian experience the claim of the natural law as *law*—in the sense of the contrast between Law and Grace? Christians are ministers of a new covenant, not of the letter, but of the spirit: 'for the letter killeth, but the spirit giveth life' (II Cor 3.6).

In answer, a distinction must be made between the social-religious and the ultimate-religious meanings of law. The Christian needs the social discipline and guidance of law as much as his neighbour, and he is ready to acknowledge the positive value of law as a means to right and fruitful conduct. In the ultimate-religious sense, however, the Christian is not in principle under law at all, but under the power of that grace which needs no law. Law is there as signposts to action, not as constraint. In practice, unhappily, the Christian is not yet wholly freed from the condemnation of law. He falls from his high calling to where the constraint of the law is necessary to make him see the call of God. The Christian lives by grace, but he must acknowledge honestly those aspects of his life where he allows himself to fall under the condemnation of law.

What, then, is the authority of the Bible in the complex social and political decisions which have to be taken? The authority of the Bible is central inasmuch as it testifies to the meaning of that revelation of God by which Christians live. The Bible, firstly, testifies to the Word of God and to that characteristic response to the Word of God in Israel and in the Church, which is created by the Word itself. It is in the setting of the response to the Word in the Bible that we know the Word. And this characteristic response to the Word of God exhibits its fruits in the transformation of personal relations. Hence, what we learn in and through the Bible is not only the Gospel of Jesus Christ but the distinctive way of life which he creates among men. And we must continually re-learn its meaning in concrete situations.

But also, we cannot properly read the Bible and seek its guidance upon social and political issues without an understanding of the long years which contributed to its growth, and the many changes in standards, and customs, which it reflects. It tells a story of mingled defeat and victory set against a background which had many radical changes to record. This is in part a pure gain. It must be emphasised strongly that those who think of the Bible as of one piece and all equally relevant to every situation, cannot do justice to the social teaching of the Bible and cannot understand those parts of the Bible whose content is specially rooted in social situations.

But the question arises whether the Bible is time-conditioned in a way which makes it difficult for us to learn social standards from it. The question applies with especial force to the New Testament. Now, the Church must be prepared to consider honestly the sociologically limiting factors which affect the Bible. We must not, however, accept what appeals to our prejudices and reject the rest; we must be prepared to admit, if the facts warrant, not only that the truth of New Testament teaching is *more* affected than we might have supposed; and we must continue to assert that the Bible does set out a characteristic quality and direction of human living which is distinctive, and authoritative, and unaffected by changing conditions. Yet this characteristic quality is created in the response to the Lordship of Christ, and its living meaning under modern conditions comes through a response in Christ, and not by the application of something which in principle can be detached from him.

It has been said that the function of the Bible is to bear testimony to the *quality and direction of human action*. The phrase I borrow from Professor C. H. Dodd's lecture, *The Gospel and the Law of Christ*, but I must justify my own use of it. What we have in the Bible is testimony to actions which are appropriate for believing men. Such actions may be divided into (*a*) public actions which could be written into the public law of any society, and (*b*) the secret intents of the heart, which are matter for religious exhortation, but which cannot be made a matter of social regulation. What matters about the specific injunction of the Bible in both cases is not primarily the precise action, but the indication of a certain quality of mind and heart and of a certain direction in which action should move.

We find this characteristic quality and direction in the Old Testament as well as in the New. For example, on the public side, there is a concern for the well-being of a man's neighbour, in Deut. 22.1-4, 24.10-13, 17-18 which is desirable in any human society, and rightly kindled by the worship of God. In Deut. 15.7-11 there is a warning against the lack of generosity of spirit towards our neighbour, which anticipates the Sermon on the

Mount. The quality of generous concern for others is indissolubly linked with the faith of the Bible.

But the Bible is a varied collection of literature, and there are in it many incompatible injunctions to action. The quality and direction of human action commended in the Bible is not uniform. Is, for example, Acts 5.1-11, to be taken as a standard of discipline in the life of the Church? We must answer that the Bible must be read from its centre in Jesus Christ crucified and risen, and that actions and injunctions must be judged by the degree of their conformity to that characteristic quality and direction of life which is the distinctive product of the Gospel.

Parts of the Bible may be far removed from the central testimony, and yet, because they bear the imprint of the Word of God and of the response to that Word in Israel and in the Church, may convey in concrete form that quality of action which we need to embody. Christians need, therefore, to steep themselves in the teaching and atmosphere of the Bible, because we are constantly being misled as to the quality and direction of human action, and need to be recalled to the events in history by which the power of God was released then, and is released again for us. We must not think of our Christian awareness of the quality and direction of human action as something which we can take for granted. On the contrary, in face of concrete decision, we must consult our Bibles afresh, not to find a mechanical answer to our problems, but in order that we may become aware of new resources in the Word of God of which we had not been aware.

The relation of the Christian concern for the quality of human action to the complex factors entering into decisions may be seen in Matt. 6.14-34. The paradox of human action lies not in the rejection of the general human concern with food and drink and clothing. Where this happens, and the shaping importance of the means of production are ignored and the Kingdom of God sought first in a false spirituality, then the power of Christian action is lost. It is from within a living awareness of the urgency and inescapability of the demand for food and drink and clothing that the claim of the Kingdom of God is to be asserted as central. How that is to be done cannot be answered in a formula, but can only be worked out in the obedience of faith. But the meaning of the Kingdom of God—which is given to us through the Bible—must control our answers to the problems which others as well as ourselves are engaged in answering.

In such situations it is possible, and indeed legitimate for Christians to differ on the solution of social and political issues. But we must be clear about the strict limits of such difference. All Christians in their social and political action are bound by the quality and direction of human action which the Bible declares. Unless even across the widest diversity of outward action there is a unity of which Christians can be conscious, unless even in the differences of actual decision the impress of the Biblical testimony to the Christian way of life has stamped itself upon Christian believers, then the truth of the Gospel has been set aside. We are bound by the Word of God in our actions as Christians, and although this does not mean a clear-cut unity in social and political matters, the Word does not return to God void.

A parallel issue is raised by the divergences of Christian teaching and practice in different periods of history. We may, of course, hold that God has never in fact allowed his Church to err, and that under changing circumstances the Church has always made the right witness. Even so, we are faced with the practical problem of how far Christian witness in social and political matters ought to change with changing circumstances. But real divergences in tradition do occur, and continuity in Christian social and political witness is not maintained directly, but is re-established across upheavals in the functioning of civilisation which necessitate the re-thinking of all the habits of life. But unless a real unity can be discerned even in the most unforeseen breaks with customary Christian tradition, the truth of the Gospel has at some point been set aside. For there is a unity of decision in social and political action which God gives to his people even in radically diverse centuries.

What, then, is the relation of church-tradition to the Bible in social action? The tradition of the Church—in the ordinary sense of the word 'tradition'—is important not as an additional source to determine what the Gospel is, but as the fruit of the working of the Gospel in the life of the Church. It would be ignorant and presumptuous to ignore the tradition of the Church, as though the Lord Jesus Christ had made no impact upon the life of the world before our appearance. But it would also be a denial of the present claim of God to our obedience, and failure to recognise an element of error in the witness of the Church in ancient times, if we rightly equated the past tradition of the Church with the present claim of God upon us.

It is wrong to set the Bible and Church over against one another as though they were separate. The Bible must be understood in the content of the Church and the Church is judged and renewed by that revelation to which the Bible testifies. But there is a broad difference between the authority of the Bible and the authority of the tradition of the Church. It is from the Bible that the content of the Christian revelation is known and the social and political details given are significant for us as examples of the impact of that revelation rather than as detailed answers to specific problems. But the tradition of the Church shows us how the Church worked out the answer to the problem of the meaning of Christian witness under specific conditions.

This had advantages and disadvantages. It has advantages in that if we want Christian guidance on particular problems, then we are given much more detailed treatment of the issues. It has disadvantages inasmuch as changing conditions make the detail irrelevant. Whatever continuity there may be in Christian doctrine, it is quite clear that there is considerably less in Christian witness in social and political issues.

The tradition of the Church is, in fact, ambiguous. This is not wholly due to the limited extent of the unequivocal testimony of this tradition in the Church to which the Bible testifies. The ambiguity of the tradition is inherent. In part, the tradition of the Church has, as over against the fluidity of the present, a content of actualised Christian truth before which we must be humble, and therefore the tradition of the Church may act not only as the means of preserving essential Christian witness in days of decline, but also as a means of reforming the Church according to the Word of God. But in part also the tradition of the Church has, as over against the fluidity of the present, a rigidity which may both stifle the freedom of a living response to a living Lord and bind upon the Church habits and standards which are irrelevant to a changed situation. The tradition of the Church may then be the means whereby the meaning of the Revelation of Christ is apprehended in its impact in social and political matters. But if so, this is because through the tradition the Revelation of God in

Christ becomes real to us, and not simply because it is in fact the tradition of the Church. Yet we need to heed the tradition of the Church if we do not want to set aside the guidance of God.

How, then, are we to know when the tradition of the Church gives us the guidance of God? The answer must be, Through the Holy Spirit. But it is equally clear that there are no formal criteria by which we can know what the Holy Spirit says without the responsibility of decision. The *testimonium spiritus sancti internum* is a certain guide, but we cannot know that we have it. We can, of course, know that Christ is faithful, but not that we are infallibly right.

We are all agreed in principle—no Christian can be found who will deny the guidance of the Holy Spirit. But agreement as to what this guidance means is extremely difficult. It is precisely by means of the witness of the Holy Spirit that we respond to the revelation of God in the Bible, and discern the true tradition of the Church. But how are we to know the witness of the Holy Spirit? Only by means of the revelation of God in the Bible and in the tradition of the Church. If this reasoning is circular, the circle is not a vicious circle, but an indication of the fact that we are not thinking about a fact within the control of man, but about the revelation of the Living God.

There are two main sources of error, apart from our own sinful hearts. One is the pressure of false assumptions which are currently held. We have been solemnly warned by our Lord that we are held responsible for discerning the signs of the times, but we know the difficulty of meeting this requirement. The other main source of error is that in our immersion in the complexity of detail we are not always aware of how far we have been carried from those ends of human action which we must be concerned as Christians to fulfil. It is from the Bible, as we constantly listen to the Word God speaking through it, that a living awareness of the true quality and direction of human action must be renewed.

We are concerned here about the witness of the Holy Spirit to the authority of the Bible in social and political matters. It is not the authority of the Bible in itself that is in question, but the Bible as a specific direction for a new situation. Where such guidance of the Holy Spirit means that a central Biblical conviction is obviously illuminated in a given situation, we may find it easy to be confident that this is right. But the witness of the

Holy Spirit may be to convince us of a line of action which appears irrelevant to and contradictory of Biblical conviction. We may in fact fail in a true obedience to Biblical truth by clinging to what is formally Biblical instead of accepting the true guidance of the Holy Spirit to what may not be formally Biblical at all. At the point of action the truth of the *testimonium spiritus sancti internum* cannot be seen. It can only be believed in fear and trembling. The witness of the Holy Spirit will also reinforce the tradition of the Church, in that it will open the way to that obedience which renews and re-establishes the tradition of the Church. But this does not mean a simple conformity to the existing tradition. Simple conformity may indeed be the way of Christian discipleship. But Christian discipleship may also mean dissent from existing tradition, that the living tradition of the Church may be newly manifested. In the life of the Church actual obedience to the *testimonium spiritus sancti internum* always involves an element of loneliness and difficulty. The Bible not only testifies to the way of God, but also to how that way must be discovered and re-discovered in human history.

4

A BAPTIST CONTRIBUTION

by

VINJAMURI E. DEVADUTT

I. *The basic difference between Hinduism and Christianity*

This chapter has a limited scope. It attempts to discuss the question of Biblical authority in relation to a situation where the Christian faith is confronted by an ancient religion which claims the allegiance of millions of people, viz. Hinduism. The chapter will displease the Hindu and some Christians. But an honest attempt has been made to see things clearly, and to get behind superficial agreements to the basic problems that make these two faiths two and not one. Our motive, however, has not been a negative one. We have attempted to show how the two can understand each other and in this understanding there may be the possibility of 'conversation'.

In the great religious systems of the Hindus, the question of 'authority' occupies an important place. Many of these systems are frankly authoritarian, though reason and experience are given quite an honourable place. This has produced in the course of the evolution of the Hindu religious systems certain very interesting results. By 'authority' is meant usually the canonical scriptures, i.e. the Vedas. Systems of religion or philosophical thought, however much they may differ from one another in their fundamental beliefs and practices, may still claim inclusion in the general system of Hinduism, provided they accept the authority of canonical scriptures. Hinduism, as its students know, is neither one religious system nor one type of philosophical thought. A wide variety of 'Sampradayas', i.e. traditions, often at great variance with one another in essentials and fundamentals, compose the complex called Hinduism. There is very little in common between Vaishnava Sampradayas and the Advaita

System. The former are essentially theistic and the latter, while accommodating religion for the benefit of the weak-minded, looks upon Religious Reality, i.e. a personal God, as a subordinate Reality, even phenomenal in character. The highest Truth according to the Advaita is the impersonal and non-qualitative Brahman. And yet both are included in Hinduism and are treated as orthodox! Though Buddhism and Jainism have had their origin in India, they are treated as heterodox, not primarily on the ground of the doctrinal peculiarities of those two systems, but because they disowned the authority of the Vedas. This position of the Hindu makes him take a certain attitude to the claims of the Christian faith in India. Many modern Hindus are prepared to grant the uniqueness of the Person of Christ, but they profess that they do not understand why the Indian Christian should not be considered free to treat the Vedas or the portions of them called the Upanishads as his Scriptures. The modern Hindu contends that while the history of the Jews and the deposit of sacred wisdom of this race, as embodied in the Old Testament, may undoubtedly be inspiring, he cannot see what relevance all this has to non-Jewish races, especially to races which have an equally long religious history and scriptures of even greater antiquity. And furthermore, and this is the real contention, all that is worth while and really valuable and inspiring from a purely religious point of view in the Jewish Scriptures is found in the Hindu scriptures and tradition, and while the Christian need not surrender any of the doctrines he considers essential and material to his faith, he can find all the 'authority' he needs for his theology in the latter. He may feel reasonably that he needs the New Testament, and he may retain it as additional to the Vedas, and the modern Hindu is himself prepared to recognise an intrinsic worth in at least certain portions of the New Testament.

This readiness of the modern Hindu to accommodate the Christian faith to the Hindu systems is a constant challenge to the Indian Christian theologian. One need not suspect any unworthy motive on the part of the modern Hindu in this attitude. The nationalist sentiment, with the pride that it involves in all that is a national possession, may be there. Psychologically an element of romantic nostalgia for the heritage from the past of one's own country may also be there; but both these elements are by no means peculiar to the Hindu mind. Even certain types of Christian tradition unhappily manifest them. The attitude is essentially traceable to the modern Hindu's basic religious philosophy, a philosophy that has its roots in the Upanishads, the most important part of the Vedas. It is not necessary to examine this basic philosophy in detail. But the idea of syncretism must be considered at the deepest level, since some Indian Christians, and also some Western students of Indian religions, are attracted by what seems an essentially reasonable and generous attitude on the part of the Hindu, his readiness to accommodate the Christian faith in the Hindu systems. The real danger of such syncretism is the fact that the Hindu expects the Christian to make equal concessions, by recognising the Vedas as a source of inspiration and authority side by side with the New Testament. This point we must take up.

The substance of this basic religious philosophy is the following:

A. Reality is One. If Reality is One, then the Many cannot be also at the same time real. The Many at best are only provisionally real. To gain a vision of the One, we must discipline ourselves to turn that vision away from the Many.[1]

B. If Reality were really One and if it really transcended the Many and is thus a Unity, then our apprehension of it is never through intellectual categories. Intellectual categories emerge from and operate only in the context of an epistemological dualism, i.e. in the context of an antithesis between the subject and the object. But if Reality were One and a Unity the dualism implied by the subject-object relationship is excluded from its unitary integrity, and with it any possibility of intellectual apprehension. All intellectual apprehensions and all affirmations arising from the experience that is rooted in the subject-object antithesis pertain only to the realm of the Many, i.e. to the realm that is only provisionally and pragmatically true.[2]

[1] 'There is on earth no diversity.
He gets death after death,
Who perceives here seeming diversity.
As a unity only is it to be looked upon,
This indemonstrable, enduring Being.'
Brihadarnyaka Upanishad 4.4:19-20. Hume's Translation.

[2] 'There the eye goes not;
Speech goes not, nor the mind,
We know not, we understand not
How one would teach It.'
Kena Upanishad 3. Hume's Translation.

C. All deliverances of our experience, intellectual and otherwise, even the profoundest of them, having this strictly limited reference to the realm of the provisionally or pragmatically true, never carry with them the stamp of ultimate truthfulness. They may not be untrue, for the Many being provisionally true does express partially the nature of Reality. In other words they are both true and false. They are true in the sense that they partially express the nature of Reality; they are false in the sense that no intellectual truth or truths apprehended in experience ever express the nature of Reality in any adequate sense.

D. Since what is said above applies equally to religious experience, all religious affirmations are both true and false. They are all true, however divergent they may be from one another; they all emerge from an experience that operates in the realm of the provisionally true and share its character. Furthermore, never having access to Reality in our normal experience, we dare not say that any affirmation is untrue. They are false also, for they can never express the total or true nature of Reality.[1]

From the above summary it can be seen wherein lie the roots of the toleration and the accommodating spirit of the modern Hindu. All religions are equally true and equally false.[2] If this is the nature of religion *qua* religion, to assess the relative merits of various religions is stupid. Let them live in amity. As for the Christian faith, it has great merits, but its claim to sole apprehension of truth is insufferable and its propagation among the Indians disrupts the Indian society. Let it, however, accept the Vedas as its scriptures and thus reorientate itself to the great stream of Indian tradition, and within this tradition it can enjoy whatever freedom it desires.

[1] 'Into blind darkness enter they
That worship ignorance:
Into darkness greater than that as it were
That delight in knowledge.'
Isa Upanishad 9. Hume's Translation.

[2] 'Even as a tree has a single trunk, but many branches and leaves, so is there one true and perfect religion, but it becomes many as it passes through the human medium. The one Religion is beyond all speech. Imperfect men put it into such language as they can command, and their words are interpreted by other men equally imperfect. Whose interpretation is to be held to be the right one? Everybody is right from his own standpoint, but it is not impossible that everybody is wrong.' Mahatma Gandhi in an article on 'Tolerance, i.e. Equality of Religions', printed in a collection of his speeches and writings entitled *Christian Missions*, Navajivan Press, Ahamadabad, India.

In the light of what is said above, it ought to be clear to such Indian Christians as see a real opportunity in the invitation by Hinduism to the Christian faith to a free alliance, that the invitation is not so simple as it seems. The invitation arises in a deep and fundamental religious conviction of the Hindus; this conviction is the strongest of all convictions entertained by the modern educated Hindu.[1] But the conviction is at fundamental variance with the major convictions of the Christian faith. In other words, the theologies of both differ fundamentally. One believes in a supra-rational, supra-personal unitary Reality, which according to some not only transcends in its own nature everything known in experience or apprehended in thought, but which even annuls all such in its unitary integrity. The other believes in a personal God, 'Father Almighty, maker of heaven and earth'. The realm of the Many is his creation and the sphere of his purposive action.

II *History and revelation*

The Christian faith is based on a revelation. Hinduism also professes to be based on revelation. But when we examine their respective views of revelation they diverge. According to the Christian view, revelation is the self-disclosing activity of God. Revelation is something that takes place. It is in and through an event. Revelation is not intuitive insights of men into the nature of Reality, though to be sure these insights have a supreme value. Revelation is a movement from God's side. The Christian believes in the revelation of God in the history of the Hebrews and in Jesus Christ.

The Christian view of revelation as the activity of God presupposes two things. In the first place, it presupposes that God is a personal Being. Activity, directed deliberately and consciously toward fulfilment of purposes, belongs only to personal beings. Where reality is viewed as impersonal and devoid of conscious purposes, where it is looked upon as transcending good and evil, there you cannot expect the type of activity implied by revelation in the Christian sense. Reality which is just Being, and a static identity with no history, cannot reveal itself and show a purpose. If the word 'revelation' is used with reference to such a reality, as it is sometimes in the Advaita, the word stands for

[1] Ramakrishna Mission, a body that is a typical representative of the best in modern Hinduism, insists that its adherents express no criticism of a Faith or Way which they themselves do not agree with.

mystic intuition in which the distinction hitherto falsely thought to exist between Reality and the individual is abolished, and the undivided Reality stands self-shining with nothing to look at and nobody to look at it. It would not be true, of course, to say that all systems of Hindu thought believe that Reality is impersonal and is a Unity. The one system that is uncompromisingly monistic or non-dualistic is the Advaita. There are Hindu systems which have no sympathy with the Advaitic point of view. Nevertheless, it would be true to say that the Hindu mind is generally more inclined toward the Advaita than toward the systems that are nearer the theistic point of view. Even where the theistic point of view is entertained, in many cases it is only provisional, for it is believed that beyond the theistic point of view there is a higher point of view, where man's mind ceases to use personal categories and learns in an intuitive vision and mystic contemplation that Reality is beyond personality, beyond change, beyond speech and understandings. The theistic point of view, it is contended, is a helpful discipline but does not 'deliver the goods'. The Bhagavad-gita, the bible of the modern Hindu, sets both the theistic point of view and the point of view of philosophical monism side by side. Though we believe that it is possible for a discriminating mind to see that the characteristic point of view of the author of the Gita himself is what might be termed the 'Purusha Gati', i.e. the theistic point of view, he is too shy to declare it clearly and plainly, and accommodates alongside his theism 'Akshara-Gati', i.e. the point of view of philosophical monism. Modern commentators on the Gita accordingly believe that the theism of the Gita is only one side of its teaching and that the Gita believes that Reality essentially transcends personal existence. Thus Radhakrishnan writes: 'Of course the Gita does not tell us of the way in which the absolute, as impersonal non-active spirit, becomes the active personal Lord creating and sustaining the universe. The problem is considered to be insoluble. The mystery clears up only when we rise to the level of intuition. The transformation of the absolute into God is maya or a mystery. It is also maya in the sense that the transformed world is not so real as the absolute itself.'[1]

In the second place, the Christian view of revelation assumes that history is real, though not ultimate, for the activity of God is

[1] S. Radhakrishnan, *Indian Philosophy*, Vol. I, 2nd Ed., p. 539.

in history. History is the sphere of God's purposive action. But if someone's view of Reality is that it is impersonal, with no conscious activity of its own, history cannot be real to him. History is a scene of activity; it is a realm of change. And as an order representing activity and change, it is antithetical to Reality, which is changeless and immutable. At the highest, history has only a pragmatic reality and one who has gained the mystic intuition does not retain any traces of association with the historical order, for the order is completely annulled to him. Revelation in the Christian sense is completely meaningless on this reading of history. Of course, the theistic systems in Hinduism should not find it difficult to accept the reality of history. But while they repudiate the Advaita interpretation of history, even they find it difficult to treat history seriously. Creation is due to the *Lila* of God, a sportive impulse in him. While *Lila* does not imply meaningless playfulness, it expresses the Hindu shyness in ascribing to God purposiveness in creation. Purposiveness implies a working toward ends, and working toward ends implies that there is something that is yet unrealised—something that is in the 'end' only. But to God and in God there is nothing that is unrealised. There is no lack in him and so it is contended that we cannot ascribe purposes to God. Accordingly there is nothing even in the theistic Hinduism comparable to the Christian conception of the Church, or the Kingdom of God, both these taken to represent the Christian belief in the partially realised will of God in the temporal order, though both having a futuristic and eschatological reference. Furthermore, the law of moral economy in the world is the Law of Karma. No doubt the Law of Karma in a sense expresses divine purpose, but once having been ordained by God for man's good, it operates with as absolute an autonomy as the causal law in the physical realm. So in the end no active and present Divine purpose need be resorted to to interpret history. And on the whole man's duty is to turn away from history, to escape from the cycle of births and deaths and gain *Mukti*—release. On this view also revelation, interpreted as the self-disclosing activity of God in great historical events, is impossible. In all the Hindu scriptures there is no event parallel to the deliverance of Israel from the Egyptian bondage, to the Exile and to the return from it.

One of the persistent teachings of the Puranic literature, it might be contended as against what we have said above, concerns the intervention of God in the affairs of men when these affairs go wrong. This thought is also the thought, in a measure, of the Epics. The Gita, which forms a part of the Mahabharata, teaches that whenever there is a decline in morality, and evil triumphs, God comes into the world to restore order. The Puranic stories of Avataras are an illustration of this teaching of the Gita. Here we confront a crucial issue. On the subject of Incarnation, Christianity and Hinduism come very near each other in theory and yet they divide vitally on this subject. The Christian believes that the revelatory activity of God culminated in Incarnation—in the incarnate Jesus. And the author of the Fourth Gospel avers, perhaps against the Gnostics, that 'the Word became flesh and made its tabernacle among men'.[1] Incarnation is an intractable event in history according to the Christian faith, and there would be no Christian faith but for this event. And the words 'the Word became flesh' have to be taken seriously. Though the idea of Avatar is quite a familiar idea in Hinduism, the Hindu mind seems to shy away from attaching any reality to Avatar as an event. Thus, for instance, Professor D. S. Sarma writes: 'The Hindu Scriptures deal with ideal truth and not with historical truth. Their validity does not depend on any historical fact. This is very well illustrated in the accounts we have in the Puranas of the various Avataras. For these are intended only to give an imaginative representation of God's help rendered to man at different stages of his evolution'.[2] Thus, the intuitive insight of the common man that his Creator is vitally concerned with his and his fellow-beings' affairs and that he, thus conceived, does deign to come into the world, is explained away.

In the Christian faith, revelation and redemption are inseparably linked. According to the Old Testament, revelation is to be seen primarily in the great acts of God's judgment and redemption. The revelation of God in Jesus Christ is both a judgment of man and a means of his salvation. Nothing in all human knowing is a more severe condemnation of man's sin and a more poignant revelation of the forgiving heart of God than the Cross—an event in the history of Incarnation. The Cross condemns and reconciles at once. The Law of Karma and redemption through vicarious suffering are irreconcilable. The

[1] John 1.14. [2] D. S. Sarma, *Primer of Hinduism*, p. 15.

Law of Karma is the causal law in the moral sphere; nothing and nobody can interfere with its autonomous operation, not even God who is its author. Even Ramanuja can only concede that God helps man to live a good life that his debt to the Law of Karma may eventually be wiped out. The Law of Karma, let it be admitted, expresses the Hindu faith in the integrity of the moral universe. The assumptions behind it, however, are very different from the Christian assumptions centring round the Cross. The Cross is not a condemnation primarily of man's moral failure, though to be sure eventually it is. Moral failure is only an effect of something else and it will not be cured unless its cause is removed. This cause is man's alienation from God, a wilful straying away from his presence and rule. The Cross is a condemnation of this alienation and enmity and that is why it can reconcile, removing the enmity. The enmity is the sin, and moral failure is the result of the enmity. The Christian emphasis is on a personal relationship, the breach in which is man's trouble. The emphasis of the Law of Karma is on an autonomous moral universe. The universe may express the will of God; nevertheless, it is autonomous, sovereign and impersonal. Moral failure is the violation of the laws of the moral universe and its immutable laws take care of all violations. Because sin in the Christian faith is conceived as arising in a breach of a personal relationship, its cure is conceived as consisting in the restoration of that personal relationship, and revelation as a means of redemption is utterly intelligible in such a context. But where sin is identical with moral failure only, and where the moral person is related only to an impersonal moral universe, there revelation as connected with redemption, has no meaning. The Cross indeed is foolishness, for how can the death of one man wipe out the sins of many, even when the very will of God which has ordained the moral universe cannot interfere with the operation of its immutable laws?

We have seen in sharp outline some of the differences between Christianity and Hinduism. But while these differences on the theoretical level are stubborn and irreconcilable, there is an overwhelming portion of the Hindu community to whom these theoretical considerations are of no consequence. Their religion is a warm-hearted one; their devotion is to a personal God and it glows with a fervour that would put many a Christian to shame. The God they worship is not only personal, but is supremely a moral Person. The attitude that philosophic Hinduism takes to the religious insights of these people is one of benevolent tolerance, but it would if it could, if only in a friendly way, explain away most of these insights. One of these insights is that God is supremely concerned with the affairs of men and that therefore he deigns to come into their midst taking a mortal form. Recall how Professor D. S. Sarma seeks simultaneously both to retain and dismiss this insight. According to him, the Hindu Scriptures deal only with ideal truth and not with historical truth, and while there is truth in the Puranic accounts of the Avataras, that truth is only ideal truth. But the common man who believes that God by his nature is such that he does reveal himself to men, to answer their longings for him, by actually coming into their midst, does not subscribe to the theory of Professor Sarma and people of his way of thinking. Is Professor Sarma seeking an escape from the historical improbability of the reported Avataras? But if there is any truth-value in the insight, it does not behove one to explain it away in the way that Professor Sarma does. It is an insight that millions of people share in India. At one time in Indian history people who shared this insight rebelled and turned against the abstractions of philosophic Hinduism—a rebellion which resulted in the Bhakti movement. The weakness of the belief of these Bhaktas and the particular insight of the movement that we are considering, is that there is nothing in Hinduism on the level of fact to answer to the implication of this insight. The historical improbability of the Avataras should not turn one to idealisation. Should Hinduism content itself with ideal truth only? Of what value is the conception of Avatara if it only represents an ideal possibility in the Being of God? Why does not the Hindu thinker, as a searcher after truth, examine impartially and without prejudice the claims of the Christian faith? He may find in the Christian belief in Jesus Christ the answer on the level of fact to the implications of the insights of the Bhakti movement.

III *Record and Revelation*

Revelation in Hinduism is really equivalent to the Scriptures. The official Hindu doctrine of revelation is the doctrine of *sabda*. The meaning of *sabda* is 'sound'; but it is not mere sound, but significant sound, i.e. sound embodied in meaningful words. Words are the medium by which men exchange their thoughts and make their purposes known to each other. Words reveal one mind to another mind. The mind of God is revealed by words communicated by him to seers and sages. Revelation thus is by means of words. And the words, communicated by God to Rishis and embodied in the Scriptures, i.e. the Vedas, constitute revelation. We believe that, except to a few, to those in the Christian faith the Scriptures and revelation are not identical. Revelation is not through words, not through propositions and not through communication of knowledge. Revelation is through action. Words can say something about an action, but they can never contain it. Accordingly, our view is that the Christian Scriptures are the record of revelation and not the revelation itself. Anyone with even a superficial acquaintance with the religious literature of the world knows one characteristic feature of the Bible—its concern with history. The Old Testament attempts to present history, the history of a small nation. No other religious literature in the world concerns itself so largely with historical events or what were thought to be historical events. This preoccupation with history in the Old Testament has offended many people and even many good Christians. What significance can the history of a small nation have for others and what message has it of universal application? History by its very nature is local both in regard to and space, and the experiences of any given people in any given period of time therefore cannot have a universal message. This last contention is true in a sense, but there is here a complete misunderstanding of the motive and the method of the historian of the Old Testament. The point is that the Old Testament writers are interested in history because to them it is made up of God's acts—the great acts of judgment and redemption. Understood in this sense the Old Testament as a historical narrative is not the history of a nation as such, but largely a record of the acts of God in relation to a nation. If revelation is through action, then there is much to be found in the Old Testament concerning revelation. As we have stated above, the Book itself is not revelation. Much that is human interposes in the actual recording, but the central theme is more often than not the activity of God. Those who say that they are repelled by the Old Testament confess often to a feeling of being more at home in the New Testament. The reason given is that the alleged cramping limitations of a narrowly historical point of view are absent in the New Testament and that in it we deal with ideas. No doubt there is history of the personality of Jesus, but such history is said to be incidental. We are primarily concerned, it is contended, with the ideas of this unique personality and the ideas of his followers about him. There is a profound misunderstanding here also. In a good part of the New Testament, also, we are primarily dealing with historical narrative and the rest of it revolves round a historical event—the act of God in coming into history. The New Testament narrative begins with a mighty event in history; if that event did not occur, there would be no New Testament. The New Testament writers do not play around ideas for their own sake, but they deal with ideas in so far as they are related to this historical event. The feeling that in the New Testament we are not moving in the alleged atmosphere of a narrowly historical point of view, is due to the fact that whereas in the Old Testament every act of God was understood as having a primary significance for the Hebrew nation alone, in the New Testament the acts of God for the first time in the whole range of Biblical writing, are unreservedly and totally conceived as having significance for the whole human race and not because it deals with ideas. The New Testament also is a record primarily of the acts of God—a record of the mightiest act of God, viz. his coming into history in Jesus Christ. Thus the Old and New Testaments are records of revelation.

The Bible is the only report and record of revelation of God in the history of the Hebrew race and in Jesus Christ and its value is determined by its character as such a record. As a record of revelation it is authoritative in relation to this revelation and all that this revelation means by implication. Revelation itself has an authority that is absolute, otherwise it would cease to be revelation. If we accept that God has revealed his will, we are bound to accept that revelation. The Bible as the record of revelation possesses the same authority as revelation in so far as that revelation is concerned. What we mean is this: while the authority of the Bible is absolute in matters that are made manifest to us in the revelatory activity of God, and also in matters that are strictly deducible from this activity, it would be illegitimate to extend its authority beyond them directly. It would have an indirect authority in regard to these other matters in that the ultimate point of view for the Christian in anything is a religious point of view, and that is based on the Bible.

In speaking about the value of the Bible as determined by its character as the record of revelation, we seem to involve ourselves in a difficulty. We know of the revelation of God only because the Bible witnesses to it; it is the only source of our information concerning the self-disclosing activity of God, and it seems illogical to determine its value by that to which it witnesses. Without the Bible we should have no information concerning revelation and it is the latter that determines the value of the Bible. This seems to be arguing in a circle. Formally perhaps it is. But we often judge the worth of a reporter by that which he reports. The Bible itself is not revelation, but it is authoritative by virtue of the inherent worth of that which it reports and records. And if we take revelation seriously we have to accept its authority; and if we accept its authority we have to accept the authority of that which witnesses to it and makes a record of it. This authority is binding, subject to the delimitation indicated earlier.

The Bible is an inspired record of revelation. When we say it is inspired we mean that the people who had a share in its writing were under the guidance of the Spirit of God. Inspiration is not verbal communication, making of the writer merely a pen for the Divine Spirit. Inspiration is that which moves and guides. It is such an inspiration of the Divine Spirit which enabled the writers of the Bible to see God's activity. Being an inspired record of revelation, the Bible has the power, when reverently read, to make that revelation vital to our experience. The word of the Bible when read in faith becomes the living Word of God and as the living Word of God a power unto our salvation.

The question is often asked whether, granting that the Bible is a record of revelation, it would be true to say that all the portions of it are such a record and equally authoritative. We have maintained that the revelation of God is through his judging and redeeming activity. It is clear, however, that the recognition of the redemptive movement of God in particular historical events is not always easy. Historical process is determined both by the activity of God and man's response to that activity. The Hebrew recognised this. Though he believed that there would be no history without God's activity, he did not believe that history was solely and automatically determined by such activity. The Hebrew never attributed every historical phenomenon to God solely. Such a thing would reduce man's status to that of an automaton. Man's resistance to God's purposes brought forth moral and spiritual degradation in society, and man alone was responsible for such conditions and therefore merited God's judgment. But he could co-operate with God by turning away from his evil ways and by walking humbly with him and thus allow God to hasten the bright day of hope. History is thus determined by God's activity and man's response to it. Now, the writers of the Old Testament were not always able, despite this recognition of the nature of the historical process, to disentangle man's share in any given historical event. But we have a principle by which we can do this, at least with a better measure of success. The judging and redeeming activity of God culminates in the incarnate Jesus. It is the testimony of the Bible itself. God who has always been acting, now acts in Jesus Christ. Jesus Christ is God in the fulness of his judging and redeeming activity. In order therefore to see the human and the divine factors involved in the historical process, we must continually refer to Christ as the true criterion and standard. The historical Jesus is the temporal manifestation of the eternal Christ, who in the indivisible being of God constitutes his purposes for mankind, both creative and redemptive. And Jesus Christ, being the highest possible embodiment for men of the revelation of God, becomes the key to understanding other revelatory acts of God. Christ is the value judgment on the record of revelation. Now, to the question if all the portions of the Bible are equally authoritative, we reply in the affirmative in so far as they stand the test explained above. This test is not something imported from outside the Bible. It is derived from the Bible itself, from the purpose of its narrative.

IV *Authority in the realm of ethics*

The main interest of this chapter is to show the relevance of the Bible to the Church's social and political message—indeed, not merely its relevance, but its authority concerning this message. We are to discuss the question, not, however, in a general way, but with particular reference to problems in the Indian situation. Social and political problems in the end are ethical problems. Social and political objectives are conceived in relation to the 'good' that is to be obtained for the individual and society through social and political organisation. The determination of the 'good' is based essentially on an ethical outlook, whatever that ethical outlook might be. An ethical outlook or an ethical point of view needs to be undergirded by a more inclusive and wider outlook. An autonomous ethic is a myth. In determining what constitutes the ethical good, you need at least to take into consideration human nature and human needs. To the extent that such a consideration is needed, to that extent at least an ethical outlook is dependent on something other than itself. The question really is, what should this other be? Secularism and humanism have really failed to give us firm foundations on which to base our ethics. And yet to many educated Hindus, humanism and secularism seem the only alternative to the religion of their fathers and, being dissatisfied with the latter, they are being driven to the former. Why does this dissatisfaction arise? We may guess at one or two reasons.

In the first place, for a long time and till recently, the Hindu ethical system for the common man was mainly that implied by the concept of the Varna Dharma, i.e. caste duty. Of course, he had also the ideal of Sadharana Dharma, i.e. common or universal virtues, such as truth-speaking, abstaining from causing injury, the practice of charity, friendliness to all creatures, purity, continence, etc. But what was plain to everyone was the Varna Dharma, and the connection between religion and ethics was more clearly seen here than in the case of Sadharana Dharmas, for the latter could be conceived even by 'natural conscience' without establishing any connection between them and religion. But in modern times, for a variety of reasons, people began to rebel against Varna Dharma. But rebellion against an ethical system which has its roots in a religious outlook involves inevitably at least a sceptical attitude toward that religion. To quite a few enlightened Hindus, humanism was the alternative. But perhaps there is another reason too why to many educated Hindus secularism and humanism are more attractive than any religion. Some forms of renascent Hinduism, in their desire to purify Hinduism of popular and indefensible beliefs, shifted the emphasis greatly from religion to philosophy, which task, of course, was not difficult, in view of the Indian tradition, where both have always walked hand in hand. We see actually a revival of the Upanishadic tradition in this, and the emphasis is on an idealistic monism. We have examined earlier a few of the assumptions of this philosophy. In regard to ethic, the attitude of idealistic monism is that ethical value as such really belongs to the realm of evaluation, and not to the realm of value at all. Reality which is a unitary integrity is by virtue of that character above good and evil. When you relegate the ethical value to the realm of evaluations, to the realm which is real only provisionally and pragmatically, you necessarily weaken its claims. If ethical value belongs only to that which is real only pragmatically, the sanctions of morality are reduced to expediency and prudence. The 'ought' of the moral law is replaced at best by 'the must'. Many advocates of modern Hinduism are sensitive to this criticism. They of course, have no intention that the sanctions of morality should be those of prudence and expediency. They believe the ethical outlook of the Hindu is well taken care of by some very inspiring teaching coming down from ancient days. But what is not realised is that you cannot expect people not to draw the plain conclusions from a given point of view. You cannot expect people to have one view of reality and another view in regard to morals. They are connected or linked together. To those with a social idealism and passion the philosophical point of view, which consigns ethical value to the realm of evaluations, is unsatisfactory. But if, to be religious, one ought to accept this particular position, it is better to abandon all religion. On purely secular grounds one can at least determine scientifically man's needs and understand the 'good' in relation to those needs.

At the moment, when caste is definitely breaking down and its sociological and religious assumptions practically repudiated, and renascent Hinduism with its dominantly philosophical outlook is unable to supply the incentive and motive for a satisfactory and enduring ethic, there is absolute confusion and chaos in the ethical outlook of the people in India. It is admitted by all honest people in contemporary India that ethically our national life has perhaps touched bottom. Corruption in public life is increasing at an alarming speed; public spirit is conspicuous by its absence. If this were all due to deliberate perversity in the people, the situation would not be serious, for the wicked can always be reformed, at least one hopes so. The tragedy of the situation is that many do not show any evidence of possessing any sense of moral discrimination and do evil in good faith. The man who travels on a railway without a ticket and believes that there is nothing inherently wrong in it, has lost or has no sense of moral discrimination. The situation is so alarming that it is time for the leaders of Hindu thought to give up their defensive role and attempt to face facts squarely. This is a pathetic situation in a country which till the other day was under the leadership of a unique moral personality—Mahatma Gandhi. Why has Gandhian leadership, a leadership that cast an absolute spell during the life-time of the leader, failed? The reason is not far to seek. Mahatma Gandhi claimed that he was a Hindu. It is stupid to contest this claim. Nevertheless, with the greatest amount of goodwill, it is difficult to substantiate his claim that his ethical teaching, at any rate, was derived from the Gita. This is not to say that Mahatmaji was dishonest. No Indian, no matter to what faith he belongs, can charge the Mahatma with this failing. But whatever the reason, his claim was not true. We do not imply by this that his ethical teaching was derived from the Christian sources. It was derived from many sources, the Christian being not the least among them. But the tragedy lies in the fact that though he claimed to base his ethical teachings on the Gita mainly, he could never relate them integrally to the religion he professed, viz. Hinduism. Of course the doctrine of Ahimsa is quite an ancient Hindu doctrine, but certainly not taught in the Gita in the way that Mahatmaji taught. After the death of Mahatmaji, people turned more readily to the Christian Gospels, especially to the Sermon on the Mount, than to the Gita to understand the meaning of this great man's teachings. Even orthodox Hindus found it difficult to refer to his death and explain it in terms of the doctrine of Karma. As a matter of fact, one never heard the word 'Karma' during all those days when the whole nation was mourning his death; rather, one often heard the word 'Cross' in the many speeches during this period. The Hindu found some meaning in the death of Mahatma Gandhi when he attempted to understand that death in the light of the Cross. Whatever the value of such a thing may be, the one thing that remains as clear as daylight is that the Hindu could not recognise either in the ethical teachings or in the death of Gandhiji anything that he was accustomed to as a Hindu; therefore while he mourned the death genuinely and sincerely for some time, he soon forgot him. Gandhian leadership failed because in its ethical qualities there was something that was said to be typically Hindu, but which the Hindu could not recognise as being Hindu. If India is to be saved from the disastrous effects of the present confusion in ethical and moral standards, she and her leaders must give serious and urgent attention to the need for an ethical and moral education of the people of the land.

The Hindu may repudiate the religious faith of the Christian. He may show active antagonism to the effort of the Christian to spread his faith. He has actually done both with a certain amount of vigour often enough. But we have not yet come across one single instance of the Hindu opposition to Christian ethical teaching. The criticism of the Hindu rather is that the Christian is not Christian enough in his ethical practices. He is furious at the suggestion that is sometimes naïvely made that Western culture is Christian culture. If Western culture is Christian culture, then there must be more in it than is seen.

Would the Hindu accept the Christian ethic? Perhaps he would, provided it is commended to him without the religious assumptions behind it. And yet the Christian ethic has no legs to stand on without the religious assumptions of the Christian faith. When Jesus commended to his disciples the virtue of benevolence to their enemies, the reason he gave was that God himself always acted benevolently toward all, and that this is shown in his impartial administration of his providence—'for he maketh his sun to rise on the evil and the good, and sendeth rain on the just and the unjust'. In other words, God's nature is to be the ground of man's moral action or, to put it in the language of the philosophers, the moral law arises in something inherent in the nature of reality. Christian religion and Christian ethics are integrally connected and related. If the Christian ethic has no legs to stand on without the religious assumptions of the Christian faith, the latter's authoritative source being the Christian Scriptures, the former's authoritative source is also the Christian Scriptures. The failure of Gandhian leadership—a leadership of unprecedented stature in modern times—must be a warning both to the Christian and the Hindu that confusion in regard to the sources and basis of one's teaching, and the lack of any authority behind it, except that of a human individual, however great he may be, achieves no enduring results, though the teaching itself be of high quality.

V *The Authority of the Old and the New Testaments in ethical matters*

One of the obvious difficulties to the Hindu and to many Indian Christians is the place and authority of the Old Testament, both in regard to religion and ethics. Is the Old Testament necessary for deriving the content of the Christian ethic? Now, when we accept the Bible as the ultimate visible authority for the Christian faith, we accept it as a whole, subject to the remarks on this point earlier in the chapter. The Bible is a unity and the Testaments are organically related to each other. The principle of the unity of the Bible is the purpose of it as the record of revelation. The Bible is a report and record of the revelatory acts of God, and its unity is in this report or the purpose of it. The unity of the Bible is not a unity of conception. There is hardly any developing philosophy of theism in the Book. The unity is not a unity of conception, but of divine action. We do not approach the Bible from the angle of man's vision of God—if we do this the Bible will fall apart into incoherent bits—but from the angle of what God has been doing for man. The Bible is a record of this and its unity is in this. Those who accept the authority of the New Testament must recognise that the New Testament itself accepts the authority of the Old Testament. We have admitted that, as a record, much that is human interposes in it. But we have also stated the principle with the aid of which we can disentangle, with some measure of success, the human from the divine element in the Biblical record. But, having stated that the Bible is a unity, we proceed to recognise within its larger unity both continuity and discontinuity simultaneously. This may seem paradoxical, but only apparently. While the whole movement of God's activity in the history of Israel culminates in one event, viz. the coming of God in Jesus Christ, there is something novel in Jesus Christ himself. God's revelation in Jesus Christ is unique. We need not enter into any elaborate argument to prove this. This novelty in God's revelation in Jesus Christ, and its uniqueness, make the revelation different from that recognised in the Old Testament. But at the same time it is the continuation of the Old Testament revelation, for it is the culmination of one movement, a movement of redemption.

The discontinuity between the Old Testament and the New Testament in so far as their respective ethical points of view are concerned may be broadly defined in this way: while the matrix of the ethical code of the former consists in the conception of justice, that of the latter consists in the conception of love. But while there is this discontinuity there is also a continuity. Jesus Christ himself seems to affirm a continuity when he says simultaneously that his mission is not to abrogate the law, and yet that in the new dispensation the conduct expected of its members should go beyond the minimum requirements laid down in the law. The point is, *love does not exclude justice*. It includes it, but it goes beyond it. This is so at least in so far as the positive aspects of justice are concerned. Roughly, if justice were rendering unto each man his due, and love rendering more than what is due, the rendering of more would include also the rendering of what is *due*. My love for my neighbour may induce me to do all sorts of things for him, but it would certainly include the rendering of what is due to him as a *person*, and this is justice. The opposition between justice and love arises when justice is viewed as expressing something merely legal and is identified with a *narrow* conception of *retributive justice*. Retributive justice, however, is only one aspect of the total nature of justice, the other aspects being those that concern themselves with the securing and maintenance of those conditions necessary for the welfare of the human individual and society, such as the four freedoms of the late President Roosevelt. In this larger understanding of justice there is no essential opposition or antithesis between it and love.

Though there is no essential antithesis, there is more in love than in justice. But this 'more' creates certain practical difficulties. Justice is based on the recognition of the claims and rights and duties and obligations of people, and it operates to see that these are fulfilled. It does not hesitate to use justifiable coercion to see itself fulfilled. On the contrary, a world of claims and counter-claims, of rights and duties, is a totally alien world to 'love'. Love is giving without any consideration of the merits of those on whom it is conferred.

In this context let us recall to our minds the source of the Christian conception of love. The early Church used a word of its own for 'love', viz. *agape*, in contrast or in preference, it would seem, to the words of more common usage at that time, viz. *philia* and *eros*. While it is said that *philia* and *eros* stood for love that in some measure looks for response, *agape* characterises an attitude of spirit that spends itself regardless of the merits of those on whom it spends itself.[1] In other words, the early Christians felt that the 'love' they felt constrained to exercise in their mutual relations was one of a quality totally different from that known in normal intimate relationships among men. This conviction regarding its new quality arose in the new experience they had at Pentecost—the experience of a saving grace flowing freely into their hearts. Having experienced this, the redeemed community felt it could exercise nothing less in the mutual relations of its members than that which had been exercised toward its members by God. In other words, the constraint to exercise love of this quality arose in a deeper constraint—the constraint of God's love active in their souls. This constraint of God's love alone was the sanction for the exercise of *agape* toward one another. In point of fact 'love' can never have any other sanction but that of love. And for this reason, the world of claims, rights, duties and obligations and of sanction for them is utterly alien to it.

But the early Church realised also that there was a world outside it—a world ignorant of the constraint of God's love in Christ, a world yet unreconciled to God. We can picture the problem that the early Church had to face. In the world outside the Church, life is generally institutionalised. Human society is not a fellowship where everyone is anxious to serve his neighbour. Often discordant purposes dominate human affairs, bringing in their train chaos and conflict. Institutional organisation emerges to bring order into society, and with a view to securing the general welfare of people, both material and moral. But the ethics of an institution are very different from the *ethos* of a fellowship, and this cannot be helped. There is a 'natural recognition' that men have certain claims and rights and duties and obligations, individually and corporately. But in this recognition the individual as such disappears. He becomes a common denominator. Each individual is an x and is a member of a society of x's. As an x along with other x's, he has these claims and rights and duties and obligations. That they may be duly fulfilled is the primary concern of human institutions. In other words, life in institutions is entirely impersonal (with exceptions like the family); their *ethos* is based on a natural conception of justice and for the due

[1] Cf. Nygren, *Agape and Eros*.

fulfilment of justice they arm themselves with sanctions which are largely legal and penal. Some of the institutions are voluntarily formed and some are of historical antiquity, native to the emergence of mankind into a society. The entry of man into the latter type of institutions is involuntary and inescapable.

The *ethos* of a fellowship like the Church is, on the other hand, based on personal relationship of a more or less intimate character and to the early Church at any rate it was an *ethos* of *agape*.

What was the early Church to do, faced with two orders—the order of grace and the order of nature? They did not run away from the latter. They recognised, for instance, the necessity of the State. And, further, they were born into it and they could not escape it.[1] While it was clear to them from the very beginning that the *ethos* of the Church could not be abandoned under any circumstances by the believers in their mutual relationship,[2] they felt that as members of the second order they were subject also to its *ethos*. They paid taxes and usually paid the State such obedience as did not interfere with their religious freedom. No doubt they keenly felt the tension arising out of the dual membership, but they hoped for its eventual resolution in an eschatological consummation.

The experience of the early Church offers guidance for us. The two orders are there for us today. While as members of the order of grace we can have only one ethic and none other, viz. the ethic of *agape*, as members also of the natural order and having a spiritual and moral responsibility for it, we must also work for an ethic for this order, an ethic which, while falling short of the ideal of love, nevertheless shows the greatest approximation to it. Here then is the need to take the whole Bible, the Old and the New Testaments as the basis for an ethical code. When Jesus Christ was confronted with the question of divorce, and when his questioners referred to the sanction of the Mosaic Law for divorce, he replied that Moses gave the sanction because of the hardness of the heart of the people with whom he had to deal. In dealing with a world yet unreconciled to God, while ever holding before it in the practice of our own life in the fellowship of the Church, the peculiar *ethos* of the order of grace, may we not

[1] As a matter of fact, St. Paul took pride in his Roman citizenship.

[2] Recall how St. Paul upbraids the appeal to a court of law by two brethren in the church at Corinth.

be obliged to work out an ethical code that would come as near it as possible? Jesus Christ said that he did not come to abrogate the law but to fulfil it. The law and the prophets are still indispensable to us today, although, through our unremitting efforts to reconcile men with God, we should always look forward to their transcendence in an ever-expanding order of grace.

5

A REFORMED CONTRIBUTION

by

BARNABAS NAGY

Translated from the German by Dorothy Barton

I *Concerning the authority of the Bible as the Word of God*

The Bible is the Word of God for the Church, and through the Church for the whole world. As canonical it claims to be the sole universal and self-validating witness of revelation. By canonising the Bible the Church did not create this immediate authority but merely acknowledged and ratified it.

The authority of the Bible is the living, concrete authority of Jesus Christ who speaks by means of it as the Lord and King appointed by God and who bears witness to himself as the *Dei loquentis persona* through the word of his prophets and apostles in the power of the Holy Spirit. In this way Jesus Christ is the centre of the whole Scripture. The Old and the New Testaments witness in their unity and entirety to Christ. Therefore the two Testaments can only be understood in the light of their living mutual reference to each other as witness to the Messiah who is coming, has come and will come again.[1] Accordingly, when we recognise the authority of the Bible we mean that all we say about God and his will is in substance testimony to Christ, although formally it is exposition and application of Holy Writ. To understand the Bible in this way is not to assert an unbalanced principle, but to bring out the clear yet mysterious way in which the Bible interprets itself.

[1] Cf. Luke 4.21, 18.31, 24.25-27, 44; John 5.39, 46; Acts 10.43; I Cor. 15.3-4; Heb. 1.1f.

To understand the Bible thus simply as witness to Christ by no means implies that we pay less regard to the first and third 'Persons' of the Trinity and place them in the background. On the contrary, a true knowledge of God, the One in Three, of his reality and his will, can only be preserved by the Christological understanding of the Bible. For Christology is synonymous with Trinitarian theology. God the Creator can be known only in the Son, as the Father of Jesus Christ.[1] And the Spirit of God is known when through him we recognise Jesus Christ as Lord.[2]

We accept the Bible as witness to Christ when we hear the message of God's present and future kingship, *basileia*, which is realised through the Messiah, Jesus. This is the source of the authority of the Scriptures, for in them that kingship is manifest, testified in faith, for faith. Hence too the significance and authority of the Church; in her, in the congregation, this King is accepted by faith because he is recognised from the Bible, the Word of God. Here His grace and His will, based on the Scriptures, are proclaimed for the whole world. This Kingdom of God, manifested in Jesus Christ and realised by Him,[3] to which the Bible testifies as the ultimate standard and authority, cannot be indifferent to any human concerns, which include social and political affairs. One can only appreciate rightly the authority of the Bible, especially in this sphere, if one bears in mind that this Kingship of God has on the one hand already been realised in the Incarnation, the Cross and the Resurrection of Christ, and even earlier in the life of the Old Testament people, but that on the other hand it still awaits its eschatological fulfilment (cf. below, pp. 94ff., para. V).

Listening to the Bible witness to Christ, we are protected from wishing to make, in casuistical fashion, neat, cut-and-dried answers to all our questions. It is not that the Bible hands to us some kind of miraculous social and political solutions; but that the Bible, and it alone, testifies with divine authority to the mystery of God's grace and lordship in Jesus Christ, and that in this 'history of salvation' it sets forth, in a manner which creates faith and demands obedience, the fundamental doctrines and the decisive precepts for man's life in community. It is only

[1] Matt. 11.27; John 1.18; Col. 1.15, 2.9.
[2] John 15.26, 16.14; I Cor. 12.3; 1 John 4.2f. [3] Matt. 28.18-20; Heb. 2.8f.

when we bear constantly in mind the series of great revealing acts in the Bible that the current problems of man's life-in-community are brought under the full light of God's Word. It is idle to turn to the Bible in the expectation that it will confirm any preconceived idea or any ideology learned elsewhere. Here God himself wishes to be our master. Anyone who forgets that it is above all we ourselves who are questioned and called to account will never hear the message of the Bible. Nor must we detach particular parts of the Bible's witness, e.g. the Biblical doctrine of nation, society and State, from the central witness of the Bible to Christ, and turn it into a Biblical 'outlook'. For then the vital nerve of this witness would be severed and we should hold only dead limbs in our hand. Man can only too easily, to his sorrow, apply such a 'Biblical outlook' to his own purposes. In this case too there would be no witness to God's gift and God's command, and we should stop our ears to the real authority of the Bible. The unique and basic importance of the Bible, for social and political problems as for others, is that, being the Word of God, it relates all problems to this one centre, the Kingdom of God realised and to be realised through Jesus Christ.

The Bible is a witness—indeed, the sole, paramount and normative witness—to God's will, once for all revealed, and to his commandment. In contrast with casuistical interpretations of the Scriptures, and with all other forms of misusing them, God's commandment rings out from this witness in the power of the Holy Spirit with an ever fresh note and demands to be heard and obeyed in faith. The Bible has therefore no mechanical authority for the right ordering of social and political life, set out in paragraphs like a legal code, but a spiritual and religious authority. It tells us how Christ wishes to make his Kingship prevail here and now in these spheres. For his Word is his royal sceptre.

It is often objected that the Bible has in fact little to say about the problems which oppress us today. But might not that afford a hint that it is contrary to the spirit of the Bible to treat these problems with such absorbing passion as we generally do? If so, the seeming silence of the Bible might be an eloquent summons to God's authority, an appeal to turn back (*metanoia*) to the right road. When this *metanoia*, when the sovereignty of God's Word has been accepted for all our thinking and living, then in the free and responsible Christian conscience the right solutions will be found.[1]

In contrast to the casuistical interpretation of scripture, we note finally that the Bible, as witness to God's revelation, testifies to his person and to his great acts. The Bible is no communication of 'timeless or eternal truths' complete in themselves, but always a 'kerygmatic' word, demanding to be proclaimed in its saving dynamic. For this proclamation is a part of God's Word. It is always the living God addressing himself to man. In this address or meeting of persons God makes himself and his will known. The social and political spheres of life are included in God's message of salvation; to them too his sovereign command is proclaimed. By claiming them for himself, God sanctifies them as an integral part of his true service. The recognition of God and of his works involves our recognition and praise of him as the Giver and the Lord of his gifts. This is part of our faith. But only the Bible, as the Word of God, can be the rule and norm of this faith, and so of this confession and this obedience.

In the social and political sphere this personal approach of God to us indicates that God manifests himself in Jesus Christ as the true and living God over against the false gods, and calls man into fellowship with him and to obedience. It is in this way that the Bible, or rather the living God in Jesus Christ, through the Bible, exercises its authority in these spheres. Through God's Word, attested in the Bible, the false gods who would like to lord it in public life are disarmed and his kingdom and goodness prevail, to his sole honour and the salvation of man.

When God approaches us he tells us not only who he is and what he desires, but simultaneously and inseparably who and what man is and what is his duty according to God's will. 'Acceptance of the Gospel alone can give us an authoritative doctrine of man' (A. de Quervain, *Kirche*, *Volk*, *Staat*, 1945, p. 255). This is very important in determining correctly the authority of the Bible in social and political questions. For behind every political system and every social ideology there is a definite anthropology, i.e. a definite idea of what man is and ought to be, of what can be made with him and out of him. According to the Scriptures, man can only know what he himself is through the Word of God. Therefore the Biblical-Christological anthropology is the ultimate

[1] Matt. 6.33 and 4.4.

criterion for all other doctrines and conceptions of man. The Bible forbids man to withdraw any sphere of his life from the Kingship of Christ. The divine command, by claiming all, restores the wholeness and unity of his existence—hopelessly broken by sin. The Bible forbids man to split his being, to tear himself apart unrealistically and to lose himself in one or other of the parts. The Bible affirms clearly that man must hear, that God does not leave him alone, but draws him to a meeting and life in fellowship with himself and makes him stand and act responsibly before him. The Bible alone affirms with the authority of the prophets and apostles that the realm both of nature and of history, and man himself, body, soul and spirit, are subordinated in the past, present and future to the Kingship of Christ and will be subject to the eternal, immortal Kingdom of God. The Bible restrains man both from making an absolute of social and political relations, and also from irresponsibly neglecting them. The true God-given dignity of social and political affairs can only be recognised aright in the light of the Bible. That is its authority in these spheres. Social and political activities must concern themselves with reality and with persons; this attitude can only be achieved and preserved if man and his destiny are seen in the light of the great facts revealed in the Bible—creation, the fall, the atonement, the redemption—and if the Bible's revelation of and testimony to God's will are accepted for the social and political life of man. So the absolute authority of the Bible for the social and political sphere finds expression in its unique message about man in his relation to Christ.

The Holy Scriptures, being the Word of God, enable us to recognise, in the light of God's revelation, the meaning and destiny in God's plan for human life-in-community and its fundamental 'orders', i.e. marriage, the family, nationality, work, economic activity, law, the State, etc. At the same time, in God's law and commandment, they show them to us at their truest and highest. The Bible reveals to us the ultimate presuppositions by which these orders can be shaped in accordance with their destiny and the divine purpose. For they cannot be grasped and regulated as though they were independent basic ordinances. Their meaning, their secret and their final expression must be clarified by the Christian revelation. In its light they must be seen as divine gifts and human tasks, always dependent on his consecration, on heeding his command and his claims.

So the Bible, being the witness to God's revelation, gives us the fundamental knowledge and the decisive directives for the social and political spheres. In this sense these important human relationships belong to the revelation found in the Bible. Questions requiring technical or expert information cannot, of course, be answered directly out of the Bible, nor may one try to dispose of such matters by Biblical quotations. When expert information is required, we must remind ourselves that God's Word is not opposed to human reason. So we must deal with these questions, as they are dealt with everywhere else, by scientific methods. The relationship of such scientific techniques to Biblical knowledge and of scientific truths to Biblical revelation can certainly not be a quiet, static synthesis, for their connection must always be thought of in a dynamic, highly critical temper. Because reason is inclined all the time to set itself up as an absolute standard, and to close its ears to the truth, which is Christ, it is impossible for us to have faith in reason and in science. But for Christ's sake and in Christian freedom we regard reason and science too as gifts of God.

The Bible message with its questions and answers, always tries to open up and keep before our eyes a fresh horizon. It points forward, acting as a prophetic sign-post. God's Word to us on social and political problems must be worked out afresh for each generation in relation to the whole Biblical witness. In all this the Bible appears not as backward-looking, but as pointing forward prophetically. We need never feel anxiously concerned for the Bible, for it will always hold its own, if only we are ready to hear the whole message—that is, its witness to Christ.

God's Word in the Bible is also the criterion of all philosophy concerned with 'orders', e.g. all political and racial philosophy. These orders must not be idealised, but their nature, ordained and given by God, is definitely good and wholesome, useful and affording protection for life and for mankind. Their sinful distortion and disfigurement is something accidental, an accretion. It is not evil but God's appointment that brings the state into being. As we are concerned in these matters with gifts of God, they must be always hallowed afresh in our hands through His Word and by means of intercession, so that they may be shaped in accordance with the revealed will of God. The Christian society must always say to the secular society 'that for it too there can be no other manifest and in the strict sense authoritative word of God, no other obligatory form of divine government than is to be found in the Holy Scriptures' (K. Barth).

The witness of the Bible reveals to us God's command in the contemporary situation.[1] Its conclusion and real meaning cannot, of course, be found in selected texts, but in the whole message of Christ. But within this framework, now this, now that section of the Bible can become especially relevant and significant. There is no part of the Bible which fails to fulfil this promise. If we treated it otherwise, we should be placing ourselves not under but above the Bible.

II *Natural law?*

If, accepting the testimony of the prophets and apostles, we take seriously the authority of Holy Writ as being the Word of God, we must, after critical consideration, reject every kind of natural theology and law, or at least put it in parentheses. Though we recognise that reason is one of God's gifts to men (see p. 87), yet to accept natural law as the foundation and standard of law would undeniably lead to the recognition of a second source of revelation. This it can never be, just because nature and reason, human perception of truth and justice, etc., are themselves gifts of God. We do find in human history a phenomenon, an undeniable and apparently inevitable feature, which may be called 'natural law'. But the community, which is the Church of God's Word, cannot recognise this phenomenon as its highest standard and ultimate authority. For this recognition would imply that man is exalted to be the measure of all things and that his reason and nature are considered as absolute; whereas he ought to stand before God in his inexcusable guilt and utter relativity. All doctrines of natural law have a general character of rationalist and speculative philosophy with a complete disregard of Christ. They always depend on a non-biblical conception of human nature. If they attempt to be Biblical or Christian, they fix their attention exclusively on an abstract belief or theory about creation. The essential inner relationship with Christ's redemption and with eschatology is absent. But if, on the contrary, the orders and institutions of man's life-in-community are thought of as

[1] Cf. Micah 6.8.

based from the beginning, as the Bible teaches, on God's covenanted grace, and so on Christ, as existing and ordained through him and for him, then there is no room for the idea of natural law. We must point out, though detailed proof[1] cannot be given here, that no system of natural law can be derived from the Bible.

Consequently Christian social ethics must not be founded on or guided by natural law, but only on and by the Bible and Christ. At the present time we are realising more clearly than ever before how dangerous it is to mix divine revelation and human speculation. So the task of the Churches of the Reformation in the ecumenical conversation of today must be to ensure that the Biblical principle is recognised afresh and emphasised in opposition to natural law. There is no question here of any abstract and rigid Biblicism, but of confronting the most burning social and political questions of the day with the whole of the Biblical revelation. As we are all, so to speak, born professors of natural law, we must wage this battle ceaselessly against ourselves also, so that our thinking, teaching and living may be determined even more completely by the Bible.

III *The authority of the Church and the witness of the Holy Spirit*

If the unconditional authority of the Bible as God's Word is rightly recognised and asserted, then the authority of the Church, i.e. of its teaching, its doctrines, its confession, its attitude, can only be essentially relative and limited in comparison with that of the Scriptures, and must in fact be determined by them and subject to them. It is only by obedience that the Church can have a real and valid authority as compared with the Bible. The word of the Bible is God's own Word, as the witness of those who themselves saw and heard his revelation; the word of the Church can only make this claim at second-hand, relying on the word of the first witnesses. The position of these two authorities must never be reversed, nor may they be put on the same level. No church revelation may be set up side by side with the Bible as a source of revelation.

This is not to deny that in a restricted sense it is both true and admissible that without the Church there is no Bible. For the Bible is the Word of the Lord of the Church, and as such has

[1] E.g. Rom. 2.14ff.; Acts 10.35f.; Matt. 7.12, 22.40, etc.

power to found, to sustain and renew the Church. But Jesus Christ is not Lord in and for himself alone, but in and for his flock; he lives as God-with-us, not apart from his body, but in his body; through his Word he calls into a living fellowship with himself an obedient people, listening in faith; consequently, there can be in actual fact no Bible without a Church, without a congregation of the faithful, without a Communion of Saints. In so far as the teaching and message of the Church was and is drawn actually from the Word of God, the Church has actual authority. Looked at the other way round, it is only as members of the congregation, of the *communio sanctorum*, that we have the promise and the hope that we shall hear the Word aright. Therefore we must not disregard the doctrines and confessions of the Church, but we must recognise them as the valuable commentary of the Church on Holy Writ. Only the authority of this tradition is determined entirely by the extent to which it really expresses God's revelation as testified in Holy Writ. In so far as it does this, it is to be valued; in so far as it fails to do this, it must be criticised and corrected in the light of the Bible.

If we listen seriously in this way to what the Fathers tell us, they will not hinder, but help and indeed compel us to hear the Bible message *hic et nunc*, whatever the circumstances of the moment, to interpret it and to apply it afresh. The Fathers' obedience should be our example for practical obedience in our day to God's Word. But their example must never become a barrier which might, humanly speaking, block the way, as God's Word brings us a fresh message here and now out of the Bible in the power of the Holy Spirit.

In this connection the question is usually raised whether the authority and correct interpretation of the Bible does not depend on the witness of the Church. To this view the Churches of the Reformation have opposed the doctrine of the *testimonium spiritus sancti internum*, by which they intended to maintain not any private judgment but simply the absolute authority of God's Word and the relative authority of the Church.

This doctrine is based on the nature and subject-matter of the Bible itself. For Holy Writ is actually concerned with the revelation of God. But God can be recognised in his revelation only through God, the Father in the Son through the Holy Ghost; therefore, the authority of the Bible can be decisively established or proved in no other way than by the sovereign act of grace of the God who reveals himself. Consequently the Bible is never surrendered to human subjectivity; on the contrary, we assert that the Bible, in theory and in practice, first and last, is exalted high above all human attempts to control it. In it God controls us in His sovereign grace through his Word and Holy Spirit.

The Holy Spirit reveals to us this living Lord through his mysterious inner hidden activity, which cannot be apprehended or controlled by introspection or by any other psychological or transcendental method. He makes the letters, the words, the texts of the Bible into a living witness, so that the living Lord Jesus Christ stands before us: God's Word in the human word.[1] In just the same way he binds us to the witness of the Prophets and Apostles. So the inner witness of the Holy Spirit must not be understood and conceived as having its origin in us, in the experiences of our faith, but in Jesus Christ, in his kingship and in the saving acts which he performed. In this way the kingship of the ever-present Lord is made actual for each individual member of the Church and for every age. The Lord himself promised his Church that the Holy Spirit would lead them into all truth.[2] It is by means of this Spirit that the Word of the Bible, 'the word of the Spirit and of life', addresses itself in a living way to the Church, and through the Church to the world. The Holy Spirit alone is the true interpreter of the Scriptures. He reveals their meaning; in him the *Exousia* of Christ, the Teacher, is continued. He makes it a personal, real and effective thing to know and follow the will and all the commands of Christ. He reveals and unfolds the inexhaustible riches and the eternal freshness of Holy Writ, the Word of God, and its astonishing and staggering relevance to the present day. A church which surrenders itself to this Word and to this Spirit will again and again lose its own authority for the sake of the ever fresh external witness of the Word, and the ever fresh internal witness of the Spirit, in order to find it again. In so far as the Church lives by the Word and allows itself to be led by the Spirit, it can itself become an example and a witness of God's Word in the world.[3] In this way the community of Christ will lead a 'life' which is exemplary for its environment of society and of the political community; and this community has the commission, and also the authority,

[1] Luke 10.16; Acts 1.8. [2] John 16.13. [3] Matt. 5.13-16.

to be a power in the fleeting world, to transform as well as to conserve it according to the measure of the Word of God.[1]

IV *The dialectic between gospel and law*

The whole content of God's Word can be described as 'Law and Gospel'. Both are revealed in all their fullness through Jesus Christ. They cannot be apprehended elsewhere than in the revelation of God given in Jesus Christ, i.e. in the single authoritative witness of Holy Writ.

Law and Gospel must be distinguished within the unity of the revelation in Christ; but they must be neither confounded nor divorced, for the sake of any dialectical equipoise. They can only be correctly distinguished and the danger of confusion can only be averted if Gospel and Law do not have an equal weight assigned to them and are not held in a logical balance; but if the scales are weighted, so to speak, on the side of the Gospel. The free grace of God must give the decisive pressure. In form and content, in its nature and in reality, God's Word is Grace. Even the Law is no more than its servant. So priority belongs to the Gospel, even in the social and political sphere.

Thus the correct sequence is Gospel and Law. If we hold to this, we shall banish the false idea that in the social and political sphere law is significant, but not the Gospel. We must not maintain that the Law is concerned with the State and political orders, and that the Gospel has no say in them. For that would leave a Gospel of consequence only for personal and individual piety; while on the other hand the Law, divorced from the Gospel, could no longer be understood as the Law *of God*.

The whole of Christian ethics, including social and political ethics, must be based, according to the Scriptures, on God's gracious election. Man's action in society is based on this action of God in society, by which God chose and appointed man to be his partner. According to Calvin, not only justification and sanctification, regeneration and eternal life, but all that is needful for human life, including the political order, must be thought of as of the benefits of Christ. Therefore by actual definition they

[1] It must be borne in mind that the Church has this authority only if it is constantly driven by God's Word to repentance. Here the Church, therefore, sees not only the disorder of society, but also, and most of all, its own sins and omissions. Only a Church which is ready to repent can exercise real authority in social and political affairs.

are not secular, for they stand under God's grace and merciful ordinance. Seen from the point of view of the Kingdom of Christ, since all power has actually been given to him, earthly kingdoms and the political powers are the signs of his Kingdom and stand in his service. Through his death and resurrection, in the renewal of their original creation in him and for him, Christ has brought them back again into the order of their divine appointment. Therefore the proclamation of this glad message about the orders of the State and of politics is a part of the Gospel necessary for its completion. Only when seen from that point of view can the nature of the State be understood as a good, holy and wholesome ordinance of God; only when seen in this way can it be recognised that in and in spite of all the distortions of the political order, God is continuously establishing something of this, his original benefit.

The unparalleled authority and significance of the Gospel in regard to social and political matters is also to be seen in the call, ever marvellously new, to the liberty of the children of God. The Gospel tells us that in these spheres too we may step from the bondage of sin into the liberty of God's children. We may liberate ourselves from the constraint of a worldly outlook and all the ungodly shackles of the world, for the free service of God's creatures (cf. the Second Thesis of Barmen in Niesel's *Bekenntnisschriften-Sammlung*, p. 335), and help right, justice and freedom to flourish according to his will. We can reverence every person as a recipient of this call to the liberty of God's children and treat him accordingly. We can declare to everyone under all social and political conditions: 'You are God's children; be reconciled to him, for he is reconciled to you.'

The Law is the form of the Gospel, inseparable from it. The Law reveals God's will; but this will appeared and was revealed in all its fullness in Jesus Christ, because he came to be the *end* and goal of the Law in order to fulfil it. Therefore the Law and each of its commands is in the first place a witness to Christ, and must be heard and understood as fulfilled in Christ. He gave it truly binding validity and authority. The perfect rule of all righteousness and of all goodness is the Law as fulfilled by Jesus Christ, as it is attested and revealed in the whole of the Scriptures, more precisely in the Ten Commandments and summarily in the twofold commandment of the love of God and one's neighbour.

The relation of the Law to the question of human justice need not be discussed here in detail, as a special contribution by Erik Wolf in this volume is devoted to the subject, and I am in full agreement with it. The relationship between the Gospel and the Law had to be discussed here only because, if the Gospel and the Law were torn apart, the authority of all the Scriptures in the social and political sphere would be involved. Now it was for a long time just the Churches of the Reformation which tore them apart in such a way as to neglect the significance of the Gospel in this sphere; so I have taken particular pains to demonstrate the falsity of this thesis. When the authority of the Scriptures is claimed for the social and political sphere, it must denote, not only that of the Law, but also and above all that of the Gospel. On the other hand, the significance of the Law, both in its content and in its relevance for social life, would of course have to be developed in its threefold application (*usus paedagogicus—politicus—didacticus*): firstly, as a mirror of social and political sins; secondly, measuring all human laws by the standard of God's Law; thirdly, guiding men to new obedience to God in social and political life. In this way the permanent significance of the social legislation contained in the Old Testament, and of the social message of the prophets, would be made clear.[1] The authority and validity of the Law must be recognised afresh in the light of the Gospel.

V *The Biblical doctrine of the two ages and its significance for the correct understanding of the Scriptures*

We defined the message of the Bible earlier in this paper as the message of the present and future Kingdom of God (*Basileia*), which is realised through the Messiah, Jesus. It is obvious that the view we take of this message will determine the meaning we attach to the authority of the Bible in social and political questions and the interpretation we give to the Bible. If stress is laid on the fact that this Kingdom is to be realised in this world, is so to speak already realised in principle, we shall constantly try to apply the Bible as directly as possible to the circumstances of our life. But if, on the contrary, we emphasise that we must not expect the Kingdom of God to be realised in this world, but must understand

[1] Owing to lack of space we merely indicate the writings of W. Eichrodt, B. Balscheit and W. Lüthi. Compare also E. Sutz, *Die soziale Botschaft der Kirche,* 1945.

it as an eschatological event, we shall always bear in mind that a direct 'application' of the message of this Kingdom to the circumstances of our life is impossible. In either case the message is relevant; but in the latter it must be understood above all as an announcement and a promise of something which cannot be fulfilled now. It is for this reason that the Biblical doctrine of the two ages is conspicuously significant when considering the authority and the correct interpretation of the Scriptures in the social and political sphere.

We are of opinion that neither the conception of a purely immanent Kingdom of God nor the purely eschatological conception is Biblical. When the New Testament mentions the present and the future age, it is said: the Kingdom of Christ, embracing heaven and earth, is come already as a reality. But it is hidden, recognised and known only through the Word of God in faith, and not yet visible. In the period between Christ's Ascension and his Second Coming, his Kingdom does indeed already embrace the whole world, including the State and society, but it is only in his Church that it is recognised, believed and proclaimed. The powers of this world are already subject to Christ, instruments in his hand. At present they have a certain amount of scope in which to break away at times from obedience to Christ. But in the age to come all these instruments will be put out of use, i.e. destroyed. Then God will be all in all; his Kingdom will be completed and his rule made directly and universally manifest.[1]

Thus the two ages must be kept strictly separate in their temporal sequence; but we must insist that Christ is already in this age the lawful Lord and King over the universe. There is no sphere of man or of the world even in this age which is not subject to his power and his Lordship. By his death and Resurrection Christ has freed the world from the power of the evil one. We must bear this in mind, if we wish to be believed when speaking of the authority of the Bible, i.e. of the infinite significance of Christ's message in the social and political sphere.

The Bible teaches that Christ's death and Resurrection certainly ushered in the final phase of this age. This reveals the battle-atmosphere, charged with highly dynamic tension, in which the Church of Christ has to live until the second coming of its Lord. It is armed with the Word of God for this fight[2] and it must use

[1] I Cor. 15.24-28. [2] Eph. 6.17.

the remaining time to proclaim the Gospel and the call to repentance to all mankind.[1]

The Church is already closely bound up in this age with the age to come,[2] though strictly speaking the age to come is the Kingdom of God coming to fulfilment at the time of Christ's Second Coming. The social and political orders must undoubtedly be considered as instituted by God for this transient age. So this Biblical doctrine has crucial significance for our group of problems. For instance, the Bible teaches us to see all the phenomena of this world, including its social and political successes and achievements, under two aspects. They have a provisional character. They are determined not only by God's grace, but also by the power of the evil one, which is not yet completely annihilated in this age.[3] This is the realism of the Bible, which reminds us that in this age everything is in permanent danger from the powers of anti-Christ. Christ rules in this age, in Calvin's striking phrase, as it were from under the reproach of the Cross. The social and political message of the Church will always be in this world a *theologia crucis*. The world which resists the message of Christ's Kingdom will certainly see to this. But the Church of Jesus Christ must and can remain under all circumstances unshakably convinced of the truth and the victory of its Lord.

The recognition that in this age everything in the social and political sphere is provisional and temporary does not lead to indifference and irresponsibility. On the contrary, the only true and genuine responsibility is eschatological, because it alone takes God's judgment with real seriousness.[4] We can only appreciate the authority of the Scriptures in the social and political sphere if we keep a firm hold on the Biblical eschatology, and thereby on the one hand save ourselves from fanciful illusions, and on the other are conscious that our responsibility in public life is a serious matter.

The uniqueness of the Bible as an authority and standard in social and political affairs is ultimately emphasised, in short, by the fact that it teaches us to pray. It urges us to intercede for the authorities and for all men.[5] It demonstrates that the decision does not rest with us, but with God alone, with His mercy and

[1] II Peter 3.9. [2] II Cor. 5.17; Heb. 6.5. [3] I Cor. 7.31; I John 5.19.
[4] Matt. 25.31ff.; I John 2.17; II Cor. 5.10. [5] I Tim. 2.1ff.

judgment. It is through the Bible that the Holy Spirit teaches us to pray aright: to ask that the good, well-pleasing and perfect will of God may be fulfilled, as in heaven, so also on earth. Holy Writ, and the Holy Spirit himself in it, teach us that the divine gifts and benefits of the social and political orders are hallowed in our sinful hands through right prayer, thanksgiving and intercession. Are we already such a praying Church? Let us seek first the Kingdom of God and his righteousness; then we must and we may remain steadfast in watching and prayer.[1] Appeal, praise, hope, preservation, shouts of victory, a new heaven and a new earth—all this is summed up in one cry, the last cry of prayer in the Bible: 'Amen, come, Lord Jesus!' This shall be our last word too on our subject.

[1] I Thess. 5.17ff.

6

A LUTHERAN CONTRIBUTION

by

REGIN PRENTER

Translated from the German

I *The authority of the Bible is based on its relation to the revelation of the living God. This revelation—God's action in this world—is concealed from men, who have fallen into sin and death; but through the message of the prophets and of the apostles it may be perceived here and now by the sinner who has faith, and it will be revealed to all men when they are made perfect. At the same time the authority of the Bible is the authority of the witness which points away from itself to God's revelation of himself as the triune God, who is himself the sole real authority.*

The authority of the Bible is based on its relation to the revelation of God. This is the sole factor which determines how and to what extent the Bible speaks with authority today. So the authority of the Bible is considered solely in relation to its own contents.

The one dominating theme of the Bible is God's revelation of himself. The Bible describes this revelation by narrating a history: the history of the world and of man, which begins with the creation of all things, describes the fall of man and his salvation in Jesus Christ, and ends with the renewal of all things. This history is a description of God's revelation of himself, because the Bible describes the events as his acts. The revelation described in the Bible is essentially the action of the Living God in the history of the world.

But the Bible does not describe the action of the Living God as something which can be directly understood by the minds of sinful men. His actions are hidden behind the impenetrable veil of natural and historical events, and this is strikingly emphasised by modern science's insistence on the unbroken chain of cause and effect throughout the whole actual world. The action of God cannot be proved; it can only be proclaimed and then believed, in faith. That is why the Bible does not represent the history of the world, and of man, as an account of events, but as a prophetic and apostolic message. The Bible does, indeed, give an account of natural and historical events, not as pure facts, however, which can be objectively noted down, but as part of the *proclamation* of God's action, which must be believed in faith.

In the Old Testament an account is given of the creation of the world and the election of the Children of Israel. Here facts are stated, but they are stated as part of a prophetic message, describing the action of the Living God through these events, and claiming the unconditional faith and obedience of the people to him.

In the New Testament an account is given of Christ's life, death, resurrection and ascension, and of his reign in glory in and through the new Israel; this is followed by an account of the renewal of the world with the second coming of Christ. Here again facts are stated, but only as parts of an apostolic message, which describes the decisive, ultimate action of the God of Israel, and thereby insists on unconditional repentance and unconditional faith.

Hence it is only through the prophetic and apostolic message that natural and historical facts are recognised as the action of God. This message itself is therefore part of the revelation of God through events. Not only the events described by the Bible as actions of God, but the prophetic message itself, is also an act of God, derived from him as the First Cause of all things.

The revelation of God, described in the Bible, is a living reality, full of tensions, which cannot be compressed into a rational conception. On the one hand the revelation is the hidden action of God in this world. By creating this world and ruling over it actively, God has come out of his own isolation and is together with the world, although he is not of the world.

Even the creation and sustaining of the world is thereby a revelation of God (Rom. 1.19-20). But it is precisely in this revelation that God is concealed from the sinner and not recognised by him nor worshipped as God (Rom. 1.21). Only through the message of the prophets and the apostles is the hidden action of God made manifest to us. But even in this message of revelation

God is still concealed from the understanding of the sinner. For what the message says about God's action is not visible in this world, nor can it be grasped by human understanding. The selection of Israel as God's chosen people, and the incarnation of God, are not facts which can be directly grasped; they are the mysteries of faith whose final revelation is still to come, and they will be revealed on the day of judgment when God fulfils his promise, and manifests their hidden meaning to risen men in the visible form of his created and redeemed world, by making all things new and destroying the power of sin, of death and of evil for ever.

But it is one and the same God who created and sustains the world, who appointed Israel as his chosen people and promised their redemption in Jesus Christ, and who will finally make all things new. There are not three different gods. The God revealed in the Bible is the triune God: the sovereign will concealed behind everything that happens, the Word of revelation which manifests him and his acts to the believer, and the renewing spirit which unites the outward form of the creation and the inward meaning of the Word in the vision of the resurrected life.

The authority of the Bible is not the authority of the book nor the authority of its authors, but the authority of the content of its message, the authority of the witness to the self-revealing action of the triune God, who is himself the real authority for the validity of the Bible.

II *The authority of the Bible excludes any so-called 'natural' theology, because its message is determined by the revelation of God and itself determines every announcement of that message here and now.*

The witness of the Bible concerning the nature of God includes realisations which are very important for understanding its authority. At the very outset it must be stressed that the Bible's message concerning the revelation of God excludes all kinds of 'natural' theology, by making itself the sole authority for determining the content of every pronouncement concerning his nature. Natural theology is man's attempt, through his own intellect, to arrive at knowledge of the Creator through knowledge of the created world. This attempt has been made again and again. It is the nature of human thought (which is always of a relative character) to be directed towards the Absolute, from which it is itself derived. In philosophy this tendency occurs again and again in all sorts of different forms, as research is made into this or that province of the human mind to discover the First Cause. But if philosophy goes beyond raising the *question* of the Absolute (this question implying that it is impossible to deny the existence of the Absolute), i.e. if philosophy goes beyond determining the *category* of the religious, if it goes on to speculate about the nature and action of the Absolute, thus practising natural theology and announcing a 'God', then 'natural' theology of this kind is not to be brought into relation with 'revealed' theology, as a first step towards the latter; this 'natural' theology is then to be rejected as the doctrine of a strange god. The god of natural theology is the god of deism, standing behind this world, the absolute World-Cause—not the God of the Bible, the Living God who works through history, the God of providence, of salvation and of renewal, the triune God. And when this god of human speculation is regarded as synonymous with the God of the Bible, the result can only be to obscure the message of the Bible concerning the Living God. The more closely preaching adheres exclusively to the message of the Bible, the greater will be its authority, owing to the clear picture it gives of the nature and action of God.

III *The authority of the Bible does not exclude, but confirms, the reality of a relationship between God and all men. It thereby presupposes that God exercises authority over men even apart from the message of the Bible, namely in his creative will governing all his creatures (particularly man). And it thereby excludes an intellectualistic, legalistic interpretation of the Bible, distorting it to apply to moral or political and social problems. This interpretation is inherent in the degeneration of the direct recognition of God's creative will, and of God's relationship with all men, into a moral (political, social) Absolute. The right relationship between the authority of the Bible message and the authority of the perception of the will of God the Creator (as revealed direct to man) is expressed in the dialectic of Law and Gospel, which excludes both theocratic fanaticism and secularistic emancipation.*

The exclusion of natural theology, and the exclusive authority of the Bible message in proclaiming God's revelation, does not mean that there is no relationship of any kind between man and God except through hearing and believing the Bible; nor does it mean that all men may not have a consciousness of God which is not derived from the Bible. The first book of the Bible states that God created all men and rules over them. In the New Testament it is also assumed that God is in contact with all men and that he sustains and rules over them (Acts 14.15-17; Rom. 1.18-2.16; 13.1-7). All men are subject to the will of God the Creator, and are therefore 'without excuse' if they oppose his will (Rom. 1.20). That is why, on the Day of Judgment, the conscience of the Gentiles will also bear witness, 'accusing or else excusing one another'. The law was written also in the hearts of those who never knew the laws of Moses (Rom. 2.14-16). Even those who worshipped heathen gods were (like the Israelites) in bondage to the elements of the world, from whose curse Christ redeemed them, when he became subject to the Law (Gal. 4.4-10).

The consciousness of God, bestowed together with the universal relationship of man with God, and manifested also in the worship of heathen gods (cf. Acts 17.22-23), cannot, however, be developed into a natural theology, i.e. an affirmation concerning the nature and action of God. Here the same thing applies as what we have just said concerning the philosophical consciousness of God. The universal consciousness of God has its origin in the consciousness of God the Creator, whose claims are directly apprehended. It is, as Luther says, a recognition of God's laws, a *cognitio legalis Dei*. The philosophical consciousness of God is, moreover, only a particular form of this *cognitio legalis Dei*, a reflective, thinking variety of the unreflective, active consciousness of the will of God the Creator. Just as philosophy, through thought, cannot perceive the nature and actions of God, but can only raise the question of a religious category which is undetermined—so the unreflective, active consciousness of God expressed in the law cannot perceive his nature or actions, but can merely fulfil or resist his demands, thus showing that the existence of an Absolute Authority is undeniable. Although the universal consciousness of God does not open the way to natural theology, it is nevertheless a means by which God can exercise his authority. In this sense the authority of the Bible is not exclusive. The Bible itself states that the authority of God may exist outside the Bible. The authority of the Bible is exclusive in its assertion of the nature of God; but that assertion is addressed to men who are already subject to the authority of God the Creator—a fact which is presupposed in the Bible message.

This is of decisive importance in understanding the authority of the Bible in relation to the political and social message of the Church today. Since all men are able to perceive God's will directly, apart from the Bible message, it is impossible to twist the authority of the Bible in an intellectualistic or legalistic sense in applying it to the Church's social and political message. The Bible does not contain any direct political and social instructions which are immediately applicable and which absolve the human reason from its normal task of finding solutions for these difficult problems. Neither the laws given in the Old Testament, nor the Sermon on the Mount, nor the example of the characters in the Bible, not even the example of Jesus himself, nor the moral exhortations of the apostles, can be understood in this way without forcing the historical meaning of the Biblical texts. On the other hand, the Bible contains the witness of God's revelation, which is not identical with the miraculous solution of social and political problems through supernatural communications.

But that does not mean that the Bible's witness of God's revelation has no bearing upon the Church's social and political message today. On the contrary! Just because the Bible does *not* contain definite political and social instructions, but something quite different, it is of the *greatest* importance for the Church's message today.

In the first place, the Bible's witness to God's revelation confirms man's direct consciousness of the will of God the Creator —let us call it outright the moral reason. The Bible regards man as God's creature, who is responsible for using his reason, and cannot relegate this responsibility to any infallible instructions contained in the Bible. Jesus does not bring a new Law: he points to an already known commandment—that of love. But it is man's own responsibility, through his direct dealings with his neighbour, to discover for himself how love is to be interpreted in practice (Mark 10.17-31; Luke 10.25-37). In the same way Paul exhorts the churches to think on 'whatsoever things are true, whatsoever things are honest, whatsoever things are just' (Phil. 4.8), and to love one another and to work with their own hands (I Thess. 4.9-12), as only God could teach them. The requirements of the Law must be fulfilled in immediate contact with one's neighbour, but not learned from the Bible parrot-fashion.

In the second place, the witness of the Bible contains a criticism of modern reason. The Bible not only speaks of God as man's Creator, but also of man as God's fallen creature, who lies under the power of sin, death and Satan, until Jesus Christ, the Redeemer, bursts the chains of the powers of evil. Even if man apprehends the will of the Creator and tries to carry it out by the light of his own moral reason, he still lies in the power of sin, death and the devil. In that case the sinner is not carrying out the Law in the way that God wills him to do. He is doing what he has to do, under the pressure of the Law, not out of love to God and to his neighbour. He does what the Law demands from the selfish motive of thereby asserting his own virtue; or he *refuses* to obey the Law in order to assert his own will. In both cases his motive is self-love. And this love of self is precisely the bond of sin, death and evil. In this way God's Law becomes a fourth power of corruption, which increases still more the enmity between God and sinner. The Law may make man outwardly respectable, and may compel him to serve his neighbour. But at the same time his own heart grows more and more wicked, because in his self-assurance or in his despair he is rebelling against God and thus cutting himself off from his neighbour. Salvation from this curse of the Law is to be found only in the liberating and renewing action of the triune God in Jesus Christ through the Holy Spirit. It is only through faith in Jesus Christ in the love of the Holy Spirit, that the sinner achieves the right attitude to God, the Creator; this enables him to hear the Law and to carry it out, not from motives of self-assertion, but acknowledging his own sin by seeking refuge in Christ, and as a spontaneous gift to his neighbour.

Actions are therefore never justified in themselves. Actions are good because God commands them. Man is good, not because he does good deeds, but because he condemns himself and takes refuge in Christ, his Redeemer. Between the good action of a sinner and his own better self there always stands his death and Resurrection. When he dies his good actions die with him; when he rises again, it is Christ who rises as his own better self. This criticism of all the acts motivated by the moral reason —a criticism of the Law of the Creator—is indissolubly bound up in the Bible with the confirmation of that same moral reason and of that same Law.

The critical light thrown on the moral reason by the Bible message prevents the moral reason from being regarded as something absolute. Where men, who live under the law, are deprived of this criticism, there is always a danger of the human reason being regarded as absolute. This may assume many different forms, from pharisaical moralism to exaggerated hero-worship. The criticism of the whole field of human activity in the light of the message of the redemption and resurrection of fallen man renders a great service: it reduces the whole of human activity to the purely practical matter of *what our neighbour needs*, and destroys all the dreams of an earthly paradise built by human effort. It is absolutely clear what a message, which expresses this critical view, has to say concerning the illusions of the usual political and social utopians.

The unity of the Bible's attitude towards the moral reason—partly confirmatory, and partly critical—is expressed in the Lutheran doctrine of the difference between and the inseparability of Law and Gospel. A sharp distinction must be drawn between the Law and the Gospel in the Christian message, but on no account must they be separated. If one looks for the laws of life on earth in the Biblical message, instead of directly apprehending the will of God the Creator through one's moral reason in contact with one's neighbour, then one is confusing the Law and the Gospel, by making the Gospel, the Bible message, into a new law. Of course, this does not mean that there are no commandments in the Bible which may clarify the practical commandments of the Creator of man's moral reason, e.g. the Decalogue, the commandment to love God and one's neighbour, the moral exhortations of the apostles, the social preaching of the Old Testament prophets, etc. Everyone sees that immediately. But the Bible throws light on this question by describing the Creation of men and the life of God's Son when he became man; which makes it an eminently human book. In this message the Bible is in complete accord with the world as a whole. Such words in the Bible have authority as laws for our lives, not because they are printed in the Bible (*lex scripta*)—in contrast to the commandments which are understood directly by the moral reason in our contacts with our fellow men (*lex naturae*)—nor because they express a higher moral standard. The relationship between the two channels of revelation is precisely the other way round, as Luther often emphasised. The commandments of the Bible have authority as laws for our lives because they coincide with what our moral reason already tells us. The commandment to love our neighbour does not express a higher moral standard than our reason realises directly to be the Creator's claim upon us, when, for instance, we come across a man who has been robbed by thieves and half beaten to death. Any attempt to interpret the Sermon on the Mount as a higher, specifically Christian morality turns the message given there into a new law. The necessity of making a sharp distinction between the Law and the Gospel is expressed in the Lutheran doctrine of the first use of the Law (*usus civilis*). The external life of the citizen comes under the jurisdiction of the law, and the Gospel has nothing to do with it. If we let the Gospel take control of political and social life, we are falling into the theocratic mistake of confusing the Law and the Gospel and making the Gospel into a new law, under which the Church (which preaches the Gospel) wants to rule the world, instead of serving it humbly with the glad promise of the Gospel.

But although this Law in its first application is distinguished so sharply from the Gospel, it cannot be separated when the Gospel is preached. The Law is often accepted and carried into effect without the Gospel, but it should never be preached without the Gospel. The preaching of the Law, in conjunction with the Gospel, always leads to its second application (*usus proprius, spiritualis*). The same law, which rules the lives of men on this earth and controls their actions, becomes a damning and deadly power when it is preached as if it were identical with the Gospel. If God himself, as the Lawgiver, is revealed through the preaching of the Law and the Gospel, then all human justice breaks down and there is only one hope for man's salvation from eternal damnation: the Gospel of Christ. In this second use of the Law Christ prepares man for the work of the Gospel. The Law destroys man as an alien work of God, so that the Gospel can reawaken man as the true work of God. The Law crucifies man with Christ, so that the Gospel can raise him up again with Christ. It is clear that in this function the preached Law cannot be separated from the preached Gospel any more than the Crucified Christ can be separated from the Risen Christ, nor the Old Aeon from the New Aeon. The destructive work of the Law is the act by which God ends the Old Aeon, in order to usher in the New Aeon (cf. Gal. 3.22-4.7).

But it is of the greatest importance to remember that the Law as mentioned in the second use of the law is exactly the same

Law as was mentioned under the first use of the law. So while the Church preaches the Law as the destructive power which prepares the way for the new Creation ushered in by the Gospel, at the same time it must uphold the justice and the authority of the law in social life. For it is precisely in his life in this world that man stands before God as a sinner, and that he is reawakened by the Gospel to fresh service and fresh hope. Just as in preaching the Christian message the Law and the Gospel must not be separated, neither must the first and the second application of the law be separated. By pronouncing God's judgment on man's sins and calling him to repentance, this teaching does not lead man into an 'inward' world of religious experiences, but out into the life of the world, where the law (in its first application) will crucify him every day in service for his neighbour. It is there, amid the ordinary life of men, that the Gospel will find him, raise him up and give him hope and consolation. There God's mercy and loyalty will be with him from hour to hour, until the Old Aeon has passed away, the Resurrection has taken place and there will be no more law and no more death.

The inseparability of Law and Gospel excludes all possibility of dividing life into two spheres, the secular and the religious.

The separation of Law and Gospel is seen in all forms of moral (or political and social) secularism. It is the nature of secularism to desire to protect the life of men (in morals, culture, politics, etc.) against the inroads of God's judgment and God's promise by means of the Gospel. We must therefore distinguish between paganism and secularism. We can only speak of secularism where the Gospel is preached. In the strict sense, we can only speak of secularism in the Church, in Christian preaching, and in theology. In modern Lutheranism (especially in Germany), Luther's doctrine of the two realms (*regnum civile* and *regnum spirituale*) is misinterpreted, so that cultural, social and economic life (the whole sphere of civic life) is sharply separated from religious life and is regarded as a '*law unto itself*'. Christian preaching is allowed to apply only to the religious life; while in the affairs of this world the will of the State is regarded as absolute.

The misconception does not lie in the distinction between Law and Gospel, nor in the anti-theocratic assertion that the political authorities are entitled to respect and do not require nor tolerate any interference from ecclesiastical advisers. The misinterpretation lies in the complete separation of Law and Gospel in the preaching of the Christian message, and the resultant division of life into isolated spheres. If the laws of life are formulated in conscious opposition to the criticism of the Gospel, those independent laws are bound to develop into complete lawlessness. For a legal system which opposes in principle the criticism of the Gospel (and thereby every other kind of criticism also) can never serve the true Law of the Creator; its very nature is a distortion of all real Law.

When the preaching of the Gospel (with its judgment and its promise) is not given free play in everyday life, there is no room for the voice of the *real* Law to be heard. When the Gospel is confined to a narrow religious sphere, then the many voices which ought to give expression to the moral reason through free discussion are usually silenced also. A law which speaks only through a dictator is just as false as a Gospel which confines itself only the religious sphere. The Law can only be rightly understood if the Gospel is also given freedom to follow the Law. The mere presence of the Gospel challenges every political power with the decision whether it shall be a despotism or a just State. A theology which tries to protect the legal system from the criticism of the Gospel thereby becomes a factor in favour of despotism.

IV *The speculations of natural law and of Church traditionalism (including orthodox Biblicism) have one thing in common: they both replace* the free operation of the Holy Spirit *in the Word of revelation given in the Law and the Gospel* (testimonium spiritus sancti), *which is itself an act of the Living God here and now, by truths gained supernaturally (through Scripture and tradition) or naturally (through natural law) and which are regarded as infallible. The Church, which trusts itself to the power of the Holy Spirit, can never recognise infallible truths of natural law, of tradition or of Scripture; but it can recognise the historical interpretation of the historical revelation (with its tradition), and empirical science. The victory of God's truth over human relativity is ensured by the power of the Holy Spirit, perfecting the Creation.*

In what has been said hitherto, when we have spoken of the direct perception of the will of God in the Creation, we have purposely refrained from using the expression 'natural law' (*lex naturae*), so frequently used by Luther and others. This expression has too many associations with ancient and modern speculations concerning natural law. 'Natural law' is a piece of natural theology (or metaphysics) which tries to develop and extend the direct perception of the will of God the Creator into a system of immutable moral and legal principles. But the will of God the Creator is concrete and individual in a double sense, and can therefore never be *comprised* within a natural law. In the first place, a particular action can never be worked out logically from the rule, but the rule must be adapted to the particular situation in free responsibility.[1] In the second place, the positive rules of morality and justice are always in need of revision and reformation.

Behind the speculations concerning natural law stands the theory of Deism. God's Creation is regarded as a completed whole, from which God himself has departed, but whose inner moral structure can imitate natural law. In that case the moral reason is not understood as the concrete awareness of the Creator's will at this moment, but as an intellectual ability which can discover the moral structure of existence. It is the same as everywhere else: the deistic conception of God gives rise to an intellectualistic conception of spiritual matters.

The moral reason, of which we have spoken here, assumes that God is quite different. God is the Living God who is constantly at work in his Creation. Hence the moral reason is not intellectual ability, which leads to speculation about natural law: the moral reason is man's readiness to receive the practical will of God the Creator for his own life, the Law of God here and now.

Speculation about natural law easily leads to an authoritarian idea of the State. If the basic rules of moral or political and social life are laid down in advance in natural law, there is no sense in giving citizens responsibility for the government of the State. On the other hand if the Law of God, and the moral reason, are understood in their historical and individual application, then political, social, moral (and cultural) decisions are made only through balancing different interests in the practical conflict between man and man; then 'natural law' is not interpreted in the lonely speculations of the intellect but in the living intercourse between man and man. A democratic form of State fits in with this conception much better than an authoritarian one. The organ

[1] 'And be not conformed to this world: but be ye transformed by the renewing of your mind' (Rom. 12.2).

of the moral reason is not abstract speculation but practical discussion. By *listening* to the other man one becomes *responsible*.

Here a word must be said concerning the importance of knowledge for understanding the practical will of God. Knowledge which assumes a speculative character is out of the question here. On the other hand, a knowledge derived from contact with real facts (as in the case of the experimental sciences) always holds significance for the moral reason. This is true of every branch of experimental science. Every fresh scientific achievement involves fresh moral (or political and social) problems and offers fresh means of solving them. For instance, the task of international understanding has assumed world-wide proportions through the development of modern communications and modern military technique, whereas in earlier times this problem was confined to relations between neighbour-states. The Church must never be indifferent towards 'secular' science, which may be more relevant to theology than a great many theocratic-allegorical expositions of Scripture.

Closely related to the speculations of natural law are confessional traditionalism and orthodox Biblicism. They are also forms of abstract speculation.

The tradition of the Church is the recollection of earlier occasions on which the Word of the Living God was heard, and God himself was actively present. But in order to bear witness to the revelation of God, the Church must hear his living Word at all times, here and now. Hence tradition is never an absolute, infallible truth which can be passed on as it stands, but a recollection of previous occasions which may be used to interpret—but only to interpret—what is heard here and now. Tradition is only a means of interpretation, a relative authority, a *norma normata*. The *norma normans* is the living Word of God itself. When—as in the Roman Catholic Church, and in Lutheran Confessionalism—the Pope or the Confessional writings are regarded as infallible authorities on doctrine, then the living Word of God is really being stifled by the recollection of the past occasions on which it was heard.

Orthodox Biblicism (Fundamentalism) is only a derivation from traditionalism, because the idea that Scripture is infallible—as a collection of revealed truths—actually turns Scripture itself into a tradition.

The idea of revelation which lies behind traditionalism (or Biblicism)—namely revelation as the supernatural communication of infallible truths—postulates the same deistic conception of God and the same intellectualistic idea of the spirit as the speculations of natural law. The idea is that God is not actively present in his revelation, but stands behind and aloof from it, after having deposited it (so to speak) in tradition (in the Bible, the Pope or the Confessional writings).

If we realise the revelation to be the *living* Word of God, the action and the message in which the living God is actually present, then this living Word must take priority over natural law, tradition or Scripture. If we realise the revelation to be the *living* Word of God, and realise also that the Bible and tradition are witnesses to this revelation and means of guiding us to God's living Word, then we shall never misinterpret the Bible in a fundamentalist way, as if it were a collection of supernaturally revealed truths; on the contrary, we shall realise that the Bible (aided and interpreted by tradition) as the witness of the prophets and the apostles to God's revelation can never be the authority for the Church's message today unless it is read *historically*, i.e. unless it is made abundantly clear that the Biblical text, *and* our contemporary interpretation of it, are both conditioned and limited by history. Neither the Biblical text, nor the explanation of it, can claim super-historical infallibility, because the revelation itself is historical, not super-historical—because the God of the revelation is not the deistic First Cause but the Living God of the Bible. It is only when the Bible is read in this way, in relation to history, that its message can be comprehended and interpreted. A collection of super-historical truths is not a message, and cannot be the source of any message.

The testimony of the Holy Spirit (*testimonium spiritus sancti*) is the way in which God helps a Church which has the courage to preach the message of God's revelation without possessing an infallible Bible and an infallible interpretation of the Bible. The testimony of the Holy Spirit is the divine miracle by which the message can be heard here and now, in divine truth, in spite of human relativity and insincerity. Firm confidence in the testimony of the Holy Spirit is the only thing which can give the Church courage to embark upon the adventure of preaching the message of God's revelation in every age.

7

AN ANGLICAN CONTRIBUTION

by

ALAN RICHARDSON

I *Some preliminary considerations*

When one attempts to deal with such questions as are raised in the effort to relate the Bible to the modern world, one must approach them from the standpoint of a particular tradition. The theologian cannot lift himself above all schools and traditions and judge of such things from an absolute perspective. The present writer, at any rate, will make no pretence of having attained a universal or impartial point of view, but will attempt the humbler task of asking what insights are to be found in his own tradition or confession which may be of value in the ecumenical discussion of Biblical authority in political and social matters. At the outset he must point out that he cannot and does not speak for all Anglicans, or for 'Anglicanism' as such. Indeed, he is inclined to agree with those recent writers who have urged that there is no such thing as Anglicanism, and that the word (not yet one hundred years old) should be allowed to die. There is no dogmatic system which can be labelled 'Anglican'. There is only an Anglican Communion which derives its direction and spirit from the temper and outlook of the divines of the sixteenth and seventeenth centuries who after the Reformation enunciated the controlling principles of Anglican order, worship and doctrine.

An outstanding characteristic of the island-Church in seventeenth-century England was its abhorrence of insularity. There were to be no distinctively English or 'Anglican' doctrines. The doctrine of the Church of England, so far as humanly possible, was to be that of every century and country. This attitude remains the basic Anglican contribution to ecumenicity. The English Church was nothing other than 'God's Catholic Church' as it manifested itself in a particular nation at a particular period of history; it was, in the fine phrase of Bishop Cosin of Durham (1594-1672), 'Protestant and Reformed according to the Ancient Catholic Church'. Its Reformation had amounted only to a rejection of novelty and a recovery of ancient Catholic truth. It possessed no system-maker, no Luther, no Calvin, no Pope: 'we call no man Master upon earth', boasted William Chillingworth in the days of Charles I. Consequently its doctors were happy to learn truth wherever they found it, and a doctrine was not untrue simply because Calvin or the Council of Trent had endorsed it. Similarly Anglicans today are willing to learn from Barth or Maritain or anyone else, although they would doubtless endorse Hooker's reservation: 'the law of common indulgence alloweth us to think (our own ways) at least half a thought better because they are our own'. The fact that we think our own ways best, says Hooker, should not lead us to draw any indictment against the ways of others: we may even think commendably of them also.[1] As with every other Christian tradition, whether the fact is recognised or not, 'our own ways' are ours because of our particular history and experience: in their concrete 'givenness' they could not be anyone else's. The Anglican attitude towards Biblical authority in political and social affairs arose out of a particular historical experience, and it has a contribution to make to ecumenical understanding precisely because it was 'given' in the particular and local setting of English history. It is one aspect of the wholeness of the ecumenical Christian tradition, neither more nor less than that.

The Anglican attitude (like that of every other tradition) can be understood only against the background of a particular history. It was not evolved in an abstract or leisurely manner (any more than was, for instance, Lutheranism) by theologians sitting in their libraries. It was hammered out in the midst of a social revolution, when the mediaeval system was giving place before the pressure of the new insurgent middle classes, when Parliament was asserting its authority over King and Church, when the fear of the military power behind the Papal claims lay

[1] *Ecclesiastical Polity*, IV, xiii, 10.

like a dark shadow over English life (as fear of the military power behind Communism does over Western Europe today), when fanatical sectaries from the Continent were propagating novel theories, when Presbyterians and Puritans were seeking to replace the ancient government of Church and State by new and strange forms. It is in such periods of historical decision that insights are born and attitudes are formed—a truth which we learn from the Bible itself, but also from Church history. As with every other tradition, we can understand why Anglicans think like Anglicans (and not like Lutherans or Presbyterians) only by understanding something of Anglican history. The mutual understanding of one another's traditions is a task of the highest ecumenical importance. A confessional position cannot be understood apart from its general economic, political and social background. In the next section therefore we shall say something about the Anglican background before we turn to our central theme.

II *The social background of Anglican thought*

The Reformation in England was remarkably conservative in character. 'There are few things known to be good', said the greatest of Anglican divines, 'till such time as they grow to be ancient'.[1] In doctrine, in liturgy, in church order and in social and political outlook nothing was altered unless it could be shewn to be contrary to the teaching of the Bible as interpreted by the Fathers of the ancient Church. In the words of the note on Ceremonies at the end of the 1549 Book of Common Prayer, 'Newfangleness is always to be eschewed'. In the century between 1549 and 1649 the naturally conservative temper of the Anglican divines was, not surprisingly, stiffened by the ruthless plundering of church property at the hands of the new revolutionary classes, who had discovered that by means of the attack upon 'superstition' they could gain rewards in this life as well as lay up treasure in heaven. The taint—if taint it be—of conservatism has clung to Anglican political and social thinking from the Reformation until today. 'The Spirit of the Anglican Reformation', writes the present Bishop of Durham, 'was, socially, strongly conservative and authoritarian. It would have been strange if it had been otherwise, for the dominant powers of the State from the

[1] Richard Hooker, *Ecclesiastical Polity*, V, vii.3.

Sovereign downwards had made great profit out of the destruction of the mediaeval system and were deeply involved in the security and policy of its supplanter'.[1]

Until quite recently the view of the Whig historians was generally accepted uncritically, that the social outlook of the Anglican divines from Elizabeth to Charles I was entirely reactionary. Contemporary historians are redressing the verdict. It is now pointed out that the Anglican divines were consistently the champions of the poor against the encroachments and enclosures of the new rich: Laud's Court of High Commission was unpopular not with the lowly but with the well-to-do. Moreover, social justice was the concern of many of the sermons of the most eminent churchmen of the period. Indeed, the social theory of the Anglican divines, though it was destined to be swept away by the triumph of the new individualism, may now perhaps after three hundred years be seen to be more truly Biblical and Christian than the types of Christianised political secularism which succeeded it. For the Anglican divines, society was essentially an organism, not a collection of individuals banded together voluntarily or involuntarily by a 'social contract'.

It was a necessary corollary from this organic conception of society that Church and State were fundamentally one body, not two. The Church was the nation on its religious side. Even in Hooker's day this assertion was scarcely true in actuality, and Archbishop Laud (executed in 1645) was doubtless the last churchman to believe that the theory could be made to work. During the three centuries which have elapsed since the execution of Charles I (1649) the break-up of the religious unity of the English people has led to the setting up of several religious 'denominations'. Laud would have regarded this solution of the conflict as blasphemous and intolerable, and, whatever we may think of his policy of trying to secure religious unity by means of legislation, it is possible even for others than Anglicans to regard him as a martyr for the unity of the body of Christ in his country. At the Restoration (1660) it was possible to secure no agreement between Anglican and Dissenter, save perhaps a grudging agreement to differ. Since then, the majority of English Christians have complacently condoned 'our unhappy divisions' with the aid of a specious doctrine of 'toleration' which owes more

[1] A. T. P. Williams, *The Anglican Tradition*, 1947, p. 25.

to the rationalism of the Enlightenment than to any genuinely Biblical insights. But the Anglican divines saw more clearly than do most modern Christians that there *can* be only one Church, since Christ is not divided, and that the unity of the Church must be made visible in the Church's fellowship and order: according to their understanding of the Bible it is of the *esse* of the Church that it should be one, and it is by its visible unity that all men should know that Christ is come forth from the Father. Furthermore, they well knew that the State exists for a spiritual end, and that a secular State is not in truth a State at all. There are no economic laws which operate in their own right, no political principles which must not be tested by a spiritual criterion. The Bible has no word, save that of judgment, for a secular society, and it is only in so far as the State is realising its true function and end in and with the Church, only as citizen and churchman are brought together in the same person, that the Bible has any relevance at all in political and social matters. To this conception we shall return.

III *Law*, *tradition*, *reason*, testimonium spiritus

A consideration of the question of the law of nature illustrates the statement that the Reformation in England did not involve a radical break with mediaeval thought. Hooker takes over the Thomistic conception of reason and the natural law: 'The general principles (of the Natural Law) are such as it is not easy to find men ignorant of them. Law rational therefore, which men commonly use to call the Law of Nature, meaning thereby the Law which human nature knoweth itself in reason universally bound unto, which also for that cause may be termed most fitly the Law of Reason; this Law, I say, comprehendeth all those things which men by the light of their natural understanding evidently know, or at least may know, to be beseeming or unbeseeming, virtuous or vicious, good or evil for them to do.'[1] But from this point onwards Anglican moral theology develops along very different lines from those taken by post-Tridentine casuistry.[2] Broadly speaking, the view that the law of nature—or what we should probably today call the moral law—is known by our

[1] Richard Hooker, *op. cit.*, I, viii, 9.
[2] See H. R. McAdoo, *Caroline Moral Theology*, 1949.

God-given faculty of reason has remained characteristic of the Anglican tradition. Obviously such a view has the most important consequences for the understanding of the political and social authority of the Bible. The matter may be illustrated historically, for it led to the sharpest conflict between the Anglicans and the Puritans. It should perhaps be added that the descendants of the Puritans today no longer hold the views of their forefathers, and that this cause of the disruption of the religious unity of the English people no longer disturbs us.

In general, the Puritans held that all things which the Bible did not explicitly permit were forbidden; the Anglicans held that all things which the Bible did not forbid were allowed, unless they could be shewn to be contrary to reason or (which comes to the same thing) the moral law. Thus, the Puritans attacked such things as the wearing of surplices or the playing of organs in churches, the sign of the cross in baptism, games on Sunday, the government of the Church by bishops, the use of the classics in education, scientific experiments, and all forms of democratic liberty. The Anglicans put up a determined resistance to this rigid scripturism (i.e. the attempt to regulate all details of life by scriptural precepts). It mistook the whole purpose of the Scriptures, which was to make us 'wise unto salvation', not to teach us how to dress or how to conduct the practical details of our daily lives, nor yet to teach us political science or natural philosophy. God had given us reason and expected us to use it. Custom (or tradition) was also along with reason to be used in the ordering of our life and worship. The question of the use to be made of the Scriptures in matters of government arose most acutely over the problem of the government of the Church itself—whether, as the Presbyterians alleged, the Scriptures must be searched to provide a model of ecclesiastical polity, or whether long usage and tradition should be allowed to affect our political arrangements. Here the Anglicans firmly refused to admit that such questions could be settled by distilling constitutions from Biblical texts. 'I deny that (Scripture) doth set down any one certain form of government of the Church, to be perpetual for all times, persons and places without alteration', said Whitgift (Archbishop of Canterbury from 1583 to 1604). Hooker himself, though he thinks that the New Testament envisages a threefold ministry in the Church, admits that the evidence of Scripture by itself is indecisive, and therefore he appeals to the age-long consent of the Church's tradition of episcopal government. This brings us to the question of the authority of tradition.

In all such cases of doubt the Scriptures must be interpreted by tradition. For the Anglican divines tradition is not a separate authority to be set alongside the Bible, as it was for post-Tridentine Romanism. They would have agreed with Aquinas that nothing was to be received as necessary to salvation which could not be proved by 'most certain warrants of Holy Scripture'.[1] But tradition, which represents the mind of the universal Church down the ages, is the best guide for interpreting the sense of Scripture, especially at those points (such as the question of church order) where the evidence of Scripture is ambiguous. Tradition thus understood is clearly of the utmost importance for a Church which seeks to assert no distinctive doctrines of its own, but to adhere only to that which may reasonably be held to be *quod semper*, *quod ubique et quod ab omnibus*. This understanding of the nature of tradition explains the Anglican devotion to the ancient Fathers of the undivided Church. Reasonable and traditional forms, ceremonies and social customs were not to be rejected merely because they had no explicit Biblical sanction. A convenient illustration of the Anglican appeal to tradition lies to hand in the matter of the dispute with the Puritans over the observance of Sunday. The Puritans, as is well known, were fanatical in the matter of Sunday-observance. But, alas, there is no Biblical text which enjoins it, and thus the Puritans ought according to their own principles to have forbidden the observance of Sunday, just as they forbade the observance of Christmas and Saints' Days. Therefore the Puritans identified Sunday with the Jewish Sabbath, and a rigid Sabbatarianism resulted. The Anglicans rejected this exegesis, maintaining that the Christian observance of Sunday does not rest upon the Fourth Commandment, but upon the tradition and usage of the Church which goes back to the days of the Apostles themselves. It was in this way that tradition supplements the Bible. Once tradition is repudiated, it is necessary to manipulate Biblical texts in order to regulate the details of social life and church life; this leads to a new-fangled Biblicism and to novel absurdities of all kinds. The Biblical teaching is always to be interpreted by reason and tradition: apart

[1] *Articles of Religion*, VIII.

from reason and tradition the Bible can be manipulated to support any kind of nonsense or heresy.

The Anglican divines accept unquestioningly the doctrine of the *testimonium Spiritus Sancti internum*. They are well aware that it is a truly Catholic doctrine. Archbishop Laud, for example, says that in conversing with the text of Scripture 'we meet with the Spirit of God inwardly inclining our hearts, and sealing the full assurance of all three (i.e. Scripture, tradition and reason) unto us. And then, and not till then, we are certain that the Scripture is the Word of God, both by divine and infallible proof.'[1] The characteristically Anglican introduction of tradition and reason into this context is worth noting. The doctrine must not be used (as some Puritans used it) as a means of denigrating tradition and reason.[2] The true function of the Spirit's witness in our hearts is to convince us of specifically religious truth—that God is revealed in his Christ, and that Jesus of Nazareth is he. The Spirit will not witness against the universal tradition of the Church, nor will he reveal to us in Biblical texts novel instructions for setting up a new ecclesiastical and social order, such as the ancient Fathers never knew. Questions about the guidance of the Bible for political, social and ecclesiastical affairs are not to be settled by the intensity of our convictions that we are being led by the Spirit: this is mere subjectivism. They are to be settled by the best scholarship that we have, or, in other words, by reason and the wisdom of the past. The Anglicans abhorred every pretence of an 'inner light' or 'guidance' which could not be checked by reason and tradition. The authority of the Bible lay in the fact that it contained the witness of the prophets and apostles to Christ, that he is the Word of God. A *word* is a rational utterance, addressed by one rational being to another. God's Word is addressed to our reason. It is not given to us to enable us to lay reason aside in attempting to solve our scientific, historical, social, political, economic and technological problems. Hence we are not to look in the Bible for economic laws, political programmes and constitutions, social policies, or even for solutions of our practical moral problems. The claims of some of the extreme Puritans (and later especially of the Quakers) to be able to answer all such questions by an appeal to scriptural texts were based upon a

[1] *Works of Laud*, Library of Anglo-Catholic Theology, Vol. II, 1849, p. 130.

[2] Richard Hooker, *op. cit.*, III, viii.

mistaken notion of the authority of the Bible and of the function of the Holy Spirit. 'By these and such like disputes', said Hooker, 'an opinion hath spread itself very far in the world, as if the way to be ripe in faith were to be raw in wit and judgment; as if Reason were an enemy unto Religion, childish Simplicity the mother of ghostly and divine Wisdom.'[1]

IV *Christian humanism*

The Anglican tradition of Christian humanism is based upon the continuing Anglican respect for the doctrine of Creation. The Puritan over-emphasis of the doctrine of the Fall was repugnant to Hooker and his successors. God's image and likeness is still present (though defaced) in man's reason and conscience; his everlasting power and divinity are still manifest in the world which once he saw to be good. Divine grace is given to Christian man that he may use reason and conscience aright, that the image of God may be restored in him. The Church is God's 'new creation', in which the effects of the Fall are, through sanctification, being done away. This attitude is closely connected with the Anglican respect for the law of nature. Law is essentially the expression of the divine nature. God's commands are not arbitrary. They only seem so to the mind which is immature and must be subjected to an external discipline; in essence they are rational. God's nature is rational, and his laws are the expression of His nature. This statement must not be taken in any Hegelian or 'idealistic' sense: to say that God's nature is rational does not mean that in its divine essence it can be known by our reason as such. It cannot. But it can be known in part. It can be known in so far as it has been revealed—made known—to us by God's rational Word. From the revelation which God has vouchsafed it can be known by us that law is not only the manifestation of God's power but also of his loving, rational wisdom. For Hooker the whole Universe is governed by God's law, and in so far as we by grace understand this law, we are understanding God's working and God's purpose. Not all of this wonderful divine law can be known by us, but, says Hooker in a memorable phrase, 'that little which we darkly apprehend we admire; the rest with religious ignorance we humbly and meekly adore'.[2]

Wherever reason and conscience operate, even beyond the

[1] Richard Hooker, *op. cit.*, III, viii, 4.

[2] Richard Hooker, *op. cit.*, I, ii, 5.

Jewish-Christian revelation, there is the knowledge of the law of God (cf. Rom. 2.14f.). Such knowledge may be rudimentary, but it is still knowledge of God. Nor does this broadly humanistic (Augustinian) point of view imply that the mighty acts of God of which the Bible tells us could be known apart from the Biblical revelation: it is the Bible which gives us the knowledge of our salvation, and makes explicit what is at best only implicit in such knowledge as the Gentiles have. Still less does it imply that these mighty acts of God are merely illustrations of general laws, which could have been known by 'unaided' reason. God's revelation comes to us uniquely through the witness of the prophets and apostles to those once-for-all acts by which our salvation was accomplished. But once we have received this witness, God further reveals himself to us through the Church's worship, liturgy, sacraments and common life—not by way of adding anything to the Biblical revelation but as the means by which the Biblical truth is brought home to us. And beyond this the knowledge of God is mediated to us in the complex business of political, social and family life: in seeking justice, truth and beauty. If this is Pelagianism, it is Biblical Pelagianism (cf. Jer. 22.15f.). It is not in books of divinity but in seeking God's will in the affairs of the common life and in worshipping his name in the congregation of his people that the knowledge of God is attained. The knowledge of God is thus essentially a lay (not a clerical) acquirement. It involves the diligent application of Biblical insights to everyday affairs by means of the unrelenting exercise of reason and conscience. It is by means of reason and conscience that we not merely perceive the relevance of the Biblical injunctions to our daily life, but also are enabled to distinguish between the relative value of the various Biblical injunctions themselves (e.g. between, say, Exod. 20.14 and Exod. 22.18). The Bible is not a code-book, still less a puzzle-book, by means of which, if we are religious enough, or clever enough, we may discern divine instruction for the regulating of modern social, political and moral life. The Anglican divines of the classical period lived long before the birth of Biblical criticism, but by their firm rejection of Scripturism and their insistence upon the appeal to sound learning, they prepared the way for a balanced assessment of the new scientific methods when they burst upon Christendom in the nineteenth century. Dr. Paul Elmer More has rightly claimed that the line of distinguished scholar-bishops, who welcomed the new Biblical learning of the nineteenth century and made it serve a fully scriptural and Catholic theology, are the true successors of the seventeenth-century Anglican divines. It was such men as Frederick Temple, Lightfoot, Westcott, Gore and William Temple who continued the genuinely Anglican tradition of scholarship, openness to new truth and toleration of a wide variety of opinion on all questions save the central affirmation of the Incarnation of God in Christ. It was because these men (and many others) continued in the direction set by the sixteenth- and seventeenth-century divines that the word 'liberal' in the English theological vocabulary has never meant simply 'liberal Protestant' and is not today merely a term of abuse: to be Catholic and to be liberal is the heritage of Anglican divinity.

V *The Political and Social Teaching of the Bible: Law, Order and Obedience*

The Anglican divines believed that their conception of the organic unity of mankind was derived from the Bible. Church and State are not two societies, but one. They are complementary aspects of humanity as the Bible understands it. Into that one humanity divisions have entered with the Fall; but the fundamental truth, though obscured, remains. The Old Testament is the source of revelation in the matter of the relation of the Church and society, since the separation of the Church and State which existed in New Testament times and until Constantine was not normative, but abnormal. Both the Church and the civil society are the work of the *Logos*, by whom all things were made. The Church is as old as Adam, or as old as Noah, through whom God made a covenant with all mankind; and though the Gentile 'churches' (i.e. the descendants of Ham and Japhet) perverted the knowledge of God, they were not left wholly in darkness or utterly cut off from God. According to the Bible, society is not an undifferentiated mass of individuals: it is divided into tribes and nations. The invisible head of all these parts of society in their totality is Christ, the *Logos*. There is no visible king or priest over all of them; each part has its own ruler and priesthood. The Jewish high priest was not a priest for all nations, neither was David or any other Jewish ruler king over all the world. Christ, though his headship was invisible, was the true priest and king of all the 'churches' and all the kingdoms of the Gentiles. The *Logos* became flesh in order to fulfil the purpose begun by him in the creation of the world and continued in its various religious and civil societies. The purpose of Christ in his Church is to gather into one all the divided nations and 'churches' of the Gentiles, to re-create the unity of mankind which had been lost at the Fall. Thus, the Church is not in essence something alien to the civil (or 'secular') order. 'The Church is not something imposed externally on civil society; the Church is civil society when through the baptism of all its members it has reached the terminus of its potentialities', says Canon G. W. O. Addleshaw, summarising the traditional Anglican position in his book, *The High Church Tradition*[1] (a book to which the present writer is indebted in the making of this summary). The idea of an undifferentiated world-church is repugnant to the intention of the *Logos*, as this is made known to us in the Old Testament revelation. The Church Universal is visible *per partes*, each part being under a Christian sovereign, who (according to due law and order, not despotically) exercises on earth Christ's kingly power. The King (or sovereign authority, of whatever form) must not usurp Christ's priestly office, which is given to the *Laos* and exercised through its responsible ministry ordained for that purpose. Though it is the purpose of the *Logos* to re-create the lost unity of mankind, this does not imply the setting up of a world-wide, uniform system of church-government or of a unitary world-state. It implies the achievement of unity and communion amidst diversity and local autonomy. 'Only as the Church envelops and absorbs civil society and lifts it up into the divine life does it fulfil the historical process marked out for it since creation. For the Church is built up out of humanity; it is not a select group of individuals called out of the world; it is humanity in the mass, toiling, struggling, sweating, with all its efforts to live an ordered social life, which is to form the mystical Body of Christ.'[2]

This organic conception of society seems to many in our day, in England as elsewhere, to be a visionary and impracticable ideal. There are those, however, including the present writer, who believe that such a conception is truly Biblical and that it can and must become the basis of an ecumenical reconsideration of the

[1] G. W. O. Addleshaw, *The High Church Tradition*, 1941, p. 156.
[2] G. W. O. Addleshaw, *op. cit.*, p. 158.

true relation of Church and society. If we believe that what the Bible teaches is authoritative, then we must seek to make that teaching the foundation of our efforts towards unity. Two primary causes have led to the almost total eclipse of the older Anglican view since the end of the seventeenth century. The first of these, of course, is the growth of sectarianism which has resulted from the break-up of the religious unity of the English people. (It may be added that, alas, the divisions which sprang up during and after the English Civil War have been exported all over the world, but especially to North America.) On the whole, the *sect* type of Christianity has attempted to set up the New Testament as normative in social and political matters, and has come to accept the notion of a Christian minority in a secular society: this is involved in the very conception of 'Free Churches'. But the setting up of 'Free Churches' falsifies even the New Testament doctrine of the Church, for the idea that two or more separate 'churches' or 'denominations' can exist side by side in one country or city is as repugnant to the New Testament as it is to the traditional Anglican conception of the Church. Even to Christian people it comes to appear incredible that the Church can be the instrument of the re-creation of the unity of mankind in an age in which she is unable to manifest unity even among Christians themselves. Denominationalism necessarily obscures the political and social authority of the Bible and makes its teaching appear irrelevant and inapplicable. And, secondly, as we have already said, the rise of secular individualism and its influence since the days of John Locke has so permeated the climate of opinion in our times that the older Biblical categories seem even in Christian circles to be old-fashioned and useless for today.

It is through denominationalism and the disappearance of the traditional Biblical-Christian teaching that Christian civilisation is decaying in the 'Western' world. For instance, since the disappearance of the old Christian teaching about *duty* in one's calling, statesmen are today at their wits' end to discover substitute 'incentives' that will cajole workers of all ranks to do an honest week's work for a reasonable wage. With the disappearance of the traditional teaching about political *obedience* a more rigid control by a vastly extended bureaucracy becomes increasingly necessary to enforce social conformity to the multiple regulations of a ruling group. The traditional Biblical-Christian (and Anglican) teaching was that the supreme social virtue was obedience to lawfully constituted authority: disobedience or rebellion is the ultimate social sin. Both rulers and ruled alike are subject to the sovereignty of law; unless men in society obey the laws of righteousness, civilisation is doomed. But when the conception of a divinely appointed lawful order is forgotten, and law becomes merely a matter of convenience, or of the enforcement of the will of the majority, it ceases to command respect in the hearts of the people. This conception of obedience, of the due discharge of the proper functions of one's station, is essential to any truly organic view of society. A measure of coercion to enforce obedience to authority will, of course, always be necessary in any human society as a result of sin; but where obedience has ceased to be regarded as a virtue, authority becomes ever more coercive, until at last every vestige of respect for human freedom and for the value of the individual has disappeared. It is only by teaching again the full Christian social ethic of obedience, duty in one's calling, responsibility in one's station, and the acceptance of the rule of law, that such things as respect for human personality and individual liberty can be secured. It is only on a basis of Biblical ethics that government by consent and the rule of law can be maintained. But today the 'churches' have been so denominationalised and secularised that they have forgotten what is the Biblical teaching and lost sight of the authority of the Bible in political and social affairs. Nevertheless, it remains true that the characteristics of Christian civilisation are that in it obedience is willingly rendered, duty is gladly performed, and honest toil is not shirked. Rulers for their part must model themselves on Christ's example and govern according to God's righteous law, as far as possible in the spirit of persuasion and love.

To secular liberalism society is not thus an organic unity but an alliance of equal and independent beings. Obedience is not a positive virtue, but a regrettable necessity, involving infringement of personal liberty. In order to secure the requisite measure of social conformity, it becomes necessary to cultivate the habit of submission to the government. This can be done in various ways, all unhappily familiar in the modern world: by economic sanctions, by police measures, and above all by propaganda. In an age in which each man grasps at equality with every other man and no one is willing to take the form of a servant, it is necessary to delete by any means the unpleasing sensation of being governed and to delude people that they are really governing themselves. The function of journalists and demagogues (often, alas, ably seconded by Christian preachers) is to generate forms of enthusiasm which will serve as substitutes for the Christian virtues of obedience and duty in one's calling. The Bible gives us no rule-of-thumb guidance for the ordering of our political and social life. But on the other hand it is supremely authoritative in those spheres. It tells us of God's purpose in Christ not only for the Church—or at least not only for the Church apart from society—but also for civil society as a whole, in which man's vocation is to fulfil the law of nature which God has ordained for his *Logos*-created world.

Part Two

BIBLICAL THEOLOGY AND ETHICS TODAY

A Survey of the World Position

BIBLICAL THEOLOGY AND ETHICS TODAY

A Survey of the World Position

by

WOLFGANG SCHWEITZER

Translated from the German by J. K. S. Reid

I *Historical and theological interpretation—an ecumenical problem*

In the chapters of the symposium that follow, the attempt is made to deal with the questions of Scriptural interpretation on the basis of ecumenical co-operation and to give examples of an interpretation of Biblical texts showing their relevance to modern times. This requires some justification. Fifty years ago such an attempt would probably have been held to be pointless. We do not yet know whether it will be applauded today. But the theological study of recent years has brought us unexpectedly close to one another. This will be outlined in what follows. It is evident that completeness is not attainable. Nor will the presentation try to be 'objective': critical remarks have not been suppressed—if only they may open the door to counter-criticism and so to co-operation.

The work of the historical and critical investigation of the Bible was carried on from its beginnings on an international and interdenominational basis. This was only natural: serious investigators in one country could not ignore results reached in other countries and in other languages. Here then, one may say, an ecumenical co-operative work had been carried on for a long time, even if it were not regarded consciously as a part of the ecumenical movement. But is not this co-operation of a purely departmental and historical kind, like the co-operation of other historical sciences, so that we can hardly speak of a really ecumenical and ecclesiastical significance? The objection is not valid, because even the 'purely' historical discussions have unavoidable consequences of an ecclesiastical and theological kind, and are always based on certain theological presuppositions.

The most important feature of the present situation is that within Biblical theology more and more weight is being laid on the theological interpretation of Scripture. In America as well as Britain, in Scandinavia as well as on the European continent, the demand is made that historical and critical study must advance to an adequately theological interpretation. This demand signifies little so long as we are not of one mind about what an adequately theological interpretation of Scripture is.

In the above sentence, a negative definition of the idea of 'theological exegesis' is first of all included. This definition can perhaps be stated thus: We will not confine ourselves to historico-critical study of the Biblical texts; our study must be put at the service of the Christian proclamation. Thus we should restore that fruitful co-operation between the several theological disciplines (historical, systematic and practical theology) that for long enough has been lost. While exegetical work upon Scripture constantly recalls theology as a whole back to Scripture, it puts itself at the service of the other disciplines.

But in what sense can exegetical theology recall us to Scripture? Evidently not in the sense that it leads us into the past and seeks to make us into Christians of the earliest centuries. Rather the contrary: interpretation will show that and in what sense the Bible contains a message that is valid today. To attempt to do this and to accomplish it are clearly two different things. So long as we proceed without certain rules, we shall always hear and interpret the Gospel differently. Can we in common set forth such rules? This question, the question of a Biblical interpretation, then becomes a key problem of ecumenical Biblical reflection.

But at this point we find ourselves in a dilemma arising out of the nature of the matter. To set out rules of interpretation means asking the question: What are the methods of interpretation that are best fitted to the whole of the Biblical message? Hence we must already understand this message as a whole before we can set out rules for interpreting the single texts. The consequence of this logical circle is that in fact interpretation of

Scripture and rules for its interpretation must always mutually enrich and correct each other.

Since then our understanding of the whole message of Scripture is constantly influenced by the ways and means by which it has been hitherto transmitted, we cannot give a universally acceptable positive definition of what 'theological interpretation' is. This would presuppose that the various confessions and schools had already achieved unanimity about the whole of the Gospel. For ecumenical co-operation there arises the question: Is it unavoidable that in the theological interpretation of Scripture we should separate again from one another? And to this it must be added that, in spite of what is said in other parts of this volume, the lines of division referred to here appear to run obliquely across many confessions.

We maintain that we are not thus compelled to divide when we listen in common to the message of the Bible. Scripture will then teach us two things, both what adequate theological interpretation is, and also how in obedience we can practically attain it. We shall now try, in view of these questions, to clarify for ourselves the position of Biblical theology on the one hand, and the latest developments in the systematic theology of the most important confessions on the other.

II *The position of New Testament study*

It is no accident that today many Biblical scholars are among the first to raise the demand for a theological interpretation of Scripture. We have to see in this the consequence of a history of New Testament study that has been full of tension. Without going into details, we can set forth the final important stages on this road. It is to be understood of course that (unhappily) the development is not so direct and simple as in the description that follows.

The historico-literary investigations which began in the nineteenth century led to a long-continued process of *analytical enquiry*. In the course of this, almost all elements of the New Testament were dissolved into their component parts, and their genuineness called in question. Radical views, such as the denial of the historicity of Jesus, were not able to stand up against exact study. Others in the course of time were much modified. But the most important problem proved to be almost insoluble: What rôle did Jesus himself play in the emergence of the Christian faith as it is described in the varying terms of the New Testament? The older historical school regarded the 'religion of Jesus' or the 'teaching of Jesus' as the climax of a religious evolution. Hence the later New Testament writings had to be considered as being of minor value—a conception not of course in harmony with the original evolutionary theory itself. Everything that failed to correspond to the above picture of Jesus was invalidated as supplementary addition. It was thus accepted that religious development from Jesus had been retrogressive.

It is well known that Albert Schweitzer (following J. Weiss) in his *Quest of the Historical Jesus* (1st Ed., 1906, *Von Reimarus zu Wrede*) had epoch-making influence, inasmuch as he destroyed the liberal picture of Jesus, for which especially the eschatological features in the Gospels had the force of merely unimportant additions. Schweitzer in this book, which was followed in 1911 by *History of Pauline Research*, and in 1930 by *The Mysticism of the Apostle Paul*, affirmed that the eschatological features could not be forced out on to the margin of the New Testament but formed an integral and constituent part of the central message of Jesus and the Apostle Paul, and so too of the whole primitive Church. This demonstration sensibly widened the gap between the Biblical scholars and the systematic liberals. For systematic liberalism now found itself in an almost insoluble dilemma. Either it followed Biblical theology and reckoned seriously with eschatology—and so ceased to be liberal; or it retained the liberal picture of Jesus—and then (as with Schweitzer himself) the whole conduct of systematic theology must be undertaken in complete independence of the results of Biblical research. It was not fortuitous that the liberals who took sides with Schweitzer could not come to terms with his historical enquiries.

It must not be overlooked that Schweitzer in matters of method remained an advocate of the analytic method which is employed in studies of comparative religion. Ultimately he emphasised the differences between the various levels of the New Testament more strongly than the foundation they had in common and here the problem of the transition from the world of Judaic apocalyptic ideas to that of Hellenic mystical ideas particularly attracted his interest.

In respect of method, a new turning was reached with the

technique of examining the genus to which texts belong, and the subsequent form-criticism. Here the question was: What led the authors of the New Testament to compose their writings? One began to enquire how for example the Gospels developed out of the apostolic preaching. This procedure is manifestly significant in a formal respect to begin with; but it also brought important theological consequences with it, which have by no means been fully worked out yet.

If one makes a start with the affirmation that the New Testament Scriptures arose out of the apostolic preaching (the *Kerygma*), the question must be considered: What then was the core of this preaching? In this way the short confessional formulas, in catechetical form, for example, achieved heightened significance. We meet them in all the Scriptures of the New Testament (I Cor. 15.3ff. is one of the best-known examples; cf. also, however, I Tim. 3.16 and I Pet. 2.21-25). Analysis by Form-Criticism helps us to discover numerous such formulas, which were probably used in the divine service of the primitive Church. Theologically it is very significant that these formulas are uniformly *Christological* in content. They affirm that Jesus of Nazareth died and rose for us, and he is the Lord and Christ promised in the Old Testament. Hoskyns has tried to demonstrate that this *Kerygma* is to be met at all levels in the New Testament, e.g. even in the different levels of the synoptic Gospels. The Christological declarations of Jesus concerning himself according to the synoptic sources affirm really nothing else than what, e.g., I Pet. 2.21-25 says. Thus Hoskyns came to the conclusion that 'the critical method has itself revealed most clearly the living unity of the documents' (*The Riddle of the New Testament*, 3rd Ed., 1947, p. 180). The critical enquirer dare not make himself judge of belief and unbelief; all he can do is finally to affirm that the New Testament poses the question of faith: What kind of man was Jesus?

One must, of course, not overlook the fact that it was not only considerations of method that led to this issue. As in the earlier stages of the historico-critical enquiry, it was rather the fundamental conception of the nature of history that played a decisive rôle, even in the development of methods. If Hegelian conceptions brought into being the analytical process from the days of F. C. Baur, so at present the tendency is observable to apply the modern *organic understanding of history*. The consequence is that many no longer care to separate event and meaning from one another, as happened earlier. Thus Hoskyns says that 'the first task of criticism is, therefore, to explain the material as it now exists. For some reason or another, perhaps for many various reasons, the story of the life and death of Jesus came to be recounted in its present form. The judgments responsible for this form may have been true or false. In either case the fact that they were made has to be explained' (p. 54).

Thus while the historico-critical enquiry was developing ever better methods of its own, it became conscious of its own limits. One cannot separate the 'religion' or the 'religious consciousness' of Jesus from the faith of the primitive Church that this Jesus is the Christ of God. This does not mean that we had to admit the impossibility of further historical research, so that Jesus himself remained veiled in mysterious darkness. The proper 'riddle of the New Testament' is rather Jesus' own faith that he fulfils the promises of the Old Testament. This is connected with the astonishing fact, to some degree in His lifetime and in any case shortly after his death and resurrection, that a numerous community arose, which held this claim valid and proclaimed it. Historical enquiry can only formulate this as a question, and demand that it be answered theologically. So long as the answer is not forthcoming, the real object of our endeavour has not been achieved, viz. the interpretation of Scripture. While the historico-critical enquiry finally poses this question concerning Christ, it indicates at the same time the point at which alone really theological interpretation can begin: the proclamation of Jesus, the crucified and risen Christ. We must put ourselves at the service of this proclamation if we will expound the New Testament.

III *The position of Old Testament study*

In the study of the New Testament, the historical enquiry led to the conclusion that the older pure 'religion of Jesus' must be freed from later accretions. It was also held that the development had been retrograde. The position was reversed in the case of the Old Testament. Here the view prevailed that the monotheism of Israel developed only gradually out of earlier heathen stages and that Israel's religion finally reached its climax in the religious morality of the prophets, which abhorred the cult of sacrifice.

With closer historical research the picture completely altered. It became more and more clear that Moses had to be regarded as the founder of Israel's covenant religion, and that as a religion of divine election it stood from the very beginning in contradiction not only to naturalism but also to the demonism of heathen cults. Thus also from the very beginning, the Decalogue (to which the prophets later harked back) formed a permanent part of this religion. The prophets introduced nothing new; they rather combated infidelity towards a God who had chosen his people at Sinai.

No one disputes that the Old Testament contains relics of earlier stages of religion. But just as the New Testament employed pictures of the ancient mystery religions and the like in the service of the *Kerygma* concerning Christ, e.g. the image of rebirth, so the older material incorporated in the Old Testament is employed in the service of a central idea, which was to be held fast by means of a fixed written form. How is this centre of the Old Testament to be more closely defined? Clearly it is necessary to advance here in an order the reverse of that employed in New Testament study. 'In the case of the New Testament, recognition of the smallest units was important, because we were shown that their character of witnessing to Christ was not imprinted on them by the work of collators and theologians, but that this character already belonged to the smallest units. In the case of the Old Testament, however, we are shown how these small units acquire their meaning through the collators and collectors' (H. W. Bartsch). It is this historical study of the literature and its sources that permits us to recognise the centre and the unity of the Old Testament.

According to the view of many Old Testament scholars, it is neither the doctrine of monotheism nor the code of morals deposited in the Decalogue, that constitutes the centre. The dominating and binding element in all the Old Testament is rather the idea of Covenant: historical books and tales of the patriarchs, the prophets and also the psalmists, hold before them, as the most valuable and at the same time the constantly threatened jewel, the Covenant which God made with Israel. It is this realisation that has resulted in recent times in the attempt being made, e.g. by Eichrodt, to present the theology of the Old Testament, not (as hitherto customary) according to any of the standpoints usual in Christian dogmatics, but to set out with the idea of Covenant as a uniform method.

Some on this point go even further: they emphasise that this Covenant idea is in fact at the centre of the Old Testament; but since we are members of the New Covenant founded by Jesus Christ we have to interpret the Old Testament from this standpoint. The result is that the Old Testament is to be considered and to be interpreted as the charter of the New Covenant: the difference between the two withers away: one tries here to read the Old Testament as Jesus read it, that is, as witnessing to himself, and in the sense of the primitive Church, which transmitted it for this reason and was of opinion that in itself the Old Testament promises of a renewal of the Covenant were fulfilled. The methods of the theologians who follow this second way are various: in most cases exposition is typological, following the example given by the New Testament in its 'scriptural proofs'.

Of course, these interpretations encounter considerable difficulties in connection with modern literary research. But on the other hand we must ask whether a Christian theologian can even for a moment work as if Christ were not yet born. Can we at all put ourselves in the position of the old synagogue? And if so, what value would this have for us? Putting the question in even sharper form: What meaning has Jesus for us if he had not applied the Old Testament to himself and so 'fulfilled' it?—a question quite independent of our modern critical investigations into the original meaning of the relevant Old Testament passages.

Finally, everything depends on what Christian theology makes of the idea of *Heilsgeschichte* (salvation history). The old Covenant can from the Christian standpoint be understood only as preparation. This does not exclude but rather presupposes that we must first of all understand it as it was understood in this preparatory time. Since it is from this point of view alone that we can reckon not only with historico-critical research but also with the demands of theology mentioned above, this view of the matter must in the long run generally assert itself.

It is evident that Old Testament theology besides its special problem has to wrestle with a problem which has pursued all

Christian theology ever since the days of Marcion: the problem of the *theological unity of the whole of Scripture*. In the light of what has just been said, it is for New Testament theology a matter of decisive importance that we do not unloose the Christian proclamation from its connection with salvation history. While Christ is the last goal of all Biblical theology, it must therefore constantly warn systematic theology against certain errors by which the importance of history is under-valued. A. Wilder mentions here especially the danger of harmonising and allegorising which some have failed to avoid, in consequence of a false application of the sentence that Christ is the 'centre of Scripture'. This error is a special threat where 'certain writers make a too simple distinction between the common underlying message and its various "forms of expression"' (*New Testament Theology in Transition*, in *The Study of the Bible Today and Tomorrow*, ed. H. R. Willoughby, Chicago, 1947, p. 433); or in other words when one acts as though he could dispose of the Gospel as he wishes, though indeed we can understand it only in its historical context. With this question we now turn to systematic theology.

IV *Critical description of the most important interpretative rules used today*

In Section I above, it was pointed out that our understanding of the whole message of the Bible at the same time determines the rules for its interpretation. If in what follows we set out the interpretative rules employed by various theological schools, this will be relevant to the whole of Christian doctrine current today. A purely formal analysis is impossible here. Since our chief interest is directed to social and political ethics, the same ecclesiastical and theological groups are viewed again under this special aspect in the last part of this paper. It then appears that certain safeguards must be observed for interpreting Scripture within these spheres—safeguards that correspond to the special dangers to which systematic theology when dealing with ethical problems is exposed. We separate general interpretation from these questions of interpretation that concern Christian ethics. But even though we do this, it has always to be borne in mind that they belong to one another fundamentally, just as practical corollaries also emerge in every case.

The first question which we must set before individual

theologians and schools of ecclesiastical thought is as follows: What is the connection in the Bible between the Word of God and the human word? On the answer given to this question depend the rules for interpretation which from time to time are worked out and applied.

(*a*) Ecclesiastical authority and the interpretation of scripture

In Part I of this volume, a consciously ecclesiastical interpretation of Scripture was demanded from different quarters. Hence we have to deal briefly with the question of what interpretative rules arise from this fact. For the sake of clarity, we deal also with the doctrine of the Roman Catholic Church, though it was not represented in Part I. At the same time we remember that all confessions and all theological tendencies (so far as they are committed to work ecclesiastically) are confronted today with a new urgency by this question. It is by no means only a matter of the so-called 'Catholic' groups within the different Churches.

The first matter of debate is the question concerning the freedom of scientific Biblical criticism. The first encounter between liberalism (modernism) and the doctrinal authority of the Church led, as it is well known, to the condemnation of the former. The defenders of Church doctrine were at pains, often rather spasmodically, to salvage what in their view could be salvaged of the authority of the Bible.

This attitude, however, has meantime greatly changed almost everywhere. In these groups, it is explained that all critical research is welcomed; the foundation of the faith is not affected adversely by such research, but can rather only be reinforced. Just because the foundation of the faith stands secure, research into the Scriptures—so it is said—can be undertaken with all the greater freedom.

But fundamentally the external freedom of critical research is not the decisive problem in the ecumenical debate, though it is so represented by many liberals even today. Those who make repeated attacks against the Roman Catholic Church, from this angle are justified in their appeal to the 'Scriptural principle' of the Reformers only if they apply it in the same way as the Reformers. Whenever this happens, it is no more the freedom of critical research into the Bible that is at stake; it is rather the freedom and authority of Scripture over against the existing human attempts at interpretation. This sovereignty of the Word of God cannot be defended where the theologian, before he even opens the Bible, is already committed to an obligatory doctrine of the Church about the truth of the Word of God, whether it be the resolutions of Councils, Papal encyclicals or Protestant confessional documents. Thus the question is whether Biblical theology has the right to amend at any time the systematic doctrine and the practical proclamation of the Church. The question is whether we open the Scriptures without expecting that the will of God, perhaps in a quite new and unprecedented way, will be revealed to us in his Word. Who is Lord in the Church?

In answer to these questions, it is usually pointed out from the Roman Catholic side that the distinction which the Protestant makes between Christ and his Church is an artificial one. Being the Body of Christ, the Church is identical in a mystical way with its Lord, and consequently the authority of the Church cannot but coincide with the authority of Christ and the authority of Scripture. In addition, Catholics say that the room for free play within the limits set by doctrinal decisions is very wide. Within this room anything is possible, and in fact there are in the Roman Catholic Church evident tendencies which concern themselves with a dogmatic and an ethic newly orientated towards Scripture. But is the freedom within this area really true freedom? Can a genuine listening to the Gospel take place where escape from this area is regarded as fundamentally impossible? Does not the doctrinal system prove to be overwhelming for the individual—or rather, not only the doctrinal system, but also the 'stream of life' (*Lebensstrom*) which through all the centuries binds individual Christians in the Church with Christ?

The idea of this living stream appears to achieve meaning just at the point where the form and content of the Gospel to be preached to the present generation is disputed. The aim is here to unfold with an ever-fresh concern the fulness of that which Christ has committed to his Church; everything which has been thus unfolded during the centuries was, in its essence, already inherent in the message of the primitive Church and in Scripture. Just as Christ is present not only in Scripture, but also and chiefly in the Church, so the witness of the Church today is understood to be the direct continuation of the witness that lies in Scripture. What need can there be of escaping outside this? On this view tradition has really the same meaning as has Scripture for the present-day witness of the Church, and the concern to be justified by it accordingly plays almost a more important part in this theology than an adequate interpretation of Scripture.

For the ecumenical debate, there emerges the relevant fact that representatives of these confessions and tendencies are able to agree completely on the presentation of interpretative rules; but in practice they do not draw the same conclusions as their debating partners.

Protestant criticism must not, of course, shut out the view that responsible church interpretation of Scripture may not as such be condemned (cf. below, pp. 150ff.). It *can* be a genuine tie with the Gospel of Jesus Christ, and can thereby help towards the understanding of Scripture from its own centre. The interpretation of Scripture that is ostensibly free of presupposition and shuns all Church ties—as is to be shown below—leads in fact to the setting up of maxims of Scriptural interpretation that are not only foreign to the Bible, but even quite un-Christian. Evangelical Christians have no cause to prize this kind of outward freedom.

Protestant thought is properly directed, not against Scriptural interpretation being prosecuted in Romanism from within the Church, but quite the reverse: against the danger here present that connection with the *Lord* of the Church is denied. It is this that ought always to be meant when one talks of the Church. The Roman identification of the Church with its Lord, Protestantism objects, can finally lead only to the word of man being put in place of the Word of God. To be tied to the word of man, or even to the multifarious forms of church life, is, strictly speaking, no ecclesiastical tie; in fact, it only opens the door to human arbitrariness and licence. The discipline of the *magisterium ecclesiae* (which in practice desires before everything else to hold the doors open on all sides by means of careful formulations) is at this point no real security. For instead of the *magisterium ecclesiae* or the life of the Church being constantly corrected by Scripture, the two stand here over against each other, and so the Church in fact is dependent on itself alone. In contrast to this, genuine church interpretation of Scripture must mean that we let ourselves be led by the Church's proclamation of Scripture ever anew to the living head of the Church, to whom Scripture witnesses, in order that we may interpret this witness in obedience to him. Since Scripture witnesses to this Lord, the Church, and so also the interpreter, are tied to it alone.

(*b*) The fundamentalists

This last demand influences specially the fundamentalists. Nothing is here sought but the tie binding us to Scripture—and yet even so the possibility of really listening to its message is lost. For here, between the human witness of past days by which the Bible has been transmitted to us on the one hand and the Word of God on the other, a false identification is made.

The impregnable maxim of the extreme fundamentalists is the doctrine of verbal inspiration. This determines what are the rules for exposition: God is the author of Scripture; men are involved only as his organs or instruments. It follows, for example, that it is unimportant how the human authors—perhaps the prophets—themselves understood or could have understood what they wrote down at the Command of God. Even when they did not conceive their prophecies as messianic in the thought of God, they are none the less intended to be messianic, and hence are to be so understood by us.

Thus at this point it is already clear that certain dogmatic presuppositions determine the course of interpretation. The fundamentalist believes that he knows what God 'really' wants to say, even when the report given of the Word of God in the mouths of men is faulty. Where then does he find the standard with which to measure the declarations of Scripture? It is clearly not attained by historico-scientific methods. Only the words of men may be analysed by such means. Only with them can questions of genuineness of a tradition or the sources of an idea have any meaning. But here the identity of Scripture and the Word of God is emphasised so starkly and strongly, that this kind of procedure must appear illegitimate. Since, then, historical criteria must be discarded, everything depends solely upon the dogmatic system which the fundamentalist brings with him when he opens the Bible.

The fundamentalists deceive themselves when they believe that they can tie themselves purely to the Word of God. Even they are unable to free themselves of all presuppositions. The tragic result is that, contrary to their intentions, they too do tie themselves to human words. When this occurs without reference to church doctrine, one frequently falls into a boundless sectarian capriciousness. Any part of Scripture or a certain interpretation of a certain text once accepted is proclaimed as the only norm with astounding obstinacy. This principle, as in the case of the tie with church doctrine, can accompany a legitimate safeguarding of the Christian *Kerygma*. But since this starting point for the understanding of Scripture is not attained by means of constant critical wrestling with the human witness of Scripture, many fundamentalists go fearfully wrong again and again: anything that stands on the edge of Scripture is thrust here or there into a central position.

As the fundamentalist declines to take the Bible as a human word seriously, it has little or no importance for him that the Biblical proclamation should be transferred into the thought of the present day. Accordingly there is here fundamentally no interpretation, but at most only a systematising and harmonising of Biblical affirmations. The message of the Bible is not interpreted; the sentences are merely collected and repeated in a certain relation. Frequently also certain texts, especially out of the prophetic and apocalyptic parts of Scripture, are 'applied' to the present with a light-hearted directness. That these sentences thus repeated are hard for modern man to understand is not regarded as a problem for method, but as a problem of fact: according to the witness of Scripture itself, the Word of the Cross is for the world in any case a 'stumbling-block', so long as no 'conversion' takes place.

This last sentence is, of course, good theology; but it can lead to a dangerous deception. What if the stumbling-block be put at a point where, so far as the Gospel itself is concerned, it need not stand? Christ became man at a certain time and in a certain place. Must not the message concerning him (so long as it remains really and only this Gospel) take today a form which makes it possible for modern man to listen to it? It is only too easy for modern man to be confirmed in the suspicion that Christianity wants nothing but to conserve antiquated ideas and heat them up.

(*c*) Liberal theology

The naïve Biblical faith has for the liberal theologian been destroyed by the scientific work of the last 150 years. Now he sees that the Bible is a historical document like other human documents. As preacher of the Gospel he, therefore, stands in a dilemma, which in the long run he cannot conceal from his congregation. They wish to hear God's Word; but he can only proclaim a human word. Must he not simply set the Bible aside?

Most liberal theologians—one cannot, of course, tar them all with the same brush—try to evade this consequence by trying to take the Bible seriously as evidence of the historical evolution of religion, from a really primitive religiosity (anthropomorphic representations of God, human sacrifice, etc.) through the 'moralistic' religion of the prophets, up to Jesus, the great 'teacher' and 'master', who profoundly deepened the ancient idea of God, so that his disciples 'found in him God' (Christ's Sonship of God is interpreted thus), who teaches a new morality and speaks of forgiveness in such a way that it makes all ideas of sacrifice superfluous. After Jesus—so runs the opinion—the development becomes again retrogressive: Judaic-apocalyptic and Hellenistic influences obscure the picture of the master even in the later books of the New Testament—nay, even in the synoptic Gospels, out of which happily we can extract the form of the 'Jesus of history'.

From this fundamental view, common to liberal theology, different possible relations to the Bible emerge. This may serve as the typical liberal opinion, that one confines himself to presenting the life and especially the teaching of Jesus so clearly, that even our generation may be 'followers of Jesus'. On this view, metaphysics and dogmatics are ignored as far as possible, and the ethical side of Christianity is strongly emphasised. It cannot be overlooked that this was once done with the greatest eagerness, and that it is still done with rather diminished zeal. Relations with the Bible remain fundamentally very loose, or indeed very 'free': we must not be bound by the letter of the Bible. 'We have the mind of Christ' (I Cor. 2.16) becomes the confident slogan of Christian freedom. Anything that the Bible contains beyond the ethics of Jesus is regarded from this angle as antiquated scaffolding or as temporary and gloomy background: we have at most to go through all this in order to extract the bright light of the 'teaching of Jesus'. Where this is done, only parts of Scripture have any present-day meaning. Accordingly one does not trouble oneself radically to find one interpretation for (the whole of) Scripture. One does not on this view interpret; one selects.

We have nevertheless to recognise that here the problem of an understanding of the Bible appropriate to the present day is grasped consciously and with relentless sincerity. Naïve pre-critical faith in the Bible has been struck from the grasp of the liberal theologian, and he therefore tries to make clear to himself what (even today) remains obligatory in the Biblical message. This is the only possible method for the solution of the problem of interpretation, so long as a relevant standard is applied. And the next step also was taken in the right direction: the obligatory element is to be found where Scripture speaks of Jesus. What is then found and proposed as solution is, of course, itself antiquated, for the liberal picture of Jesus is itself illusory (as has been briefly indicated above). By applying this technique of choosing, which is really determined by idealistic presuppositions, the liberal school prevents access to the message of the Bible at a decisive point. Both its disparity from Scripture and its inability to press forward to a real interpretation are explicable from here.

Opposition between liberals and fundamentalists has in many parts of the world died away already. But on the other hand, in North America, it still plays a considerable rôle. In general, however, new possibilities are being sought, in order to win a way out of this opposition, without disregarding either the historico-literary criticism of the Bible or its theological interpretation.

(*d*) Religious significance of history—first solution

For the liberal theologian the Bible became a witness of human history. Could it not, however, be that this human history is at the same time the history of God with men? Thus the special character of Christianity would lie in the fact 'that it is born out of history'. And thus too 'it is religion that was born of history. It was not merely mediated through historical persons. It was mediated also through the events of history' (H. H. Rowley). In this case, the events in the Bible, in which God deals with men, are to be taken with the same seriousness as human reactions to these events. Both are inextricably entangled with one another: the divine acts and the human experience of these acts, the speech of God and the answer of man—these neither can nor ought to be parted from one another.

It is immediately clear that this conception not only can but must make use of historico-critical study. On the assumption that the relation of 'religion and history' is rightly seen, a theological interpretation of Scripture is here evidently possible. Similarly, it also appears possible from this standpoint to make the Bible relevant to modern man. The transition from Old Testament to New Testament completes itself here with comparatively little difficulty. The experiences which the people of Israel and the primitive Church underwent are also our experiences. Or rather, we shall experience their reality as soon as our eyes are opened by Scripture.

It is apparent that Scripture here becomes the key to our history. Will the witness of Christ, the proclamation of the person of Jesus as the incarnate, crucified and risen Lord, be really heard in this case? Its significance lies chiefly in the fact that in these events the whole scheme of God's judgment and mercy is revealed as the ground scheme for the whole of history. This scheme necessarily becomes more and more influential on further development, and the person of Jesus retreats more and more into the background. We saw indeed that this interpretation started out from a new conception of history. It is therefore not surprising that ultimately it fails to overcome its limitations.

The nerve-centre of this interpretation is the question of the meaning of Biblical eschatology: since the Cross and the Resurrection of Christ are understood finally in the last analysis only as revelation through the acts of God in history, the eschatological meaning of God's acts in Christ, which signal the end of the history of this present world, cannot receive its due Biblical recognition. It is no chance that more is said in this connection of 'realised eschatology' (C. H. Dodd) than of what still remains to be fulfilled.

If Scripture is here to reveal the meaning of history, the converse of the sentence used above is readily applied: history, and especially in this case the history of the Church, illustrates Scripture for us. Here the relation between Bible and Church receives a positive evaluation: only in the Church (where the history of salvation is continued) can Scripture be a living thing; or more exactly, only in the Church can that become a reality which Scripture itself witnesses. The Church in this case is the most important instrument by which God acts in history.

The decisive question to be put to the representatives of this tendency is as follows: Is not the relation of revelation and history here misunderstood in a rationalistic sense? Or is it not rationalism when we pretend to recognise this *schema* of judgment and mercy as clearly as is done here? We must make no mistake: this *schema* can be a very useful key to the understanding of Scripture. But it can also very easily lead to arbitrary interpretation.

It is perhaps not a mere coincidence that many theologians today, under the influence of the views described above, have turned to *typology*. There can be no doubt that typological tendencies are present within Scripture itself, especially when the authors of the New Testament refer to the Old Testament. So long as this is meant to say that the Old Covenant leads up to Christ, this is in fact a genuine Christian understanding of history. We must reckon with this, even if we cannot, on historico-critical grounds, accept the typological meanings accorded to individual passages. On the other side, we must heed the warning of those who fear that a preoccupation with 'types' and their developments could lead us into speculations quite foreign to the Bible. Finally, all typological interpretations of Scripture are based on the rationalistic presupposition that God's acts with men must have been repeated at different times and are still repeated, since he himself remains the same. But, over against the false meaning of history that is deduced from this, this word has validity: 'My thoughts are not your thoughts, neither are your ways my ways, saith the Lord' (Isa. 55.8).

(*e*) The solution of existentialist philosophy

In the year 1941 Rudolph Bultmann made the proposal to restate the mythological elements in the message of the New Testament in a new way. He had in mind to develop a principle of interpretation which did not eliminate the New Testament *Kerygma*, but really set it forth in interpretative terms. He saw in this the difference between his own attempt and that of liberal theology. He is at one with it in holding that the Christian message in the New Testament has so strongly mythological a form, that in this form it can no longer be transmitted to men of today. But we are not dependent on this form since, according to Bultmann's view, the *mythos* has no other significance than that of expressing a certain understanding of man's existence, and so must be interpreted existentially. The Cross and the Resurrection of Christ achieve meaning for the individual only when they lead him to a genuine decision, to a new understanding of himself and thereby to a new life.

In the debate which arose over Bultmann's proposal, the most important question was whether the *Kerygma* would not again be surrendered as *Kerygma*, in this case to existential philosophy. Whereas in the case just described a certain understanding of history seemed to overshadow the uniqueness in character and occurrence of the event of Christ, it is here the existential understanding which Bultmann holds to be the key of his exposition which leads to a similar result. His conception encounters difficulties as soon as the *mythos* is regarded not only as the expression of a certain understanding of man's existence. It could of course be the expression of a certain understanding of the world or of history; liberation from mythological elements would then have to run on different lines from those he proposed.

(*f*) The dialectical Christocentric solution

It is unjust to regard dialectical theology as the resuscitation of fundamentalism. Recourse to Scripture takes place not because there is need to hold on to what has been transmitted, but quite the other way round: because all has become dubious, and because in consequence the position of the preacher of the Gospel has also become dubious. In this profound crisis, questions in the foreground concerning the validity of single scriptural words and so on lose more and more of their meaning, over against the radical fact that the Bible is God's Word to men, that as we deal with the Bible God speaks to us even today and that he addresses precisely those that despair. The 'Word of God' here becomes not identical with the very letter of Scripture; it is rather in a literal sense God's act of speaking with us, his claim upon us, or as the Reformers used to say *viva vox evangelii*. Not only the too precipitate systematisation of ethics, but also the too precipitate systematisation of dogmatics, are sharply criticised here.

At the same time, the Bible is understood quite unambiguously as a human word. Hence we must hear and reckon with this human word, as it has been spoken, since it is of prime importance that the message of the Bible be received. The historical and literary work done on the Bible is fundamentally approved and regarded as part of the task of interpretation. Whenever we hear the Word of God in the human word, the message of the Bible becomes no longer a message out of the past, but an event in the present. It then happens that God speaks and man hears, and this means that he accepts the message of Jesus Christ: 'The Bible becomes clear where it becomes clear that it says this one thing—that it proclaims the name of Jesus Christ and therewith God in his riches and mercy, and man in his need and helplessness . . .' (Karl Barth, *Dogmatik*, I, 2, 808). The decisive demand of this theology is accordingly apparent in that justice is done to the message of Christ as the centre of Scripture.

Where the authority of the Word of God was threatened by the corruption of liberalism, the dialectical theology is rightly regarded as a liberating break-through to reformed theological fundamentals. Its influence goes far beyond the narrow limits of the dialectical school, properly speaking. If many have won their way back to the thought that in theology and Church we have to do, not with the fulfilment of human longings, but with obedience to God himself, they have to thank the direct or indirect influence of Karl Barth. Many of Barth's opponents even have learnt from him—or at least have allowed themselves to be reassured by him that the claim of God upon us in Scripture confronts us in both a human and a divine way. This tension, in contrast with fundamentalist and liberal thought, is expressly affirmed in this theology. In this sense we are faced here with a Christological understanding of Scripture.

It was seen above that the same tension has, in the case of C. H. Dodd and others, led to the attempt to interpret history from the standpoint of the Bible. Since dialectical theology is concerned above all with the claim of God, eternal and also 'here and now', it necessarily follows another way. The result is that the representatives of the tendency described under (*d*) above criticise it for its constant uncertainty in regard to the problem of history. According to the opinion of these 'historically orientated theologians' (if we may use the term), the fundamental Christological principle for the interpretation of Scripture in dialectical theology is exaggerated. All Scripture is understood as witness to the event of Christ; the history of God with men is compressed into this one point (cf. Karl Barth, *Dogmatik*, I, 1, 119). This appears especially clearly in its interpretation of the Old

Testament. That there is here a history of God with man, i.e. a succession of *different* acts of God upon men and through men, is in fact not taken seriously. The result is that this theology does not reckon seriously with the incarnation of the Word; it has no safeguard against docetism.

(*g*) Consequences and questions for further study

We have tried to review the present situation of the ecumenical debate concerning the fundamental rules of interpretation. But it would be false to believe that this represented a complete cross-section of what is being discussed today. For beside the groups here named there are numberless other interpreters of Scripture in all confessions, who do not fall into the categories of school and tendency. For instance, if one were to class the New Testament scholar J. Schniewind (who died in 1948) as a pupil of the 'Biblicists' M. Kaehler and A. Schlatter, it would have little significance for our discussion here. For these German 'Biblicists' are not at all interchangeable with the 'fundamentalists' mentioned above, if only for this reason, that they have a far more positive attitude towards historical research than the 'fundamentalists' have.

If we disregard these 'lone wolves' who belong to all lands and every confession, it appears that the present struggle in theology described above in IV (*b*)-(*f*) is a struggle for the recognition of the liberty and sovereignty of the Word of God against historicism. Hence the theologians who have been and are influenced by Kierkegaard should be the first to break the ban upon historicism and the evolutionary ideas bound up with it. (P. T. Forsyth, the English theologian who died in 1921, is to be remembered in this connection.) In fact the issue at stake in this conflict is the meaning of the historical for the fundamentals of theology and within the theological system. This problem is not identical with the question of the right of historico-critical research to live, though it is not wholly separable from it.

In the defence against historicism, many were led to emphasise more strongly the existential or matter-of-fact character of the Word of God. The pendulum seems, however, to have swung too far here. Great care has recently been taken to discover the Scriptural understanding of history. Here perhaps O. Cullmann's book, *Christ and Time*, ought to be mentioned. The discussion of this subject has, in fact, only begun, and its results for interpretation have still to be formulated. Recognition of the proposition that Christ is the centre of Scripture must not mislead us to believe the old problem of the relation of revelation to history solved. On the contrary, it stands now with greater theological urgency before us.

V *Christ as the centre of Scriptural interpretation, of dogmatics and of ethics*

We have affirmed that New Testament research leads out into the question: 'Who was, or who is, Jesus Christ?' We have already noted the special difficulties with which systematic theology has in dogmatic questions to wrestle, if it is concerned to reckon with the fundamental proposition: Christ is the centre of Scripture. We must in conclusion try to follow out this line into the sphere of Christian ethics, since it is with this that this volume is specially concerned.

It may not be clear at the outset to everyone that the way of dogmatics must be followed here. Is it not a diversion? Liberal theology was certainly, as we saw, of the opinion that Christianity is above all an ethical religion, and that the most important thing was to develop and as far as possible apply the highest ethical principles out of Scripture. It was apparent, however, that this view was nourished too exclusively on an optimistic idealism, which did not take into account the egoism of human nature. Thus from 1914 there was experienced in increasing measure the 'problem of ethics today' (cf. Karl Barth in *Zwischen den Zeiten*, 1923). Our generation stood 'helpless, perplexed and uncertain' before the ethics familiar to an earlier generation. It is characteristic of the present ecumenical discussions that this realistic outlook is increasingly recognised in all countries and confessions. Our ethics have no solid basis, so long as we fail to proclaim credibly to the men of our time the Gospel of forgiveness in Jesus Christ, and to see them in the light of the Bible as they really are, and as they may become in Christ.

In addition it follows that no development of ethical principles from the Bible, and no direct application of them to present problems, are possible. At the ecumenical Study Conferences of 1946 in London, 1947 in Bossey and 1949 in Wadham College, Oxford, which all addressed themselves to this subject, no one gave expression to Biblical literalism. In the sphere of social and political ethics, a direct application of isolated Biblical passages could have only disastrous results. The significance of the Conference at Bossey can be said to consist in this, that those who took part unanimously agreed that every Biblical interpretation has to set out from Jesus Christ. At the Wadham College Conference the attempt was made to develop this fundamental principle in its details in the *Guiding Principles for the Interpretation of the Bible*, which are reprinted in our volume. The unanimity at this Conference was astonishing (cf. especially the concluding sentences of the Declaration of 1949). But we still have a long way to go with one another, before we find real unanimity about the *application* of the message of the Bible (cf. below, p. 241, I (*g*), and p. 243, IV (*c*). Where do the difficulties to understanding lie?

In those groups that referred to the theological meaning of history and experience, the opinion still survived with certain modifications which we have characterised above as typically liberal. The ethical instructions of the Bible are regarded as time-conditioned. In place of direct application, the attempt is made to make 'the mind of Christ' relevant to the present day. Thus, so-called 'middle axioms' are formulated, to bridge the gulf between the Bible and the modern world. The attempt to develop ethics afresh out of the centre of the Biblical message has for the most part not yet been made. One has the impression that the problem of the historical discrepancy between the Bible and the present day has forced itself into the foreground. Consequently, 'Christian' ethics is in practice founded more on the idea of natural law and similar general humanistic conceptions than on the Bible.

Contrast both with this Protestant type of foundation for ethics, and also with the Thomist ethics (with its systematisation of the relation between the natural and the supernatural) is offered by Karl Barth and the majority of the so-called dialectical theologians, who develop Christian ethics persistently out of the very centre of the Christian message of Jesus Christ. Hence the way *via* dogmatics is not for them regarded as circuitous, since there is a valid method of advance from Scripture to ethical problems. In all dogmatic questions, ethics stands ready to be discussed as the other side of dogmatics. Consequently, there is for Barth an inner connection between the doctrine of election (man is chosen in Christ to be partner in a covenant) and the fundamental questions of Christian ethics: 'For church dogmatics, the ethical problem consists in the question whether and how far human action is praise of God' (*Dogmatics*, II, 2. 600). The humanity of Jesus Christ becomes correspondingly the standard of theological anthropology. The humanity of man consists in the fact that he, as Christian, was made for the service of his fellow men (*Dogmatics*, III, 2. 264ff.).

The most important feature of this type of ethics, of which Karl Barth, A. Quervain and D. Bonhoeffer are exponents, is that Gospel and Law are seen in the closest connection. The start is made not with the imperative, but with the indicative: God has chosen us in Christ, and hence we must and can be obedient to him; God's deed makes our obedience possible. It follows that Christian ethics has to proclaim the Lordship of Christ over all spheres of human life without compromise. In the opinion of many critics, this has some unhappy consequences: on the one hand, the distinction between the pre-Christian or non-Christian world and the Kingdom of God cannot be clearly defined any more. Since all rights are to be derived from justification in Christ, the existence of rights based solely upon the gracious will of God to maintain his universe are denied. On the other hand, the distinction between this old world and the Kingdom of Christ is in practice levelled out.

These exegetical and dogmatic conclusions are paralleled by the interpretative method proposed by Barth, especially as developed in *Christengemeinde und Bürgergemeinde*. On the basis of a certain correspondence between the Kingdom of God and the State visible to the Christian, Barth develops, by way of analogy and quite tentatively, Biblical directions for the life of the civic community. Barth's critics point to a fundamental weakness in this method, e.g. that from the same dogmatic hypotheses quite different and in fact contradictory analogies can be drawn. Thus this pamphlet is only another illustration of the difficulties by which these studies are faced.

In view of the opposition of the Barthian theology outlined above, it becomes understandable why the problem of the relation between 'Law and Gospel' and the question of the correlation of the Kingdom of Christ to the social and political realms always play an important rôle in the ecumenical debates on these questions. For as soon as other fundamental dogmatic judgments are passed, the method of Christological analogy, for example, becomes questionable. Hence at the Conference at Bossey in 1947 the Scandinavian Lutherans held fast to the Lutheran doctrine of the two realms. According to this, a realm independent of the Law of God need not be proclaimed, but the Biblical doctrine of the two aeons must be seriously reckoned with (so especially A. Nygren). The old world does not become the new world through the proclamation of the Lordship of Christ. This is promised nowhere and cannot be seriously proposed by a Biblical scholar. The new age does indeed invade the old in the Gospel of Christ, but the old age must continue to live its life according to the will of God, until in fact it reaches its end. Applied to politics, for example, this means that politics cannot be controlled by the Gospel, but that as long as this earth continues, government must be by the sword. Every mixture of Law with Gospel can only breed fanaticism as its consequence.

Hence there arises a tension for the Christian in public life, which we cannot in this world avoid. It is necessary on the one hand to co-operate with all one's strength in the building up, maintenance and constant improvement of the organisations of the social life of man—flight from this into the sphere of 'inwardness' would only mean that this public life would be surrendered to the anarchic powers that would injure both ourselves and the whole of mankind. On the other hand, the Christian has the task of proclaiming the dawn of the Lordship of Christ—a Gospel which must be regarded by natural man not only as a support for his own strivings, but also and chiefly as the intimation of the end of the world and hence as a threat.

Out of this tension there arises the double character of the prophetic function of the Church. So long as the world is ready to listen to the proclamation of the will of God, the Church can render a very positive contribution to the present ordering of human society. But where the world attempts to evade its responsibility before God, prophetic proclamation will become the witness of suffering.

The weightiest objection against this doctrine is that it completes itself in two 'compartments', and this in practice can only have the consequence that concessions have to be made to the apparent autonomy of this world and its 'institutions'. It is not to be denied that certain Lutherans, especially in Germany, succumbed to this temptation in the past, while the new impulses, which, for example, A. Nygren set in motion, were not yet developed systematically and in detail.

In spite of all these differences, certain fundamental ideas can be affirmed to be becoming more and more the common convictions of many of those who take part in ecumenical discussion. First, the demand that the Church should not withdraw itself from its social and political responsibility. It is part of man's responsibility in the eyes of God that we must be 'our brother's keeper' in the social and political sphere. The Church must not confine itself to the cultivation of the 'inner life'.

Further it appears that Christian ethics should ultimately recognise no tie with any kind of social and political system, but only with the will of God himself. This will of God can never be static, since God is not an abstract principle, but a personal God; and what counts is that we *today* hear and accept his voice when we *today* sin against him. What can be held to be thoroughly good in the systems of yesterday must perhaps be most sharply condemned today, if a blind and reckless adherence to the past were to lead to injustice today.

It is important that we constantly seek to know this will of God. The movement back to the Bible, which is observable in all confessions and in all parts of the world, clearly shows that there is a new readiness to receive direction from Scripture. Even where we often do not appear to be unanimous about fundamental questions, there is evidence that, by listening in common to the message of the Bible, we may be able to proceed to a common interpretation and so to a common proclamation of the good news which it offers.

Part Three

PRINCIPLES OF INTERPRETATION

1

THE RELEVANCE OF THE BIBLE

by

C. Harold Dodd

The Bible did not descend from heaven all complete (like the Koran, as they say), and it was not dug up from some long-buried archaeological deposit (like the Egyptian Book of the Dead). It has indeed an archaeological aspect, for it is bound up with the life of remote epochs in the past; and in another aspect it comes to the believing reader direct from God this moment. But in plain fact the Bible is the book which you hear read in church—any church in Christendom—on any day, now or for many centuries past. We receive it from the Church: there is no other source from which we can receive precisely *these* writings in *this* setting, which make up the canon of Scripture. It is also the book which contains the history out of which the Church emerged. The Scriptures are concerned with the continuing life of an historical community—the people of God. This community remains self-identical through many changing historical forms—Hebrew clan, Israelite kingdom, Jewish dispersion, Catholic Church. Every part of that long history—down to the present day—is relevant to the acceptance and understanding of the Bible as the Word of God. Bible and Church are correlatives. The attempt (since the Reformation) to set the authority of the Bible over against that of the Church, and the authority of the Church over against the authority of the Bible, results only in obscuring the nature of this authority, which resides in both together.

The Church offers the Bible as ἅγιαι χράφαι τῆς παλαίας, τῆς καινῆς διαθήκης the sacred documents of the Old and New Covenants respectively. The basic idea is that of a covenant between God and man. *Diatheke*, it is true, is not *syntheke*, a contract on equal terms between two parties. The initiative lies wholly with God, who alone fixes the terms of the Covenant and offers them for man's acceptance. But the acceptance is of the essence of the matter, nevertheless. In all statements of the *diatheke*, in both parts of the Canon, there are two aspects: first, the action of God on behalf of man; then the demand for responsive action from men. Thus, the Decalogue begins: 'I am the Lord thy God, which brought thee out of the land of Egypt' and goes on: 'Thou shalt. . . . Thou shalt not. . . .' In later Jewish exposition of the Torah the two aspects are in some sort represented by the distinction between *haggada* and *halacha*. In the New Testament they correspond with the distinction between *kerygma* and *didache*. The divine action is always the basis of the Covenant; and this action, again, has two aspects: the negative, which is judgment, and the positive, which is mercy or forgiveness.

The pattern of the Covenant is most fully drawn out in the prophetic interpretation of events from 760-530 B.C. (or thereabouts): God's judgment is manifested in the disasters inflicted by his 'rod'—Assyria and Babylon—upon an unfaithful people: his mercy is manifested in the salvation of a remnant and the restoration of the Jewish community; and the prophetic interpretation of the whole process culminates in a call to repentance and obedience to God, which leads to the reformulation of the *Torah* in the post-exilic community. The same pattern is made visible, through prophetic interpretation, in the Covenant at Sinai and the call of Abraham. In the whole of the Old Testament picture, however, there is a sense of incompleteness and inconclusiveness, pointing forward to a 'new Covenant'. Finally, in the New Testament the pattern is 'fulfilled', i.e. completely embodied in historical action, which results in the emergence of the Christian Church as the New Israel, the final, 'eschatological' people of God. 'Fulfilment' of the old Covenant in the new is on one side its abrogation, and on the other side its total reaffirmation upon a new level.

As the call of Abraham and the Exodus are understood for what they really are only in the light of the (later) prophetic crisis of Israel, so the entire history of the old Covenant discloses its full meaning only in the light of the new Covenant. The twofold rhythm of judgment and mercy in God's approach to man in history received its final embodiment in the death and resurrection of Christ, and his call to men is God's final demand upon them.

Such is the pattern of the history in which God's Covenant with men is established. It has two elements: (*a*) a direction of events, and (*b*) an interpretation of these events. These two elements interact. The message of the prophets arises out of the course of events which they experienced, and interprets these events; and because they interpreted them just *so* and not otherwise, the history of God's people after the Exile took *that* form and no other; and so all through. The decisive significance of this interaction is accounted for upon the Biblical postulate that God is *both* the Lord of history *and* the Interpreter of his own action to the mind of man. ('The Lord will do nothing, but he revealeth his secret unto his servants the prophets', Amos, 3.7) One might put it in the form that the God of creation is also the God of revelation—but for the fact that creation is itself a revelation, and that God's revelation of himself to men is creative of history.

This total structure of event and interpretation in continual interaction is God's Word to man. Since God is the living God, his word is action, 'quick and powerful', and action in history, so that movement in time is of the essence of the matter. At the crucial point of history (τὸ πλήρωμα τοῦ χρόνου) the Word attained complete and final embodiment in history (ὁ λόγος σὰρξ ἐγένετο).

The outcome of the whole process—more properly of its 'fulfilment' in Christ—is the existence of the Church, which is also the standing witness to the reality of God's Word. In the life of the Church the pattern reappears. The Church continually stands under the judgment of God, *and* praises him for his great salvation. In the Eucharist (which is specifically the sacrament of the new Covenant), the Church places itself within the *Heilsgeschichte*. It remembers the events of Christ's coming, his Cross and Resurrection, and remembers also, by implication (explicitly in some ancient liturgies) the entire course of the divinely guided history of God's people which was there fulfilled. It thus exposes itself to the word of judgment and mercy which that history embodies. At the same time it acknowledges the immediate, 'contemporary' presence and action of God in the coming of Christ to his people ('*Benedictus qui venit in nomine Domini*'). This 'coming' is at the same time his remembered coming in humiliation, and his expected coming with angels and archangels and all the company of heaven. Thus history re-enacts itself, and its meaning is reaffirmed and countersigned by the faith of the Church.

It is in the *koinonia* of the Church, this meeting-point of eternal meaning with historical actuality, that the *testimonium spiritus sancti internum* must primarily be sought. τὸ πνεῦμα ὅπου θέλει πνεῖ, it is true (John 3.8), and God's witness to himself cannot be put under any restriction. But the same evangelist who records that word also records this other: οὔπω ἦν πνεῦμα, ὅτι Ἰησοῦς οὐδέπω ἐδοξάσθη (John 7.39). That is, the witness of the Spirit may be most confidently and fully acknowledged within the *koinonia* where Christ, crucified and risen, is glorified before his people. The Spirit is, primarily, God's gift *to his Church*, by which the 'things of Christ' are made known to us.

Here, then, in this indissoluble unity of Bible and Church, we seek the seat of authority. From this point of view, we see that the relation of the New Testament to the whole is unique and sovereign. The New Testament alone exhibits the effective meaning of the Old Testament, and it is the arbiter of the living tradition of the Church. The Old Testament looks forward, the history of the Church looks backward, to the Cross and Resurrection, which constitute the *centre* of history. If in the Old Testament we have foreshadowings of the Gospel, so in the successive historical experiences of the Church we have 'after-shadowings' of the same.

It is within this structure of divine revelation—*Heilsgeschichte* re-constituted in the *koinonia* of the Church—that the warnings, precepts and promises of Scripture take effect. Outside this *koinonia* they are in danger of being misinterpreted and misapplied. This does not mean that the tradition of the Church imposes an arbitrary meaning upon the words of prophets and apostles. They are our 'fellow-citizens' in the people of God, and we allow them the παρρησία which belongs to the free citizen, and listen with a decent humility while they speak for themselves. Each spoke to a particular situation, and their words come to life within that situation—but that situation, whether in the eighth century B.C. or the first century A.D., is *contemporary* with us in the *koinonia* of God's people (in the same sense in which we are in the Eucharist contemporaries both of the Cross and of the *parousia* of Christ), and the prophetic and apostolic word receives fresh illumination within that *koinonia*.

* * *

So far we have been occupied with the *particularity* of the divine revelation, particularity inseparable from the nature of history. *Heilsgeschichte* is the history of God's *chosen* people, from the call of Abraham onwards to the constitution of the Church at Pentecost and the gathering-in of the Gentiles. But the Bible places this history of the people of God in a setting which is deliberately made universal and human in the widest sense. The call of Abraham, which is the initiation of God's Covenant with his people, has behind it the symbolic myth of the Covenant with Noah, the ancestor of all existing races of men, a Covenant established 'with you and with your seed after you, and with every living creature', a Covenant 'between me and the earth'. Similarly the close of the *Heilsgeschichte* melts into the symbolic myth of Doomsday, when all nations are gathered before the Judge of quick and dead.

The Noachian Covenant is in Jewish tradition the Covenant by virtue of which the fundamental commandments of God are binding upon all men. Thus, all men are ἐνδιαθήκοι. That is why Jesus can ask, Τί ἀφ' ἑαυτῶν οὐ κρίνετε τὸ δίκαιον; (Luke 12.57). It is this Covenant that justifies Paul in speaking of a law which the Gentiles possess written upon their hearts and attested by their conscience. Accordingly, in the judgment scene of Matt. 25.32, πάντα τὰ ἔθνη are arraigned under a law which is in fact a law of simple humanity, though it is also (though they do not know it) the Law of Christ. There are not two laws, but one. The Word by which the world was made, which is in the world though the world knows it not, which came to God's own people in history, is also the Word that is made flesh. It is from this standpoint that we apprehend the 'Law of Nature' and it is by the Church that this law is interpreted in its universal obligation.

Thus the Church, God's people chosen out of mankind, appears as the ἀπαρχῆ of a race which as a whole is under a universal Covenant with God, and is destined to be 'summed up in Christ'. The historical beginnings of the Church in the past are known; its specific modes of action in the present are clearly defined—the preaching of the Gospel and the celebration of the Sacraments—and these are the basis of its *koinonia*. But the frontiers of the *koinonia* cannot be traced short of the boundaries of the human race. The Church is trustee, under the Covenant of Sinai and of the Cross, of the benefits of that Covenant on behalf of all mankind.

Hence the Bible is relevant to *all* history, though the relevance may be concealed from the eyes of men. The faith and witness of the Church not only re-constitute the *Heilsgeschichte* within its own *koinonia*, they also reveal in the contemporary historical situation the perpetual pattern of God's dealing with men in his Word of judgment and of renewal, which is an approach to men demanding a response of obedience. By the impact of his Word the elements of the existing 'secular' situation are transformed. It is thus the task of the Church, not only to reconstitute the *Heilsgeschichte* within its own *koinonia*, but also to mould the existing historical situation in the world in terms of the Word of God. In doing so, it secures the relevance of the Law of Christ to the history of our own time. The attempt to dictate the Christian ethic directly to a non-Christian world has little prospect of success. That world must first know itself to stand under God's providence of judgment and mercy, to be within the Covenant established with 'all flesh', and consequently to be under obligation to the Law of God, who is Creator and Redeemer of all mankind.

2

REVELATION AND INTERPRETATION

by

GEORGES FLOROVSKY

For what if some did not believe? Shall
their unbelief make the faith of God
without effect?—Rom. 3.3.

I *Message and witness*

What is the Bible? Is it a book like any other intended for any occasional reader, who is expected to grasp at once its proper meaning? Rather, it is a *sacred* book addressed primarily to believers. Of course, a sacred book can be read by anyone as well, just 'as literature'. But this is rather irrelevant to our immediate purpose. We are concerned now not with the letter but with the message. St. Hilary put it emphatically: *Scriptura est non in legendo, sed in intelligendo*. Is there any definite message in the Bible, taken as a whole, as one book? And again, to whom is this message, if any, properly addressed? To individuals, who would be, as such, entitled to understand the book and to expound its message? Or to the community, and to individuals only in so far as they are members of that community?

Whatever the origin of particular documents included in the book may have been, it is obvious that the book, as a whole, was a creation of the community, both in the old dispensation and in the Christian Church. The Bible is by no means a complete *collection* of all historical, legislative and devotional writings available, but a *selection* of some, authorised and authenticated by the use (first of all liturgical) in the community, and finally by the formal authority of the Church. And there was some very definite purpose by which this 'selection' was guided and checked. 'And many other signs truly did Jesus in the presence of his disciples, which are not written in this book. But these are written, that ye might believe that Jesus is the Christ, the Son of God; and that believing ye might have life through his name' (John 20.30-31). The same applies, more or less, to the whole Bible. Certain writings have been selected, edited and compiled, and brought together, and then commended to believers, to the people, as an authorised version of the divine message. The message is divine; it comes from God; it is the Word of God. But it is the faithful community that acknowledges the Word spoken and testifies to its truth. The sacred character of the Bible is ascertained by faith. The Bible, as a book, has been composed in the community and was meant primarily for its edification. The book and the Church cannot be separated. The book and the Covenant belong together, and Covenant implies people. It was the People of the Covenant to whom the Word of God had been entrusted under the old dispensation (Rom. 3.2), and it is the Church of the Word Incarnate that keeps the message of the Kingdom. The Bible is the Word of God indeed, but the book stands by the testimony of the Church. The canon of the Bible is obviously established and authorised by the Church.

One has, however, not to overlook the missionary background of the New Testament. 'The Apostolic Preaching', therein embodied and recorded, had a double purpose: the edification of the faithful and the conversion of the world. Therefore the New Testament is not a community-book in the same exclusive sense as the Old Testament surely was. It is still a *missionary* book. Yet it is no less fenced-off from the outsiders. Tertullian's attitude to the Scriptures was typical. He was not prepared to discuss the controversial topics of the faith with heretics on the Scriptural ground. Scriptures belonged to the Church. Heretics' appeal to them was unlawful. They had no right on foreign property. Such was his main argument in the famous treatise: *De praescriptione haereticorum*. An unbeliever has no access to the message, simply because he does not 'receive' it. For him there is no 'message' in the Bible.

It was no accident that a diverse anthology of writings, composed at various dates and by various writers, came to be regarded as a single book. *Ta biblia* is of course plural but *the Bible* is emphatically singular. The scriptures are indeed one Holy Scripture, one Holy Writ. There is one main theme and one main message through the whole story. For there is a story. Or, even more, the Bible itself is this story, the story of God's dealings with his chosen people. The Bible records first of all God's acts and mighty deeds, *Magnalia Dei*. The process has been initiated by God. There is a beginning and an end, which is also a goal. There is a starting point: the original divine *fiat*—'in the beginning' (Gen. 1.1). And there will be an end: 'even so come' (Rev. 22.20). There is one composite and yet single story—from Genesis to Revelation. And this story is history. There is a process going on between these two terminal points. And this process has a definite direction. There is an ultimate goal, an ultimate consummation is expected. Every particular moment is correlated to both terms and has thereby its proper and unique place within the whole. No moment therefore can be understood except in the whole context and perspective.

God has spoken 'at sundry times and in divers manners' (Heb. 1.1). He was revealing himself through ages, not once, but constantly, again and again. He was leading his people from truth to truth. There were stages in his revelation: *per incrementa*. This diversity and variety should not be ignored or overlooked. Yet it was ever the same God, and his ultimate message was ever the same. It is the identity of this message that gives to the various writings their real unity, despite the variety of manners. Different versions were taken into the book as they stood. The Church has resisted all attempts to substitute a single synthetic Gospel for four differing Gospels, to transform the *Tetra-evangelion* into a *Dia-tessaron*, in spite of the difficulties implied in the 'contradictions of the Evangelists' (with which St. Augustine was wrestling). These four Gospels did secure the unity of the message well enough, and perhaps in a more concrete form than any other compilation could afford.

The Bible is a book about God. But the God of the Bible is not *Deus absconditus*, but *Deus revelatus*. God is manifesting and revealing himself. God intervenes in human life. And the Bible is not merely a human record of these divine interventions and deeds. It is a kind of divine intervention itself. It carries with itself a divine message. God's deeds constitute themselves a message. No need therefore to escape time or history in order to meet God. For God is meeting man in history, i.e. in the human element, in the midst of man's daily existence. History belongs to God, and God enters human history. The Bible is intrinsically historical: it is a record of the divine acts, not so much a presentation of God's eternal mysteries, and these mysteries themselves are available only by a historical mediation. 'No man hath seen God at any time; the only begotten Son, which is in the bosom of the Father, he hath declared him' (John 1.18). And he declared him by entering history, in his holy incarnation. Thus the historical frame of the revelation is not something that ought to be done away with. There is no need to abstract revealed truth from the frame in which revelations took place. On the contrary, such an abstraction would have abolished the truth as well. For the Truth is not an idea, but a person, even the Incarnate Lord.

In the Bible we are struck by the intimate relation of God to man and of man to God. It is an intimacy of the Covenant, an intimacy of election and adoption. And this intimacy culminates in the incarnation. 'God sent forth his Son, born of a woman, born under the law' (Gal. 4.4). In the Bible we see not only God, but man too. It is the revelation of God, but what is actually revealed is God's concern about man. God reveals himself to man, 'appears' before him, 'speaks' and converses with him so as to reveal to man the hidden meaning of his own existence and the ultimate purpose of his life. In Scripture we see God coming to reveal himself to man, and we see man meeting God, and not only listening to his voice, but answering him too. We hear in the Bible not only the voice of God, but also the voice of man answering him—in words of prayer, thanksgiving and adoration, awe and love, sorrow and contrition, exultation, hope or despair. There are, as it were, two partners in the Covenant, God and man, and both belong together, in the mystery of the true divine-human encounter, which is described and recorded in the story of the Covenant. Human response is integrated into the mystery of the Word of God. It is not a divine monologue, it is rather a dialogue, and both are speaking, God and man. But prayers and invocations of the worshipping psalmist are nevertheless 'the Word of God'. God wants, and expects, and demands this answer and response of man. It is for this that he reveals himself to man and speaks to him. He is, as it were, waiting for man to converse with him. He establishes his Covenant with the sons of men. Yet, all this intimacy does not compromise the divine sovereignty and transcendence. God is 'dwelling in light unapproachable' (I Tim. 6.16). This light, however, 'lighteth every man that cometh into the world' (John 1.9). This constitutes the mystery, or the 'paradox' of the revelation.

Revelation is the history of the Covenant. Recorded revelation, i.e. the Holy Scripture, is therefore, above all, history. Law and prophets, psalms and prophecies, all are included and, as it were, woven into the living historical web. Revelation is not a system of divine oracles only. It is primarily the system of divine deeds; one might say, revelation was the path of God in history. And the climax was reached when God entered history himself, and for ever: when the Word of God was incarnate and 'made man'. On the other hand, the book of revelation is as well the book of human destiny. First of all, it is a book which narrates the creation, fall and salvation of man. It is the story of salvation, and therefore man organically belongs to the story. It shows us man in his obedience and in his obstinate rebellion, in his fall and in his restoration. And the whole human fate is condensed and exemplified in the destiny of Israel, old and new, the chosen people of God, a people for God's own possession. The fact of election is here of basic importance. One people has been elected, set apart from all other nations, constituted as a sacred oasis in the midst of human disorder. With one people on earth only did God establish his Covenant and grant his own sacred law. Here only a true priesthood has been created, even though but a provisional one. In this nation only true prophets were raised, who spoke words inspired by the Spirit of God. It was a sacred, though hidden centre for the whole world, an oasis granted by God's mercy, in the midst of a fallen, sinful, lost and unredeemed world. All this is not the letter, but the very heart of the Biblical message. And all this came from God, there was no human merit or achievement. Yet, all this came for the sake of man, 'for us men and for our salvation'. All these privileges granted to the Israel of old were subordinate to the ultimate purpose, that of a universal salvation: 'For salvation is of the Jews' (John 4.22). The redeeming purpose is ever universal indeed, but it is being accomplished always by means of separation, selection or setting apart. In the midst of human fall and ruin a sacred oasis is erected by God. The Church is also an oasis still, set apart, though not taken out of the world. For again this oasis is not a refuge or shelter only, but rather a citadel, a vanguard of God.

There is a centre in the Biblical story, or a crucial point on the line of the temporal events. There is a new beginning within the process, which does not, however, divide or cut it into parts, but rather gives to it an ultimate cohesion and unity. The distinction between the two Testaments belongs itself to the unity of the Biblical revelation. The two Testaments are to be carefully distinguished, never to be confused. Yet they are organically linked together, not as two systems only, but primarily in the person of the Christ. Jesus the Christ belongs to both. He is the fulfiller of the old dispensation and by the same act that he accomplishes the old, 'the Law and the prophets', he inaugurates the new, and thereby becomes the ultimate fulfiller of both, i.e. of the whole. He is the very centre of the Bible, just because he is the *archē* and the *telos*—the beginning and the end. And unexpectedly this mysterious identity of the start, the centre and the goal, instead of destroying the existential reality of time, gives to the time-process its genuine reality and full meaning. There are no mere happenings which pass by, but rather events and achievements, and the new things are coming to existence, that which never existed before. 'Behold I make all things new' (Rev. 21.5).

Ultimately, the Old Testament as a whole has to be considered as 'a book of the generation of Jesus Christ, the Son of David, the Son of Abraham' (Matt. 1.1). It was the period of promises and expectation, the time of covenants and prophecies. It was not only the prophets that prophesied. Events also were prophecies. The whole story was prophetical or 'typical', a prophetical sign hinting forward towards approaching consummation. Now, the time of expectation is over. The promise had been accomplished. The Lord has come. And he came to abide among his people for ever. The history of flesh and blood is closed. The history of the Spirit is disclosed: 'Grace and truth came by Jesus Christ' (John 1.17). But it was an accomplishment, not destruction of the old. *Vetus Testamentum in Novo patet*. And *patet* means precisely: is revealed, disclosed, fulfilled. Therefore, the books of the Hebrews are still sacred, even for the new Israel of Christ—not to be left out or ignored. They tell us still the story of salvation, *Magnalia*

Dei. They do still bear witness to Christ. They are to be read in the Church as a book of sacred history, not to be transformed into a collection of proof-texts or of theological instances (*loci theologici*), nor into a book of parables. Prophecy has been accomplished and law has been superseded by grace. But nothing has passed away. In sacred history, 'the past' does not mean simply 'passed' or 'what had been', but primarily that which had been accomplished and fulfilled. 'Fulfilment' is the basic category of revelation. That which has become sacred remains consecrated and holy for ever. It has the seal of the Spirit. And the Spirit breathes still in the words once inspired by him. It is true, perhaps, that in the Church and for us now the Old Testament is no more than a book, simply because the Law and the Prophets were superseded by the Gospel. The New Testament is obviously more than a book. We do belong to the New Testament ourselves. We are the People of the New Covenant. For that reason it is precisely in the Old Testament that we apprehend revelation primarily as the Word: we witness to the Spirit 'that spake through the prophets'. For in the New Testament God has spoken by his Son, and we are called upon not only to listen, but to look at. 'That which we have seen and heard declare we unto you' (I John 1.3). And, furthermore, we are called upon to *be* 'in Christ'.

The fullness of revelation is Christ Jesus. And the New Testament is history no less than the Old: the Gospel history of the Incarnate Word and the beginnings of church history, and the apocalyptic prophecy too. The Gospel is history. *Historic events* are the source and the basis of all Christian faith and hope. The basis of the New Testament is facts, events, deeds—not only teaching, commandments or words. From the very beginning, from the very day of Pentecost, when St. Peter as an eye-witness (Acts 2.32: 'whereof we are all witnesses', *martyres*) witnessed to the fulfilment of salvation in the Risen Lord, apostolic preaching had emphatically an historical character. By this historical witness the Church stands. Creeds have an historical structure too, they refer to the events. Again, it is a sacred history. The mystery of Christ is precisely in that 'in him dwelleth all the fulness of the Godhead bodily' (Col. 2.9). This mystery cannot be comprehended within the earthly plane alone, there is another dimension too. But historical boundaries are not obliterated, not dimmed: in the sacred image historical features are clearly seen. Apostolic preaching was always a narrative, a narrative of what had really happened, *hic et nunc*. But what happened was ultimate and new: 'The Word was made flesh' (John 1.14). Of course, the Incarnation, the Resurrection, the Ascension are historical facts not quite in the same sense or on the same level as the happenings of our own daily life. But they are no less historical for that, no less factual. On the contrary, they are more historical—they are ultimately eventful. They cannot obviously be fully ascertained except by faith. Yet this does not take them out of the historical context. Faith only discovers a new dimension, apprehends the historical *datum* in its full depth, in its full and ultimate reality. The Evangelists and the Apostles were no chroniclers. It was not their mission to keep the full record of all that Jesus had done, day by day, year by year. They describe his life and relate his works, so as to give us his image: an historic, and yet a divine image. It is no portrait, but rather an ikon—but surely an historic ikon, an image of the Incarnate Lord. Faith does not create a new value; it only discovers the inherent one. Faith itself is a sort of vision, 'the evidence of things not seen' (Heb. 11.1: St. John Chrysostom explains *elenchos* precisely as *opsis*). The 'invisible' is no less real than 'visible'—rather more real. 'And yet no man can say that Jesus is the Lord, but by the Holy Ghost' (I Cor. 12.3). It means that the Gospel itself can be apprehended in all its fulness and depth only in spiritual experience. But what is discovered by faith is given in very truth. The Gospels are written within the church. In this sense they are the witness of the Church. They are records of church experience and faith. But they are no less historical narratives and bear witness to what had really taken place, in space and in time. If 'by faith' we discover much more than what can be detected 'by senses', this only discloses the utter inadequacy of 'senses' in the knowledge of spiritual matters. For what had really happened was the mighty deed of the Redeeming God, his ultimate intervention in the stream of historical events. One should not divorce the 'fact' and the 'meaning'—both are given in reality.

Revelation is preserved in the Church. Therefore, the Church is the proper and primary interpreter of revelation. It is protected and reinforced by written words; protected, but not exhausted. Human words are no more than signs. The testimony of the Spirit revives the written words. We do not mean now the occasional illumination of individuals by the Holy Ghost, but primarily the permanent assistance of the Spirit given to the Church, that is 'the pillar and bulwark of the truth' (I Tim. 3.15). The Scriptures need interpretation. Not the phrasing, but the message is the core. And the Church is the divinely appointed and permanent witness to the very truth and the full meaning of this message, simply because the Church belongs itself to the revelation, as the Body of the Incarnate Lord. The proclamation of the Gospel, the preaching of the Word of God, obviously belongs to the *esse* of the Church. The Church stands by its testimony and witness. But this witness is not just a reference to the past, not merely a reminiscence, but rather a continuous rediscovery of the message once delivered to the saints and ever since kept by faith. Moreover, this message is ever re-enacted in the life of the Church. Christ himself is ever present in the Church, as the Redeemer and head of his Body, and continues his redeeming office in the Church. Salvation is not only announced or proclaimed in the Church, but precisely enacted. The sacred history is still continued. The mighty deeds of God are still being performed. *Magnalia Dei* are not circumscribed by the past; they are ever present and continued, in the Church and, through the Church, in the world. The Church is itself an integral part of the New Testament message. The Church itself is a part of revelation—the story of 'the Whole Christ' (*totus Christus: caput et corpus*, in the phrase of St. Augustine) and of the Holy Ghost. The ultimate end of revelation, its *telos*, has not yet come. And only within the experience of the Church is the New Testament truly and fully alive. Church history is itself a story of redemption. The truth of the book is revealed and vindicated by the growth of the Body.

II *History and system*

We must admit at once that the Bible is a difficult book, a book sealed with seven seals. And, as time runs on, it grows no easier. The main reason for that, however, is not that the Book is written in an 'unknown tongue' or contains some 'secret words that man may not repeat'. On the contrary, the very stumbling-block of the Bible is its utter simplicity: the mysteries of God are framed into the daily life of average men, and the whole story may seem to be all too human. Just as the Incarnate Lord himself appeared to be an ordinary man.

The Scriptures are 'inspired', they are the Word of God. What is the inspiration can never be properly defined—there is a mystery therein. It is a mystery of the divine-human encounter. We cannot fully understand in what manner 'God's holy men' heard the Word of their Lord and how they could articulate it in the words of their own dialect. Yet, even in their human transmission it was the voice of God. Therein lies the miracle and the mystery of the Bible, that it is the Word of God in human idiom. And, in whatever the manner we understand the inspiration, one factor must not be overlooked. The Scriptures transmit and preserve the Word of God precisely in the idiom of man. God spoke to man indeed, but there was man to attend and to perceive. 'Anthropomorphism' is thus inherent in the very fact. There is no accommodation to human frailty. The point is rather that the human tongue does not lose its natural features to become a vehicle of divine revelation. If we want the divine word to ring clear, our tongue is not to leave off being human. What is human is not swept away by divine inspiration, it is only *transfigured*. The 'supernatural' does not destroy what is 'natural': *hyper physin* does not mean *para physin*. The human idiom does not betray or belittle the splendour of revelation, it does not bind the power of God's Word. The Word of God may be adequately and rightly expressed in human words. The Word of God does not grow dim when it sounds in the tongue of man. For man is created in the image and likeness of God—this 'analogical' link makes communication possible. And since God deigned to speak to man, the human word itself acquires new depth and strength and becomes transfigured. The divine Spirit breathes in the organism of human speech. Thus it becomes possible for man to utter words of God, to speak of God. 'Theology' becomes possible—*theologia*, i.e. *logos peri theou*. Strictly speaking, theology grows possible only through revelation. It is the human response to God, who has spoken first. It is man's witness to God who has spoken to him, whose word he has heard, whose words he has kept and is now recording and repeating. Surely this response is never complete. Theology is ever in the process of formation. The basis and the starting point are ever the same: the Word of God, the revelation. Theology witnesses back to the revelation. It witnesses in divers manners: in creeds, in dogmas, in sacred rites and symbols. But in a sense Scripture itself is the primary response, or rather Scripture itself is at once both the Word of God and the human response—the Word of God mediated through the faithful response of man. There is always some human interpretation in any Scriptural presentation of the divine Word. So far it is always inescapably 'situation-conditioned'. Is it ever possible for man to escape his human situation?

The Church has summarised the Scriptural message in creeds, and in many other ways and methods. Christian faith has developed or grown into a system of beliefs and convictions. In any such system the inner structure of the basic message is shown forth, all particular articles of faith are presented in their mutual interdependence. Obviously, we need a system, as we need a map in our travels. But maps refer to a real land. And any doctrinal system too must be related to the revelation. It is of utter importance that the Church has never thought of her dogmatic system as a kind of substitute for the Scriptures. Both are to be kept side by side: a somewhat abstract or generalised presentation of the main message in a creed or in a system, and all particular documents referring to the concrete instances of revelation. One might say a *system* and the *history* itself.

Here a problem arises: how, and to what extent, can history be framed into a system? This is the main problem of theological hermeneutics. What is the *theological* use of the Bible? How should the divers and concrete witnesses, covering hundreds of years, be used for the construction of a single scheme? The Bible is one indeed, and yet it is, in fact, a collection of various writings. We are not entitled to ignore that. The solution depends ultimately upon our conception of history, upon our vision of time. The easiest solution would have been indeed if we could simply overlook or overcome the diversity of times, the duration of the process itself. Such a temptation faced Christianity from an early date. It was at the root of all allegorical interpretations, from Philo and Pseudo-Barnabas to the new revival of allegorism in post-Reformation times. It was a permanent temptation of all mystics. The Bible is regarded as a book of sacred parables, written in a peculiar symbolical language, and the task of exegesis is to detect their hidden meaning, to detect the eternal Word, which happens to have been uttered in divers manners and under divers veils. The historical truth and perspective are irrelevant in this case. Historical concreteness is no more than a pictorial frame, a poetical imagery. One is in search of *eternal* meanings. The whole Bible would be then reconstrued into a book of edifying examples, of glorious symbols, which point out the super-temporal truth. Is not the truth of God ever the same, identical and eternal? In that mood, it is but natural to look in the Old Testament for the evidences of all distinctive Christian beliefs and convictions. Two Testaments are as it were melted into one, super-temporal, and their distinctive marks obliterated. The dangers and shortcomings of such a hermeneutical approach are too obvious to need an extensive refutation. But the only real remedy against this temptation would be the restoration of historical insight. The Bible is *history*, not a system of belief, and should not be used as a *summa theologiae*. At the same time, it is not history of human belief, but the history of the divine revelation. The basic problem remains, however, still unsolved: for what purpose do we need both system and history? By what reason and for what purpose did the Church keep them always together? Again, the easiest answer to this question is the least satisfactory: one may suggest at once that the Scriptures are the only authentic record of the revelation, and everything else is no more than a commentary thereupon. And commentary can never have the same authority as the original record. There is some truth in this suggestion, but the true difficulty we have to face is elsewhere. Why are not the earlier stages of the revelation superseded by the later ones? Why do we still need the law and the prophets even in the new covenant of Christ, and, to a certain extent, on the same level of authority as the Gospels and the rest of the New Testament writings? I mean, as chapters of the same unique book, as it were. For, obviously, they are included in the canon of Scripture, not as historical documents only, not as chapters on the stages of history already passed away. This applies particularly to the Old Testament. 'For all the prophets and the law prophesied until John' (Matt. 11.13). Why do we still keep both the law and the prophets, and in what sense? What can be the right use of the Old Testament in the Church of Christ?

First of all, it needs to be an historical use. Yet, again this history is a sacred history—not a history of human convictions and their evolution, but a history of the mighty deeds of God. And these deeds are not disconnected irruptions of God into human life. There was an intimate unity and cohesion. They led and guided the chosen people into God's supreme purpose, unto Christ. Therefore, in a sense, the earlier ones were reflected, as it were, or implied in the later ones. There was a continuity of the divine action, as there was an identity of the goal and purpose as well. This continuity is the basis of what was called the 'typological' interpretation. Patristic terminology was at that point rather fluent. Still, there was always a clear distinction between two methods and approaches. 'Allegory' was an exegetical method indeed. An allegorist dealt primarily with the texts; he searched out the hidden and ultimate meaning of Scriptural passages, sentences and even particular words, behind and beneath 'the letter'. On the contrary, 'typology' was not an exegesis of the texts themselves, but rather an interpretation of the events. It was an historical, and not merely a philological method. It was the inner correspondence of the events themselves in the two Testaments that had to be detected, established and brought forward. A typologist looked not for the 'parallels' or similarities. And not every event of the Old Testament has its 'correspondence' in the New. Yet there are certain basic events in the old dispensation which were the 'figures' or 'types' of the basic events in the new. Their 'correspondence' was of divine appointment: they were, as it were, stages of a single process of the redemptive Providence. In this manner 'typology' was practised already by St. Paul (if under the name of an 'allegory': Gal. 4.24: *Hatina estin allegoroumena*). There is an identical purpose of God behind all his mighty interventions, and in full it has been revealed in Christ. St. Augustine put it very clearly: '*in ipso facto, non solum in dicto, mysterium requirere debemus*' (*in ps.* 68, *sermo*, 2, 6). And 'the mystery' of the Old Testament was Christ; not only in the sense that Moses or the prophets 'spoke' of him, but primarily because the whole stream of sacred history was divinely oriented towards him. And in this sense he was the fulfilment of all prophecies. For that reason, it is only in the light of Christ that the Old Testament can be properly understood and its 'mysteries' unveiled—they were, in fact, unveiled by the coming of him 'who should come'. The true prophetic meaning of the prophecies is clearly seen only, as it were, in retrospect, after they have been actually fulfilled. An unaccomplished prophecy is always dim and enigmatic (so are the prophecies of the Book of Revelation, which point to what is still to come, 'at the end'). But it does not mean that we simply put arbitrarily a new meaning into the old text: the meaning was there, though it could not yet be seen clearly. When, for instance, we, in the Church, identify the Suffering Servant (in the Book of Isaiah) as Christ the crucified, we do not simply 'apply' an Old Testament vision to a New Testament event: we detect the meaning of the vision itself, although this meaning surely could not have been clearly identified in the times preceding Christ. But what had been first just a vision (i.e. an 'anticipation') has become an historical fact.

Another point is of utter importance. For an 'allegorist' the 'images' he interprets are reflections of a pre-existing prototype, or even images of some eternal or abstract 'truth'. They are pointing to something that is outside of time. On the contrary, typology is oriented towards the future. The 'types' are anticipations, *pre*-figurations; their 'prototype' is still to come. Typology is thus an historical method, more than a philological one. It presupposes and implies intrinsically the reality of history, directed and guided by God. It is organically connected with the idea of the covenant. Here the past, the present and the future are linked in a unity of divine purpose, and the purpose was Christ. Therefore typology has emphatically a Christological meaning (the Church is included here, as the Body and the Bride of Christ). In practice, of course, a true balance was never strictly kept. Even in patristic use typology was variously contaminated by allegorical deviations or accretions, especially in the devotional and homiletic use. What is, however, of importance is that in the catechetical tradition of the Early Church, closely related to the administration of the sacraments, this balance was always kept. This was the tradition of the Church, and deviations were due more to the curiosity or imagination of individual scholars. The Church was, in full sobriety, historically minded. Along with a presentation of the doctrine (i.e. a system) the Holy Bible was always read in the churches, with the deliberate purpose of reminding the faithful of the historical basis and background of their faith and hope.

St. Augustine suggested that the prophets spoke of the Church even more clearly than of Christ himself, i.e. of the Messiah (*in ps.* 30.2, *enarratio*, 2, M.L., 36, 244). In a sense, this was only natural. For there was already a Church. Israel, the chosen people, the people of the covenant, was much more a Church than a nation, like other 'nations'. *Ta ethne*, *nationes* or *gentes*—these kindred terms were used in the Bible (and later) precisely to describe the heathen or pagans in contrast to the only nation or people that was also (and primarily) a Church of God. The Law was given to Israel just in her capacity as a Church. It embraced the whole life of the people, the 'temporal' as well as the 'spiritual', precisely because the whole of human existence had to be regulated by the divine precepts. And the division of life into 'temporal' and 'spiritual' departments is, strictly speaking, precarious. In any case, Israel was a divinely constituted community of believers, united by the Law of God, the true faith, sacred rites and hierarchy—we find here all elements of the traditional definition of the Church. The old dispensation has been accomplished in the new, the covenant has been reconstituted, and the old Israel was rejected, because of her utter unbelief: she missed the day of her visitation. The only true continuation of the old covenant was in the Church of Christ (let us remember that both terms are of Hebrew origin: the Church is *qahal* and Christ means *Messiah*). She is the true Israel, *kata pneuma*. In this sense already St. Justin emphatically rejected the idea that the Old Testament was a link holding together the Church and the Synagogue. For him the opposite was true. All Jewish claims were to be formally rejected: the Old Testament no longer belonged to the Jews, as they had not believed in Christ Jesus. The Old Testament belonged now to the Church alone. Nobody could any longer claim Moses and the prophets, if he was not with Jesus the Christ. For the Church was the New Israel and the only heir of the promises of old. A new and important hermeneutical principle was implied in these rigoristic utterances of the early Christian apologist. The Old Testament was to be read and interpreted as a book of the Church. The book *on* the Church, we should add.

The Law was superseded by the truth, and in it has found its accomplishment, and thereby was abrogated. It no longer had to be imposed upon the new converts. The New Israel had its own constitution. This part of the Old Testament was antiquated. It proved to be basically 'situation-conditioned'—not so much in the sense of a general historical relativity as in a deeper providential sense. The new redemptive situation had been created or inaugurated by the Lord: a new situation in the sacred perspective of salvation. Everything that belonged essentially to the previous stage or phase had now lost its meaning, or rather kept its meaning as a prefiguration only. Even the Decalogue perhaps was not exempt from this rule and was overruled by the 'new commandment'. The Old Testament is now to be used solely in its relation to the Church. Under the old dispensation the Church was limited to one nation. In the new all national discriminations are emphatically abrogated: there is no more distinction between a Jew and a Greek—all are indiscriminately in the same Christ. In other words, one has no right to isolate certain elements of the old dispensation, apart from their immediate relation to the life of the Church, and set them as a Scriptural pattern for the temporal life of the nations. The old Israel was a provisional Church, but she was not a pattern nation. One may put it this way. Obviously, we can learn a lot from the Bible on social justice—this was a part of the message of the Kingdom to come. We can learn a lot about a particular political, social and economic organisation of the Jews through the ages. All that may possibly be of great help in our sociological discussions. And yet it is hardly permissible to detect in the Bible (viz. in the Old Testament) any permanent or ideal pattern of political or economic settlement for the present or for any other historical realm at all. We may learn quite a lot from Hebrew history. This will, however, be only a historical lesson, not a theological one. Biblical fundamentalism is no better in sociology than anywhere else. The Bible is no authority on social science, as it is no authority on astronomy. The only sociological lesson that can be extracted from the Bible is precisely the fact of the Church, the Body of Christ. But no reference to the Bible in 'temporal' affairs can be regarded as a 'Scriptural evidence'. There are 'Scriptural evidences' only in theology. It does not mean that no guidance whatever can be found or even sought there in the Bible. In any case, such a search will not be a 'theological use' of the Bible. And perhaps the lessons of the old Hebrew history are on the same level as any other lessons of the past. We have to distinguish more carefully between what was permanent and what was but provisional (or 'situation-conditioned') in the old covenant (and first of all we have to overcome its national limitations). Otherwise we would be in danger of overlooking what was new in the new covenant. In the New Testament itself we have to make a clear distinction between its historical and prophetical aspects too. The true theme of the whole Bible is Christ and his Church, not nations or societies, nor the sky and the earth. The old Israel was the 'type' of the new, i.e. of the Church Universal, not of any particular or occasional nation. The national frame of the provisional Church has been done away by the universality of salvation. There is, after Christ, but one 'nation', the Christian nation, *genus Christianum*—in the ancient phrase, *tertium genus*—i.e. precisely the Church, the only people of God, and no other national description can claim any further Scriptural warrant: national differences belong to the order of nature and are irrelevant in the order of grace.

The Bible is complete. But the sacred history is not yet completed. The Biblical canon itself includes a prophetical Book of Revelation. There is the Kingdom to come, the ultimate consummation, and therefore there are prophecies in the New Testament as well. The whole being of the Church is in a sense prophetical. Yet, the future has a different meaning *post Christum natum*. The tension between present and future has in the Church of Christ another sense and character than it had under the old dispensation. For Christ is no more in the future only, but also in the past, and therefore in the present also. This eschatological perspective is of basic importance for the right understanding of the Scriptures. All hermeneutical 'principles' and 'rules' should be re-thought and re-examined in this eschatological perspective. There are two major dangers to be avoided. On the one hand, no strict analogy can be established between the two Testaments, their 'covenantal situations' being profoundly different: they are related as 'the figure' and 'the truth'. It was a traditional idea of the patristic exegesis that the Word of God was revealing himself continuously, and in divers manners, throughout the whole of the Old Testament. Yet all these *theophanies* of old should never be put on the same level or in the same dimension as the incarnation of the Word, lest the crucial event of redemption is dissolved into an allegorical shadow. A 'type' is no more than a 'shadow' or image. In the New Testament we have the very fact. The New Testament therefore is more than a mere 'figure' of the Kingdom to come. It is essentially the realm of accomplishment. On the other hand, it is premature to speak of a 'realised eschatology', simply because the very *eschaton* is not yet realised: sacred history has not yet been closed. One may prefer the phrase: 'the inaugurated eschatology'. It renders accurately the Biblical diagnosis—the crucial point of the revelation is already in the past. 'The ultimate' (or 'the new') had already entered history, although the final stage is not yet attained. We are no more in the world of signs only, but already in the world of reality, yet under the sign of the Cross. The Kingdom has been already inaugurated, but not yet fulfilled. The fixed canon of Scripture itself symbolises an accomplishment. The Bible is closed just because the Word of God has been incarnate. Our ultimate term of reference is now not a book, but a living person. Yet the Bible still holds its authority—not only as a record of the past, but also as a prophetical book, full of hints, pointing to the future, to the very end.

The sacred history of redemption is still going on. It is now the history of the Church that is the Body of Christ. The Spirit-Comforter is already abiding in the Church. No complete system of Christian faith is yet possible, for the Church is still on her pilgrimage. And the Bible is kept by the Church as a book of history to remind believers of the dynamic nature of the divine revelation, 'at sundry times and in divers manners'.

3

HISTORY AND INTERPRETATION

by

JOHN MARSH

I *Is there any central reality or concept within the Biblical revelation which provides a major hermeneutical key?*

This is not a real question, for the existence of such a key is given within the Bible itself. 'Ye search the Scriptures, because ye think that in them ye have eternal life; and these are they which bear witness of me' (John 5.39). 'And beginning from Moses and all the prophets, he interpreted to them in all the Scriptures the things concerning himself' (Luke 24.27). 'Christ died for our sins, according to the Scriptures . . . he hath been raised on the third day, according to the Scriptures' (I Cor. 15.3f.). 'These are written that ye may believe that Jesus is the Christ, the Son of God; and that believing, ye may have life in his name' (John 20.31). In face of all this it is clear that our question should be, is it possible nowadays to retain and to employ the hermeneutical principle given in Scripture itself?

But perhaps we ought not in these days to accept the testimony of the Scripture to itself? Yet to refuse its testimony is really to be unscientific, for the first requisite of science is to take each thing for what it is, and not another thing. And that means, in the study of the Bible, at least to make the attempt to accept the Bible at its own valuation and with its own presuppositions, and to see whether in the end that process does not make more sense of it, and of our understanding of human life, than any alternative method.

The Scriptures themselves profess to witness to Christ, to

speak of him. It is this which enables us to speak of them as God's Word, for the Word of God is Christ (John 1.1-14). It is thus Jesus Christ himself, our incarnate, crucified, risen, ascended, reigning Lord, who is the 'key' to them. In what sense can this be true?

The most fundamental thing is that when we say Jesus Christ is the key to the Bible, we mean first and foremost that the key consists in the gracious, redeeming activity of God. 'God was in Christ reconciling the world to himself.' If Jesus Christ be the key, then, and if he alone can unlock the door to the meaning of the Bible, we must understand that the Bible is in the first place the story of God's action, his initiative both in creating the world, and in redeeming it. Behind all the story of the Bible lies this one fact: God is the prime agent in all that goes on; his activity is fundamental, his indeed the only *action*, all else being *reaction* to what he has done.

Next, when we say that Jesus Christ is the key to the Bible, we mean inescapably that the key to understanding it lies also in man's response to God's gracious and all-determining activity. As man, Jesus Christ made response to God's will and demand in his obedience, becoming 'obedient even unto death, yea, the death of the cross' (Phil. 2.8). This is the key to the understanding of our own empirical nature as men, for we are disobedient, and to the new hope for us that exists in Jesus Christ, 'for as through the one man's disobedience the many were made sinners, even so through the obedience of the one shall the many be made righteous' (Rom. 5.19).

Then when we say that Jesus Christ is the key to the Bible, we mean that he takes the central and interpretative place in its history. What has gone before finds its climax and its consummation in him, and what comes after receives form and fashion from the fact of his coming, and the subsequent reactions of men to his reign. 'When the fulness of the time came, God sent forth his Son' (Gal. 4.4). Jesus said, 'The time is fulfilled, and the kingdom of God is at hand; repent ye, and believe in the gospel' (Mark 1.15).

And when we say that Jesus Christ is the key to the Bible, we mean that its story, and the story of this world, are inexplicable save for the fundamental and basic reality of a world that is beyond history, yet most intimately related to it. It is the world where dwells the 'lamb . . . foreknown before the foundation of the world' (I Pet. 1.20); the world from which he came, and to which he returned (John 13.3), the world which is the coming consummation of our own historical order.

The key we have to use, then, is complex, and not simple. It does not warrant us in taking as the *Biblical* meaning of any passage any application of a text that seems to fit our modern situation, which might provide much excellent hortatory material, but would give us much pernicious guidance as well. The Bible is concerned to state the wholeness of the drama of God's dealings with and coming to man; and it is not until we have made every situation to yield to that wholeness that we can hope to reach its central meaning. In particular, we must remember that both history and human response are part of the key to the Bible. Thus in the history which finds its climax in the life and death of Jesus there will be much that is crude and ethically imperfect. Historical development is a real thing, must be a real thing if the Biblical story is to have a centre in Jesus Christ. Its reality derives very much from the fact that history consists not only of God's action, though that is the primary and constitutive thing, but it consists also in man's reaction; and man's reaction, like all other creaturely things, is capable of development. But the standards of judgment are to be found, not in our human nature, empirical and fallen, but in the perfect humanity of the 'proper man'.

But to say this does not mean that we may not, that we must not, judge an action in its historical setting and use it as a criterion for our own, without having first subjected it to the scrutiny and judgment of what God did in Jesus Christ. We can see, in a study of history, why men's reactions to God's action have differed and to some extent developed. But God's claim and promise and demand have not altered. He offers always the same grace, he claims still the whole self, he promises still the same life. At any point of his dealings with men, had there been a perfect response in obedience, the gates of everlasting life would have been opened. If not, then the conviction that the issues have always been those of life and death have been base deceptions. In historical fact, only in Christ, only in God's Son was perfect obedience possible and found.

Thus it would seem that the existence of different ethical and religious and theological levels in the Bible do not prevent, but rather necessitate, the use of the central hermeneutical key that the Bible gives. The central principle is given and valid; what needs discussion and elucidation is how to apply that principle today. (See Part III.)

But there is another set of problems that in an age of positivist science of history militates against the integrity of such a Biblical key. Is it possible for the Old Testament to 'witness to Christ', to 'speak of him'? Do the Scriptures themselves demand to be understood as a unity; and if so, in what way? This essay seeks to bring forward some of the evidence which needs to be taken in review.

First, the writers of the New Testament are quite clear that the Old Testament belongs to them, in the sense that the events of which they write—the events that constitute the birth, life, death, Resurrection and Ascension of Jesus Christ—are 'according to the Scriptures'.[1] Nor is this conviction simply an invention of the Early Church, for it derives from the teaching, and indeed from the conviction, of Jesus Christ himself. It is important to point out that Jesus's post-resurrection teaching is not a new thing, but that it is clearly presented in the synoptic Gospels as part of the instruction given to the disciples before the Passion began.[2] What such teaching means is to be understood in the light of wider evidence as to Jesus's own conception of his divine-human destiny. That this consisted in a profound belief that the history of his people *as recorded in the Scripture* was to find its climax and fulfilment in himself is clear, not only from his assertion in the Synagogue at Nazareth[3] that a scripture of Isaiah was fulfilled in that day, not only from such manifestly prophecy-controlled actions as the 'triumphal' entry into Jerusalem, but even more profoundly in the understanding of his whole life's work in terms of a Messiah who was also Isaiah's 'Suffering Servant'. The evidence for this is not part of the Evangelists' adornment of

[1] See e.g. I Cor. 15.3, 4; Rom. 16.26; II Tim. 3.15; Acts 8.35; the many references to the Scriptures in the Gospels indicate the same thing in another way.

[2] Luke tells us explicitly that one of the predictions of the Passion was prefaced by a statement that in Jerusalem 'all things that are written by the prophets concerning the Son of Man' would be accomplished. This is probably not the original form of the saying, which is more likely to have had the form of all the other predictions of the Cross—the simple statement that the Son of Man is or shall be delivered into the hands of men to be crucified, and to rise again.

[3] Luke 4.21.

the narrative, but rather lies embedded in the story itself, and it is clear that for Jesus himself there was a continuity between the story of his people and his own story, in which his own life became at once the climax, the meaning and the fulfilment of all that had happened hitherto.

Jesus was unique in seeing a fulfilment of Jewish history in a Messiah who was also a Suffering Servant: but he was not unique at all in expecting a fulfilment, and a Messianic fulfilment of that history. Many scriptures were given a Messianic interpretation before the time of Christ, and the Rabbis were hardly distorting their texts when they understood them as expressive of a certain incompleteness in Jewish history and religion, and as pointing forward to a Messianic fulfilment still to come. 'I see him, but not now; I behold him, but not near; a star has arisen out of Jacob, and a sceptre is established in Israel.'[1] So is the Old Testament a self-confessedly incomplete and therefore in the last resort an unsatisfactory book. It speaks of things yet to happen, of one still to come. Yet, the historical process being what it is, the Old Testament writers cannot refer expressly to the New, or to the events recorded in it: and so it happens that within and without the Church there is much debate as to whether and in what manner the Old Testament alludes to the New. Can it, with any respect for historical integrity, be held to refer to Christ, to speak of him? Is it possible, in this age of self-conscious, historical method, as in previous ages of the Church, to admit the New Testament claim that Moses, the prophets and the psalmists all speak of Christ?

In answering this question in the affirmative, it would seem that the Bible itself leads us to formulate four propositions in justification thereof. They are these:

(1) The same God is the subject of the story of both Old and New Testaments. The Church has always believed this, though not without recurrent doubts and misgivings. But unless this proposition be true, there is an end of any specifically Christian faith as trust in the God and Father of our Lord Jesus Christ. Unless he be the one and only God, Creator of all and Disposer of all, the trust we are asked to put in him is vain. Certainly to believe that the same God revealed himself in the story of Israel and the story of Jesus Christ is not without difficulty: but the

[1] Num. 24.17 (J).

difficulties are not in the change of God from one sort of being to another. Throughout the story God's name—that is, his very essence and person—is love. The one unchangeable divine love has taken many forms, and our own experience of human love helps us to understand how multiform the manifestations of love can be. But the point for which we are contending is not generally a difficulty, nor is it much contorted—the same God is at work in both Testaments.

(2) The same God offers in the two Testaments the same salvation. Both Testaments record certain divine acts in history, different indeed in execution and import, but one in their basic aim, viz. to create a people of whom God can say, 'I am their God, they are my people'. Man's first estate, as created in God's image, is one in which there is direct communion and fellowship with God. Sin and its rebellion caused estrangement between God and man, and it is the purpose of God all through history to re-establish the fellowship that sin had broken. The constant promise to Israel and her leaders is: 'I will be with thee.' The successive crises of the long and tragic history of the chosen people all turn on the question whether those who are not wholly given to God's will can live with him. In the New Testament we read of the constitution of the New Israel, the Israel of God, in him who was 'Immanuel', God with us. There is indeed a difference between the two Testaments as they tell of what God has done to create and preserve a people for himself; but they are one at least in this: that the gift which God was waiting to give to his Israel-after-the-flesh was nothing less than life-with-himself which is his gracious gift to his Israel-after-the-Spirit. In both Old and New Testaments it is made abundantly plain that the issues raised by the divine activity in history are those of life and death, not indeed physical life and death, but spiritual. 'See, I have set before thee this day life and good, and death and evil', writes the Deuteronomist.[1] And the fourth Evangelist, from a profounder insight, affirms that 'God so loved the world, that he gave his only begotten Son, that whosoever believeth on him should not perish but have eternal life'.[2]

The content of the salvation that is offered—eternal life, life with God in his kingdom—is the same in both Testaments. But so is the manner and the means of salvation—God's forgiveness

[1] Deut. 30.15. [2] John 3.16.

of sins. What hinders man from enjoying the richness and fullness of the divine presence is his sin, and there is no means by which man can remove that obstacle himself. The sinful act cannot be undone. God has never pretended that our sins did not matter, as if there were nothing to forgive. But neither was sin for him the irremovable thing that it is for us sinners: 'The day of the Lord is great and very terrible, and who can abide it? Yet even now, saith the Lord, turn ye unto me with all your heart, and with fasting, and with weeping, and with mourning: and rend your heart and not your garments and turn unto the Lord your God: for he is gracious and full of compassion, slow to anger and plenteous in mercy'.[1] Thus Joel in the days of the old covenant: and when Joel's words were proclaimed as fulfilled on the day of Pentecost, and men asked what they should do, Peter replied: 'Repent ye, and be baptised every one of you in the name of Jesus Christ unto the remission of your sins.'[2] The salvation that is offered in both Testaments is the same—life with God through the forgiveness of sins.

(3) In both Testaments the same God offers the same salvation by the same Saviour. This proposition can only be known retrospectively from the time of the events which the New Testaments records. The *locus classicus* is the prologue to the Fourth Gospel, where the writer tells us that the Word, which in due time 'was made flesh and dwelt among us' was also 'in the beginning with God', was the agent in creation, active in the world and its history, and especially in the history of 'his own' people.[3] This does not deny—on the contrary, it implies—that the Word has had a multiform manifestation in history. It is quite consistent to follow John's prologue with the opening of Hebrews and say that 'God, who at sundry times and in divers manners spoke in time past unto the fathers by the prophets, hath in these last days spoken unto us by a Son'.[4] The same Saviour acts in both Testaments, and we can see this if we keep clearly in mind that this is in the order of reality and not in the order of knowing.

But, further, the Christian Church identifies her Lord Jesus with the Jewish Christ or Messiah. A pre-Christian Jew could not have done this, for this was an 'historical possibility'[5] only

[1] Joel 2.11ff. [2] Acts 2.38. [3] John 1.1ff. [4] Heb. 1.1.

[5] I use the term without compromising my belief that a divine possibility is also involved. Faith is the work of the Holy Spirit.

after the events constituting the Incarnation had taken place. And yet the Jews had a doctrine of a Messiah, and interpreted many prophecies (often the same that Christians used) in reference to Messiah. A Messianic prophecy was thus clearly an unfulfilled prophecy: but an unfulfilled prophecy was most clearly, as the Old Testament shows, a false prophecy.[1] If a prophecy remained both unfulfilled and believed in, it could only be because a reality was already apprehended 'afar off' indeed, but really and effectively. In the light of later happenings, Christians can now say who was the object of those pre-Christian insights; and it therefore becomes possible, with due reserve, to speak of the prophets of the Old Testament as having seen and spoken of Christ.

And there is a more general consideration than the simply Biblical. God, Christians hold, has acted decisively to save man in Jesus Christ. But that one act of God was possible only through a whole series of historical events, which centred indeed in the life and death and Resurrection of Jesus Christ, but which of necessity included more. There were several 'moments' in the life of Jesus, but it was not until they were all past that the apostles could proclaim him as 'Lord and Christ'.[2] That is, the various events that had occurred as separate items of an historical sequence had to be seen for what they were—one divine act by which God had reconciled man to himself.[3] Similarly, the disparate historical events by which God had both offered salvation to Israel and prepared the way for his Son have to be seen as moments in the one divine act of man's redemption, as indeed the prologue to the Fourth Gospel presupposes. But this is to say that ontologically, though not sequentially in history, the agent that was active in the beginning of man's redemption was the same as that which effected it securely in history, and will consummate and crown it at the end. Just as the apostles at Pentecost saw for the first time that the many events they had experienced with and through Christ were but parts of one whole event which now became the content of their good news, so they later came to see, as we may come to see, that not only the events of Christ's own life are part of the divine act of redemption, but

[1] Deut. 18.22. [2] Acts, 2.36.

[3] Calvin, in the *Institutes* (I, 16,5-19), attempts to show how the various 'moments' of the divine salvation take their place in the one saving act.

that from creation one God has been working his one gracious work. In both Testaments the same salvation is offered through the same Saviour.

(4) In both Testaments the same God offers the same salvation by the same Saviour through the same actions. This, I think, is the most difficult proposition to state clearly, or without arousing misunderstanding. Let me begin by affirming that to hold this proposition does not involve a denial of the uniqueness, the once-for-all-ness of Jesus Christ as that which is quite 'new' in the New Testament story. But in the New Testament record we have many an indication that to the mind of Jesus and to the disciples, as well as to the Evangelists, this was presupposed.

In the account which Luke gives of the Transfiguration he tells us that Moses and Elijah spoke to Jesus of the 'Exodus' he would accomplish (or fulfil) at Jerusalem.[1] What is meant by such fulfilment is indicated e.g. in the story of the preaching at Nazareth when, after reading Isaiah 61.1f., Jesus boldly claimed, 'This day is this scripture fulfilled in your ears'.[2] This can only mean that for the first time that which was uttered in promise has now become reality. Likewise, to fulfil the Exodus at Jerusalem would mean that in his death on the Cross the deliverance that was promised in action at the Red Sea was for the first time really enacted. It is indeed a remarkable thing how around this theme of the Exodus the whole life of the people of God has been built. At the Exodus, by the miraculous deliverance at the Red Sea, Israel had been, according to the surviving tradition, constituted as God's people. By going down into the waters and coming out on the other side, the old tribes now became one people, on their way to new life in the promised land. What more natural than that later, when proselytes were added to Israel, they should be required not only to submit to circumcision, and so share in the Abrahamic covenant, but that they should also be baptised—go down into the water and emerge to a new life with God's people, looking with them for the fulfilment of their hopes in the land of promise. And what more natural, when Messiah came, than that he should likewise submit to baptism—go down into the waters and emerge again, and thus once and for all constitute the true Israel of God, in his own person embodying the repentance of the people for their sins, and in his

[1] Luke 9.31. [2] Luke 4.21.

own life exhibiting the fruits of the new powers of the 'age to come' that had indeed come in him. And, again, what more natural than that he should see in his passion and death a new baptism,[1] into the waters of which he would go down, and from whose depths he would emerge to new and resurrected life. No wonder also that Paul, following his experience in Damascus after his conversion, should be the New Testament writer to interpret baptism in these very terms of dying with Christ and rising again with him.[2] So it would seem that the fulfilment both of the deliverance at the Red Sea and of the baptism of the Christian, the one place where these prophetic historical actions really came to pass, is in the life, death and Resurrection of Jesus Christ. This is not to deny the reality, in historical sequence, and in historical events, of the passage of the Red Sea, or the baptism of any believer: but it is to recognise that God could not effect at the 'baptism' of Israel at the Red Sea, any more than he can effect now at my baptism, the immediate deliverance which is his gracious and constant intent to bestow. Indeed, not even at the baptism of Christ could that be done. And the reason is always the same. Man's sin meant that instead of a direct journey to the land of promise, there must be forty years wandering in the desert. My sin means that I cannot be made perfect at my baptism: man's sin meant that even for Jesus there was no direct road from his baptism in the Jordan to his triumph and glory. Indeed it is plain from the reference to the Servant Songs, by the voice he hears from heaven at his baptism, that Jesus himself knew at that time that the road to his 'promised land' lay through shame and suffering and death. So he comes to speak of his baptism later on as his ordeal of the cross: from that baptism there *is* immediate access to the victory and the Kingdom. *Regnavit a ligno Deus*. So the fully real and the really full event, of which the Red Sea and my baptism are only historical promise, that in which they are fulfilled, or become for the first time *real*, is the life and death and Resurrection of Jesus Christ. As Dorothy Sayers has put it, this is 'the only thing that has ever really happened'.[3] For all our sense of the reality of history, this event alone has reality in the

[1] Luke 12.50.

[2] Rom. 6.3ff. Paul after his conversion was three days without food and drink or sight, and was on a couch—as near a corpse as a living man could be. He wakes at the word of Ananias to be baptised and begin a new life in God's true Israel in Christ (Acts 9. 9, 18).

[3] Dorothy Sayers, *The Man Born to be King*, p. 37.

full and final sense; for here alone is the historical sequence really given absolute significance, not only possessing temporality and succession, but is taken up into eternity and the amazing oneness of God.

The Eucharist itself, as we now celebrate it in the various parts of Christendom, is another constant witness to these things. The Last Supper, whether it were Passover or Kiddush or Chaburah meal, was without doubt set in the context of the events associated with Passover—the deliverance from Egypt and the crossing of the sea. Thus whenever Christians 'do this' in memory of him, they are reaffirming that the unity of the context of Passover, Exodus, Lord's Supper, Baptism is central to the Christian tradition and the Christian life. And once more the situation is not that at the Eucharist an historical event is remembered in symbolic action. That was not true of the Passover. That event had not obtained its proper reality, had not fully 'occurred', until Christ broke bread and poured out wine, went to his death upon the tree, and was raised again in glory. Only then did it become real, and *fully* historical. And our celebration of the Eucharist is itself not real save as it enables us with efficacious symbols to be at that one real event when God saved the world. As Dr. Dodd has well put it in his Appendix to *The Apostolic Preaching and Its Development*: 'At each Eucharist we are *there*—we are in the night in which he was betrayed, at Golgotha, before the empty tomb on Easter Day, and in the upper room where he appeared; *and* we are at the moment of his coming, with angels and archangels and all the company of heaven, in the twinkling of an eye at the last trump.'[1]

From this point of view we can understand the purpose and motives of the Evangelists, who by implicit reference to prophecy or by letting the Old Testament story shape their own form of the tradition about Jesus, tried to make it plain that the life of the Incarnate Word brought the past into its full historical reality, as God willed. 'How many soever be the promises of God, in him is the yea: wherefore through him is the Amen, unto the glory of God through us.'[2] The flight into Egypt 'fulfils' the

[1] The future reference within Scripture is, of course, in the picture Revelation gives of the 'marriage supper of the Lamb' (Rev. 19.6-9).

[2] II Cor. 1.20. The promises, as we have seen, may be by word or event, as we should now say. But that is a modern distinction: when the A.V. was translated, 'conversation' meant behaviour generally (Latin: *conversatio*).

settlement of the tribes in Egypt, and so on. Jesus giving the 'new law' on the mountain fulfils Moses' legislation for Yahweh at Sinai. Detailed applications such as these are possible and are made because, as the Evangelists believed, what was done in promise before is now done in fulfilment by Christ. In both Testaments the same God offers the same salvation by the same Saviour through the same actions.

Such ways of thinking about time and history are indeed strange to us. We are so conditioned in our apprehensions and our reasonings by our experience of history as *passage* or *succession*. Further, our historical criticism, both of the Bible and of secular history, has proceeded from a conception of history that has not been subjected to scrutiny in the light of the Biblical conceptions of time and eternity. But if we take what evidence the Bible has to give us, it seems that we find throughout an understanding of time very different from ours, profoundly theological, and well adapted to the Christocentric historiography of the New Testament writers. It is impossible in a short space to set out all the evidence, but one or two pointers may help.

First, there is the thought that there is a human time and a divine time, and that it is when these two coincide that real history is made. A simple and clear example is found in Numbers when Yahweh answers Moses' doubts about his ability to feed the Israelites on flesh while they are in the desert. God says:[1] 'Now thou shalt see whether my word shall fall in with thee [meet thee] or not.' Moses has his own course of action—his own 'times', for times were known by their contents; but God's Word, once spoken, also has reality, and when it 'meets' Moses it will become effective and then the time of God's action within the context of Moses' life will have come. This conception of a significant event being conditioned in both the human and divine 'times' is characteristic. 'My prayer is unto thee in an acceptable time', says the Psalmist,[2] echoing Isaiah. The word of prophecy which comes from God himself ('Thus saith the Lord') is likewise fulfilled when the utterance of the prophet is met by God's own action. 'I am the Lord . . . that confirmeth the word of His servant . . . that saith of Jerusalem, She shall be inhabited . . . and to the temple, Thy foundation shall be laid.'[3]

[1] Num. 11.23. [2] Ps. 69.14: cf. Isa. 49.8.
[3] Isa. 44.26f.

But while for man history can never lose its successive character, it is plain that he derives from his experience of the divine activity in history knowledge of another quality altogether. This can be seen in the use of the phrase בעת ההוא, 'at that time', in Deuteronomy. It is used fifteen times altogether, entirely within the first ten chapters.[1] Many things happen 'at that time': Moses appoints judges; briefs Joshua and the Israelites for their campaign; intercedes for Aaron, and so on. Some of the events are separated by long intervals of time. Three possibilities confront us. First, the phrase 'at that time' may be, at any rate on occasion, simply the survival in an edited narrative of a temporal reference to a context now lost, or irrecoverably misplaced. Second, we may try to find a particular historical reference for each occurrence of the phrase. Third, we may think that the unity of meaning is bestowed theologically, not chronologically. The first method is in danger of solving difficulties by avoiding them. The second demands some drastic analysis of the editorial work in places, without offering a sound reason why narratives should be so divided up. The third alone gives real unity and provides a satisfactory reason why these usages are found here. For Deuteronomy, though a patchwork, has a certain definite aim. We might call it the first Zionist tract, and regard it as seeking to make itself effective by reminding the Israelites that there had been a 'golden age' in the past when God had acted in their history to constitute them a people. The references in these ten chapters are to 'times' within that series of events by which God called and formed his people. That is why they can all be said to take place 'at that time'—at the time, namely, though it be a time covering many years of history, when God acted. Times are known by their contents. God had not made Israel all at once, but many events went to constitute his forming of the nation. So those many events could be and had to be thought of as one event, because they were, in terms of what they disclosed of the divine action and nature, one act of God. God's one act when it 'fell in with' the tribes of Israel resulted in those diverse historical events which together made up the divine formation of the one people of God.

It is part and parcel of this same mode of thinking that the future activity of God to restore his people should also be thought

[1] Deut. 1.9, 16, 18, 2.34, 3.4, 8, 12, 18, 21, 23, 4.14, 5.5, 9.19, 10.1, 8.

of as taking place 'at that time'.[1] And it is at least conceivable that this manner of thinking of human and divine time lies behind the whole Christian proclamation of 'the time' having been fulfilled at 'that time' at which God acted in the successive events of Christ's life to perform his one act by which he has saved the world. Certainly it is not until all the events of the Incarnation are complete—birth, life, death, Resurrection, Ascension, gift of Holy Spirit—that the apostles themselves understood the *one thing* that God wrought. And, if we may hazard the opinion, it will not be until the whole historical order is brought to its final consummation in Christ that we shall be able to see just how the manifold of history has been one perfect work of God.

But do our four propositions, even if true, really matter? Surely.

First, they are, it would seem, the final and satisfactory answer to Marcionism, ancient or modern. We cannot cast the Old Testament away, because it writes of the same God as the New. But the God of the two Testaments is One who is known in his acts, and these must be in either case of the same event-pattern, else we could not confidently ascribe them to the same God, any more than we could ascribe a Corot painting to Van Gogh.

Second, they seem necessary to a real understanding of the Incarnation. God's Son, the 'very image of his substance',[2] can be acclaimed as such only if the event-pattern of the life and actions of the New Testament Son fulfil and crown the event-patterns of the divine activity in the Old.

Third, unless the same God offers the same salvation, the divine history of the world is deprived of all its drama—all really *crucial* issues between life and death. God's offer has always been that of life; he has not offered salvation on an instalment or hire-purchase plan. At every crisis of history the ultimate issue is posed for man, whether man discern the 'signs of the times' or not. God has certainly spoken 'in divers manners' before he spoke in his Son; but he had always spoken a word of life. The drama of history does not 'work up to' a life-and-death issue; it is there from the beginning. What happens new in Christ is that the issue is decided. And with that decision all history is fulfilled, i.e. made real.

[1] E.g. Isa. 18.7; Jer. 1.4, etc. [2] Heb. 1.3.

II *The relationship of historical discipline to ethics*

In both Testaments the distinctive teaching about the roots of ethics and human behaviour not only consists in the fact that the moral imperative is regarded as a divine command, but in the fact that the springs of conduct are in the things that God has done to redeem mankind and constitute a people for himself. In the New Testament this is represented by such a text as 'be ye kind one to another, tenderhearted, forgiving each other, even as God also in Christ forgave you' (Eph. 4.32). The Old Testament expresses it in such a saying as 'Just balances, just weights, a just ephah, and a just hin, shall ye have: I am the Lord your God, which brought you out of the land of Egypt' (Lev. 19.36). The recital of what Yahweh had done in bringing Israel from the ghettoes of Egypt was calculated to move them to a recognition of his favour towards them, and a consequent obedience to his Law, so that the divine-human community could be established in fullness and power. The constant appeal of the prophets is to what God did who 'brought you out of the land of Egypt'. Likewise it is the recital of what God did in Christ to reconcile the world to himself that is calculated in the New Testament to move men universally to a recognition of the all-embracing and ineluctable divine purpose, and a consequent obedience to the demands that Christ makes upon those who enter his Kingdom. The good news that Jesus Christ was born, was crucified, was raised from the dead and exalted to God's right hand is the accepted content of Christian preaching from the earliest days. (See Dodd, *The Apostolic Preaching and Its Development*.) As we have seen, the acts of God in both Testaments are a fulfilment-identity, and it would therefore seem that we may understand the ethics based upon these actions as standing in a like relationship to each other. We would thus describe the ethics of the two Testaments as standing to one another in a relationship of fulfilment-identity.

While in both Testaments the determinative principle of ethics consists in the acts which God has done to constitute a community of responsible persons to share fellowship with him and to partake of his blessedness, ethics proper consists in the actions of men. Further, just as the two Testaments stand in a relation of fulfilment-identity in regard to the actions of God, so do they in regard to the actions and behaviour of men. If it be true that the Exodus never really happened until Jesus 'fulfilled' it in his death and Resurrection, then we may say that Israel was never really constituted until the New Israel was constituted in the blood of the New Covenant and by the death and Resurrection of Christ. Thus the social and personal ethics of both Testaments have terms in common, which stand in the same fulfilment-identity relationship to each other. Social terms such as 'covenant', 'people', 'kingdom', 'flock', 'father', 'son', 'peace', 'justice'; personal terms such as 'holiness', 'forgiveness', 'truth', 'righteousness', 'purity'—all these occur in both Testaments, and, like the stories of God's actions in either Testament, must be understood in relation to each other. But here, as there, the centre and the 'norm' is Christ.

It is perhaps important to make some attempt to enunciate some of the principles by which, in the ethical sphere, we may apply the given fundamental principle that Christ is the central hermeneutical principle of the Bible. And first, because to assert his centrality is to assert the importance and the integrity of the historical, we must take every precaution to ensure that we have discovered the proper historical setting of our text. Christ cannot be the Lord of the lives of men who live in history unless they look for his guidance in and through the medium where they themselves need it—in historical situations. Every historical aid is of importance to the Christian who would understand the ethics of his religion, though he must remember that he may not accept the historian's conception of the nature of the historical without applying it to the test of the insights given by the Bible as to what history is.

Second in the resultant historical situation, we must try to penetrate beyond the historically relative forms of experience to the essential demands made by God and the manner of man's response. Difficulties are unavoidable. For each period of history has its own special circumstances which condition and modify man's apprehension of the divine. It is important to pass beyond the naïve view which counts some Biblical stories as good ethical material because they accord with our modern practice and other stories as bad ethical material because they affront our contemporary moral sensibilities. Both 'good' and 'bad' material will show that every human apprehension of God's will is relative to historical conditions. But such a pervasive relativity cannot justify disobedience to the divine will as historically understood, though it will free us from the conceit that our present hearing of God's command is free from relativity. Obedience and error are twin ingredients of every historical situation, infected as it is by temporality and by sin. But universal relativity will not justify moral scepticism, for we know one who in all things did his Father's will. In moral action, as in prophecy and in Biblical history, Christ is the fulfiller. He alone knew God's will perfectly, and gave it perfect obedience. This constitutes the hope of men who know God's will imperfectly and imperfectly respond. For Christ's last word for those who thought their obedience to God lay in crucifying him was: 'Father, forgive them, for they know not what they do.' Man must trust in Christ's righteousness; his own is as filthy rags.

So we come to the third principle of application of the basic hermeneutical principle, viz. that we must relate the actions of God and men which we have discovered in the given historical situation to the action of God in Christ and the reaction of Christ as man.

Fourthly and lastly, we must use both the historical situation we uncovered and the judgment that Christ passes on it to estimate our own historical situation today. This will involve us in making many hazardous judgments, often without much clear guidance, and never with a supernatural aid to relieve us of thought and travail. Guidance, like the power to heal, will come by prayer and fasting.

If, instead of dealing with a single text or passage, we propose to enquire what the Bible has to say about a certain ethical notion or duty, then it would seem right to concur in the theses propounded by the Bossey Conference in 1947[1]—that we should trace the problem from the New Testament to the Old, and back again. We begin with the New, because it is only in the light of the New that we shall understand the Old aright (though to approach the Old from the New does not discharge us of our duty to apply historical criticism to the record before us in the Old Testament), and we return to the New from the Old, because it is only as the consummation of an historical process that we can understand the New.

[1] See footnote on p. 243, *infra*.

4

THE INTERPRETATION OF THE BIBLE

by

JAMES MUILENBURG

The first task of the interpreter of the Bible is to recognise the presence of both diversity and unity in the Bible, and to discern the relationship between the two without doing violence to either. Of these two features which characterise the sacred writings from beginning to end, it is unity that is central and controlling. But we must first do justice to diversity if we are to avoid the errors and distortions of a premature theological interpretation. For Biblical revelation is *historical*, and nothing can liberate us from the task of coming to terms with the concreteness and uniqueness of historical events. Yet the 'history' of the Bible is not like other history, either secular or sacred. It is unique in its understanding of time, in its discerning of the relation of the divine action in time, and in the relation of the 'people' to time. The 'history' of the Bible is understood from its own characteristic point of view, and so it is impossible for the interpreter to separate the historical event from its interpretation. The cleavage between the interpreter as historian and the interpreter as theologian is intolerable. For the problem of hermeneutics is one problem, not two. It is precisely this inextricable unity between history and interpretation that constitutes the crux of the hermeneutical problem.

I

We begin with diversity, then, not because it is the more important, but rather because we are interested in understanding the unity of the Bible *dynamically*, in relation to all the variety and uniqueness of word and event. Among the diversities which must be taken seriously, none is so important as the *diversity of time*. To understand the Biblical view of time and event, to see how *word* and *event* are related, and to discern how *past* and *present* and *future* are apprehended is to enter the world of the Bible. *Diversity of authorship* reflects the variety of experience and personality that lies within and behind the Biblical writings. The Biblical writers are no neutral or passive mediators of divine revelation. At every level Biblical revelation abhors a stereotype. Similarly, *diversity of literary form* reveals also not only the highly dynamic character of Biblical revelation, but also discloses how meaning is bodied forth among a people where form and meaning were intimately connected. More important is the *diversity of the Biblical message* itself, which is explained in part, at least, by the particular historical context. The great value of recognising these diversities is the startling and moving way in which they witness to the unity of Scripture in Jesus Christ. So profound is the reality of this unity in Christ which the Church confesses that it is often proposed that we must begin with the recognition of this prior unity. This must not be denied, but there is a living witness which the individual passage gives in its relation to the whole of Scripture and the Christ who binds the Scripture into a unity, and it is a loss when the witness is obscured.

Yet a too exclusive emphasis upon diversity has been attended by grave deficiencies. Too often the modern interpretation of the Bible has rested with these diversities and has not perceived their relation to the dominating unity of Scripture. Too often an attempt to give an 'objective' historical construction of the development of Biblical religion has taken the place of Biblical theology. Not infrequently humanistic presuppositions have guided the interpreter's thought so that we were given the dubious gifts of *principles*, *insights*, and *ideals* instead of the Word of God which the Bible in reality gave. Man became the subject in a Scripture where the only subject was God. Evolutionary or Hegelian constructions of development comprehended the Biblical materials in a structure which was completely alien to the Bible itself. Thus the uniqueness of Biblical revelation itself was lost. The Bible is more than history, and the history of the Bible is not the kind of history that men have often supposed. It must be understood in its own categories if it is to be understood at all.

Our second task is to recognise the unity of the Bible. Our aim is to show various lines of unity and to show how they are related to the one central unity of the whole Bible.

(1) First of all, there is *the unity of the divine purpose* which controls the Bible from beginning to end. Let us take two examples. As soon as the first Hebrew appears on the scene of the Biblical 'drama', he is confronted by Yahweh and his word:[1]

> Get thee out of thy country, and from thy kindred, and from thy father's house, unto the land which I will show thee: and I will make of thee a great nation, and I will bless thee and make thy name great; and I will bless him that blesseth thee, and him that curseth thee will I curse: and in thee shall all the nations of the world bless themselves.

This word of *command* and *promise* reveals the purpose of God, and its significance is grasped by recognising the context in which it occurs after the preceding chapters of Gen. 1-11. It provides the key to an understanding of the whole Yahwist epic. It persists beyond this particular source throughout the whole Old Testament, but presses beyond the old Covenant into the new. The Apostle Paul reads the command and promise to Abraham in the light of its fulfilment and realisation in Christ:[2]

> And the scripture, foreseeing that God would justify the Gentiles by faith, preached the gospel beforehand unto Abraham, saying, In thee shall all the nations be blessed. So then they that are of faith are blessed with the faithful Abraham.

The call of Abraham does not stand by itself, but persists through the whole of the Bible. The promises are not fulfilled in the Old Testament but in the New. Christ has broken down the middle wall of partition (Eph. 2.14); with him 'there cannot be Greek and Jew, circumcision and uncircumcision, barbarian, Scythian, bondman, freeman; but Christ is all, and all in all' (Col. 3.11). In him all the nations of the world are blessed.

In another passage the Lord speaks to Moses concerning his people Israel:[3]

> Thus shalt thou say to the house of Jacob, and tell the children of Israel: you have seen what I did unto the Egyptians,

[1] Gen. 12.1-3. [2] Gal. 3.8-9. [3] Exod. 19.3-6.

> and how I bear you on eagles' wings and brought you unto myself. Now therefore if you will obey my voice and keep my covenant, then you shall be my own possession from among all peoples: for all the earth is mine: and you shall be a kingdom of priests and a holy nation. These are the words which thou shalt speak unto the children of Israel.

Like the call of Abraham this passage does not stand alone. It is related to the whole history of the covenant people, and supremely to the New Israel, who are 'built up as a spiritual house to be a holy priesthood, to offer spiritual sacrifices, acceptable to God through Jesus Christ'.[1] In the Book of Revelation these covenant words receive their culmination in the singing of the eschatological song before the throne of God.[2]

Beginning and *end* are the two foci of divine revelation. In the beginning God initiates his purpose and will; in the end he brings them to realisation. The whole of Scripture lies under God's *initiating* and *completing* event and Word. All beginnings naturally expect an 'end' in which the purpose of God will be achieved. Creation, the new creation after the flood, the call of Abraham, the Sinaitic covenant, and similar events anticipate a conclusion. The dynamic character of Biblical history is understood by its reference to the divine purpose. Israel is the people of God, *called*, *chosen* and *redeemed*, but her calling, election, and redemption have behind and within them the mighty purpose of God. The prophetic faith of the Bible will not rest until the consummation is achieved in *the new exodus*, *the new occupation of the promised land*, and *the New Israel* born into the new covenant. Thus the messianic hope is a cardinal feature of the Christian understanding of Scripture. The 'end' does not arrive until the messianic age and the coming of the Messiah. From the Christian point of view, the whole Bible is orientated eschatologically. In the Old Testament this is most clearly seen in the prophecies of Second Isaiah, where the whole tradition (the Exodus, the call of Abraham, the everlasting covenant after the flood, and the creation of heaven and earth) is read in an eschatological context. The prophet looks forward to the messianic age and the Servant of the Lord whom Christians rightly interpret as the Messiah.

(2) The Biblical category which does the greatest justice to the

[1] I Pet. 2.5. [2] Rev. 5.9.

persistence of God's activity among his people is *the covenant relation*. In the covenant Israel understands the meaning of her existence. The Bible is pre-eminently the book of the covenant. The old covenant not infrequently anticipates the new (Hos. 2.12-23; Jer. 31-34; Isa. 55.3-5, etc.), and the new covenant is interpreted by reference to the old (Luke 22.20; I Cor. 11.25, II Cor. 3.4-9, 12-16; Heb. 8.8-12, 9.15, 10.16-18). The institution of the new covenant is a recollection of the old covenant. The nature and reality of the covenant are understood by the relation that the old covenant bears to the new and the new to the old, and understands it at those historical moments where it provides maximum illumination for the meaning of history and the life of the nation under threat of destruction (e.g. 750-722 B.C., 650-621 B.C., 625-586 B.C., 550-538 B.C.). Hosea, the writers of the Deuteronomic Code, Jeremiah, the Second Isaiah become supreme witnesses to the meaning of the covenant in these chasms of history.

Again the covenant relationship between Yahweh and his people is *contingent*. The will of God is therefore at all times the supremely relevant issue of history. The Law with its demands and claims, the prophetic oracles, and the requirements of the cult are all rightly understood when they are read covenantally. Even the Creation must be read in relation to the covenant. Both from the historico-critical and from the theological point of view, Creation claims no independent status. Its *raison d'être* is the covenant. Finally, the covenant-promises constitute the matrix in which the future is anticipated with expectation and hope. In the course of Israel's history, the covenant people becomes the remnant. The remnant is the *waiting* community (Isa. 8.16-18; Hab. 2.1ff.; Isa. 40.28-31; Psalm 130, etc.; cf. Rom. 8.19ff.). The *waiting* community is the bearer of the continuous movement which looks forward to the resolution of the inequities and conflicts and corruptions of history. The promises to Israel give history a direction and a goal, and constitute a defiance of alternative interpretations which seek to reduce history to the cyclical round of recurring seasons. It is the waiting community which looks forward to the coming of a messianic age and the Coming One.

In the covenant relationship Israel confesses God to be her sovereign Lord. That God is King of his people is the assumption of the whole Bible. The passages which cast the greatest light upon the Kingdom of God appear before and after the destruction of the nation and, indeed, in all the situations where the people of God face the threat of extinction. In a very early passage (Jud. 8.22-23), Gideon rejects the proffered kingship: 'I will not reign over you, neither shall my son reign over you, but the Lord shall reign over you.' This is an authentic expression of Israel's understanding of her existence, and is inconceivable outside the covenant relation. In a later passage (I Sam. 8.4-9) God addresses Samuel concerning Israel's request for a king: 'Listen to the voice of this people according to all that they say to you; for they have rejected me from being king over them.' Such a passage makes clear what is implicit throughout the history of the covenant people, that its historical existence stands in tension with its faith in the sovereignty of God. Israel's story is the story of a broken covenant, but the sovereignty of her God cannot be escaped. He is Lord and King both in judgment and in the grace which transcends all judgment. In certain respects the most revealing section of the Old Testament on the divine kingship appears in the prophecies of Isaiah of Jerusalem. His inaugural vision reaches its climax in the overwhelming outburst, 'For the King, the Lord of hosts, mine eyes have seen!'[1] The prophet's faith in God's sovereignty in history dominates his whole message to Israel. From the beginning to the end of his career, the prophet is involved in the crisis of the kingdom. His messianic utterances look forward to the messianic King.[2]

> For to us a child will be born, to us a son will be given; And the government will be upon his shoulder, and his name will be called 'Wonderful Counsellor, Mighty God, Everlasting Father, Prince of Peace'. Of the increase of his government and of peace there will be no end, upon the throne of David, and over his kingdom, to establish it, and to uphold it, with justice and with righteousness, from henceforth and forever. The zeal of the Lord of hosts will do this.

Christians read these messianic words of Isaiah in the light of the coming of the Messiah in Jesus. Those who confess him as the Christ see these words in relation to his coming, although it must always be remembered that the Christ who came was more than all of Israel's purely messianic expectations and appeared as

[1] Isa. 6.5. [2] Isa. 9.6-7.

a suffering Redeemer. After the fall of the Kingdom of Judah in 586 B.C. the faith in the divine sovereignty asserted itself afresh. This is clearly seen in the eschatological message of Second Isaiah. The opening lines already anticipate the coming of the divine rule (Isa. 40.10), and the climax appears significantly just before the poem on the Suffering Servant of the Lord.

> How beautiful upon the mountains are the feet of the heralds,
> Who bring good tidings of peace, news of salvation,
> Who say to Zion, 'Your God has become king!'

Not only the word 'gospel' but its reality is profoundly anticipated in such passages as these.

The divine purpose and the covenant relationship in which the sovereignty of God is revealed and established in the life of Israel are aspects of one and the same reality. This is also true of a third category of unity, *the continuity of the divine revelation*. The reality of divine revelation is most powerfully expressed in the succession of theophanies. The theophanies reveal the divine purpose and occur within the category of the covenant. God reveals himself to the patriarchs, to Abraham and to Jacob-Israel; he reveals himself to Israel at Sinai; he reveals himself to the charismatic deliverers like Gideon; he reveals himself to his servants the prophets, like Isaiah and Jeremiah and Ezekiel. But the supreme theophanies come at the beginning and end. At these points God reveals his mighty Word and event. Again it is Second Isaiah who portrays the time-fulfilling, world-embracing event of the divine epiphany in language and thought that does justice to the meaning of Israel's past tradition and history and to the future of the people of God:

> Behold, your God!
> Behold, the Lord God comes in power,
> and his arm shall rule for him,
> Behold, his reward is with him,
> and his recompense before him.

In this supreme event the purpose of God will be revealed, his election of Israel will be demonstrated, his righteousness vindicated, his redemption accomplished, his grace made known, his Kingdom will come, and his glory appear. Nowhere is the dynamic, living relation between the old covenant and the new more clearly revealed than in the use that the New Testament makes of the prophecies of the great prophet of the 'exile'. But above all, in these poems the Servant of the Lord offers himself for the sins of the world. Even if, as seems probable, the prophet was referring to Israel, it was Jesus who fulfilled the prophecies. All the true meaning of Israel, the people of God, is revealed in Christ. Christ is the final meaning of Israel.

II

The foregoing discussion has concerned itself primarily with the Old Testament. We have described three major continuities within the old covenant: the purpose of God in history; the covenant relation of God with his people, who are called, chosen, redeemed, and covenanted by him; and the reality of the divine revelation which is expressed supremely at the beginning and the end. In each instance the Old Testament was found to be incomplete and insufficient in itself. The resolution of forces within the life of the covenant people is not to be found in the Old Testament. The old covenant is fulfilled in the new. The creation of the world, the fall of man, the call of Abraham and of Jacob-Israel, the covenant relationship itself, the words of the prophets, the rituals and practices of the cult, and Israel's existence as a holy people are fully apprehended by the Christian only when he sees them in the light of Jesus Christ. The prophets view the covenant with Israel as a *broken covenant*. Therefore they look to a time when the divine justice and the divine mercy will be fully revealed. The new covenant is realised in the death and Resurrection of the Christ, yet it is also future in its anticipation of his coming again in the *Parousia*.

The first words of Jesus in the Gospel of Mark already point to the fulfilment:[1] 'The time is fulfilled, and the kingdom of God is at hand; repent, and believe in the gospel.' The Kingdom is not yet proclaimed; its reality is present in Jesus Christ. The Bible is a covenant book from beginning to end; from beginning to end it is the book of the Kingdom of God. Finally, only in the New Testament is the meaning of the people of God fully understood. Many of the books of the Old Testament are occupied with the nature of Israel's covenant life with God,

[1] Mark 1.15.

books like Hosea, Deuteronomy, Jeremiah, Ezekiel, Second Isaiah, and Daniel, but the final meaning of the true Israel is revealed in the birth and teachings and life and death and Resurrection of Jesus Christ. The reality of Christ is not absent from the Old Testament. He is present because the Old Testament expects the coming of the messianic age and the Messiah. But he is also present in the interior meaning of many passages. The new covenant of Jer. 31.31-34 is fulfilled and completed in the revelation of the Lord's Supper. Moses' request to see the glory of God is not viewed in its full range until we look upon the face of the Christ (II Cor. 4). The domestic tragedy of Hosea adumbrates the cross of Christ. Even so primitive a passage as Gen. 6. 1-8 with its description of sin and judgment and grace receives its full commentary in the revelation of the Cross.

Having established the unity of the Bible, the organic relationship between the Old and New Testaments, it is essential that we recognise the difference between the two Testaments. The first thing to be said about the New Testament is that it is *new*. The coming of Christ is the new event. It is an event as the revelation of the Old Testament is event, but it is the unique and final event. The New Testament does not only continue the record of the Old; it does not merely pursue the story to its close. It bears witness to the one decisive event in the light of which all other events are fully grasped. When we read the Old Testament without the New, 'the veil remains unlifted, because only in Christ it is taken away'.[1] In the face of Jesus Christ we see 'the light of the knowledge of the glory of God'.[2] Christ gives us a new law, a new word, a new people, a new redemption. The creating, living, revealing, and redeeming Word becomes incarnate in Him.[3] 'Grace and truth came through Jesus Christ.'[4] 'In many and various ways God spoke of old to our fathers by the prophets, but in these last days he has spoken to us by a Son, whom he appointed heir of all things, through whom he also created the world. He reflects the glory of God, and bears the very stamp of his nature, upholding the universe by his word of power.'[5] Our interpretation of the Bible is determined by the completeness of God's revelation in Christ. We interpret the whole Bible in the light of our faith in God's revelation in Christ. The Bible is both sacred history and faith-history, *Heilsgeschichte*

[1] II Cor. 3.14. [2] II Cor. 4.6. [3] John 1.1-14. [4] John 1.17. [5] Heb. 1.1-3.

and *Glaubensgeschichte*. As sacred history it is apprehended through faith in Christ, the Son of God who died and gave himself for us. We do not interpret the Bible as bondsmen of the letter. We do not interpret it as Law but as Gospel. It is misleading to speak of the Old Testament simply as Law and the New Testament simply as gospel. Law and Gospel are present in both Testaments. But it is the Gospel which liberates us from bondage to the Law and permits us to interpret the Bible in the light of faith. The revelation in Christ does not shatter the meaning of the Old Testament. It casts an ultimate light on all that we read. The original meaning is not lost, but is finally and fully illumined. Faith does not mean that we can now read a passage as we choose so long as it gives us some affirmative word, even about Christ; faith in Christ, if we know what we are saying when we say 'Christ', means that the original words as they were meant by their original writers are understood in the context of the revelation with which they are organically related. The historical revelation is taken seriously, but the work of Christ transforms the revelation of the old covenant into something new. Jews and Christians inevitably interpret the Bible in different ways, for they have differing conceptions of the movement and culmination of the religion.

III

The following principles of interpretation grow out of our recognition of the diversity and unity of the Bible. The task of all exegesis is to understand the meaning of the transmitted text. Hermeneutics seek to show how the Bible must be approached to make it intelligible, how it must be dealt with, how the original meaning may be communicated, and what instruments are available for interpretation. A knowledge of the original language is indispensable. No translation is ever a sufficient guide, for no translation is a perfect rendering of the original. Every interpreter will be his own translator; he will turn the alien speech of the original into the words and forms of his own language which most adequately reproduces the original.

(1) *The establishment of the text.* The first task is to establish the wording of the text. Where the Hebrew or Aramaic or Greek is insecure, the help of the versions will be enlisted. Where there are alternate readings, the criteria of textual criticism will be

applied. The character and value of each version and of the different manuscripts will be taken into account and their witness evaluated.

(2) *The determination of the meaning of the words and their relationship to each other*. Our purpose is to recover the mind of the original speaker or writer. We must know what he meant when he wrote, and must seek to understand his words as his original listeners understood them. We cannot assume that the words bore the same meaning to the original writers as they do to us. For arriving at the meaning of the words all the means of linguistic and philological study are available to us: dictionaries, word studies, etc. Such a work as Kittel's *Theologisches Wörterbuch zum Neuen Testament* is indispensable to the interpreter of both Testaments. It is especially important to have a feeling for the connotations and associations which the original words have, and to recognise that the same word may have a wide range of meaning. The competent interpreter will have a sense of the nuances and shades of meaning of words, for among such a people as the Hebrews words have a more living and elemental quality than they do among ourselves. After the meaning of the words has been made clear, the interpreter will study the relationship of the words within a sentence. He will study the grammatical function and the syntactical relations of the text. He will observe very closely the order of the words in the original text, for the order of the words often shows where the emphasis lies. He will be careful to notice how sentences are related to each other and how key phrases are repeated in fresh contexts. The whole passage must be subjected to close linguistic, syntactical, and grammatical scrutiny.

(3) *The Biblical world of thought*. The Bible has its own anthropology and psychology and sociology. We must not confuse ancient Semitic forms and modes of thought with those of the modern, western world, which have been so much influenced by Greek conceptions. For example, the significance of anthropomorphisms must be explained. Words like *face*, *arms*, *hands*, *eyes*, *ears*, *heart* must be understood in their original associations. The importance of the body and the various parts of the body must be felt and explained. Words like *soul*, *spirit*, *blood* cannot be simply taken over; they must be interpreted. Again, the *family* terminology of Scripture should be understood. Both the solidarity

of the family in the Bible and the meaning of various relationships within the family must be clearly recognised. The meaning of the father-son and husband-wife relationships must be appreciated. When the reality of the family is understood, new light will be shed on many passages (e.g. the genealogies). Finally the interpreter will explain the significance of the *word* in Biblical thought, the relation of word to *soul*, to *thing*, to *event*, and the effect that words exert in relationships.

(4) *The literary form*. Literary form often reveals the purpose of the writer and helps us to articulate the movement and structure of the thought. The first task here is to identify the literary unit by discovering its beginning and end. The distinction between poetry and prose will be observed. Where strophic structure is present in a poem, the strophes must be separated and carefully analysed. The particular literary type (*Gattung*) will be identified, and its function in the life of the community or individual understood. Our exegesis will be affected by the recognition of the literary genre. We cannot, for example, deal with all psalms in the same fashion. The hymn, lament or song of thanksgiving have different aims in view. In the prophetic literature, which is especially rich in the variety of literary form, the literary guise must be observed. The relation between an invective (*Scheltrede*) and a threat (*Drohrede*) often gives us a key to the proper interpretation. Similarly, such a poem as Isaiah's Song of the Vineyard (Isa. 5.1-8) loses its point and force unless we know that he is employing a fertility-cult song as a vehicle for his message.

(5) *Historical criticism*. The meaning of a Biblical passage cannot be successfully or reliably interpreted unless we know the circumstances surrounding its creation. The authenticity of the passage must be established. We cannot treat words which are separated by centuries, even though they succeed each other on the same page of the Bible, in the same way. The sources of the writing must be separated, their dates determined, their provenance and destination established, and the concrete situation and occasion determined. For a religious faith where history is the mode of the divine revelation such a task is of the first importance. Biblical revelation is concrete, and it is the task of historical criticism to recover this concreteness. No theological interpretation is safe which does not take history seriously, and no historical interpretation is possible without historico-critical examination.

(6) *Historical setting and background.* Historical criticism is only the beginning of our task here. After the historical situation and authorship have been determined (so far as that is possible), the historical circumstances and conditions surrounding the writing must be explained. We cannot read the prophets unless we know the historical environment in which they prophesied. The prophecies of Isaiah would be almost unintelligible without our knowledge of Assyrian aggression during his life and ministry. The Word of the Lord is never a permanently valid principle of universal reason, but a particular Word spoken in a particular situation to a particular people, by one to whom the Lord had spoken in a concrete moment.

(7) *The later history* (*Nachgeschichte*) *of a passage.* The solidarity of the covenant people and the unity of the tradition is vividly illustrated by the way in which some passages and motifs are repeated and reinterpreted in the Bible. This reinterpretation is of great significance both for hermeneutics and for theology. Such a passage as Gen. 15.6, 'And he believed the Lord; and he counted it to him for righteousness', is reinterpreted in the New Testament and given its ultimate dimension in the revelation of Christ. The covenant promises are repeatedly interpreted in new situations and settings, and are understood in the light of their fulfilment in the New Testament. There is no question of the legitimacy of such reinterpretation.

But there are other passages, like the birth stories of Matthew and the rabbinical exegeses of Paul and the typological exegeses of the Epistle to the Hebrews, where the situation is different. What shall we say of this kind of interpretation? Whether Matthew and Paul and the writer of Hebrews were justified or not in employing such exegetical devices is one question, and whether we are permitted to follow their example is another. They were employing the exegetical devices current in their day. But the plain fact is that the Old Testament passages to which they refer did not mean what they are interpreted as meaning. This does not mean that the truth which the apostles and others sought to convey is not genuine truth. But their truth is in actuality divorced from the passages which they connect with it. For us to employ such methods is to open the door to arbitrariness and irresponsibility.

But the matter does not end here. It is often said that the

original writer meant more than he realised, that his words imply more than he knew, and that a later age was in a position to see depths and ranges of truth that were undisclosed to him. There is an important truth here, but it is nevertheless a precarious truth. New situations naturally place a passage in a new contemporaneity, and the words consequently assume a new vitality and depth. This is certainly true. Moreover, this truth is not confined to the Bible alone. The importance of tradition enters here. The use that the Church Fathers and the Reformers make of the Bible often helps us to see a more profound meaning in a passage. A wise and discriminating use of tradition may be of great assistance in the interpretation of a passage. Yet here too we encounter the problem of deciding what tradition we shall use. Should we, for example, include Origen's allegorical exegesis here, and all the predecessors and successors of Origen from Pseudo-Barnabas on? The most that we can say on this point is that in every instance we must do full justice to the sense and intent of the original writer. A careful application of all the hermeneutical principles here set forth should guide us from going astray.

(8) *The Oriental character of the Bible*. The Bible is Oriental both in its literary form and expression and in its mode of thinking. It is not easy for modern Western men, schooled in Western ways of thought and expression, to think Orientally or to do justice to the imaginative qualities of the Oriental mind. Only the imagination can interpret the imagination, as only the poet in us can interpret poetry. The imagination must assert its rights. How many futile pages have been written on the anthropomorphisms of the Bible without any appreciation of their profundity and their final relation to the Incarnation! Many commentaries show all too clearly their cultural and national provenance, Greek, Latin, German, French, English, or American. The Bible is an Oriental book, and it must not suffer violence.

(9) *The experience and personality of the writer*. The divine revelation is mediated through persons. Our protest against the extremes of modern liberal interpretation, which tended to absolutise experience, has naturally aroused a strong reaction against this kind of interpretation. However true it is that the prophets were concerned about proclaiming the Word of God, they all of them reflect the experiences through which the Word

of God came to them. We must, indeed, be cautious about modernising and 'psychologising' because it is easy to give these experiences a modern anthropocentric meaning. Moreover, we must be careful not to incorporate mystical interpretations into passages which defy mystical interpretation, as in the Old Testament prophets. Finally, interpretation through experience must be checked by all our other principles. Yet, when these dangers are recognised, it nevertheless remains true that the experiences of Moses, of the prophets, and of the apostles do help us to understand the meaning of their words. How poor we should be without the account of Isaiah's vision in the temple or the story of Paul's conversion on the road to Damascus!

(10) *The operation of the Holy Spirit.* The interpretation of Scripture is a work of grace. We cannot of ourselves hear the Word of God or receive its meaning. For the Christian the task of hermeneutics is inconceivable without the operation of the Holy Spirit. When we enter into living relationship with a passage of Scripture, when the Bible speaks to our inner condition and humbles us, we have been granted the gift of the Spirit. It is the Holy Spirit which reveals to us the word of truth. The words may lie cold and inactive on the page, always 'something out there', always an object to be examined, always an interesting religious phenomenon of the ancient Semitic world, always all the various things so many of our books have said they were. But for the Christian it is otherwise. As a member of the community of the Spirit, of the Church of God where the Bible becomes Scripture by the operation of the Spirit, the reading of the Bible depends upon what the Spirit has to communicate. This Spirit is not capricious; it is not like the wind that 'bloweth where it listeth', but it is the Spirit which is in Christ which guides to all truth. And the Spirit which is in Christ, as we have seen was present even though 'hidden' in the book of the old covenant and revealed in the book of the new covenant. The Holy Spirit which spoke through the men of old speaks today, and through these ancient sacred words addresses us in our own condition.

(11) *The total Biblical context.* Historical criticism guards and preserves the historical revelation. No principle of Biblical interpretation is valid which destroys the history in which the revelatory Word was spoken. Yet every passage belongs to a larger whole. We read a passage within the context of the whole

original writing. We interpret an oracle or confession of Jeremiah or a passage from Paul in the light of the entire book. But the books themselves belong to a single organic unity. They are part of a covenant literature. They are part of a continuing revelation which assumes for the Christian the character of a 'story' in which the purpose of God is at work in the world. In this story we inevitably read all things in the light of the beginning and end. The story is not understood until the conflict of forces within it has been resolved, yet the resolution is not understood without a knowledge of that which is resolved. We cannot select certain passages and eliminate others from this story. Otherwise the anthologist determines where revelation is present and where it is not. The coming of the Christ does not efface the historical revelation. Christ stands in organic relation with the revelation, even if it is a new revelation. The Bible is the canon of the Christian Church. All parts of it must be read within the context of the canon.

IV

We are now prepared to address ourselves to the final problem of this paper. What is the relation of the Bible to the formulation of ethics? Has our recognition of the diversity and the unity of the Bible shed any light on this question? It is agreed that the Bible is an historical revelation, and that it must be interpreted as an historical revelation. This immediately raises the question whether such a revelation, with all the diversities which characterise history, can yield us the kind of consistency and order and logical coherence that are required of any ethic? If we appeal to the major unities for a solution to our problem, then how is each of these unities to be understood in relation to the problem of ethics? How is the divine purpose of God in human history as it is revealed in the chosen people and fulfilled in Christ to be understood in relation to the contemporary problems of ethics? Similarly the Kingdom of God, which is based upon the covenant relation between God and Israel, must find some concrete expression which is intelligible to the student of ethics. How, finally, is the continuity of the divine revelation as it is focused in supreme moments of theophany to be related to ethical norms and decisions? Above all, how are we to understand the central unity of Scripture in Jesus Christ, in relation to our problem? If we succeed in recognising the ethical relevance of the Bible, there is the corollary problem of determining how we may establish authentic rapport between the Bible and ourselves.

In the first place, the nature of the Bible forbids us to find within it any external ethical system. The revelation it contains does not present itself to us in terms of permanently valid principles or ethical norms. Frequently, when such generalisations seem to be approximated, closer examination will reveal that there is little constancy and consistency maintained throughout. The demand that is made of man is characteristically existential; certainly the passages both in the Old and the New Testament which move us most deeply ethically are those which are addressed to concrete situations, such as the Word of the Lord to David in the affair of Uriah the Hittite, or the Word to Ahab after the murder of Naboth, or the story of the Rich Young Ruler, or the parable of the Good Samaritan. What is demanded in each instance is understood in a concrete historical context. Moreover we cannot *simply* apply the laws of the Old Testament or the prophetic imperatives or the Sermon on the Mount or the preaching of the apostles to our own situations. The Bible is a *sacred history*, and a distilling of permanent laws and principles from it is not in keeping with its fundamental meaning and character.

But we cannot leave the matter thus. For the Bible does offer us all kinds of guidance and direction in the discernment of our duty and obligation. The apodictic laws of the Covenant Code, the Book of Deuteronomy, the prophetic oracles, the psalter, and the wisdom literature are all undergirded by a conception of man's situation which does more than suggest how he should act in specific situations. Always man is *a responsible person.* He lives under a judgment higher than his own and must submit himself to it. He lives under a sovereignty higher than the sovereignty of nations and must yield his allegiance to it. God is Lord of the 'lords' of the earth, he is King of the kings. This responsibility is grasped within the unique community of the covenant people. There, and there alone, does man know what kind of a person he is, and it is there that he understands the nature of the obligation under which he lives. Yet all men are *intended* by God to belong to this covenant, as the movement and direction of Biblical thought demonstrate. Within the blessed community man sees what he *ought* to be and what he *ought* to do. He is the *servant* of a Lord who establishes justice in the earth, and he must labour unceasingly for the realisation of justice (Amos 5.24; Mic. 3.1, 6.8; Isa. 1.27, 56.1; Jer. 5.4-5, 22.3; Ps. 82.1-5; Job 31, etc.). This servant relationship is envisaged in the Servant passages of Second Isaiah and realised in their fulfilment in Jesus Christ.

The urgency with which the demand for justice is made becomes creative for every new situation. But the demand is always interpreted concretely in the context of a given environment. Frequently the elaboration of what justice involves for ourselves is clear, e.g. the demand that there shall be no poor in the land; the demands concerning the widow and orphan and resident alien. Further, the nature of the relation which man has to God within the covenant community is understood as a relation of the love of God to man and the reciprocal response of man in loving God and the community of men ruled by a loving God. The Book of Deuteronomy is dominated by this loving sovereignty, and by the demand that man shall implement this loving sovereignty into the concreteness of his own social situation. *Faithfulness to the covenant* lays upon him the demand to obey a God who rules his people in love. Love to man is an inevitable corollary to God's love of man and man's love of God. Therefore the concern for the individual person (Covenant Code, Nathan's parable, the affair of Naboth's Vineyard, etc.) presses on to its final revelation in Jesus the Christ.

Israel is the responsible people. The meaning of election, as of the covenant, is responsibility (Amos 3.2). Prophecy and priestly Torah join in asserting man's responsibility to man. The divisions which separate men from one another, divisions of race and nation and class, are all finally transcended in the Christ who has broken down the middle wall of partition. Man's offence against man is sin against God. This is the witness of both prophecy and Gospel.

The ethical structure can assume more definite form. We see this very clearly in the commands of the Decalogue (Exod. 20.1-17), the apodictic laws of the Covenant Code, and in not a few utterances of the prophets (Amos 5.24; Hos. 6.6; Isa. 1.27, 56.1; Mic. 3.1, 6, 1-8; Jer. 5.4-6, 22.3) and the Wisdom writers (Job 31). The demand of Deuteronomy that there be no poor in the land is one that is incumbent upon every society. The demand for justice with its concrete implementation, gives us more than general guidance. We are not left to grope after the writer's meaning. Amos leaves no question in our mind at all on this point. The recognition of the worth of the individual person characterises every major level of Scripture. The solidarity of the community could assert itself to great extremes, to be sure, but the recognition of the value of the person is so great that it is constantly breaking through the barriers and asserting itself. Again, man's body is sacred. It was fashioned by God in the body of the mother. He who created me created my neighbour also. We are all of us the work of his fingers, and are bound within a family where there is but one God and Father over us all.

In the second place, it is within the reality of the sacred history that we are to view our problem of the relation of the Bible to ethics. Israel is a holy people, called, chosen, redeemed, and covenanted by her sovereign Lord and Redeemer. This primary relation of God and Israel cannot be ignored for the sake of securing an ethical system. That is, we cannot discount or remove the essential understanding which the holy people has of its existence in order to discover universal truths relevant to all times. The concreteness of the Bible, both in its pervasive conception of historical existence and in the unique and unrepeatable moments of historical events and words, must be accepted. It is with this concreteness that we have to do. This means, that the holy community continues to be for us the holy community; the revelatory events continue to be for us revelatory events.

Church and Bible are reciprocal realities, mutually interpenetrating, so that one cannot be understood without the other. It is wrong both historically and theologically to set Church and Scripture over against each other. It is the Church which possesses the Bible. The Church treasures the Bible, proclaims its message, interprets its meaning. *Extra ecclesiam nulla scriptura; extra scripturam nulla ecclesia.* The Church is the custodian of the revelation. Within the Church the Holy Spirit is at work to reveal to its members the Word of truth. The ethical question which we ask of the Bible is asked within the Church to which the inquirer belongs. This does not mean to say that there is no light at all for him who inquires of the Bible from without. There is much light that the Bible sheds even to the sincere secular person.

It is unwise and dangerous to deny this. But if we seek to ask the Christian question, then the answer is given within the community of the covenant people, the Israel of God, the Church which is the body of Christ.

The ethical question is raised from within the community of Christ. But how can the inquirer enter into relationship with the Bible to receive the light he needs? How may he hear what the Bible is saying? As a member of the *ecclesia* of God he subjects himself to what he reads. He places his consciousness within the consciousness of the people of God. He waits to hear what they heard who first listened to the prophet and the apostle. He is himself addressed. He approaches the Bible with a prayer in his heart for God's guidance. He thinks and hopes and waits as a child of the covenant. He reads the sacred Word by faith. His faith controls his being, and he comes like a child with his question to see what it is that God has to say to him (cf. Isa. 28.9-13). He will try so far as possible to give up his own stubborn pride and self-centredness and read by faith alone (*sola fide*). And when the Word has come, he will know that it is not of his own wisdom or knowledge or piety that he has received an answer, but by the gift of God's grace (*sola gratia*). He is controlled throughout by his faith that God has spoken in the Bible and in Jesus Christ, one faith in one final revelation.

This poses, finally, the question of the relation of the Biblical covenantal manner of thinking and living to our contemporary situation. Has the Bible a word to speak to the nations? Does it speak to the harassing issues which beset our age? Or is there a chasm fixed between the world of the Bible and our own, so wide that it cannot be bridged? The Bible itself is clear on this matter. The God of the covenanted people addresses himself to Assyria and Babylonia and Greece and Rome and all the nations among whom the covenant people live, and the covenant people are compelled to understand God's righteous will in relation to the movements and vicissitudes of their own history. The Old Testament does not rest until all the nations are related to the covenant sovereignty of God, either by their inclusion within the community or by the judgment that befalls them in the light of the moral sovereignty of God, and the New Testament in its eschatological perspectives sees the purpose of God realised when all the kingdoms of the world become the Kingdom of our God and his Christ. To live in history means to live under the sovereignty of the God who reveals himself in history and is Lord of history. He is the Creator and Redeemer of history, and our lives as Christians are always confronted with the ultimate demand of his will for us in each historical situation which is understood in the light of his Creation and Redemption.

5

FROM THE BIBLE TO THE MODERN WORLD

by

G. Ernest Wright

I

The problem of Biblical interpretation has always been and will ever be a chief concern of the Church because the very nature of the Scripture makes it inevitable that this be the case. On the one hand, the Bible records the story of God's visitation of a particular people at a particular time and place in history. In order to understand such a literature we are impelled in the first instance to study the history it presents. This involves a comprehension of geography, text, language, literary relationships, indeed the whole apparatus of historical criticism. The Bible is not an abstract discussion of ideals and doctrines of universal validity. The Word of God it reveals confronts a people in their own specific history and is fitted to the occasion and context. Here the universals cannot be apprehended, they have no meaning, apart from the particular. Consequently, the interpreter who attempts to speak about the Biblical teaching on this or that subject cannot minimise the importance of linguistic, philological, and historical study. When he does so, he immediately betrays his lack of understanding of the nature of the Bible and of the God who has chosen to reveal Himself in historical events.

On the other hand, it is the Church's faith that the Bible presents the Word of God for *our* salvation here and now. God's saving acts in Israel and specifically in Jesus Christ were done on *our* behalf. The ancient story is contemporary testimony. At one and the same time the Bible is a historical record and a living Word constantly mediated to us, and formed in us, by the Holy Spirit. While this unity of the historical and the living Word has often been lost, it is the primary assumption of the Church's faith.

The most serious of the hermeneutical problems arise precisely in the attempt to interpret a historical literature as the living Word of God. On the one hand, the very nature of the writing presents peculiar problems. When we set ourselves apart from the Bible and begin to dissect and analyse it after the manner of purely objective historians, we are continually in danger of misinterpreting it through the use of tools which fail to draw out its true meaning. During the nineteenth century one such tool was the use of organic metaphors and analogies drawn from the realm of biology. The significance of the Bible was described primarily by means of the metaphor of growth. In the Scripture, it was thought, there exists a marvellous story of man's gradual evolution in the knowledge of God, which can be portrayed as developing from seed to plant, to flower, or from childhood to youth, to maturity, or from the primitive to the developed, to the culmination.

Today an increasing number of scholars are reacting against the exclusive use of this particular tool. While focusing attention on the obvious signs of progressive revelation in the Bible, the single-minded concentration on the metaphor of growth has betrayed the interpreter together with his Church. It has led him to examine the writings by means of an ascending scale of values, and to devaluate the theological significance of the early portions of the Old Testament in order to make room for the growth he desires to find. It has focused his attention on the evolution of concepts because he believes this to be the main task of his enquiry. It has emphasised historical continuity and environmental conditioning at the expense of the discontinuous and the unique. When the Church begins to look upon the significance of its Scripture solely in terms of an evolutionary scale of values, it can no longer hear the living Word of the God of history except as it finds his will expressed in those values which are rationally discernible. Yet the Bible as a textbook for values is a troublesome book; readers who use it solely for this purpose must exercise great caution in the selection of those values which belong only to the peak of the developmental scheme. Thus it has become obvious that the Church betrays the Gospel when it tries to expurgate the Bible in order to meet the conditions imposed by a faulty hermeneutical tool and in order to accommodate itself to the world on a platform of secular or pagan idealism.

The Biblical God who speaks in historical events confronts man first of all with himself and thus he reveals to him his true state as a creature. Only in this light does God reveal his will and those 'values' necessary for life. Consequently, the interpreter inevitably finds himself involved in and addressed by the document he seeks to interpret. It then becomes obvious that the metaphor of growth, while of considerable importance when used in the proper way, nevertheless fails to focus the interpreter's attention on those concerns which were of primary importance to Biblical man.

Yet, on the other hand, the Christian interpreter, who finds himself and his own existence involved in the Scripture he is trying to understand, experiences serious difficulty in appropriating its divine Word to himself and to his Church because of the distance which separates his own age from that of the Bible. The Biblical revelation is fitted to and conditioned by a history that is not his own except as he is enabled by faith to participate in it. Two major questions thus arise: (1) How is it possible for the Christian to participate in the Biblical events so that the Word there spoken is found to be addressed also to him? (2) Is there a unity and coherence existing between the different parts of the Scripture so that the reader will never become lost within it, without any guide to direct him between the essential and the non-essential? If such unity exists, what is it or what is the key which unlocks it?

(1) With regard to the first question, the Church has always used tradition, that is, the teaching of the fathers of the Christian community, as *one* of the most important, if not *the* most important, bridge between the past and the present. Those of the Protestant and Catholic communions have differed sharply over the relative authority which tradition has in deciding questions of faith, but both have nevertheless made great use of it in determining the meaning of Scripture for the contemporary Church. The creeds, for example, were formulated as summaries

of Biblical doctrines, and they have served as a steadying influence, tying the past and the present together. Yet the creeds confine themselves to matters which can be rationally discerned, defined and discussed. In themselves they do not confront us with the living God in the way that Scripture itself does. There is still the necessity for the interpreter by sympathetic imagination and faith to enter the history of Israel, for example, in order to comprehend the meaning and power of God's Word to the prophets. Only as he is able to hear the Word in that history is he enabled to hear the same Word in his own history. Only as he stands with the apostles 'in Christ' is he enabled to discern the meaning of God's work in Christ for his own day. Only as he by adoption is a son of Abraham does he become heir to the grace of life.

Biblical history is of a type for which the world offers no real parallel; it is confessional history in which fact and event are not separated from theological meaning. In the Books of Kings, for example, it is repeatedly stated that if the reader wishes to know more facts, he can go to the Book of the Chronicles of the Kings of Israel or of Judah; but the editor implies that he has given sufficient information to enable one to see the theological significance of the events described. Yet most of our histories of Israel attempt to marshal the facts, and the theories based upon them, in a secularised manner, without any serious attempt to deal with that which was the chief concern of the Biblical writers themselves. The Church cannot afford the luxury of such a seemingly 'objective' approach. Its primary aim must be to view Biblical history through the eyes of its interpreters, grappling with those vital questions of faith and meaning with which the Biblical authors themselves were concerned. This means that the Christian interpreter must take his stand with prophet and apostle in their struggle to hear God's Word of judgment and mercy in the midst of the human crisis. He cannot separate himself from them, from their history, or from their all-absorbing attention to the objective being of God, else he will not hear with them that Gospel which is nothing other than God's proclamation. In separated 'objectivity', he may be able to dissect and to analyse, but he himself will not be involved in the analysis, nor will the proclamation find him as the one to whom it is addressed. Having read the words, he will remain as one who did not hear them.

The first concern of the Church, therefore, must be to hear God's Word in Scripture, and this involves a conscious attempt to live within the atmosphere of Biblical faith, including its eschatology. Only when it does so, can the distance between the past and present, between the Gospel which called the Church into being and the message which the Church must proclaim to this day, be bridged. This means that the Church must understand, come to terms with, and perpetuate the Biblical language and vocabulary as a living factor in its life, liturgy and preaching. *The most important single function of dogmatic theology is the preservation and exposition of the Biblical language as a fitting vehicle for the Gospel as proclaimed by the Church to this day.* Unless theology is able to do this, the Church will be separated from the Biblical source of its continued enlightenment.

Now, as it happens, this point of view is one which today is much debated. Many sincere Christians believe that the Bible must be 'de-mythologised'. Its 'myth' of the will of an anthropomorphic God, of his choosing, judging, destroying, redeeming, resurrecting the people of Israel, of his raising Christ from the dead to sit on his right hand as the Lord of creation, ruling the hosts of angels and men, judging the quick and the dead—all this is felt to be a language without relevance for modern man. The Church's interpretative effort should be to extricate the essence of the Gospel from its mythical and metaphorical trappings; when this is done, it will be in possession of a message which it can proclaim to the world, perhaps in a variety of languages and vocabularies. Liberal idealism of the nineteenth century was perhaps the most successful in this effort. Yet, as previously mentioned, the result was an emphasis on emergent value and on the use of metaphors drawn from organic evolution which separate us sharply from those central claims which the Bible makes for itself.

More recently, certain theologians who emphasise the existentialist nature of the Biblical point of view have concluded that the mythological framework of the Bible may be safely set aside provided we retain the core of the Gospel message, which is to help man understand his own existence in a new way and thus enable him to live a new life. The Cross and Resurrection have little meaning in themselves except as they become concrete or contemporaneous in the life of the faithful. What is essential in the Bible is God's confrontation of man in his existential situation. What are narrated as historical events are without relevance to us except as they bring conflict in the soul and a new understanding of the self in relation to God.

The justification for this type of 'de-mythologising' process (*Entmythologisierung*) depends entirely on what is assumed to be the centre of the Biblical message. The truth which the position contains should not blind us to its one-sided nature. Can such a view come to terms with the Biblical conception of time and history and thus avoid the dangers of docetism? Is there not a hermeneutical danger here of allegorising history and reducing it to religious psychology? There is surely something in the Bible which is prior to confrontation and self-understanding. That is an objective work of God in the history of Israel as a nation and in the historical person of Jesus Christ, a work which shows the impossibility of true life in the *old* order and yet which makes it possible in the *new* order of Christ. Must not the Christian's vocabulary stem from his double status as a pilgrim and sojourner here in this age and also as a member of the new age, inaugurated by God in Christ, which though actually present now is yet to be consummated in all its glory? The Christian cannot avoid or set aside the Biblical view of time, which, though it occasions severe difficulties in the modern mind, is nevertheless the foundation on which the Biblical dimension of faith is placed. Without it one has no means of interpreting the meaning of history, other than as the secular order in which he lives provides it, and he must live without hope in the future which will redeem the present by the power of the God who is the directing Lord of time.

On the other hand, it is a question as to whether the new view has successfully avoided the myth and metaphor it desires to evade. Man does not 'meet' God in precisely the same way that he meets a friend, nor can he 'hear' him with the same ears or 'obey' him with the same obedience. Is not the theme of existential confrontation in itself a form of 'myth', or at least necessarily expressed in terms of metaphor? No religion can exist without the use of metaphor simply because it is impossible for a finite being to speak of the Ultimate in any other way. In speaking of God Biblical writers are openly and frankly anthropomorphic; indeed what more daring and vivid anthropomorphism could be used than that of the Incarnation of Jesus Christ! Our problem, and that of the Biblical writers, is not one of avoiding metaphor but of deciding what type of analogy may best be used to bring out the true nature of God as we know him from his historical revelation. 'To whom then will ye liken God, or what likeness will ye compare unto him?' (Isa. 40.18). It is no accident that the particular metaphors chosen by Israel were used as a weapon against the current naturalisms. The validity of the selection was tested and proven in the warfare against other gods. So rich and many-sided is the selection that it is to be doubted whether the Church can devise any significant improvements. On the contrary, the Church must preserve the original metaphors on which its faith rests, striving always to make clear just what is meant by them and what is not.

Furthermore, since the foundation of the Bible lies in a particular conception of time, it is inevitable that the witness should be interested in both the first and the last things of earth. But in depicting them stories and pictures are used which to the sophisticated of mind have appeared oftentimes as trivial and naive. Yet we possess no other way of speaking of these matters, unless we rob them of the power and beauty which hold our attention and lead us to awe and to reverent worship. To 'de-mythologise' them is to do away with them with nothing to put in their place; and the result is a docetic view of Biblical time. In Biblical faith picture, poetry and reality are inseparably fused. To do away with the pictorial and to translate the poetry into abstract prose means either to do away with the reality or else to create a literal rationalism after the manner of certain extreme fundamentalists which resolves the tension between the known and the unknown.

The problem of the Church, therefore, in bridging the gap between Biblical and present time is not to be resolved by a process of 'de-mythologising'. Instead, it is one of preserving and expounding the relevance of the Biblical vocabulary. To be sure, the Church must never lose its sense of the mystery of God by assuming that metaphor confines or limits him. A tension must always exist between reality and the theological language used to describe it; it is a tension which can be resolved only by separating ourselves from the Biblical God and the Biblical literature which reveals him. Furthermore, there remains the question as to whether we have the right to use the term 'myth' for any portion of Biblical literature, and thus to assume that it is even possible to 'de-mythologise' that literature. When modern theologians revive the term in order to describe those portions of the Bible which deal with the supra-historical, with Creation and eschatology, they should at least make clear that they are using the word in its derived, not primary or original, sense. In the Bible, as distinct from the genuine mythology of polytheism, both the Garden of Eden and the Kingdom of God are not separated from earth or its history; they are firmly fixed within that history. While they may not fit into the framework of time by which we measure human events, they certainly fit into the Biblical sense of historical time, which is nothing else than the time of God's purpose.

(2) The unity of the Bible is not something which can be ascertained or described by a simple or single formula. The two books of the New Testament which appear to expound the Christian significance of the Old Testament by means of the simplest patterns, namely Hebrews and Revelation, are two of the books which had most difficulty in getting into the canon! The Early Church seems to have grasped the Bible's essential unity intuitively in the light of the Risen Christ. And I suspect that this unity is something which is seen most clearly only in the worshipping community, and that those most convinced of the unity are precisely those who experience most difficulty in expressing their conviction in words. We need today to make a new and vigorous attempt to define it, but I doubt that either we or the subsequent generation will be entirely satisfied with the result. That this is so is both the perplexity and the glorious mystery of the Bible which leave us searching even in our certainty.

If the Risen Christ is the fulfilment of, the centre of, and the key to the unity of the Bible, then our most critical problem is the discovery of what he means for the Church's task of interpretation. How, for example, are we to read the Old Testament in the light of Christ? Is Luther's phrase, 'What leads to Christ' (*was Christum treibet*), a principle of selection between the eternal and the temporal? To make a simple assumption that it is such a principle may lead us to attempt an analysis of 'the mind of Christ', whatever we may mean by that phrase, and then to use the result as a yardstick for measuring truth. Yet even some of the teachings of Jesus have a 'situation-conditioned' nature, and our problem is not solved by the over-simplified supposition that everything which we find in the New Testament is in itself more authoritative than anything which we find in the Old. Moreover, since the authority of the Old Testament as Scripture is never challenged in the New, we should find it most difficult to use the latter as the real canon or measuring rod by which the Old Testament may be broken up into its authoritative and unauthoritative parts.

The unity of the Bible in Christ has been demonstrated more commonly in the history of the Church by the use of Christological allegory and typology. Since Christ is the Lord of both Testaments, his Word is to be found in the Old Covenant as well as in the New. Yet in the Old Testament the passages which are clearly and unequivocally Messianic comprise but a small part of the whole. Are we entitled to read in the remainder of the literature a Christology which the words themselves do not imply and of which the authors were seemingly unaware? Taken on its own terms, the Old Testament as a whole does not present Christ to us; it rather prepares the way for Christ. In the past, Christological interpretation of the Old Testament has been tempted to read into the faith of Israel more than was actually there and to erase the Biblical conception of time with its constituent elements, promise and fulfilment.

Yet most of the Church's scholars today appear to be agreed that the key to the Bible is somehow to be found in Jesus Christ. But how is this key to be used? When we confess Christ as Lord, precisely what do we infer regarding hermeneutical method? No one today appears to have the final answer to these questions, or at least an answer which will find general acceptance. The following remarks reflect the present state of the writer's own thinking on these questions, and they must be regarded for what they are: tentative suggestions toward a solution, rather than the completely rounded and concisely argued solution itself.

To confess Christ as Lord of both Testaments is an affirmation of faith without precise content until it is further defined. We are compelled to explain what we mean by Christ in this connection, and to ask whether he achieves his true meaning apart from the doctrine of the Trinity. In itself the conception of the Trinity reveals an awareness of the complexity of the Godhead which defies oversimplified analysis. We are thus warned against the use of over-simplified formulae in the interpretation of the Scripture. The belief in Christ as Lord means little unless God himself is first of all Lord. At a time when most Christians in the World-Church are agreed on the Lordship of Christ as the faith which binds the Churches together, we must not betray the Church's doctrine of Christ by a Christomonism which in practice may resolve the complexity of the Godhead by a new kind of monotheism based on Christ.

If, on the other hand, the true meaning of Christ can be grasped only within the context of the Trinity, then we have made at least one step forward in our search for valid hermeneutical principles. When in a trinitarian context we say that Christ is the Lord of the Old Testament, we do not infer the necessity of, nor are we compelled to use, Christological allegory or typology in interpreting the Old Testament. Instead, we are asserting that Christ shows us the true meaning of what God was doing with the Chosen People, Israel, because we see the end to which all was leading. Thus the initial and intervening steps in the history do not lose their meaning for us, but instead are given new significance because the end provides the key to their intended direction. One cannot set up route markers along a road until he knows what the route is. *Christ is the destination and at the same time the guide* to the true understanding of the Old Testament.

To illustrate: When the Jew reads the Old Testament, he searches for the Law in the first five books. These books he separates from the rest and calls them *The Law* or *Torah*. The Prophets and the Writings are further separated and read solely as commentary on the Torah. The Jew is thus inevitably led to a rather legalistic and static approach to the Scripture. With Christ as the guide, the Christian makes a very different and more dynamic approach to the Old Testament. The Pentateuch is seen to contain something more primary than the Law and it is not separated so sharply from what follows. The very arrangement of the books in the Old Testament shows this difference. The Christian possesses a Bible in which the Hagiographa have been distributed. He does not stop with Deuteronomy before entering the Former Prophets. He goes from Genesis through Kings, Chronicles, and Esther. When and for what reason this order of the books came into being we do not know, though its source must ultimately be sought in the Septuagint. The point is that the Christian's attention is immediately focused, not on the Law, but on the mighty acts of God narrated in a certain and specific history, acts which find their inevitable culmination in the death and Resurrection of Jesus Christ and in the formation of the new *ecclesia*, the New Israel under the New Covenant. Furthermore, the poetic and prophetic books are seen to be more than a commentary on the Law, but actually an integral part of the revelation of God and of the people's response to it in that one history previously given.

Such a view of the Old Testament means that we are not only entitled, but compelled, to employ a rigidly careful exegesis in interpreting what it says in the light of its own historical and conceptual environment. Equally important, we are permitted to recognize God's accommodation of his Word to the people's understanding and the limitations of the people in discerning and applying what they heard. Yet at the same time the Christian doctrine of the Trinity means that even in passages which have nothing directly to do with Christ, the Holy Spirit may confront us with the true God in all his holy majesty, or with God's inescapable will, or with our sin and God's judgment upon it, until we seek and are led in repentance and faith again to Christ. *In hermeneutics we thus do not need to confuse Christ with God the Father nor with God the Holy Spirit*. Nor need we try to use 'The Mind of Christ' as a means of selection between good and bad within the Old Testament, other than as he and his apostles in the New Testament give us explicit direction. Christians have continually tried to objectify some authority so that God's will may likewise be objectified in specific and systematized teachings and programmes. But God has thwarted these efforts, and gives every indication of doing so again and again.

II

Despite the exceedingly complex nature of the problems with which this essay is attempting to deal, it is much easier to discuss them in terms of abstractions than it is actually to employ the proposed solutions as tools in exegesis. Yet the major theological problems can never be solved entirely through abstract discussion. When we try to do so, we are not confronted directly with the energizing power of God's Word, but we are inclined to spend our time in dissection and trisection of each other's opinions, prejudices and inherited patterns of thought. An inductive methodology, in which principles arise from a direct effort to interpret the text, may in the long run be much more fruitful.

Let us, then, turn from general discussion to examine certain specific illustrations of the Bible's message for the social life. In doing so attention must be focused on what the Bible says, on how the teaching of the Old and New Testaments is to be brought together, on what this teaching means for the Church today, and on how we get from the one to the other.

At the Bossey conference a group of theologians arrived at one general rule in interpretative procedure: in social and political matters we should begin with an examination of the New Testament. We should then turn to the Old Testament to study the background in which the New Testament teaching is placed. In this way we should be able 'to grasp the Biblical pattern of human life and society from the standpoint of the whole Bible whose centre is Christ' (*From the Bible to the Modern World*, Geneva, 1947, p. 112; see also pp. 150f. above).

1. Following this procedure, let us refer briefly to the Biblical teaching regarding marriage, because it furnishes a comparatively simple illustration of one type of interpretation. The place to begin is certainly with Jesus' words about the sanctity of marriage, his prohibition of divorce as a revision of Old Testament Law (Mark 10.2-12), and the Apostle Paul's discussion of our bodies as belonging to Christ (I Cor. 6.15) and of the marriage relation as a mystery, a symbol of the relation between Christ and the Church (Eph. 5.22-33). In each case quotations are made from the Old Testament as authoritative references; so we turn to the Old Testament for a careful study of the attitude towards marriage there. We discover that Israel made no radical changes in ancient marriage custom. Hebrew marriage was a civil affair, a transaction between two families which was sealed by a covenant and the presentation of gifts. Israelite Law, while it did not institute polygamy, seems to take the practice for granted (cf. Deut. 21.15-17), though several passages seem to go out of their way to describe the trouble a man gets into when he does have more than one wife. The example of Solomon appeared to later people as so

bad that Deuteronomic Law, whether obeyed is another matter, prohibited the king from multiplying wives to himself 'that his heart turn not away' (Deut. 17.17).

The most important point to consider in the Old Testament is the fact that the faith of Israel made a sharp break with prevailing Near Eastern customs necessary, at least in the minds of certain thinkers. In the tenth- or ninth-century Creation-story monogamy, not polygamy, is envisaged as ordained by God: 'Therefore shall a man leave his father and his mother, and shall cleave unto his wife, and they shall be one flesh'; that is, they shall be as one person (Gen. 2.24). This remarkable statement achieves its true significance only as it is evaluated over against Old Testament custom and the custom of the entire Near East. There is no parallel to it. All that we can say is that the writer has been led by his reflection on the meaning of God's creation of male and female to make this break with ancient custom and to see that monogamy is an institution established by God in the order of Creation. Similarly, Malachi, for theological reasons, roundly condemns divorce as a violation of God's will. It is God who is the witness of the marriage covenant with 'the wife of thy youth', and God hates divorce; it is a violation of a sacred covenant (Mal. 2.14-15).

To this background of theological principle, rather than to social custom, Jesus appealed when he was asked about divorce. As to the law on the subject in Deut. 24.1-4, Jesus says that it was given because of the hardness of people's hearts; that is, it was an accommodation to the imperfections of human nature. (And it is true that Deuteronomic Law does not institute divorce, but attempts to limit it and preclude its abuse.) But, continues Jesus, there is a higher law to be found in the Creation-story. He quotes Gen. 1.27 and 2.24 and concludes in the spirit of Malachi: 'What therefore God hath joined together, let no man put asunder' (Mark 10.2-9).

What kind of a law is it that Jesus is here giving? While phrased in terms of a legal prohibition, it is obviously not a law which can be forced upon people who live in a state of sin. Most of the New Testament Law is not law at all in the ordinary sense. It does not govern; it rather describes the relation of men in the new age, in the Kingdom of God.

The difference between the two uses of the word 'law' may

perhaps be clarified if we recall the distinction we make today between statutory law and natural law; the first governs, the latter describes. Jesus' absolute prohibition of divorce on any grounds cannot be interpreted in a juridical sense, for it is not meant for the court-room. What happens when it is so interpreted is clear from Matt. 5.32 and 19.9, where the Church has softened the prohibition by adding an exception, that of adultery. Nearly all scholars agree that when the early Church tried to apply Jesus' law as a governing law, they were faced with the necessity of adding an exception to the absoluteness of Jesus' teaching. Yet, without question, to Jesus the sacredness of marriage is something established by God; it is a divine ordering. Anything less is compromise and sin.

The dilemma facing the Church in proclaiming this message is occasioned by the fact that while it is the Body of Christ, both it and its members also exist in the old order of sin and compromise. It lives in both the new and the old ages at one and the same time. Thus most non-Roman churches proclaim the truth of the Biblical teaching, while at the same time they permit divorce in the world as it is, striving only to limit it to certain grounds among its members. Today, the vast increase in the divorce rate, even among nominal Christians, is a proof of the weakness of the Church's witness. Nevertheless, we are not in position to prohibit it entirely any more than did the Law of the Old Testament. The situation of the Church finds its parallel, therefore, in the old and new ages of the Bible. When the Law of the new age is objectified and treated in a juridical sense, as the Roman Catholic Church does in prohibiting divorce entirely, then the Law becomes the source and means of sin and compromise, precisely as St. Paul claimed the Law of the old age did. And not only church members but the Church itself becomes involved in self-righteous deception. The Roman Catholic practice of annulment seems a long distance removed from the teaching of Christ in Mark 10, even though it pretends to be true to it. The experience of the Protestant Episcopal Church in attempting to keep even the softened Matthean version of Jesus' teaching is a further case in point. This means that the Law of the old age is necessary, evolving as society is ready for it to evolve. But to achieve the absolute 'Law' of the Kingdom demands a new reconciliation with God in Christ that in him we may become a new creation. Consequently, the Church which seeks its message from the whole Bible must proclaim the Law of both the old and new ages. Yet special emphasis must be laid on the latter, because it is the will of God that the whole creation must one day find its true life in the condition that Law describes.

This illustration of Biblical interpretation raises numerous issues which cannot be dealt with here. As to procedure, we began with the New Testament, then turned to the Old, and then went back to the New. In this instance, the Word of God in the Bible as a whole comes out clearly, all the more so when we look beyond the Bible to its background in the ancient world. Critical, historical, and archaeological study have all played a role in the conclusions presented. The dilemma of the Church today is seen as parallel to that of Biblical men who knew the will of God but who in both Old and New Testaments were faced with the necessity of accommodation and compromise because they were children of faith in a world of sin.

Does God speak only in absolutes or does he also speak in the accommodating laws of the old age? This is a most difficult question for us to face. Yet there is no doubt that the writers of both Deuteronomy and Matthew believed that the will of God was also expressed in the accommodation. I suspect that our conclusion must be, however, that while the will of God for our own compromises must be earnestly sought, those which we find in the Bible have a temporal and illustrative relevance and are not necessarily binding upon us in any literal fashion.

When we say that we have found the Word of God in the Bible regarding the institution of marriage, how do we know that we are right? Is it because Christ or the Bible says so? Partly; and partly also for numerous reasonable but nonetheless secondary reasons. In the last analysis we recognize the Word of God here because it is truth, truth which God confirms in us, truth which enlightens us and apart from which we would still be in darkness.

2. A second illustration which might be treated briefly is difficult to choose. Social and economic relationships form a vast and complicated topic, but they can all be gathered together under the law of neighbourly love. This is the law which is absolutely basic to the Biblical ethic. The difficulty with it in the Church has been its exceedingly general nature so that it is so easily

converted into a sentimentality without real meaning. Yet, when the Church divides on nearly every other issue, it has always remained united in the faith that this is God's fundamental requirement of men. All the more reason, therefore, that we should search the Bible to see what specific content is given it.

In the New Testament every commandment given to govern the relations of men, including the Decalogue, is held to be fulfilled in the commandment of love (cf. Mark 12.31; Rom. 13.8; Gal. 5.14). It reaches its fullest expression in the bond which faith in Jesus Christ creates in the Christian fellowship, a bond which transcends every human barrier. Man is thus deprived of all right to think himself superior to anyone in his own generation or in past generations, for all are one in Jesus Christ whose Kingdom embraces the faithful in all generations (Luke 13.28-30, etc.). Human love in its deepest sense, therefore, is not a natural possession; it is derivative, a gift of God in Christ. As such, it deprives men of all those distinctions which occasion injustice. In substance, it is the Kingdom of God and his righteousness in which marriage, the state, and all human institutions as presently known, are done away. For, as Christ said to Pilate, 'My Kingdom is not of this world' (John 18.36).

In other words, the New Testament law of love in all its depth and profundity, is one which does not govern but describes the relations of man in the new age, the new Kingdom of God in Christ. When we fail to recognize it as such, we identify in some measure our present love with true love, the tension between the two orders of existence is relaxed, and we fall into self-righteousness. The very law of love, therefore, when treated as a juridical law of the present worldly order, becomes a breeder of sin.

Yet what are we to do? We live in the world where distinctions exist, where relative choices must be made, where men are organized in vast impersonal corporations which in the power of a technical civilization arm the corporate will into a destructive power previously unknown. Obviously, the New Testament contains no explicit programme of social action for the Church to proclaim to such a world, precisely because it is not interested in framing worldly systems. We do find, of course, instructions by the apostles to their communities with regard to earthly institutions. These are of great interest, but their authority for us would seem to be largely illustrative, clearly distinct from the authority of the central message of the New Testament. They are the Apostles' attempts to apply the Gospel, and they belong to the order of what the Apostle Paul called his own word, not the Lord's. In view of this fact, it is a question as to whether the churches possess the right to divide so sharply over certain specific New Testament teachings or practices, such as the Apostle Paul's advice regarding the Christian and the state or the orders of church government.

Be that as it may be, we should now turn to the Old Testament source from which the commandment of love is derived. There in Lev. 19 we find its context, one totally different from that of the New Testament, because the Israelite situation was totally different from that of the early Church. It is set in the midst of social legislation aimed at correcting the abuses of an organized society. We find it to be a hortatory summary of the motivation behind a detailed social ethic determined by the ordinances of God, something we sorely miss in the New Testament. In Lev. 19 we find instructions concerning gleaning, that the poor and the sojourner may get food; against stealing, false swearing, oppression; about wages, gossip, impartiality in court; about honouring the aged, helping the deaf and the blind, caring for trees, cattle and crops, forbidding sexual irregularities, mutilation of the body, unjust weights and measures, etc. The reason for all these specific regulations is given in verses 17-18: 'Thou shalt not hate thy brother in thy heart. . . . Thou shalt not take vengeance nor bear ill will against the children of thy people, but thou shalt love thy neighbour as thyself. I am Yahweh!' As the context indicates, the word 'neighbour' here (Hebrew, 'friend') actually means 'countryman' or fellow Israelite. Verse 34 (as also Deut. 10.19) extends the law to the sojourner. God's command to the Israelite is thus to love every member of his community; and further it is clear that he is to do so regardless of any attitude of love or hate exhibited toward him (cf. verse 17*b*; Exod. 23.4-5, where the enemy is specified; Prov. 25.21). While nothing is said here regarding love for those who are not members of the Israelite community, it should be noted that the Law of Israel was given for the governing, not of the world, but of the covenant people. The wider reaches of the law of love could only be faced when decisions were being made regarding the relevance of the whole Law for the governance, not of a political, but solely of a spiritual and world-wide community (cf. Mark 12.31; Gal. 5.14; James 2.8). The seeming particularism of the law, while often emphasized today, is thus not a relevant factor to be considered.

Though cast in legal form, the law is obviously not an ordinance which can be enforced by a human judge or court. Yet both lawgiver and judge are God. Before the divine Judge every member of the community has an equal status, and God's requirement of the people who acknowledge him as their Lord is that they must treat each other with a mutual respect and concern which transcend legal duty and are rooted in the recognition of a common Lord of a common humanity. While the law appears only in Leviticus, it is an excellent summary of the intent of the whole law governing social relationships in Israel, and it is the ground from which the prophetic protest against social iniquity sprang.

Now there is something very appealing about this law in its Old Testament setting. There one simply cannot sentimentalize it. Alongside every generality is a concrete illustration or application to show precisely what is meant; in fact, the general law is derived from and summarizes the meaning of the older specific laws. The reason it appeals to us is because the Old Testament is nearer the world in which we actually live. Here is the attempt by social legislation to alleviate injustice in the old order, one in which we too exist. Yet it has always been obvious that the Church cannot proclaim the *specific* regulations of the Old Testament as the Word of God for a subsequent age or another civilization (e.g. the impossibility of transferring the prohibition against interest or the institutions of the sabbatical or jubilee years, the latter never more than ideals in any case).

What, then, is the authority of the Old Testament in these matters? *First*, we are led by the Holy Spirit to a true knowledge of the centre of sovereignty in this universe, and to our state as responsible creatures, who find their true life in willing obedience to the Creator and Lord. *Second*, we are provided with concrete illustrations of what that obedience means; and the Word of God, convicting us of our social sins by means of these illustrations, impels us to follow similar paths toward the alleviation of injustice in our own order. Neither here nor in the New Testament, therefore, is the Church given a specific programme to proclaim and support in the present world, but in the light of God's revelation it must denounce iniquity and idolatry and, following the lead of the Biblical illustrations, must encourage men to seek the proper specific answers today.

Third, the one God who rules both the old and new ages has revealed his Law for the old age, a Law known to be valid because it is not set aside by Christ. Instead, the latter accepts it, takes it into the new age by deepening and fulfilling it, by writing it, not in outward codes, but on men's hearts. It is this Law which the Church must proclaim to the present world. What is it? How do we find it?

The Pentateuch preserves only fragments of Israelite jurisprudence, but all of them are interpreted as God's revealed Law for the ordering of the national life, including the religious cultus. The 'secular' or casuistic law (cf. Exod. 21.18-19 for the type) is closely related in formulation and content to the characteristic law of other people of the time, though the command or apodictic type is peculiar to Israel, expressing with its 'Thou shalt' the strong theocratic relationship between God and people which existed in the covenant.[1] Furthermore, the Law as it now stands consists not only of the original Mosaic nucleus, but also of the successive adaptations and expansions made necessary by the changing conditions of subsequent society. Consequently, it is not surprising that repeated attempts were made to distinguish the essential elements of the Law, to which all else must conform or else become a means of rebellion against the divine Lord. In Exodus and Deuteronomy it is clear from the arrangement of the material that the Decalogue was considered as the sum and heart of the Law. We know that it continued to be so considered in the early Christian community.[2] From Deut. 6.4 and 10.12-13 we infer that the requirements of the Decalogue will be fulfilled, if Israel shall exhibit an intense and unwavering love for God which shall issue in glad, whole-hearted obedience. From the prophets we infer that the essence of the Law is to hate evil and to love the good (Amos 5.14-15), to do justly, to love *hesed* (loyalty to the obligations of the covenant), to walk humbly with God (Mic. 6.8, etc.).

These brief formulations were necessary because without them

[1] Cf. A. Alt, *Die Ursprünge des israelitischen Rechts* (Leipzig, 1934).

[2] See Robert Grant, 'The Decalogue in Early Christianity', *Harvard Theological Review* (Cambridge, Mass., U.S.A.), 40 (1947), pp. 1ff.

there would have been no way by which the shifting forms of society could have been guided or interpreted. They indicate also a realization of the danger of all purely formal legalism; for it is one thing to administer the common law solely on the basis of legal precedents, but quite another to administer it with due regard for the purpose of God in the life of man. Today the Church may proclaim such brief formulations, and others it may make itself from Biblical law, as God's will for the present world. In fact, if it is to take the election of prophet and apostle seriously as a guide to its own election, the Church is compelled to proclaim this law.

Yet we should note carefully its setting. In theological circles there has been considerable discussion of natural law in its relation to revealed Law. Many scholars have concluded that we must of necessity make considerable use of natural law ethics as a supplement and ally of Biblical ethics. Yet it is quite clear that Biblical ethics are not to be sharply distinguished from natural law ethics. In ethical matters the Bible borrowed widely from every available source. The Pentateuchal Law, the wisdom of Proverbs, the rabbinical background of certain of Jesus' teachings, are excellent illustrations. It would appear that Biblical ethics must be interpreted as including and meant to include what we today term natural law ethics. The important point is the new framework or setting in which ethical teachings are placed. The significance of no culture or civilization is to be judged solely by its ethics, but by the *Weltanschauung* which gives them meaning. Ethics, whether derived from natural law or somewhere else, do not exist in a vacuum. The Biblical *Weltanschauung* transforms the setting, the meaning, and the relevance of all ethics, primarily by placing them under a new sovereignty, that of the Covenant-God.

Furthermore, the detailed ordering of man's social, economic, and political life in the Old Testament is not a part of the order of Creation, though some try in a measure to make it so in order to relate it more easily to natural law. Instead, the ordering of the common life was viewed as the great redeeming act of God which stood at the beginning of Israel's national history. Consequently, the Old Testament Torah was conceived, not primarily as a legal burden to be born, but as God's assurance of a perfect, peaceful, and fruitful life on this earth. Changes and adaptations in the form of society are thus possible, differing emphases in detail among the leaders are permitted, because all Law and all institutions must express the *active* will of the *living* God and form an adequate response to his redeeming acts. Later Judaism, against which St. Paul was arguing, tended to regard the Law as a static entity, but the prophetic criticism of all institutions, including the Law, indicates that a purely legalistic view of the Sinai covenant is not in keeping with the deepest insight concerning its meaning (cf. Jer. 11).

The unsolved problem of the Old Testament, however, is this: Is the Law, which is God's promise and guide to true life in this earth, something that man because of sin cannot keep even though he wants so desperately to do so? Is his life to be lived solely in hope, while he continually suffers punishment through divine judgment? The Law is the guide to life; but since in it man finds sin and judgment, is God's promise in the Law illusory? The New Testament opens at this point, proclaiming God's saving act in Jesus Christ for the sinner. It does not abrogate the Law, nor the essential revelation of God about life in this earth. Instead it responds to the unanswered question: how can man keep God's Law and how can he be saved from his continued sin of rebellion? The answer is the new creation, the reconciliation with God in Jesus Christ.

This treatment is necessarily brief, and it undoubtedly raises more problems than it solves. Its thesis is, however, that by means of trinitarian hermeneutics the Old Testament can be found to possess a social and political message which the Church must proclaim to this world. At the same time the Church also must proclaim the new order of salvation, the new age in Christ, toward which the world must inevitably move, because God has so determined it by his grace. This new order, grasped by faith, is now actually present in the invisible Church, even though inadequately represented in the visible churches. But the God who is Lord of both ages will not allow us the luxury at this moment, this interim, of retiring to the one order while leaving the other to take care of itself. The two orders of existence interpenetrate, and in the Cross God calls, he elects us to strive by might and main with the old age, though by faith we also live in the new. We are to do so, not through the hope of any material reward for ourselves now, but because the holy God is to be served and because life achieves its meaning in the service to which one is called.

6

GUIDING PRINCIPLES FOR THE INTERPRETATION OF THE BIBLE

as accepted by the Ecumenical Study Conference, held at Wadham College, Oxford, from June 29th to July 5th, 1949

Our conference has endeavoured, on the basis of the work of earlier conferences, to develop specific principles of interpretation, for the use of the Bible in relation to social and political questions. The Christian's authority lies in the will of God. It is agreed that the Bible stands in a unique position in mediating that will to us. In our study together we have used Jer. 7.1-15 as a test case in discovering the extent of agreement in the application of hermeneutical principles. We have found a measure of agreement that surprised us all. We submit the following statements as a general consensus:

I *The necessary theological presuppositions of Biblical interpretation*

(*a*) It is agreed that the Bible is our common starting point, for there God's Word confronts us, a Word which humbles the hearers so that they are more ready to listen and to discuss than they are to assert their own opinions.

(*b*) It is agreed that the primary message of the Bible concerns God's gracious and redemptive activity for the saving of sinful man that he might create in Jesus Christ a people for himself. In this, the Bible's central concern, an authoritative claim is placed upon man and he is called upon to respond in faith and obedience throughout the whole of his life and work. The law of love has always a binding and compelling hold upon us, and in it we encounter the inescapable will of God. On the other hand, in the more specific laws provided for the detailed organisation of the social life of a people who lived under conditions different from our own, we should through reverent and serious study seek to distinguish in the light of God's revelation in Christ the permanently binding from that of purely local and temporal significance.

(*c*) It is agreed that the starting point of the Christian interpreter lies within the redeemed community of which by faith he is a member.

(*d*) It is agreed that the centre and goal of the whole Bible is Jesus Christ. This gives the two Testaments a perspective in which Jesus Christ is seen both as the fulfilment and the end of the Law.

(*e*) It is agreed that the unity of the Old and the New Testaments is not to be found in any naturalistic development, or in any static identity, but in the ongoing redemptive activity of God in the history of one people, reaching its fulfilment in Christ. Accordingly it is of decisive importance for hermeneutical method to interpret the Old Testament in the light of the total revelation in the person of Jesus Christ, the Incarnate Word of God, from which arises the full Trinitiarian faith of the Church.

(*f*) It is agreed that allegorical interpretations which were not intended by the Biblical authors are arbitrary and their use may be a disservice to the proper recognition of Biblical authority. But Christian exegesis has been justified in recognising as divinely established a certain correspondence between some events and teachings of the Old and of the New Testament.

(*g*) It is agreed that, although we may differ in the manner in which tradition, reason and natural law may be used in the interpretation of Scripture, any teaching that clearly contradicts the Biblical position cannot be accepted as Christian.

II *The interpretation of a specific passage*

(*a*) It is agreed that one must start with an historical and critical examination of the passage. This includes:

1 The determination of the text;
2 The literary form of the passage;
3 The historical situation, the *Sitz im Leben*;

4 The meaning which the words had for the original author and hearer or reader;
5 The understanding of the passage in the light of its total context and the background out of which it emerged.

(*b*) It is agreed that in the case of an Old Testament passage, one must examine and expound it in relation to the revelation of God to Israel both before and after its own period. Then the interpreter should turn to the New Testament in order to view the passage in that perspective. In this procedure the Old Testament passage may receive limitation and correction, and it may also disclose in the light of the New Testament a new and more profound significance, unknown to the original writer.

(*c*) It is agreed that in the case of a New Testament passage one should examine it in the light of its setting and context; then turn to the Old Testament to discover its background in God's former revelation. Returning again to the New Testament one is able to see and expound the passage in the light of the whole scope of *Heilsgeschichte*. Here our understanding of a New Testament passage may be deepened through our apprehension of the Old.

III *The discovery of the Biblical teaching on a specific social or political issue*

(*a*) It is agreed that one must begin with a direct study of the Biblical text in relation to a given problem; otherwise the general principles which we establish will reflect more the presuppositions of our own time than the messsage of the Bible. Only then may we safely deduce applications for our own situation.

(*b*) It is agreed that in examining a particular modern problem we should begin with the New Testament teaching. In the light of this we should consider the Old Testament evidence as well, in order to view the problem in the light of God's total revelation. In following this procedure, historical differences in the various parts of Scripture must not be overlooked; otherwise the amassing of various texts may be done in too facile a manner and the Bible made to present a united witness on a topic which in fact it does not do. Furthermore, care should be used to see the correct proportions so that too much emphasis may not be placed on a single passage and the correct Biblical perspective be lost.

(*c*) It is agreed that the Biblical teaching on social and political issues must be viewed in the light of the tension between life in the kingdoms of this world and participation in the Kingdom of God. While there has not been time in this conference to explore our understanding of the relation of ethics to eschatology,[1] we are agreed that the scriptural teaching of the two ages has an important bearing upon the way in which a specific social or political issue is to be interpreted.

IV *The application of the Biblical message to the modern world*

(*a*) It is agreed that if we are to receive the guidance of the Holy Spirit through the Scriptures, we must discover the degree to which our particular situation is similar to that which the Bible presents. It must be remembered that absolute identity of situation is never found, and therefore the problem of adaptation becomes acute. Nevertheless in each new situation we must allow ourselves to be guided by the Bible to a knowledge of the will of God.

(*b*) It is agreed that the Bible speaks primarily to the Church, but it also speaks through the Church to the world inasmuch as the whole world is claimed by the Church's Lord. The Church can best speak to the world by becoming the Church remade by the Word of God.

(*c*) It is agreed that in applying the Biblical message to our day, interpreters diverge because of differing doctrinal and ecclesiastical traditions, differing ethical, political, and cultural outlooks, differing geographical and sociological situations, differing temperaments and gifts. It is, however, an actual experience within the Ecumenical Movement, that when we meet together, with presuppositions of which we may be largely unconscious, and bring these presuppositions to the judgment of Scripture, some of the very difficulties are removed which prevent the Gospel from being heard. Thus the Bible itself leads us back to the living Word of God.

MEMBERS OF THE CONFERENCE

Professor C. T. Craig, Madison, N.J., U.S.A.
Professor V. E. Devadutt, Serampore, Bengal, India

[1] See on this problem the report of two previous ecumenical study conferences (London, 1946, and Bossey, 1947), *From the Bible to the Modern World* (published by the Study Department of the World Council of Churches, Geneva).

Professor C. H. Dodd, Cambridge, England
Professor W. Eichrodt, Basle, Switzerland
Professor G. Florovsky, New York, U.S.A.
Professor J. Marsh, Oxford, England
Dr. G. Mayeda, Japan
D. L. Munby, Oxford, England
Professor N. W. Porteous, Edinburgh, Scotland
Canon A. Richardson, Durham, England (*Chairman*)
Professor E. Schlink, Heidelberg, Germany
Dr. W. Schweitzer, Geneva, Switzerland (*Secretary*)
Rev. O. S. Tomkins, London, England
Dr. T. F. Torrance, Aberdeen, Scotland
Professor L. J. Trinterud, Chicago, U.S.A.
Professor G. E. Wright, Chicago, U.S.A.

PRESENT ONLY ON THE LAST DAYS

Bishop A. Nygren, Lund, Sweden
Professor G. Staehlin, Erlangen, Germany

YOUTH DELEGATES

A. Adegbola, Nigeria
J. A. Atger, Saint-Martin-le-Vinoux par Grenoble, France
N. S. Booth, Boston, U.S.A.
J. Gibbs, Preston, England

Part Four

SOME SPECIFIC APPLICATIONS

1

THE CHURCH'S RESPONSIBILITY FOR THE WORLD

by

HENDRIKUS BERKHOF

Translated from the German

I *Definition of the subject*

The word 'Church' is used here to mean the community of Jesus Christ, as described in the New Testament. Its Old Testament counterpart is significant for us, but only indirectly. In the New Testament 'world' is a kaleidoscopic conception. Nor does the distinction between *Kosmos* and *Aion*, in any case slight, take us very far (*Kosmos* stresses extension in space, *Aion* existence in time). Our title implies that we are only concerned with a particular meaning of the word, namely mankind in the widest sense, but those only who do not yet, or who no longer, belong to the Church. 'World' may also refer to those whom the Church has challenged for a decision, to whom it has already completely discharged its responsibility. By its response, the world has become either the Church or 'the world' in a specific sense. In the Bible, and especially in the Johannine writings, the world often means the power that resists and hates Christ and his community (John 14.17, 15.18ff., 16.33, 17.14; I John 2.15, 5.4f.). World and Church are here in complete opposition. The Church can no longer feel a conscious and defined responsibility; she has already discharged it. The world is the result of the discharged responsibility and the consequent decision (John 15.24). In its relation with this world the Church can only suffer (John 16.33). In this paper 'world' will be used in a more neutral sense for human beings considered apart from their decision for or against Christ.

Our subject does not include, except indirectly, all that is predicted of the relation of God or Christ to the world, and finds its classical expression in John 3.16. In God's plan of salvation Church and world are related to each other in a variety of ways. The world is an object of God's care. In it the Church is enabled to live and grow, that the world may thereby become the Church. The covenant with Noah is the foundation on which the covenants with Abraham and Moses, the new covenant in Christ and the activity of the Holy Ghost may develop. Hence the intercession 'for kings and all that are in high places; that we may lead a tranquil and quiet life in all godliness and gravity. This is good and acceptable in the sight of God our Saviour; who willed that all men should be saved, and come to the knowledge of the truth' (I Tim. 2.2-4; Revised Version here and elsewhere in this chapter).

At the same time the Church is the harbinger and prophecy of the new world, the anticipation of mankind in the new aeon, created for this purpose in and from this world: 'that we should be a kind of first fruits of his creatures' (Jas. 1.18). So far no conscious, defined attitude of the Church towards the world has emerged.

Where such an attitude is indicated in the New Testament, it is primarily an *antithetic* relationship. The world, even when it is a world which does not yet know Christ and has not yet consciously rejected him, is a power of seduction. It threatens to involve Christians in its own remoteness from God and to draw them away from Christ. Therefore in the New Testament the main emphasis is placed not on the responsibility of the Church for the world, but on the command to flee from the world. 'Know ye not that the friendship of the world is enmity with God?' (Jas. 4.4; cf. Rom. 12.2; I Cor. 7.31; Phil. 2.15; Gal. 6.14; Col. 2.20; Jas. 1.27; I Pet. 1.14, 4.1-3, etc.). This antithetic relation has some bearing on our problem, but is not immediately relevant. Christians must beware lest the seduction of the world tear them away from Christ.

The question should therefore now be put in this way: Are there in the New Testament clear injunctions which should determine the relation of the Church to a world for which it is consciously responsible? The answer is certainly: yes. There are many such expressions in the New Testament which we will now review.

II *Evangelisation*

Our first reference is to the missionary commission, as we find it in Matt. 28.19, or even more explicitly for our purpose in Mark 16.15: 'Go ye into all the world and preach the Gospel to the whole creation.' This word can be taken as the epitome of all that will be said later of the responsibility of the Church for the world. Christ was speaking to the Apostles. They are his representatives (Luke 10.16): 'He that heareth you, heareth me.' As he is in the world for the world's sake, so are they, but not to the exclusion of others. The Apostles are the prototype and the pattern of the Church. As they are called out of the world into fellowship with Christ for the purpose of carrying the Gospel of Christ out again into the world, so should the Church be also; called to follow and to witness. The following is the basis of the witness, the witness is the purpose of the following. The two are as close as breathing in and out. So the community is described in I Pet. 2.9, as follows: 'But ye are an elect race, a royal priesthood, a holy nation, a people for God's own possession, that ye may shew forth the excellencies of him who called you out of darkness into his marvellous light.'

When the New Testament speaks of evangelisation and preaching, we naturally think first of the spoken word. The Church has a responsibility to the world that through its service the world may learn of God's great act of salvation in Jesus Christ. This knowledge can only be propagated through the word spoken or written. Consequently, the New Testament lays the chief stress on the responsibility of preaching. Proofs of this familiar fact need not be cited; but it would be wrong to let the responsibility towards the world be exhausted in preaching. In the light of the New Testament this would be inadmissibly simple and superficial. Here we come face to face with what has often in recent times been called 'The Exemplary Existence of the Church'.

III *The exemplary existence of the Church*

The Church of Christ, called out of the world in opposition to it, has a fully independent position of its own: '... that ye may be blameless and harmless, children of God without blemish in the midst of a crooked and perverse generation, among whom ye are seen as lights in the world' (Phil. 2.15). Though existing in antithesis to the world, the Church does not sever all relations with it; on the contrary, it enters into a new relation with it, and that not incidentally, but of set purpose. By this antithesis it intends to enter into a specific relation with the world, namely, that of opposition and evangelism. As the Church in the world, it is itself part of the message. Its mere presence makes it a witnessing Church. Its very antithesis makes it a pattern. The children of God 'are seen as lights in the world', and they may and must both know and intend this. To point to this function is to spur to action. The passage quoted starts with 'Do all things without murmurings and disputings that ye may be blameless and harmless'.

That the contrast of Church and world are directed at the world appears even more clearly in Eph. 5.8-14. St. Paul says in verse 11: 'Have no fellowship with the unfruitful works of darkness, but rather reprove them.' This reproof must be interpreted by verse 8: 'Walk as children of light.' 'But all things [i.e. these "unfruitful works of darkness"], when they are reproved, are made manifest by the light', verse 13. The Church discharges its responsibility to the world by existing as light. This fact was expressed once for all by our Lord in the Sermon on the Mount, when he said to his Apostles, the prototypes of the Christian community: 'Ye are the light of the world. A city set on a hill cannot be hid. Neither do men light a lamp, and put it under a bushel, but on the stand; and it shineth unto all that are in the house. Even so let your light shine before men, that they may see your good works, and glorify your Father which is in heaven' (Matt. 5.14-16). Here Christ himself declares that the independent existence of the community is not an end in itself. It is there to be seen, so that through the proclamation of the Gospel mankind may come to glorify God. And that is not all. The community must be conscious of its purpose. Christ is not speaking as a law-giver. He says: 'Ye *are* the light of the world.' But only by constantly remembering what it has and is in Christ can the community reach this goal. What Christ says here is said also in the First Epistle of St. Peter: 'Having your behaviour seemly among the Gentiles; that, wherein they may speak against you as evil-doers, they may by your good works, which they behold, glorify God in the day of visitation' (2.12). But this does not imply that the existence of the Church will always issue in blessing. We heard that the works of darkness are made manifest by the light (Eph.

5.13). But the darkness does not wish this to happen. It is only through God's grace that it admits it (John 3.20). The existence of the Church is effectual to save or to condemn. Noah by building the Ark 'condemned the world' (Heb. 11.7). Of course, the existence of the Church cannot take the place of the Holy Spirit. But it is used by the Holy Spirit to challenge the world. The Church discharges its responsibility by existing, if it is conscious of being used in this way, if it affirms this use, and if it lives and prays in the hope that it will be used to bless, not to condemn.

The argument of this paper does not require us to discuss at length what this existence as a pattern means in concrete terms. The Church has exactly the same temporal problems as the world. But it has its own way of solving them or, when they are insoluble, of bearing them. For it lives by forgiveness and expectation. That makes it possible for it to see and to deal with things in a different way, in the light of these divine facts. By strict monogamy, conjugal affection and the refusal of unchastity, by the treatment of women, the nurture of children and the relief of the needy, by a neighbourly relationship between master and slave, and so forth (Eph. 5 and 6, Col. 3 and 4, and elsewhere), the Church lives its own exemplary existence, lives it in antithesis to the world, but with the purpose of winning the world thereby to life in Christ.

So this existence, when its purpose is considered, must be translated into the loving service of one's neighbour, as indeed is done comprehensively in the New Testament. This translation brings out three points: how fundamental is this responsibility for the world as the expression of the Great Commandment (Matt. 22.39); secondly, how closely existence and preaching of the Gospel are bound up with each other, for evangelism is also, and indeed primarily, the fulfilment of the command to love (see the next section); and, thirdly, that the Christian knows that just as Christ lived to serve, so must he too serve his neighbour. Thereby the phrase 'exemplary existence' escapes being misunderstood by transference to some remote and ideal region. Not only is there reference to the world, but the world itself is being drawn into the existent Church. For example, 'So then, as we have opportunity, let us work that which is good toward all men, and especially toward them that are of the household of the faith' (Gal. 6.10).

In this connection, two marks of the existent Church must be specially noticed. First, the *unity* which the Church has in Christ and which is there in order 'that the world may believe that thou didst send me' (John 17.21), as Christ prayed. And St. Paul points to *divine worship*, in the spirit and orderliness of which the world should feel the presence of God: 'But if all prophesy, and there come in one unbelieving or unlearned, he is reproved by all, he is judged by all; the secrets of his heart are made manifest; and so he will fall down on his face and worship God, declaring that God is among you indeed' (I Cor. 14.24-25).

IV *Preaching and existence*

These two ways in which the Church expresses its responsibility for the world are seen in the New Testament as an indissoluble unity. One is not more or less important than the other, still less are they alternatives. The statements in Matt. 5.16 and I Pet. 2.12, that the existence of the Church should cause the world to glorify God, clearly require that existence should comprise much more than the behaviour beheld. For in its mere existence the world cannot 'see' God. That the foundation and secret of its existence is God, the Father of Jesus Christ, can only be made known to the world by means of the word, by preaching. In this connection it is significant that the existence of the Church is so often described as light. In the language of the New Testament, light is that which uncovers, which illuminates, which reveals the facts. It is one of the key-words describing God's revelation. In the Johannine writings 'light' and 'life' are intentionally placed side by side in characterising the revelation, e.g. 'In him was life, and the life was the light of men' (John 1.4). Life refers more to pure being, light to consciousness, though no pedantic distinction should be made. A Church cannot be called light merely because it exists biologically; it must aim at consciousness of its environment. The element of appealing, evangelising, recruiting is clearly implied in the texts quoted. A Church which should try to discharge its responsibility towards the world merely by its preaching or merely by its behaviour would have quitted the field of the New Testament.

Here attention must be drawn especially to I Pet. 3.15. The First Epistle of Peter refers already in 1.11 to the existence of the Church as an example, which must convict its opponents of their wickedness. In this connection, we read in I Pet. 3.15, 'being ready always to give answer to every man that asketh you a reason concerning the hope that is in you'. Here preaching as the answer to the curiosity awakened in the world by the existence, is the natural sequel. Preaching is the necessary explanation of the existence. The existence is the indispensable illustration of the preaching.

V *Intercession*

It goes without saying that to preaching and exemplary existence must be added intercession. For God alone can give power to the preaching. He alone can turn our words into his Word. He alone can lead us to obedience, to an existence which is not darkness but light, and he alone can make this existence (which in itself can be interpreted psychologically and sociologically in all sorts of ways) into a proclamation. An appeal to the world will constantly pray for this miracle of the Holy Spirit, i.e. intercede for the world that it may come to know the truth. Such intercession is frequently mentioned in the New Testament (Acts 13.3; Eph. 6.18f.; Col. 4.3; II Thess. 3.1). At the same time this intercession extends further. We mentioned at the beginning the call to pray 'for kings and all that are in high places' with the purpose that 'all men should be saved and come to the knowledge of the truth' (I Tim. 2.2-4). Definite presuppositions underlie the practice of responsibility for the world. It is in order that this responsible activity may extend to all mankind that God in his patience maintains the world in these last days (Mark 13.10; II Pet. 3.9). Therefore the Church has a very special interest in the maintenance of the world and its orders, natural as well as social. Hence the special intercession for those 'in high places, that we may lead a tranquil and quiet life in all godliness and gravity'.

VI *Action in public life*

The point just made carries us a step further. In his attitude to the orders, a Christian expresses his responsibility for the world. If he prays that chaos may be checked and the orders maintained, he will wish to exert himself for this purpose. *Ora et labora!* His first step will be grateful submission. This is the most important form it takes in the New Testament (Rom. 13.1-7; I Pet. 2.11-17). Next he will gratefully use the orders and make them serve his purpose (Acts 16.37 and 25.11). But he will do both these things with constant reference to God's design for the world and his own responsibility in it. Where the world-orders oppose this design and this responsibility, he can only disobey (Acts 4.19, 5.29), and as a consequence suffer (John 16.33; Rev. 7.13-17). It follows as a matter of course that this attitude can and must lead to positive political action to maintain and improve the world systems. This is not stressed in the New Testament, a fact which is easily understood when we consider the political structure of the Roman Empire and the social and political position of the tiny Christian communities.

VII *The Church's office as watchman*

This expression has lately come into current use to describe the responsibility which the Church has in political, social, economic, technical and cultural affairs. No only must church members co-operate in them gratefully and critically, but the Church as such should raise her voice in public life, especially where she sees that God's command is disregarded and his purpose for the orders thereby menaced. This office of the Church to be a watchman, to proclaim the reign of Christ over all spheres of life, is only an extension of what the New Testament says about the responsibility of the Church for the world. That this particular duty is hardly mentioned is natural in view of what was said at the end of the previous paragraph. But we must point out two hints: first, the remarkable appeal of the prisoner Paul to the Emperor (Acts 25.11). On personal grounds this appeal was unnecessary and this far-reaching decision hardly to be explained. Paul was determined to go to Rome. He was determined to penetrate with the Gospel to the nodal point where all the threads were gathered and decisions for the whole world made. That is why the Book of the Acts can end with apparent abruptness. Luke has achieved his object when he has related how the Gospel reached the hub of the world. For it is there, and thence to the whole empire, that the Word of God must ring out. This is no more than a hint. It would be possible to interpret Paul's appeal to the Emperor differently or not at all.

Nor is the second hint entirely clear. Paul says in Eph. 3.8, that 'unto me was this grace given, to preach unto the Gentiles . . . to the intent that now unto the principalities and the powers in the heavenly places might be made known through the Church the manifold wisdom of God'. What does this mean? The powers in the heavenly places or in the air, which are the enemies of Christ (Col. 2.15) and wish to separate us from him (Rom. 8.38ff.), appear as the so-called στοιχεῖα τοῦ κόσμου, the 'rudiments of the world' (Col. 2.8 and 20 in connection with 15ff. and Gal. 4.3 and 9). These rudiments are for instance the tradition of the Gentiles, Jewish legalism, public opinion. One might say they are the demonic orders. They can separate us from Christ, like the modern State, technics or capitalism today. But since Christ has 'made a show of them openly, triumphing over them' (Col. 2.15), the Church must demonstrate their essential powerlessness, by word and deed, by witness and resistance. Here, if this exegesis is correct, we catch a glimpse of the Church's office as a watchman.

VIII *The relation of the Old Testament and the New Testament*

At this point we can no longer dispense with the Old Testament. It is precisely the Church's office as a watchman, a mere outline in the New Testament, which is broadly drawn in the Old Testament. The Old Testament hardly knows anything of a relationship between God's people and the world. Israel is called out of the world, and only through Christ can all nations be blessed (Gen. 12.3). The nations are certainly there, but either as instruments of God's design for Israel or as vessels of his wrath (oracles of judgment upon the nations in the great prophets), or as both (Isa. 10). Evangelistic responsibility makes an isolated appearance in the Book of Jonah. But in another aspect the world is everywhere present. Israel is the closest association of Church and State. It is a nation among the nations; at the same time it is God's people, and as such exists in a double state. It has priests and a king too. And the king must not officiate as a priest, e.g. Saul in I Sam. 13.8-14; Uzziah in II Chron. 26.16-21. A prophet is associated with the king (Nathan-David, Isaiah-Ahaz and Hezekiah, Jeremiah-Jehoiakim and Zedekiah, etc.). Israel is, so to speak, an eschatological paradigm, a pointer towards the relationship God wishes there to be between the Church and the world. Here we see a piece of the world that is entirely appropriated by the Word of God and is stamped with it in every corner of its political and social life (e.g. the sabbatical year, Lev. 25). The Church's office of watchman is exhibited with enormous energy in the prophetic denunciations of political and social conditions (the major prophets, Amos, etc.).

From this point the New Testament retreats. The New Testament Church plays a missionary rôle in the heathen Roman Empire. Church and world are not as close to each other as in the Old Testament. The radius of responsibility varies with circumstances. Evangelism and exemplary existence are the primary and basic expressions of responsibility. Whether the watchman's office should be performed in public life and, if so, how, depends on the circumstances, e.g. in the Roman Empire before or after Constantine, in Russia or in Norway, in Holland or in Indonesia. The method of its performance varies at different times and under different conditions. Consequently, the Old Testament is neither directly applicable nor obsolete. It shows the high-water mark of responsibility, which the Church should steadily keep in view and ever strive to attain.

At the same time it must not be forgotten that between the Old Testament and the New Testament there stands Jesus Christ. Men have not been able to keep the Law of the Old Testament theocracy. One man only was righteous, and he was executed under the Pharisaic theocracy. His Resurrection signifies the foundation of God's reign in the eschatological theocracy. The promise of the Old Testament first came into force through Christ. In time the Church and the world will so completely coincide that there will be no more Church (Rev. 21.22), and on the bells of the horses there shall be 'holy unto the Lord' (Zech. 14.20).

In the expectation of this future, and in the power of the Holy Ghost, the Church's responsibility for the world will be extended so wide that through her witness and her service, her office of watchman, her intercession and her political action, fleeting intimations will appear of the theocracy to come.

2

THE QUESTION OF PROPERTY IN THE LIGHT OF THE OLD TESTAMENT

by

Walther Eichrodt

Translated from the German by Morvyth Evans

The following attempt to clarify the social message of the Old Testament is made with a full realisation of the special hermeneutical problems in the exegesis of the Old Testament. An 'objective' understanding of the Old Testament message, i.e. assuming that the exegete can lay aside all his own religious preconceptions, is an illusion which has too long impeded and misled the scientific study of the Old Testament. We realise today that, consciously or unconsciously, all exegesis is based on definite metaphysical presuppositions. The only mistake is that these presuppositions often have nothing to do with the subject under investigation, and do violence to the meaning. The important thing will be to find the general attitude required for the material, without which the significance and value of the details cannot be rightly assessed. But for the Christian there is only one way of looking at the Old Testament, namely in the light of God's act of redemption through Christ, if Christ's claim to be the fulfilment of Scripture is valid. Without that the meaning and the bearing of the Old Testament message are bound to remain obscure. As Christians we have no claim on the Old Testament, unless we read it as the revelation of God fulfilled in Christ. Otherwise it is nothing more than a collection of Jewish records, and has no more to do with the Church than any other sacred book of religious history.

Seen from this angle, the events described in the Old Testament assume the character of the *Heilsgeschichte*, which is striving towards a perfect form. These events are not narrated by the Old Testament writers in the form of a historical account, but in the form of a sermon whose purpose is to awaken the reader's faith. But as this sermon is based upon, and directed towards, a definite historical situation, it cannot be understood unless all possible means of historical research are applied in order to make its meaning clear and precise. The meaning of the Old Testament for today, however, does not become clear until it is confronted with the message of the New Testament. Only in this way can the standards be found by which the relevance of the Old Testament revelation can be traced for the life of the Church in the New Testament, without the Church falling into one of two errors: either autocratic disregard for the message of the Old Testament, or slavish dependence upon the letter of the law. That is why exegetical study must strive to ensure that the Church's freedom from, and subjection to, the message of the Old Testament are developed in the right way. Only then will it be able to achieve this lofty aim, first of recognising the Old Testament's contribution towards the Christian conception of God, and second, extending and deepening, but also critically limiting and correcting, the Old Testament message by means of Christ's act of redemption. In this way the authority of the whole Bible would be raised from the ineffectiveness of a dead principle and would become living and valid.

It would have been desirable if an expert in New Testament exegesis had written in the light of the New Testament material on the same questions. As it has not been possible to obtain a contribution of this kind, in spite of many efforts, this paper is obliged to confine itself to the Old Testament. That is why it seemed essential to insert these remarks at the beginning of this chapter.

In face of the widespread collapse of the social order and the social system of the nations of Europe, which we have experienced during the last few years, our age is urgently asking what are the really valid bases and fundamental principles of social life. Sometimes consciously, sometimes dimly, the fear is expressed that we have lost track of the eternal laws of life and that our insight into the fundamental bases of life has been obscured.

This makes it all the more important that we should not seek at random, but that we should go to the right source, and there investigate the soil in which our whole culture is rooted—in the world of the Biblical revelation. And this is where the Old Testament particularly claims our attention, because it gives so much space to the social and economic side of life.

When we ask ourselves what the Old Testament has to say about social life, this does not mean that we expect to find a ready-made social programme in the Old Testament which could be applied to our present troubles without any reference to the rest of the Bible. Unless we are going to misunderstand completely what the men of the Bible say about the right social order, we must bear in mind that it is inseparably connected with the basic, central theme of their message. This basic, central theme of the Old Testament is the news of the sovereignty of God and the establishment of his Kingdom. So that when man goes to the Old Testament to enquire about his attitude towards his neighbour, he is immediately confronted by the question of God. If he wishes to act aright, particularly in the exercise of his social responsibility, he must look back to the making of the covenant at Sinai in the past, and forward to the final redemption in the future. Israel's laws were formulated and carried out through faith in the divine covenant; the prophetic warnings and exhortation were sustained by their faith in God's final act of deliverance. Owing to this faith, the men of the Old Testament were able to perceive their tasks in this world, and they received new insight into the nature of man, a new realisation of his task, a new attitude towards the wealth the earth produces and the way in which it should be used. These laws are therefore witnesses to their faith; their aim is to establish rules which will preserve the faith of a community called by God. They are not a juridical system, with its numbered paragraphs, which could simply be declared valid, and adopted by our own age.

Because we share the faith of the men of the Old Testament in the God who made his covenant in the past, and who will fulfil that same covenant in the future, we want to find out what were the guiding lines which they laid down as witnesses of this God, in order to show their people the right way to that service to which their life and ours should be consecrated.

I

What is the view of the nature of man, and what is the attitude towards the goods the earth produces and their significance for our service to our neighbour, which we find in the Old Testament in the social order of the people with whom God made his covenant?

The best answer to this question is found in the oldest law of Israel, the so-called Book of the Covenant in Exod. 20-23. That is the law which is given to the people which has been brought out of slavery in Egypt (i.e. out of a condition where there was no justice at all) and which is now placed under the justice of God. These people, after their arbitrary treatment as slaves in Egypt, compelled to do forced labour, had not only seen, but had learned by bitter experience, even in their own flesh, the misery of inequality and dependence which comes from being at the mercy of the whims and fancies of those who wield power in this world. These people were therefore well prepared to understand the will of the God, who had brought them up out of this abyss of misery into freedom, when Moses gave them the first law. The legal order which was to form the framework of their life was not an oppressive burden, but it was felt as the expression of the care of the saving and sustaining God, and as a help against the destructive impulses and forces within their own hearts.

(*a*) This helpful office of the Law, with its respect for human life, comes out at once in its *estimate of man*. The structure of society in the ancient world, in which women did not enjoy full legal status and in which slavery was accepted as a matter of course, also forms the basis of society in Israel; it was not shattered by God's revelation to Israel. The effect of this new understanding of God was not to revolutionise the whole social structure; it was rather to release fresh moral forces, which were to introduce new moral standards into the existing system and thus transform the social structure from within. The new social order was, therefore, not brought about by drastic changes which had no regard for history; it adapted itself to the permanent historical process—the only way in which fresh insights can be worked out and permanently assimilated. So the individual, who receives a new status among the people of the covenant, is not an abstract idea; men are persons whose origin, history and social position differ, but who all, in their different situation, benefit from the clearer conception of society now revealed by God.

1. Here attention must be drawn to the principle which is valid throughout Israel's legal order: the equality of all citizens before the law.

Whereas in the ancient civilisations of the East—Babylon, Assyria, the Hittite Empire, Egypt—the system of class legislation was in force, which judges and punishes an offence quite differently according to whether it involves a royal official, a priest, a free man or a slave—all Israelites are equal before the law. For in this Law God himself speaks to his people, and in his sight the poor man is as precious as the rich one, the member of a small tribe or of a despised family is worth just as much as the representative of an influential family or the bearer of a high office. In the case of physical injuries the Babylonian law also demanded retribution on the principle of 'an eye for an eye and a tooth for a tooth'! But this only applied to free men; in the lower classes compensation could be paid in money. But in Israel the same law applies to all social classes, Exod. 21.23-25; there is no legal recognition of class distinctions. And this remained the same all through their history, even when the differences of class became much greater (as is shown by the later laws: Deut. 19.21; Lev. 24.19f.).

2. This equality before the Law is accompanied by a new respect for human life. Whereas in neighbouring states offences connected with property such as theft, robbery, etc., were frequently punished with the death penalty, this was no longer the case in the law of the Old Testament. The life of even the most degraded person is worth more than the richest possession; hence the law can only demand restitution of the stolen or embezzled property, which must indeed be made through hard work. The idea that depriving a man of his freedom by imprisonment was an adequate way of making amends for damage to property is quite foreign to the Old Testament. We also seek in vain in the laws of Israel for punishment by mutilation—the cutting off of the hands, or the nose, and similar cruelties, which were often perpetrated in ancient times in the name of justice. Here again, the life of guilty man is not put on the same level as any sort of material values, but enjoys the protection of the Law against all vindictive retribution.

3. And from a third angle also clear light is cast on the high view of man in the Old Testament; this is the care for the poor and weak, who live on the darker side of life, and whose rights are all too easily curtailed. The widows, orphans and strangers who cannot assert their own rights before the law—partly because of their sex (women and men did not enjoy equal rights), partly on account of their youth, or again because they do not possess full civil rights—are always the first to be exposed to the mercies of rapacious money-grabbers, unless they have a patron and advocate who takes up their cause. It is the judge himself who is called upon to be such an advocate and legal helper in the commandment: 'Thou shalt neither vex a stranger, nor oppress him; for ye were strangers in the land of Egypt. Ye shall not afflict any widow, or fatherless child. If thou afflict them in any wise, and they cry at all unto me, I will surely hear their cry; and my wrath shall wax hot, and I will kill you with the sword; and your wives shall be widows, and your children fatherless' (Exod. 22.21-24). Immediately after this comes the commandment not to seize the goods of the poor man arbitrarily if he fails to pay his debts; and in chapter 23.6: 'Thou shalt not wrest the judgment of thy poor in his cause.'

Thus God himself intervenes on behalf of the rights of those who cannot help themselves, and impresses the command to be just to the poor and weak so earnestly upon the hearts of his people, that he even regards oppression as a form of blood-guiltiness and threatens to punish it with the sword. He thus reveals himself directly as the God of the poor and unprivileged and thus urges the whole nation—which has been through the time of exile in Egypt—to pass on the benefits of their deliverance to *all* classes. The poor are to receive their rights not as a form of charitable largesse, but as a fundamental means of preserving national life and the most important provision for its safety. It is more important than big battalions and powerful allies that the nation should allow its weak and helpless members to have a share in the freedom and justice given and entrusted to them by the mighty hand of God.

In order to ensure that this commandment shall not simply remain on paper, and be fulfilled merely with pious phrases, definite provisions are laid down, stressing over and over again the duty of solidarity and of deliberate mutual help, and combating the selfish principle that 'every man is his own neighbour'. The family is mobilised, this being the most natural group in which mutual help is practised. There is the law concerning the re-purchase of land which had to be sold in times of bitter distress, in order to pay off urgent debts. Here the family of the debtor has the right to re-purchase such land at any time at the price for which it was sold; the interest on land must not drive the price up. This prevents people from being dispossessed of land and turned into wage-slaves.

But even those who suffer the bitterest fate of the impoverished and have to sell themselves into slavery, in order to pay off their debts to the creditor with the work of their hands, even they enjoy the protection of the law. Here again the family must intervene and pay off the debts of their relation. If the family cannot do so, the debtor's period of service cannot be prolonged at will, but terminates after six years, after which he can go free (Exod. 21.2ff.; Deut. 15.12ff.; Lev. 25.47ff.).

The rights of the creditor are therefore restricted to such an extent that he cannot carry on a lucrative business at the cost of his fellow citizens. And the relations of those who are in trouble are called upon to share the responsibility; they must learn to apply as a valuable privilege the principle of solidarity and mutual help to every member of the family.

These legal maxims show us clearly the object to which the legal system of Israel was directed: the human being, called by God to freedom, is the indispensable form of wealth—this is the kernel of the whole legal ideology of the Old Testament. The equality of all the members of the nation before the God who is no respecter of persons demands the same rights in working life; it calls for voluntary sacrifice by all citizens, in order to avoid inroads of inequality and oppression.

The power of this influence of faith on social action is brought before us most strikingly in one section of the Old Testament legal code where we would not expect it: namely, in the part dealing with the rights of slaves. In all ancient civilisations the slave was regarded as a piece of property, part of the household equipment, with which the owner could do as he liked. In Israel however the slave is protected against the arbitrary wishes of his own master—which meant an entirely new attitude toward the treatment of slaves. If anyone ill-treats his slave and knocks out one of his teeth or an eye, he loses his rights to the slave and must set him free (Exod. 21.26ff.). If anyone kills his slave, he is liable to a heavy punishment: he must pay the price of the slave (Exod. 21.20). We see that here the slave is no longer regarded merely as a piece of property, but as a man, and that he therefore receives legal protection even against his own master. In the same way the foreign slave, who has escaped from his master and fled to Israel, must not be handed over, as was the custom everywhere else (Deut. 23.16f.). Neither do we find any mutilation or branding of the slave; on the contrary many slaves, even when they could go free, preferred to become serfs because their lot was a happy one. Thus the respect for human life and its dignity extends even into the world of slavery, because the Israelites recognise the God who claims the poor and unprivileged as his own, and takes them into his protection.

(*b*) Where the new view of man penetrates so deeply into the traditional legal customs and demands a new social procedure, it is to be expected [illegible]hat *the attitude to earthly goods* will also be influenced by it. We [illegible] this already in the treatment of property: property was clearly [illegible]ondary importance in comparison with human life. And a se[illegible] example was given in the right to re-purchase mortgaged p[illegible]rty. Both these examples lead us to a principle of decisive imp[illegible]ce for our attitude to property: property is a gift of God, le[illegible] us in order to maintain human life; but it has no value in its[illegible] which would justify its being acquired at the expense of human [illegible]es.

1. This applies to the source o[illegible]ll profit: landed property. From the very outset it is engrave[illegible] upon the hearts of the Israelites that the real owner of the lan[illegible] is God himself (cf. the introductory speeches in Deut. 1-11; see a[illegible]so Exod. 23.11; Deut. 31.10f. and Lev. 25.23: 'Mine is the land', says the Lord). God gives the land to his people as a loan, so that they may maintain their life by enjoying its fruits.

This also means, however, that the land is not a thing which can be sold at will. Being the basis of the existence of the people, it belongs not to the individual, but to the community. Hence when Canaan was conquered it was divided among the tribes, who again divided it among the different clans and families. But the clans have a permanent prior claim on the property, taking precedence of the individual's claim. That is the other side of the law of redemption, which we have already noted from the point of view of solidarity. Since the clans can always redeem the land sold by the individual, they preserve the basis of their existence unimpaired. For the land is the most important means of production; and the Old Testament legal system is concerned with ensuring that every citizen has access to this means of production by protecting the land from private speculation and administering it as communal property. This reveals admirable clearsightedness on the part of the Old Testament lawgivers in perceiving the cardinal economic point on which the maintenance of personal freedom hinges. In the neighbouring civilisations, especially in Egypt from which they had escaped, they had an example before their eyes of the dispossession of the free farmer from his native soil, resulting in the accumulation of the means of production in the hand of the individual, giving him enormous power over his fellow citizens who have now become dependent ur him. This primary source of slavery must be stopped; that i aim of the agrarian laws of the Old Testament.

Closely connected with this are the laws erning money matters. It is true that in the Old Testa this aspect of economic life is very undeveloped, owin the conditions in Canaan being much simpler than thos the great, wealthy civilisations. Hebrew law knows noth of the business transactions of great commercial firms, wi their particular problems. On the other hand, it fully underst ds the importance of money in difficult economic situations, hen it can help people over a year of bad harvests in the f m of a loan. And here the far-reaching decision is made, th no interest is to be levied on such loans. If one bears in mind e way in which usury flourished in the countries surroundin srael, where the usual rate of interest demanded was 20 per cent. to 30 per cent., the commandment forbidding the taking of usury (Exod. 22.25), which was emphasised again and again in the later laws (Deut. 23.20; Lev. 25.36f.) is undoubtedly a reversal of the usual legal customs. The reason for this interference with the usual legal order is not any theory about money, but the same watchfulness concerning the free use of the land which we saw in the regulations about landed property. The danger of borrowing is falling into debt and being dispossessed of one's land. The object of the legislator is to limit this danger as far as possible.

So from the very beginning the Old Testament Law shows us how the lawgiver took up with determination the struggle for the protection of the freedom and security of all citizens, and endeavoured to build barriers against the torrents of self-interest and the craving for profit; this was in contrast to all precedent and custom in the countries surrounding Israel. But this struggle is entirely the outcome of faith in the Lordship of the God, who as Creator and Redeemer has chosen a people of his own and who now demands that the outer life of this people be shaped in accordance with his will.

II

It was the great mission of the prophets to protect this concern for social righteousness, this dawning development—resulting from the Hebrews' faith in God—in times of historical crisis, to prevent it from withdrawing into a false religious 'subjectivity' and to insist on its being unconditionally enforced. Their speeches therefore resound with charges against the rulers of the people, whether they are the kings and their officials, or the elders of the cities and of the clans, or the priests and false prophets who wanted to exploit the difficulties of the time in order to destroy the burdensome restrictions of God's order and to open the way to the lust for power and possessions, on the pattern of the great empires which set the fashion. So the prophets fight for equality before the law against the unjust judges, and scourge their corruptibility and their obsequiousness to the upper classes. They stand up for the rights of the economically underprivileged and constantly mention orphans, widows and foreigners as those who stand particularly under God's protection. They attack the war profiteers, upstarts and money-makers, who make profitable business out of the misery of the masses, due to frequent wars or to poor harvests; and they openly expose the tricks of the corn-usurers and land-speculators.

In all this the prophets show themselves to be loyal advocates of the old divine order of justice; and yet their social message goes further than the ancient law. This applies in cases where they show the full significance of fresh abuses which had crept in.

Four points should be specially mentioned:

1. We read in Isaiah and Jeremiah that in their time laws were framed without much thought or care, and were continually being multiplied. We are not told the real reason for this state of affairs, but we know that it is in the critical periods of a nation's history that poor statesmanship tries to prop up the tottering building with quantities of new excogitated regulations; whereas what is really required is a reawakening of the original sense of justice, and an increase of confidence and readiness for mutual help. It is an evil day for a nation when the State imposes a ruthless austerity upon the common people, squeezing the last ounce out of them by new taxes and dues, in order to fill the empty treasury. Then the laws become an unwieldy accumulation of paragraphs which simply bewilder the ordinary man, whereas the cunning quack-lawyer or usurer can always wriggle his way out of a situation, and twist the letter of the law for his own purpose. Here the law is in danger of disappearing in the impenetrable jungle of ordinances, and hence of losing its divine authority. Isaiah therefore attacks those who 'decree unrighteous decrees', and who keep on writing false statutes, in order 'to turn aside the needy from judgment and to take away the right from the poor' (10.1-4). Jeremiah, however, attacks those who are proud of their ancient law, since it has been made useless by the lying 'pen of the scribes' (8.8). These prophets are anxious that the law shall be intelligible to everyone in its simple, basic principles, and that its application by the judges shall be intelligible and convincing to the sense of justice of the masses.

2. The prophets bring to light one enormous temptation which springs from the development of the capitalist economy, and decks itself out with a showy veneer of logic and economic expediency: this is the temptation to increase the numbers of economic goods and use them for the purpose of making more profit—as if that were an end in itself—through which external culture and the power of the State can be enormously increased. It was the extension of trade and of international contacts in the time of the later kings which started this economic tendency in Israel also, long after it had gained the ascendancy in the neighbouring States. There the acquisition of capital by wholesale trade was far more extensive than in a community of wealthy farmers; in those countries, therefore, luxury became rife, in the form of huge buildings, splendid clothes, costly furniture, a

sumptuous standard of living, and produced a dazzling external civilisation. In those countries the State could get far more money out of the wealthy classes, which it used to build up powerful armaments for imperialistic purposes.

Many people in Israel thought the time had come to change over to this dazzling and profitable system, when the great wars against the Arameans and Assyrians in the seventh and eighth centuries had destroyed the social structure of the State composed of small farmers, when economic conditions were bad owing to the great loss of manpower, and the state finances were exhausted through paying tribute and through preparations for war. What did these people care, if the change could only be effected by brutal infringement of the law—by driving the distressed peasants into slavery to pay off their debts, by levying usury on corn and charging high rates of interest, by buying up their land at cheap prices? Without any regard for the 'year of release' and the right to redeem land, they formed the small holdings into enormous estates, worked by tenants and slaves, which yielded much higher profits. They finally crowned their series of lawless actions by legal murder, in order to rob a stubborn farmer of his rightful heritage—the story of Naboth's Vineyard is a case in point. This ill-treatment and deprivation of the rights of large sections of the nation was excused on the pretext of economic expediency, and in view of the visible success of the strong capitalist states; any appeals to law and justice were branded and ridiculed as antiquated provincialism, old-fashioned eccentricity, which were hostile to progress and civilisation.

The prophets fearlessly opposed this powerful current of heathen ideas and practices which broke into Israel at that time, and threatened to sweep away the law which governed the use of land. They took up the cause of the despised peasants, the backward people, and the masses who had been deprived of their rights. They exposed the delusion of thinking that progress can be achieved at the expense of one's brother and one's fellow man, and made it clear that this civilisation and economy was branded with the mark of Cain. And, *horribile dictu*, they challenged this logical and expedient economic development (which seemed to be going right through the civilised world automatically and without a pause, tolerating no exceptions) and summoned it to cease, in the name of the God-given rights of the weak and the defenceless. They urged those who wielded economic power to correct their account books in the light of the social commandment of the God of Election. Fundamentally, however, this simply means that the fundamental recognition of the nature of man, which had been given to the Hebrew faith, is being applied fearlessly to the very different conditions of Israel's later history: the realisation that the life of the free worshipper of God is worth more than any material values, and that any encroachment on that life endangers the existence of the whole community. That is wl even the economic order must be subordinate to this right of th free citizen who belongs to the people of God.

3. In this connection the prophets attack another form of idolatry of material values—namely, the unprecedented growth of a life of pleasure. Side by side with the impoverishment and slavery of the free classes of society, enormous sums were being diverted for the purpose of dazzling luxury—and this the prophets denounce as an execrable misuse of God's gifts. In so doing they make no distinction between the finer enjoyments of culture and the extravagant squandering in a coarse sensuality, for their purpose is not to extol the simple, old customs of their ancestors, nor the ascetic ideals of monks; they are concerned with the contrast between an apparently flourishing civilisation and the crying distress of the people, for whom this pleasure-seeking culture has no eyes and no understanding. The fact that the love of pleasure and luxury becomes an idol, to which men would rather offer their sacrifices than to the God of the poor and the unprivileged—this is the essential point of the prophets' scathing judgment on the civilisation of their own day.

Hence the ancient law of the nation is applied and utilised by the prophets in a new way; it proves to be a good weapon in the struggle against the dangerous forces which threaten to destroy and ruin the national life. But the prophets go still deeper and try to lead their people to perceive how inseparably service to their neighbour is interwoven with their whole existence.

4. The prophets do this by describing all the outward forms of worship as worthless, even repulsive to God, if social justice is ignored. When religious customs and solemn services of worship are no longer understood and used as a means of strengthening us for helpful action, but are performed in order to acquire merit

in the sight of God—an attitude which gives one an inflated sense of self-importance and a sense that 'we have done all that is required', and can therefore ignore our duty to our neighbour—we have relapsed into paganism and have reduced the most Holy God to the level of an idol. Hence the biting words in which such worship is rejected: 'I hate, I despise your feast days, and I will not smell in your solemn assemblies. Though ye offer me burnt offerings and your meat offerings, I will not accept them; neither will I regard the peace offerings of your fat beasts. Take thou away from me the noise of thy songs; for I will not hear the melody of thy viols. But let judgment run down as waters, and righteousness as a mighty stream' (Amos 5.21-24). 'For I desired mercy, and not sacrifice; and the knowledge of God more than burnt offerings' (Hos. 6.6). Similar passages occur throughout the prophetic writings and make it impossible to escape from God's insistence on social duties into the unreality of personal moral edification and quietism. Every solemn acknowledgment of the God of their fathers, who had brought them up out of slavery in Egypt, becomes a lie unless it leads on to the struggle for justice in human society.

Thus in spite of all the beautiful and uplifting worship, their whole high destiny as God's people may be jeopardised unless service to one's neighbour is recognised as the touchstone showing the sincerity of their faith. The classical expression for this truth was coined by Jeremiah, when he says (in 22.16), remembering the good king Josiah: 'He judged the cause of the poor and needy; . . . was not this to know me? saith the Lord'. Knowing God, i.e. comprehending his nature and standing in the right relationship of true devotion to him—that is determined by being modestly prepared to serve the weaker members of the community. Nothing else, however splendid in outward appearance, however pious it may pretend to be, can replace this element in the worship and service of God.

III

What is the significance of this message of the Law and the Prophets for our own day? Little explanation should be needed to show us how directly this message of a bygone age applies to our own times, and how the aims which men struggled to attain then are still true and valid for all who recognise the God of the

Old Testament to be the Father of our Lord Jesus Christ. Can we protect our system of justice against the inroads of heathen ideas and ideals, and against stultification by purely formal legal technicalities, except by struggling for the unconditional recognition of certain great ideas of justice in our whole national life, which are inseparably bound up with faith in the Creator and Redeemer in the Old and the New Covenant? Where will our legal development end, if it does not remember to regard man as a creature whose life is protected by God, and who must therefore be protected against arbitrary oppression, vengeance and brutal debasement? The pagan law of the Third Reich which abolished equality before the law, and reverted to a cruel and degrading system of punishment, shows us that the Biblical view of the nature of man cannot be taken for granted, but has to be constantly regained. And what can provide adequate legal protection for those who are economically, physically or mentally backward, except the Creator's desire for their welfare? Violence against such people cannot be prevented by logical arguments, nor by a general feeling of humanitarianism, when times of great crisis incite the egoism of the healthy and active to h[illegible] action. Here again we have seen with horror how the sense of humanitarianism disappears and logical arguments drive people to the elimination of the unfit.

Moreover, with regard to the Old Testament attitude to earthly goods, it is quite obvious that when economics and politics are said to be governed by autonomous laws, as if they were independent forces demanding absolute submission, no legal system can protect the weak against the triumph of materialist philosophy. It requires courage to oppose modern economic dogmas (however obvious the ruin that awaits them) with the unconditional refusal to countenance slavery in any form, and not to let one's sense of duty be influenced by arguments in favour of increased output of the political economy or national greatness. The fact that, in accordance with God's order, the life of every individual, even of the poorest, is of greater value than all material things—this fact represents an unsurmountable stumbling-block to all economic developments which make profits for the few out of human misery, both to the large-scale ownership of land and to the great capitalist blocks of trade and industry—and proves these forms of economic development to be *wrong ways*.

But this unconditional insistence that material goods must be used in order to maintain human life, freedom and independence, gives a certain colour to the idea of property. We are not required to take over the Old Testament agrarian laws in their historical (and therefore imperfect) form and apply them to our own time. The point is that we must recognise the idea behind those laws, that everyone should enjoy the profits of his own labour and not be cut off from free access to the means of production. Ownership of the means of production, if it cannot be transferred entirely to the community, must be removed from the risk of selfish misappropriation and placed at the service of all, i.e. no legal regulation should make it possible for goods, which are required for general use, to be held back from the economic process and kept in reserve, in order to obtain the highest profit. The significance of this for modern agrarian law, the present financial system, and the present exchange of goods, is obvious. A law which favours land-speculation, the hoarding of money, and the withholding of essential goods, has failed in its purpose and has become an injustice. When in the social message of the Old Testament we recognise and take to heart its faith in God's divine justice, we cannot escape the duty of helping to think out afresh in a penitent spirit all the economic and political problems which the Western civilisations must face if they wish to escape annihilation.

So the social message of the Old Testament—if we will only hear it aright—launches a radical attack on our legal system, and on our economic development, and calls us to a passionate revolt against all forms of evil and injustice which violate and debase man—man, whom God has called to fellowship with himself.

Then does this message place the solution of economic and social questions entirely in the hands of man, and expect man's goodwill to establish a just order of life from which all injustice is excluded? That is the ultimate and decisive question which we must face, if we wish to avoid the danger of becoming mere sentimentalists. Here the decisive factor is what is regarded in the Old Testament as the final and deepest reason for the injustice prevailing in the world: it is not man's ignorance and his delusions, it is not the cunning and unscrupulousness of a few people who are to be held responsible; still less is it the imperfection of the creation in which 'things come into sharp collision with one another'; but it is the power of evil which resides in every human heart as a sinful propensity and seduces the masses. No human will can overcome this power; it has taken root everywhere owing to man's wilful estrangement from God, and cannot be driven out of the present world-order. That is why the prophets set all their hope on a new creation of the world through the power of God, and rejected, as a radical delusion, the idea that a new humanity and new conditions could be created through human reforms. Their whole hope and expectation is therefore directed towards the future in which God will overcome the mysterious power of evil, and will create a man with a new spirit, a completely new people, a human race which is capable of goodness.

But this burning expectation does not make the present time, nor present action, of no account. Because God is going to create a new world, because he led his people out of Egypt into Canaan as a pledge of that promise, and because he has crowned this redeeming action by sending his Son, man is called upon to meet God half way, to give himself whole-heartedly to this renewing will of God, and through his whole life to bear witness to the fact that he believes in the victory of God's will over all obstacles. Jesus has created a permanent picture of ingratitude and lack of faith in the figure of the lazy servant who buried the talent entrusted to him in the ground, instead of using it to good purpose. So with the same seriousness with which they placed all their hopes in God's coming, the prophets called men to obedient activity, based on God's command to establish justice among men. The prophets only recognised faith as valid if it actively fulfilled God's will.

Hence the whole life of the believer is lived under constant tension: the tension between the Now and the Hereafter, between the part and the perfect whole, between defeat and triumph. For the prophets have left no doubt that the way of faith leads to suffering. The believing community does not charge forward from victory to victory; but through apparent defeat, suffering and death it bears the banner of its Master. Its faith must be bravely maintained in spite of all disappointments, in spite of all the successes and triumphs of evil. But it is able to hold firm in this faith, without losing sight of the truth and the meaning of its action, because it looks forward to the final victory of God's Kingdom. Its Forerunner and its Lord is the Servant of the Lord, who through suffering was raised up in glory. The believer can therefore keep clear of the false illusion that he possesses the unfailing means of solving all difficulties, the secret key to success in every situation. The meaning and the success of his obedient service consist not in what he does and achieves, but in the way in which his service bears witness to *God's* mighty action. He knows that he is called to be a witness to God's claim to rule the world. If he upholds the cause of God's sovereignty over the world, undismayed by success or failure, he has hoisted a signal that points to the coming King and the establishment of his Kingdom. The truth of this witness is guaranteed by him who at Eastertide broke the bonds of death and 'hath brought life and immortality to light'.

3

THE RULE OF LAW

by

ERIK WOLF

Translated from the German by John C. Campbell

The question of the authority of the Bible for the rule of law has a theoretical and a practical side.

Taken *theoretically* it belongs to the complex of questions dealing with the relation between theology and the science of law. There are, however, various possible answers to the search for a concept of justice that would be valid both in theology and in the philosophy of law. Every theologian and every philosopher of law alike will have an interpretation of his own.

Taken *practically* the question seems to admit of an even greater number of possible answers, for one must consider here the part played by factors of history and society, social ideologies, political programmes, and in addition to these the different types of church, their confessions, moral principles, doctrines, traditional ways of life and many other circumstances.

A further complication is introduced by mutual ignorance of one another's axioms and ways of thinking and also of the aims in view. The *jurist* or *economist*, e.g. as member of a statutory commission, as judge, advocate or university professor, is aware of the great variety of scientific problems and insights in his own field. He knows how legal and economic questions are entangled with historical and political problems. On the other hand he will perhaps underrate the importance of questions raised by theology, because as a 'layman' he has little acquaintance with them. The theologian, on his side, as minister, professor or church politician frequently underestimates the difficulty that underlies problems of social and legal science, because he believes that by instinct and tradition with the help of 'sound common sense' he is able to know and say what is needful on the subject. To make up for that he is well versed in the dogmatic positions and the laborious methods whereby theology passes its judgment on social questions. Thus the two parties often talk at cross purposes and fail to understand each other.

For this reason it seems useful to set out clearly the presuppositions of this problem both for theology and also for the philosophy of law.

I *Theological principles of the inquiry*

We understand the Bible as *God's Word to men*. It is the revelation of God for us because it witnesses as a whole to Jesus Christ as the unique, immediate revelation of God for men. That is to say, we have a *Christocentric* understanding of the Bible. There follows from that:

(*a*) The Bible, as we understand it, is not just a '*historical document*' interpreted by a *theology for which history as such is the medium of revelation*. The methods of comparative religion do indeed secure scientifically binding conclusions about historical facts which appear in the Bible, but such insights are not essential to the life of faith and do not bind the believer's conscience.

The observation is sometimes made that the statements of the Bible on the rule of law contain ideas stamped by the outlook and limitations of a particular period and describe institutions that are now things of the past. In the Old Testament, for example, we find usages and norms of ancient Jewish customary law and of the later priestly law. But this has no significance for us, for such an observation misses the aspect of the matter that interests us—that these statements are 'God's Word' to men. Therein lies their authority. Because it is God who proclaims here his law for men, who makes 'his' covenant with them, therefore there is a Biblical authority for these statements. Viewed simply as 'history' the ancient Jewish laws have as little validity for people of today as the Code of Hammurabi or the Hittite law-books.

It has no significance for us that in the Old Testament also there is an amalgamation of rabbinic doctrines on Mishpat and Zedaqua with institutes of Roman provincial law, and in the New Testament a dilution of the *ius gentium* of imperial times by traditional Stoic and Platonic doctrines of *dikaiosunē*. The only matter of importance is that Christ gave instruction on the subject of law and that in the prophetic and apostolic statements with regard to law 'God's Word' too is spoken in contemporary legal concepts.

(*b*) To continue, the Bible is *not* for us one of the many other documents of religion but revelation given once for all. It is a proclamation made by the Spirit of God (not of man), witness to the condescension of God to us, not to our quest for knowledge of God and human perfection. Theological liberalism which sees in it only one of the achievements of man's religious experience will be able to discover by the methods of comparative religion a parallel between Christian and Socratic or Stoic ethics, between Christian and Mohammedan eschatology, Christian and Buddhist rules of life, as well as many other 'points of contact' between Christianity and other religions. But these insights, too, which *all* rest on or lead to an (assumed) *religio naturalis*, *sc. rationalis*, are insignificant for the believer who experiences his existence as a Christian as something incomparable, in strict contrast to all 'religions'. They are not binding for him.

Understood in such a way the authority of the Bible must of necessity (and always) appear slighter than the authority of nature or human reason. A deistic interpretation of law evolved in this fashion and developed philosophically as *ius naturale* or *ius rationale* signifies therefore no answer to the question put by us. Our quest for a Biblical authority for the rule of law does not aim at establishing the legitimacy and norm of law *from the standpoint of man* (even supposing his standpoint to be religious). To settle that question is the affair of a (profane) philosophy of law and not of theology. It is no Christian concern. We are trying to find what is the *divine* guidance on law which is unknown to the independent human understanding of law (rising from natural, rational and historical sources). As a matter of fact liberal theology can never see more in Biblical guidance than a 'Christian' confirmation of the insights assumed by it at any given time or ranked superior to revealed truth as 'scientific', i.e. 'rational' insights (biological, sociological or historical).

(*c*) The Bible is for us, however, not merely a document of morality that in the (now unessential) guise of primordial myths holds a kernel of permanently valuable moral teaching and is to be held in esteem as a summary ('the best so far') of social and individual rules of moral conduct. This view leads to an arbitrary selection of 'really important' passages from the Bible. It lays the foundation of a theological moralism which easily results in an optimistic, secular belief in progress (failing to appreciate the eschatological character of the Biblical message). The element of surprise, the 'strangeness', the 'foolishness' of the Word of God then disappears, and the Bible becomes merely the confirmation of practical and sensible behaviour. There remains as a Biblical basis of law only an average, bourgeois propriety; this, however, leaves us in the lurch where the really problematic situation in which law is involved begins to appear, and where we feel it today. The authority of the Bible is then made to appear on the side of that optimistic sense of being in the right, which fails to recognise the power of sin, the inextricable entanglement of all human wit and wisdom in wrong and the seriousness of the threat of final judgment.

(*d*) Further, the Bible is for us not an 'ecclesiastical document'. It does not get its authority from the Church, but the Church from it. The opposite view, the attitude of a theology of institutionalism cannot leave to the Bible its genuine authority. For it is substituted the *imprimatur* of an ecclesiastical teaching authority.

For our problem that would mean that certain propositions of the Bible become canonical, others not. The former constitute a treasury of timelessly valid rules of the *ius divinum*, the *traditio divina*, the boundary between which and a mere *traditio humana* remains extremely vague. Despite the large measure of agreement between the content of the *traditio divina* and 'Biblical guidance' we are not able to accept this doctrinal concept of the Roman Catholic Church on account of its commingling with the *traditio humana*. According to reformed theology there is no source of divine guidance on law outside Holy Scripture.

In this context it must also be said that an interpretation of the Bible that regards as binding only those pronouncements that accord with one of the confessions that has played an effective part in church history cannot be the right way to ascertain the authority of the Bible for law. For every confessional theology will measure the Bible by its confessional standards (instead of the other way round) and in so doing will read into the Biblical guidance on law that meaning which corresponds to such standards. A confessionalist exposition of the Bible is always from the very first on the way to a purely historical approach and its theology of law merely reflects the contemporary philosophy of law with a theological background substituted for a secular one.

The content of Biblical guidance may not be 'stylised' according to Augustine, Aquinas, Luther or Calvin. It is not a question of finding out what elements in it best meet the needs o[illegible]stern or western man, European, American or Asiatic civi[illegible]ion. Neither may we ask whether and in what way the doc[illegible] of Biblical guidance on law 'fits into' one of the older or more[illegible]nt ethical systems. Least of all may we allow ourselves to b[illegible] dependent on a fashionable theology, be it historical or pneum[illegible] orthodox or liberal, confessional or ecumenical. This is the [illegible] way to prevent the authority of the Bible from being used in [illegible] service of ideologies or misused in the fight against them.

(*e*) Finally, that exposition of the Bible seems to us to b[illegible] mistaken which is consciously bound to the literal wording o[illegible] the text without observing that the Word of God is not identical with the words of the Biblical text written by men. Such a fundamentalist theology substitutes a dictatorship of the letter for the authority of the Spirit.

The meaning of what we have said is that we are never entitled to apprehend the guidance given by the Bible according to the sense of the words taken in isolation from the whole. Everything depends on the context in which a passage stands, on parallels between it and other texts of Holy Scripture and on their proper interpretation. Biblical guidance on law is also *viva vox evangelii* and not rigid formulae. It is intended to help *every* age to achieve a just order but not to keep alive artificially obsolete legal conceptions and institutions.

Following or obeying Biblical guidance does *not* therefore mean reproducing literally in life a pattern of conduct discovered in the text of the Bible, nor listening to the (so often deceitful) 'inner voice' of conscience, but making a serious attempt to listen for God's Word in the Bible and to be led by it. To find guidance in the Bible does not therefore mean performing an act of theoretical perception which could ensure action according to the insight given. It is impossible to construct a 'system' out of guidance received and by applying it save ourselves the trouble of decision. Guidance is indeed an experience of faith, but it directs us not only to examination of our conscience. Rather it indicates limits and ends to govern our assumption of responsibility, in the shape of rules for our behaviour towards our neighbour. This is something more than a philosophical *ethos* and different from it because the whole 'Word' of the Bible is in substance more and other than each of its individual words, themselves written by men. That is evident from its effect. It is not just a matter of something being heard, but of something that has happened. One cannot therefore discover Biblical guidance by looking up and selecting all the 'legal', 'moral' or 'juridical' passages of the Bible. That would mean subjecting Holy Scripture to an external standard instead of submitting to guidance from it. Thus one cannot take literally as guidance on law every saying of the Old or New Testament which says something about justice, judgment or punishment, about statute or commandment; and neither may one apply to justice in an earthly state all passages which speak of the righteousness of God. It is rather worthy of note that not every passage associated with legal matters is *ipso facto* already guidance as we understand it. It is possible for a *prima facie* quite 'unjuridical' or 'non-moral' looking statement of the Bible to contain important guidance for the social order.

To anticipate any misunderstanding we add this explanation. By 'Biblical guidance' we do not mean any substitute for the decision of the individual conscience, but rather a leading towards that; by 'Biblical guidance on law' we do not mean legal maxims but 'basic principles of law'—leading ideas for lawgivers, judges, counsel, government officials, and also for every individual citizen in private dealing with the law. Its guiding rules are not rigid, abstract principles, but active ones, requiring reinterpretation as each case arises. They constitute at once boundary marks and signposts, but not a timetable which enables us to say that only trains found in it will run.

The function of Biblical guidance on law is thus a dual one: it acts:

(*a*) As a check on man's will to assert his own right and to shape the law (for others as well) according to his free will.

(*b*) As rule and guide for social life corresponding to God's will which Holy Scripture shows to be creative of order for men.

II *Principles of the inquiry in terms of the philosophy of law*

These give an outline for a Biblical ontology of law.

(*a*) According to this we do not understand 'law' as a law of nature (independent of God and answerable only to itself):

(*i*) neither in the sense of law as an original growth (as opposed to an artificial product): what is *phusei dikaion* does not have a more valid claim to be true law than what is *nomo dikaion*;

(*ii*) nor in the sense of a law arising out of necessity of nature 'eternal' (as opposed to an arbitrarily established historical law). The *ius naturale quod natura omnia animalia docuit* has for us in principle no higher standing than the *ius civile* or *ius publicum*;

(*iii*) nor in the sense of an uncorrupted, natural, moral law (*in cordibus inscripta*) in contrast to the positive moral command tainted by civilisation and culture (*in tabulis inscripta*), for natural morality is always the expression of a *religio naturalis* of which Holy Scripture knows nothing;

(*iv*) nor yet in the sense of the Kosmos, as an ordinance of creation, which, detached from its Creator, has a life of its own ruled by 'immanent' laws. Natural law understood in this way serves only for the 'religious' embellishment and supposedly 'divine legitimation' of worldly circumstances.

(*b*) Again we do not understand law as a law of reason (indedependent of God and answerable only to itself):

(*i*) neither in the sense of rules of practical intelligence (worldly wisdom, 'sound common sense'), for they are able to develop only a superficial utilitarian morality: the rational law of utilitarianism;

(*ii*) nor in the sense of propositions of formal logic, for they can only develop a system of generalised legalised concepts formally non-contradictory: this law of reason, of rationalist philosophy, has, however, no ethical sanction;

(*iii*) nor in the sense of fundamental principles of the philosophic mind (entelechies, monads, categories), for they are valid only on the presuppositions and within the framework of the philosophical system that sets them forth: the rational law of idealism, owing to the relativity of the different cultural ideals and their *ethos*, remains without any (general) sanction.

(*c*) Finally we do *not* understand law in the sense of the historical or positivist schools of legal philosophy as a product of historical or social forces (conceived as independent of God); that is to say:

(*i*) neither as law for which tradition sets the standard, for the greater age ('laws ancient and wise') or the national character of a system of law are no guarantee for its ethical value;

(*ii*) nor as law for which reasons of State set the standard; for the mere power of a ruler or mere state interest may indeed maintain outward discipline, but the rule of law thus upheld will never serve as basis for anything more than a morally indifferent power State in which 'law' is merely equivalent to compulsory order.

(*iii*) nor yet as a right to *revolution*, as asserting that only a law giving adequate expression to the revolutionary idea is true; for this conception also remains without moral sanction, since each revolutionary ideology of law can be contradicted by its opposite (and none can be refuted).

III *Guidance and rule of law in the New Testament*

The New Testament is the starting point for the interpretation of the Old Testament also. The way, here, leads from the New to the Old and thence back to the New Testament. The New Testament is for us the Gospel of the divine revelation in the crucified and risen Christ, the Redeemer of all men who accept his grace and are justified by it. It is therefore necessary here to say a word or two about the relation between justification and law.

Justification means deliverance from sin. That is not something we can do for ourselves nor does it mean that we assume individual responsibility in order to assert ourselves. We can justify ourselves neither at the bar of conscience, nor before our fellowman, nor before God.

Justification is the work of God's grace with us, made effective through faith. We do not deserve justification. It is a gift. We have no claim to it, for it is bestowed on us by a free decision of God.

Law, however, we can deserve to have on our side, as a legal claim to something. We can earn it as a right to something; we may in some way and within certain limits make a claim to be in the right and to be put in the right; we ask also to be left in possession of our rights. It is of course a provisional and ambiguous possession when we assert: 'I am in the right; I have a right to this or that.' Nevertheless, we are able to use such language just because a right is not grace but rather (in theological terms) 'law'. It is not a gift and is bestowed on no one. It must always be won anew and defended. Law is indeed not Gospel, justice not love. The former judges and condemns; the latter sanctifies and redeems. 'Therefore we conclude that a man is justified by faith without the deeds of the law' (Rom. 3.28). That is the *articulus stantis et cadentis ecclesiae*, the proposition by which the Church of the Reformation stands and falls. Are we not then surrendering the core of the Christian faith, indeed the very Gospel itself, if we apprehend and proclaim as the object of Biblical revelation not only grace and love, but also law and justice, the order of the world as well as the harmony of the Kingdom of God? So it would appear.

Here however we must observe that the word 'right' (*ius*) is contained in the word 'justification' (*iustificatio*), which means 'putting in the right'. Philologically it is a necessary part of the word but in fact it is also an essential part of the meaning How can that be if justification is by faith alone and faith the work of God's free grace, whilst legal right is a matter of reason and human will? It is so because lawful right does not arise originally and essentially from human nature but in the sense of righteousness is an attribute of God.

The Bible speaks very clearly on this matter. In it God has revealed himself as the God of righteousness. This signifies firstly—revealed as a righteous God (*Deus iustus*) who with due cause passes judgment on men. It signifies, secondly—revealed as God who justifies himself, as the wholly 'Other' in whose presence no man's self-righteousness can abide. The Bible, however, thirdly, shows us God as One who instructs men in righteousness, who makes known to them what is to be law among them. Thus under the old covenant he has declared himself as Lawgiver and demands from men fulfilment of the law as the Lord in whose Kingdom men love judgment (Ps. 99.4). But in the New Testament also, which according to Christ's word brings not the dissolution but the fulfilment of the law (Matt. 5.17-19; Rom. 3.31), the Lord has given clear testimony that he is a God of righteousness. Christ is not only Lord of the past and of the future world; he reigns already in the present one. He gives order not only (unseen) to his community (the ecumenical Church) but also (although hidden) to society in all its forms, whether 'Christian' or 'pagan', consciously or unconsciously outside the Church.

This social world abides, it is true, in sin (even when its intentions are good) and under judgment (even where it has the name of Christian), but at the same time it is a world where law rules among men, a world which can be better or worse according to the way in which men 'keep the commandments of Christ' (John 14.21, etc). The commission to go forth to all nations shows that these commandments are valid for *all* men of *all* ages.

Naturally, there can be no doubt that Christ's commands are those of love and *inward* discipline, not those of a merely external order. He has appeared as our Redeemer and not as our Judge. It is in order to save us from the just penal judgment of God (his own judgment) that he has in his mercy taken it upon himself on the cross, accepting it at the same time as satisfaction. We must nevertheless take good care, particularly in the light of this saving knowledge, to rid ourselves of the unbiblical prejudice that law and justice are concerned only with the *external* order of life, and that because Christ laid down no basic principles on the subject he has therefore left no guidance for living under the rule of law. That, however, is something he has done, partly in express words, partly in parable form. The sacrifice of Christ, especially, as an incomparable and unrepeatable act shows that the righteousness of God is a matter to be taken seriously. Only in the light of the atoning death of Christ do we get the right conception of the holiness and majesty of the just judgment of God, as they are symbolised, for example, in Dante's great poem. It is this source, this divine origin of justice that applies a strict criterion and gives grave importance to the meaning of law in the world; therein lies the meaning that gives it binding force.

Secular anthropology and its allied sciences cannot disclose this. He who would know how God puts man in the right and judges him cannot recognise as final man's own account of himself, be it philosophical or sociological, psychological or biological in its basic principles. He may then inquire of the Bible, but only in the spirit appropriate to it, i.e. theologically; otherwise he will get nothing in answer that is not already contained in his question.

From all we have said there follows, in reply to our question whether there are New Testament statements that are binding on men living under the rule of law, this answer. The Kingship of Christ in the world (although concealed) compels us to acknowledge in him the source and goal of all human social order (including the rule of law). The New Testament has something authoritative to say both about the life of man rooted and grounded in Christ as an ordered life, and about the Christian Church built up on him as corner stone, and also about the world order in general created, and sustained by him as Creator (as he is also of men whose thinking, faith and life are 'non-Christian').

(*a*) Among the numerous instructions which proclaim the will of Christ for an ordered life there must be reckoned not only the saying of Jesus in the Synoptics, but also the words of guidance given in the apostolic writings. Apart from I Cor. 7.10 and 25 it is impossible to draw a definite line between words of the Lord and instructions of the apostles. The following distinctions are to be made:

1. Guidance for *church life*: e.g. on disputes (Matt. 18.15ff.) and on the legal status of women (I Cor. 11.3f.; 1 Tim. 2.8ff.).

2. Guidance for *Christians* as members of political groups (e.g. 1 Cor. 6.1; Matt. 22.21; John 19.11; Rom. 13.1ff.; Matt. 17.24f.; Rom. 12.7-21).

3. Guidance which is *valid for all men* and has already been recognised both in theological and philosophical teaching on social ethics, e.g. conduct towards one's neighbour (Matt. 5.22, 34ff., 18.10, 25.35f.); for business life (Matt. 6.19; Luke 12.33ff.); for propriety and good habits (I Cor. 5.11); for social peace (1 Cor. 7.20f.); and harmony (Gal. 5.19f.). It will be one of the tasks of future ecumenical study to clarify the question how these different instructions are related to one another.

(*b*) The New Testament expositions of the Ten Commandments too are more than mere personal exhortations to Christians. We find them not only in the Sermon on the Mount where Jesus speaks about marriage (Matt. 5.32; cf. Matt. 19.6, 9), about oaths (Matt. 5.34ff.), and about conduct towards one's neighbour

(Matt. 5.22, 5.34ff.; cf. Matt. 18.10, 25.10, 25.35f.), but also in many passages in the apostolic letters, especially in the 'household rules' (Eph. 5-6; Col. 3.8f.; Tit. 2; I Pet. 2; Heb. 13). To these may be added special instructions as on respect for the law among social dependents (I Tim. 6.1; I Pet. 2.18) and on the lawful duties of young people (I Pet. 5.5). These affirmations of the Ten Commandments are neither annulled nor weakened by the commandment to love in the Sermon on the Mount.

Guidance is also given in examples of legal conduct in the actions of Christ, of disciples and apostles or in the parables. We many recall again here our expository rule. One may not apply the texts literally. Here too and above all we are trying to listen for guidance and ruling coming from the text. These passages are just the ones that are particularly instructive for the position of a Christian living under the rule of law irrespective of the totally different legal standards set today. Among these passages we may reckon such parts of Scripture as follow here: Plucking ears of corn; permitted in Deut 23.25, and confirmed in Matt. 12.1ff.; payment of taxes, Matt. 17.24f.; childlike obedience, Lk. 2.51; punctual performance of ceremonial commands, Matt. 3.15, 5.17ff., 8.4, 15.6 and 19.18ff.; Mark 1.21, etc. Besides these, one should take note of the conduct of Jesus during his trial (Matt. 26.55ff., 27.11ff.) and of the behaviour of the apostles before their judges (Acts 4, 5, 7, 16.27ff., 17.4ff, 20.17ff., 21.27ff., 22.26.)

In the parables one must take into consideration the fact that whilst they sometimes describe unrighteous conduct, there always follow on it the normal legal consequences.

IV *Guidance and rule of law in the Old Testament*

Even where the Old Testament is law pure and simple, it is understood only as prophetic reference to the righteousness manifested in Christ (Gal. 3.24). It is neither annulled nor inessential, neither can it be characterised as binding only in part (Luther's distinction between *ceremonialia*, i.e. unimportant, and *iudicialia*, i.e. important, sections of the law cannot be carried through). The statements of the Old Testament on law and justice may therefore neither be ignored nor selected and used arbitrarily as instances. According to Christ's own words, the law is fulfilled by himself. Christ is therefore neither legislator of a new law, neither is he *nomomachos* with respect to the old one; He is rather *verus legis interpres* (Calvin).

The question whether statements of the Old Testament on the rule of law and the administration of justice give us guidance that is binding must therefore be answered in the affirmative, in so far as we understand it with respect to the work of Christ (the justification of sinners by his sacrificial death) and to his present activity in the world (as head over his Church *and* as *Rex Mundi* (Lord of Lords); also with respect to his future (as Lord of the new earth, the eternal city, as βασιλεύς of the βασιλεία τοῦ θεοῦ). The same question must however get a negative answer in so far as we misunderstand the Old Testament as a 'work of man' (summary of historical statutes, usages, institutions), or again as 'ritual law' (sacrificial rites, priestly hierarchy, etc.), or indeed as a means whereby individuals or peoples justify their own pharisaic fulfilment of the law, righteousness of works, messianic hope for domination over this world, etc.).

The Old Testament, too, has something authoritative to say about the rule of law. This is to be found in the first place given through the revelation of personal commandments and guidance from God. Among these we reckon above all the Ten Commandments. The Ten Commandments contain a basic order that carries out a legitimising and critical function, as *norma normans* with reference to all other Old Testament laws. They are not a code of legal principles giving us power and authority to pass judgment on men (today) in individual cases; they are, however, a summary expression of God's will to establish order among men; they are a rule for all social order of such a kind that failure to respect the Ten Commandments takes away the basis of legitimacy from every legally ordered society and claim of right. Every political power remains under their authority. It is impossible, then, to interpret too carefully or comprehensively the Ten Commandments in order to find out the significance of what they have to say about the rule of law. No exposition can in this matter be too deep or far-reaching, for God's Word has a breadth and depth of meaning far beyond all human words. But it must be on its guard against giving a legalist positivist rigidity to the maxims, and likewise against that visionary antinomianism which supposes that love annuls law. Above all, any exposition must bear in mind that it is in the light of the rule of Christ alone that we can understand the Ten Commandments as an order given by God.

As an indication of how the Ten Commandments can be understood as guidance and rule we give below two examples to suggest a line that might be followed in exposition. Our choice is the fourth and sixth commandments (taken in the order of the Heidelberg Catechism).

(*a*) The fourth commandment to keep the Sabbath holy does not provide us people of today with a prescription about worship that has a positive legal value. On the other hand, its meaning is not exhausted in pointing out as a fundamental principle—found elsewhere too—that working man has a claim to rest and relaxation. It urges on us that God has created us to praise him, that this is a reason for rejoicing and that everyone is therefore to share in this rejoicing: even a prisoner, one obliged to carry out a task or make expiation, must be allowed to have this day for reflection and edification. The fourth commandment reminds us of our equality in the sight of God and demands the rest and quiet of the holy day as the right of all alike. But the commandment lays a special obligation on us to gather together as a congregation, to abide under the Word. From that there arises guidance for society ruled by law as follows: to provide room and protection for the proclamation of Law and Gospel on the one hand, and on the other the ruling that nothing is to be done in the social, legal or political field without seeking first the guidance of the Word.

(*b*) We must scrutinise with special care the guidance of the sixth commandment. Here too we are not simply dealing with a legal maxim that forbids absolutely, say, the death penalty, military service, interruption of pregnancy or euthanasia. But we have before us a basic principle which guides in a definite direction the complicated decision on these legislative questions about which every society ruled by law must make up its mind, viz. towards a decision in accordance with the revealed will of God.[1] Setting a limit it tells us that except in cases of necessity we must not take life, and indicating a line of action that we are to protect and cherish all life created by God. As a compulsory

[1] Even if no outline of state action, no world plan can be projected on this basis (so A. de Quervain, *op. cit.*, II, 17), it does not follow that we must renounce the guidance offered here for social morality. Professional theologians continually obscure their own view into this by their positivist, rational (in other words un-Biblical) conception of law.

law the guidance of the sixth commandment could not be carried out, and as a law of love, pure and simple, it would be visionary, for we cannot exist without destruction of life (at least of plant and animal life). In addition no Christian Church has ever accused of murder the serving soldier or the executioner carrying out his legally appointed task. But taken as a genuine guiding rule the sixth commandment has much more to say to us than merely to forbid the taking of life. It aims at preventing altogether hatred of our brethren and urges life-saving effort where others are in mortal danger. Indeed it summons us to the succour of all neighbours in distress (L[illegible] 10.25-37) and of all men menaced by physical or spiritual death. 'Strengthen the things that are ready to die' (Rev. 3.2). This saying is the positive rendering of the sixth commandment, the rule to guide us in applying it. It carries in it, too, when understood in the prophetic light of a Christian's life, the promise: as one who has received grace and been redeemed and is hearkening to the guidance of God's Word, thou wilt not kill.

Over and above this the 'Thou' of the sixth commandment is to be interpreted as in the others. That is to say it concerns not only individuals,[1] but communities and nations, but especially every kind of higher power that has God's commission to call the murderer to account. It is the whole of mankind that is being addressed here in the people of God and as the people of God. Wars and executions there should not really be. God permits them only as exceptions; they are inevitable on account of our sinful condition, but as often and as far as possible to be avoided. It would be more pleasing to God and better for us men if there were no such things. In this there lies the political guidance never to glorify the killing of a fellow man, not even of enemies in wartime, neither to recommend it nor take it lightly. Here the State is told that it must neither indirectly tolerate the destruction of life nor directly advance it. This is so even in cases where we are concerned with life that from a biological or other utilitarian standpoint seems to be of inferior value. It is told in addition that it must prevent danger to life and must thus set limits to the development of technics, and especially to the 'motorisation'

[1] Calvin in particular recognised this: not simply individuals but a whole people can be chosen by God and must then be sanctified to become a *peuple saint* (C.R., 56, 64, etc.).

of traffic, where this development is becoming a growing menace to life.

Along with the Ten Commandments which contain commands and instructions proclaimed directly to persons, we find in the Old Testament numerous applications of these commandments in the warnings and exhortations of the prophets. Here we have God's will for the ordering of society proclaimed in concrete situations, but with supra-temporal validity. The particular historical element in each occasion and saying is not the essential thing for us. For us it is the exemplary factor, that is, the 'guidance' to which we must hearken.

In conclusion, attention must also be drawn in this context to the history of God's people (as a whole). Scripture shows us here how God from time to time gives a *new*[1] order to the life of this people by a 'constitution' (covenant), when the people has fallen away from him. In the gracious act of establishing such a new order (e.g. in the covenant with Noah), order is restored not only in the relations between God and man on a new standard, but along with this new constitution of the relation to God and through it, as the ground of their legitimacy, the rights that bind men together in lawful union are confirmed or receive a fresh orientation.

V *Conclusions for the Christian understanding of law*

We attempt now to develop some of the consequences of our thinking and ask first of all:—Does the doctrine of Biblical guidance contain a new and essential insight which could not be equally well derived from jurisprudence and the philosophy of law?

We answer yes, for it brings into view as a guiding rule for law three limits to the understanding of what law means, which are continually disregarded by secular thinking on the subject, by showing up as erroneous three tendencies in the interpretation of law by men.

(*a*) First is the *idolisation* of law, that is, every exaltation for its own sake of order coming 'from below' (from man), appealing to a 'divine spark' in man's nature or dreaming of a capacity of the human spirit to become equal with God.

(*b*) Second there is the tendency to attribute to law a *diabolical character* (*demonic*), rejecting it as a hindrance to the establishment

[1] J. Ellul, *Le fondement théologique du droit*, Neuchâtel, 1945.

of the Kingdom of God on earth and denying the possibility of ordering the Christian life under the rule of law. This is supported on the one side by enthusiastic exaggeration of the law of love (Tolstoi) and on the other of the doctrine of original sin (Flaceius).

(*c*) Finally, there is that *indifference* to law which treats it as a trifle, asserting that law is an *adiaphoron*, because all that matters is the salvation of the individual soul, which must sanctify itself by inward absorption in the mystery of God and separate itself from the world (the error of mysticism and of modern, romantic tendencies in the evangelical Church).

The further question whether the Bible can give authoritative guidance on law to the man of today must also be answered by yes, so long as Biblical guidance on law is clearly distinguished from every 'natural law' of a 'natural religion', and equally clearly from the 'moral laws' of philosophical systems or doctrinal propositions and from the moral theology of an ecclesiastical tradition. Neither may we identify Biblical guidance on law with the traditional conceptions of order associated with the ideas of 'Western Christendom', 'Christian civilisation', 'Christian humanism', 'the religion of civilisation', etc. Its authority may not be confused with that of Plato, Aristotle or Kant—nor supported by them, nor by any modern authorities, such as sociology, psycho-analysis or existential philosophy. The point here is to contradict decisively the urge to seek confirmation of Biblical truth from any kind of insight into truths immanent in the world, and, above all, to remain free from the influence of the 'isms'—philosophical, economic, political—and also theological.

Finally we must observe that there is authority of the Bible only through and for faith. To a man who rejects the Gospel of Jesus Christ—as it is proclaimed in Scripture—thinking to work out his own salvation or to require none, one can only proclaim the Biblical guidance on law, as the Gospel itself is proclaimed—but not thrust it on him. On the other hand we must not make the approach to this conception easy by secularising the Christian message. We cannot prop up Biblical guidance for law on an ideal of human rights with a biological, rational or historical basis (whether we call it natural law, rational law or simply the right to exist). Nor may we seek to obtain its suffrage for one of these interpretations. It does not admit of identification with a 'cosmic law', whether formulated in terms of causality, mechanism or vitalism. Reconciliation of the Christian message and modern science along these lines makes shipwreck inevitable. Neither anthroposophical cosmologies nor any kind of mundane anthropology lead the way to the Bible. The word of Scripture is not the corner stone of the Babel Tower of human wisdom but Word that shakes this construction to its foundation and brings it to a fall. As the judgment of God the Bible demonstrates human wisdom to be foolishness just at the point where its own wisdom begins. We can therefore never succeed in making Biblical authority for the rule of law among men obvious to an unbelieving jurist or philosopher of law, if he thinks that he can do without it. For Christ is the physician for the sick and not for those who think they are well or who look for other physicians. Not everyone will see that all have the same need of him. All the same, this must always be preached to them. Thus far also discourse about Biblical guidance on law will always be part of the preaching of the Gospel and will be addressed also to those who believe that they can find the way for themselves. We cannot look for more than this, but this must be done.

4

CHURCH AND STATE IN THE LIGHT OF THE NEW TESTAMENT

by

HANS VON CAMPENHAUSEN

Translated from the German by John C. Campbell

It is a continual source of surprise to the modern reader to observe how reticent, on the whole, is the New Testament in face of that entity which today we usually speak of as 'the State'. But this reticence is really not so surprising. The political question is not the supreme question of life as it regularly appears to modern thought, following in that the traditions of classical antiquity. There are, in any case, broad dominions and long periods of time for which it has not had this importance, and this is also the case for the world of early Christianity. It was only the pressure of the first persecutions that compelled Christians to think out more thoroughly the problems which this subject raises. When we, in the following pages, endeavour to assemble and interpret the relevant New Testament statements we must constantly bear in mind the working principle that no statements are to be extracted from any historical source on matters about which it was never intended to speak. This principle, as may easily be understood, is often violated in respect of the New Testament. But that does not mean that our enquiry must be condemned to theological sterility. The very caution and silence that the New Testament observes on this question can themselves be very instructive for us.[1]

If we turn first to the environment of Jesus, one thing stands

[1] From the abundant literature on the theme 'Early Christianity and the State', let us mention three recent studies in which further suggestions and discussions are

out clearly: that here in fact is a people politically disinherited and alienated from the State to the furthest degree. The Judaism of his times had for centuries ceased to know what existence as a national State was like, and in any case it had never really been a great power. At that time Palestine was broken up into different zones where delegated and little-loved authority was exercised by the grace of Rome, whilst Rome itself provided for general security and administration over all, recruited soldiers, collected taxes, ordered, confirmed and executed death sentences on criminal or political charges as occasion demanded. These were more or less the only contacts which ordinary inhabitants of Palestine had with political life. In this situation, however, the Judaism of that time was by no means really pacified and Palestine was, and for a century to come remained, highly insecure ground as far as politics were concerned. Again and again we hear of disturbances, riots, bloody conflicts, of partisan leaders gathering their bands about them in the hill country, and, on the side of Rome, of violent interventions by the occupying power, gradually losing its nerve. Behind these chance incidents, however, it is ever and again possible to discern on the part of Judaism —torn though it was by party strife—a definite passion rising against the foreign yoke. This is not simply a political rising as we understand it, a rising in order to restore national independence for its own sake, but rather a religious passion, which, it must be admitted, did encroach on the political sphere. Deprived for centuries of a political life of its own, Judaism had increasingly sought to order its existence according to the norms of a strict

to be found: Otto Eck, *Urgemeinde und Imperium. Ein Beitrag zur Frage nach der Stellung des Urchristentums zum Staat* (*Beitrag zu Förd. Christl. Theol.*, 4, 2, 3), 1940. Martin Dibelius, *Rom u. die Christen im ersten Jahrhundert* (*Sitzungsber. der Heidelb. Akad. d. Wiss. phil.-hist. Kl.*, *Jahrb.*, 1941-2. 2, Abh.), 1942. Wolfgang Schweitzer, *Die Herrschaft Christi und der Staat im Neuen Testament*, Zürich, 1948. Eck brings together all the available material in a most exhaustive review and discussion, but is not sufficiently critical in valuing and separating the meagre sources and continually yields to the temptation to try and take more out of them than they are able to give. Dibelius goes beyond the compass of the New Testament. His concise account is a model of mature, cautious and sound discussion of the details in an amply conceived context. Schweitzer starting with exegesis tries to penetrate to essential insights that have real dogmatic actuality, but in so doing seeks support in constructions which remain assailable. In addition to these monographs, there is an uncommonly suggestive collection of essays by Ethelbert Stauffer, *Christus und die Caesaren. Historische Skizzen* (1948). But it dispenses with notes and a critical apparatus. Cf. also Hal Koch, *Kirke og Oevrighed indtil Konstantin den Store.* (*Dansk Teol. Tidsskr.* 10, pp. 147-72), 1947.

piety. It had suffered from the continual violation of its religious principles owing to its cramped and enfeebled state, and now looked forward with growing eagerness to the great turning point that God was to bring to his people. The ardent expectation of a wonderful Messiah, born of David's line or descending from high heaven, destined to bring at last to God's people holiness, peace, dominion and fulfilment, realising all religious and earthly desires, is the inspiration behind the resistance and offensive movements which blaze up from time to time, even though it was only certain circles which were heart and soul in its grip. It was just such unsettling expectations as these that made the public appearance of men like John the Baptist or Jesus himself so unwelcome and dangerous in the eyes of the ruling authorities.

We know that one of Jesus' own twelve disciples bore the nickname 'the Zealot'.[1] His supporters, accordingly, came to some extent from these circles of aggressive, religio-political activism. But the message of Jesus himself was of a different character. Jesus indeed also proclaims the coming Kingdom of God which will change from the very foundation all existing relationships. He proclaims it as imminent, and all that he has to say to his own times, rightly understood is summed up in the demand to take this future seriously, to live with it in view and heeding his words to begin a new life: 'Repent for the Kingdom of God is at hand.'[2] But, it must be remembered, the Kingdom of God is for Jesus God's Kingdom in the sense that it should not and could not be brought in by human endeavours, but breaks in miraculously coming on its own from God. Indeed, in his own Person it has already come, mysteriously veiled, into the midst of the people, and will be fulfilled by his own Second Coming, the Second Coming of the Son of Man. This Kingdom is in no sense a political task for the execution of which men could be recruited. Two things follow from the proclamation of the Gospel. Firstly, there is required—think, for instance, of the Sermon on the

[1] Luke 6.15; Acts 1.13. From the word about the two swords, Luke 22.38, we may conclude with Edg. Salin, *Urchristentum u. Staat* (*Schmollers Jahrb.*, 55, 2, 1931), 27, that some of the disciples carried weapons; cf. H. Windisch, *Der messianische Krieg und das Urchristentum*. According to Acts 1.6, national hopes seem also to have been associated with the Second Coming of Christ; cf. W. G. Kümmel, *Jesus und Paulus*, Anm. 27, *Judaica*, 4. (1928), 24f. At the same time the significance of these isolated passages must certainly not be exaggerated.

[2] Matt. 4.17 = Mark 1.15. With these words Jesus takes up the preaching of John the Baptist, Matt. 3.2.

Mount—simply the most strict fulfilment of the binding commandments of God for which a new joy, impetus and power are given through confident hope in the glory to come. Secondly, there is required, through faith in the Master and his promise, readiness to dare all and to free oneself from the impeding entanglements of a world which is already unmasked as provisional by his Word and robbed at bottom of its seductive power by his coming. The significance of this for the State is shown by the one saying of Jesus that deals at all with a political problem, a saying occasioned only by a question raised by his opponents. It is Jesus' answer in the passage about paying tribute to Caesar.[1]

This passage deals with one of the so-called 'debates'. Many of these in which Jesus took part particularly in his last days have been handed down to us. His enemies—in this case the Pharisees—are trying 'to catch him in his words', to use Mark's phrase. The questioners therefore are sent out to set a trap for him and do not put their question out of genuine interest in the matter. The question of the tribute, the general poll-tax, led on as a matter of course to very dangerous ground and touched on perhaps the most delicate point in the political situation of that time. This tax, inexorably demanded by the Romans, was not only unpopular and disliked, as every tax is, but in addition it violated in a special way Jewish religious sentiment. It had been regarded as the sacred privilege of the Chosen People to pay taxes to the Temple only, and therewith to God, and indeed the introduction of the tribute had in its time provoked a revolt. Now Jesus is to be brought into the position of having to choose between loyalty to the existing powers and popularity with his own people.

The famous answer which he returned then is thus to be understood firstly as escape from a dilemma, as a deliverance due to his wonderful and brilliantly superior gift of repartee with which he compels his opponents to leave him and to hold their peace. By making the questioners themselves show him the image of the ruler on the tribute money, it is, as it were, clearly demonstrated as the latter's property, and in an almost comical way further discussion of the matter becomes superfluous. In addition, to be sure, the hypocrisy and inner dishonesty of the Pharisaic attitude is shown up in a way that covers them with

[1] Mark 12.13-17; Matt. 22.15-22; Luke 20.20-26; on the subject see E. Stauffer, *Die Geschichte vom Zinsgroschen*, *op. cit.*, pp. 118-49.

shame. In their question they cheerfully make use of the despised currency. They have not even taken offence at the image, forbidden by Jewish law, nor at the religious emblem on it. Yet surely they might have taken up the question long ago on these grounds, rather than start getting scruples of conscience only when it comes to paying the tax. And amid all this Jesus' answer goes far beyond the stated question, lifts the discussion on to quite a different level, his own level, where we are concerned with an ultimate decision in the sight of God. There, too, the pious theological scruples, about which the Pharisees busied themselves out of a sense of their own importance, fall to the ground as trifles of no value. 'Render unto Caesar the things which are Caesar's and unto God the things which are God's'.[1] This proposition does not signify a peaceful agreement to live and let live between the two spheres, each of which is to preserve its own rights; rather the *parallelismus membrorum* realised in the outward form has a definitely ironical intention.[2] As, with a wave of the hand, Jesus sets aside, far from himself, the whole of the

[1] We may not strain the interpretation of the word ἀπόδοτε to give the meaning of a civil duty of restitution or a markedly favourable attitude towards the Empire, as Stauffer, with abundant material, has striven to do most recently: *Die Geschichte vom Zinsgroschen*, *op. cit.*, p. 137. The expression, typical for the payment of debts and taxes, comes naturally here, and there is no indication that Jesus wished to emphasise it in the sense of some theory of the State or of fiscal rights: cf. Dibelius, *op. cit.*, 3, Anm. 2. Such considerations appear only since Justin (*Apol.*, 1, 17) in the Fathers, who try to use the traditional saying from the new standpoint of their own political situation. Of course, Jesus also may have been acquainted with the true facts of the situation about coinage rights and the imperial prerogative expressed by the stamp on the silver denarius. But the main point of his answer does not in my opinion rest on such considerations, but on the immediate impression and apparently unambiguous witness that the image and superscription convey directly to a simple mind. If anyone, as Irenaeus (*Haer.*, IV, 30, 2) says in a different context, carries in his belt '*Taurum et argentum et aeramentum cum imagine Caesaris*', it thereby becomes perfectly clear that someone else's, i.e. Imperial, property is meant and not one's own. For Stauffer, on the contrary, the answer of Jesus brings out the special right of the Emperor as such. According to Stauffer, in a very positive and imperative instruction, it teaches us to understand the imperial tax as 'due contribution of God's people to the maintenance of the Empire'. Its first part, in his view, envisages the 'intercessory sacrifice for Caesar' for which the Imperial tax had to make a contribution, and the second part, the Temple tax, a technical word being as a matter of fact used to denote payment of it. These are undemonstrable assumptions from which far-reaching conclusions are drawn for the theology of history: that Jesus had established a relation in principle between the Empire and the Kingdom of God. 'The *Imperium Caesaris* is the way, the *Imperium Dei* is the goal of history' (p. 146).

[2] Alb. Schweitzer, *Die Mystik des Apostels Paulus* (1930), 305; Dibelius, *op. cit.*, p. 4.

supposed difficulties and problems of this world doomed to collapse and with it the transient world of politics. Such matters day by day preoccupy and crowd men's minds and prevent them from getting to hear what is truly 'actual' and decisive. Such questions are easily answered. Let them keep their place on the circumference and receive such attention as they can get. Thus he gives men an unclouded vision of the living God, the one thing needful, whose ominous and saving nearness has even now in his own Person become reality. Jesus is concerned with other matters than daily worries[1] or the latest political sensations of the day as such. They work up all pious minds into a state of excitement, whilst to him, with the end of the world in prospect, they appear in a very different light.[2]

As a supplement, let us add at this point another narrative, handed down by Matthew only. It is not indeed concerned with any problem of the State in the proper sense of the word, but is none the less able to set in a sharper light the inward disposition and attitude towards institutions and claims of this world. The issue in it is also a question of taxation, not, however, an Imperial tax, but the Temple dues—that is to say a question of Jewish ritual law.[3] Peter has been asked by the collectors whether his Master, Jesus, is also in the habit of paying this tax and has answered in the affirmative. Jesus draws him out on the subject: 'What thinkest thou, Simon? Of whom do the kings of the earth take custom or tribute? Of their own children or of strangers?', i.e. Jesus and his disciples as children of the King of kings ought by right to be free of a ritual gift. The surprising thing now is that Peter, none the less, is told to accede to the tax demand and the necessary money is procured by a most striking miracle. Historically, the whole section must be regarded as a product of the community. It gives with some legendary frills an answer to the question whether Christians have still to pay the Jewish Temple tax or not. The gulf which separates them inwardly from this ritual system—a thing of the past for them—is naturally much wider than that in the legal order underlying the tribute question. For that reason its validity is, as a matter of fact,

[1] Luke 12.13ff. [2] Luke 13.1f.

[3] Matt. 17.24-27. The narrative appears combined with the story of the tribute money as early as the following: Irenaeus, *Haer.*, V, 24, 1; Clemens Alex., *Paid.*, II, 14, 1; Origen, *Comm. Rom.*, IX, 30.

fundamentally challenged. But the result is the same in both cases. Christians may feel that they are different, that they are moving in another direction and that in the essential things they are superior. But consciousness of this is not to stir them up to hostile resistance and argument. Rather in order to cause no offence, they accede quietly to all public demands that are still made on them as a matter of custom.

The remoteness from all questions of politics and the State in which the Fourth Gospel sees Jesus is, if possible, still greater, and is, it seems, expressly emphasised in the conversation with Pilate. The Kingdom of Jesus is 'not of this world', and the statesman sees himself forced to choose, whether he is to follow the Emperor or the everlasting King.[1] The Christians do not indeed fight against the earthly ordinances of the State, but they do not seem to feel any obligation at all to support them or give political co-operation. It is only in the Apostle Paul that we find the first word on the civil authority spoken with fundamentally positive intention. But even in his works, Roman citizen though he was, in a relatively ample literary testament of eight or nin more or less comprehensive epistles, there is only the one sectio in Romans that takes up the question of the 'powers that be' But his development of this theme here is presented with unusually marked emphasis and it is no accident that it has b again and again quoted and expounded.

The text stands in a context of general moral exhortatio rules for the Church, such as Paul usually offers as a second main section in his letters, after the more fundar lly dogmatic expositions which are never wanting. Such nical instructions generally make use of an older literature of morals and maxims, and in Paul it is the same, however strong may be the impress that the traditional material has received by being envisaged from the new standpoint of the Christian faith. Even the demand to submit to the powers that be is essentially an old

[1] John 18.29-19.16. For the interpretation, cf. my essay, *Zur Auslegung von Joh.* 19.11, *Theol. Lit. Zeit* 73 (1948), 387-92.

[2] Rom. 13.1-7. I pass over here the passage in II Thess. 2.6f. It is as a matter of fact still under debate whether κατέχον or κατεχων may mean the Roman Empire, its Emperor or not. (For this view most recently, E. Stauffer, *Die Theologie des Neuen Testaments* (1943), 66f.); but this exegesis—first offered by Tertullian—is not probable, whether it really means a mysterious mythical power (so Dibelius, *op. cit.*, 12ff.) or indeed Paul himself and his missionary preaching (so O. Cullmann, *Rev. d'Hist. de Philos. relig.*, 1938, pp. 174ff.; *Christus u. die Zeit* (1946), pp. 144ff.)

piece of Jewish tradition. The idea that the powers that be are ordained of God is also met with in this quarter, although with something else in view—namely, as a warning to rulers themselves not to exceed their powers. The practical moral significance of civil justice and power as a protection against revolt and wickedness is also brought out occasionally in rabbinic literature. Nevertheless, the clarity and firmness with which Paul recapitulates the three aspects—obedience, divine institution and moral function—the tremendous energy and awful seriousness with which he brings out man's duty and God's requirement with regard to the civil authority and preaches the same to all is unexampled, unique—in a word, Pauline, and, if you will, Christian.[1] 'Let every person be subject to the governing authorities. For there is no authority except from God and those that exist have been instituted by God. Therefore he who resists the authorities resists what God has appointed and those who resist will incur judgment. . . . For the existing authority does not bear the sword in vain; it is God's servant to execute his wrath on the wrong-doer. Therefore one must be subject not only to avoid God's wrath but also for the sake of conscience.[2] For the same reason you also pay taxes, for the authorities are ministers of God, attending to this very thing.'

How does Paul come to emphasise so strongly the significance of the civil authority and the duty of obedience, the obligation on everyone's conscience and therewith for Christians also? The old problems of the Palestinian world have long since disappeared, as the final sentence introducing tax-paying as a matter of course clearly shows. Paul is writing to a city church drawing its members from the Hellenistic population and not from Roman nationals, and for that reason also writes in Greek. No special love or proud enthusiasm for the State was to be reckoned with in their case. But Paul is not concerned with anything of that sort. What he requires is simply subordination and due respect, abstinence from unruliness and impropriety in dealings with the civil authority. The modern reader—and not only he—likes to see in these words an express veto on revolution. One is also

[1] Any dependence on Jesus' word about the tribute money seems to me non-existent. Otherwise, G. Kittel, *Christus u. Imperator* (1939), 19; W. Schweitzer, *op. cit.*, p. 44.

[2] This sentence should be omitted as a gloss, according to Bultmann, *Theol. Lit. Zeit.*, 72 (1947), 200.

inclined to think that the absolute nature of that veto is underlined by the fact that here Paul obviously had in mind pagan civil authority, and, what is more, an authority that had at that time persecuted and taken advantage of him just because he was a Christian. But that is not the way to argue here. It is clear that Paul is speaking in support of civil authority as he finds it in existence, as 'powers that *be*', so that his words give therefore no permission to overthrow existing authorities or refuse them obedience on the ground that they do not perhaps come up to the Christian ideal of a civil authority. But on the other hand in the passage before us there is obviously no assessment of possible differences in the sphere of morals, and the civil authority is envisaged rather as itself the guardian of the law and of righteousness and only as such. The whole course of the argument would otherwise lose its meaning. That is quite unambiguously shown by some further sentences passed over previously: 'For rulers are a terror not to good conduct but to bad', says Paul and draws the conclusion, 'Then do what is good and you will receive his approval, for he is God's servant for your good. But if you do wrong be afraid, for he does not bear the sword in vain . . .' and so on. Every revolution starts with the assertion that the existing authority is unjust and that its measures were keeping down the best elements. Paul could not so readily proceed from the opposite view as established fact and the ground of his demand, if such revolutionary ideas were even on the furthest horizon of the discussion. In other words, the idea of a revolutionary front lies quite beyond his horizon and nothing whatever can be taken out of the sentences of Rom. 13, as far as the problem of revolution is concerned. It should not indeed require these reflections to make it quite clear right away that the small, poor Christian conventicles, which were lost among the masses of the great cities, and had only one desire—to be left in peace and remain in obscurity, could never dream of anything so violent as political upheavals. From the whole of the first century and far beyond it there comes not a single Christian utterance that even in the remotest and most hypothetical sense has any such thing in view.[1]

The danger that Paul really wished to meet ought not to be so

[1] The possibility of violent resistance, which, however, is on considerations of principle scorned by Christians, is first asserted by Tertullian, *Apol.*, 37, 4f., with powerful, rhetorical exaggeration and transparently tactical intention for pagan readers.

hard to tell. We know indeed, e.g. from I Corinthians, but from frequent other testimony as well, what unrest and exuberance was often awakened in the young Christian churches by the sense of their new and wonderful calling. The echo of Jesus' old message of the Kingdom had not died away; on the contrary, by his Resurrection, by the outpouring of the Holy Spirit, by the new life in the fellowship of the Church, the expectation of the end of the world had now become really urgent. People felt themselves in a state of grace as members of the new people of God, called to rule with Christ and already almost over the boundary between the two ages, more as citizens of the coming than of the passing world. That sort of outlook could lead to very undesirable consequences, particularly among immature church members just recently torn from pagan relationships of a totally different character. We know how certain Corinthian Christians, under the slogan 'All things are lawful', violated all rules of morality, decency and consideration;[1] we hear how in Thessalonica some were 'unruly',[2] so that Paul had to inculcate the duty to work and commend respect for the leaders of the Church.[3] It is therefore—particularly in a letter to Rome—easy to understand that in such circumstances he sought to seize the opportunity of impressing on his hearers with every possible emphasis that their new, higher status and the imminent end of the world gave them no right at all to make light of the civil authority, still an ordinance of God, to fail in meeting its requirements and show it proper respect. Rather: 'Pay all of them their dues, taxes to whom taxes are due, revenue to whom revenue is due, respect to whom respect is due, honour to whom honour is due.'[4]

It is no accident that Rom. 13 concludes with an eschatological outlook, i.e. with a glance at the great future coming from God, in the light of which everything is to be understood: 'The night is far gone, the day is at hand . . . let us put on the armour of light; let us conduct ourselves becomingly as in the day. . . .' This demand of Paul's for upright conduct is valid also in relations with the civil authorities; but it indicates at the same time how far he is prepared to go in upholding their position. It is only authorities 'at present' existing, powers 'that be', which the Christian may not disregard. It is these same authorities whose pagan

[1] I Cor. 6.12, 10.23. [2] I Thess. 5.14; II Thess. 3.11.
[3] I Thess. 4.11, 5.12f. [4] Rom. 13.7.

representatives Paul can elsewhere qualify without hesitation as 'unrighteous', who owing to their sins would not inherit the Kingdom of God and who in the eyes of Christians are 'of least esteem'.[1] This sharp opposition of Christendom and those outside it strikes a new note alongside the preaching of Jesus which hardly yet took the pagan world into its view; but on the other hand the more profound agreement in substance between the Pauline attitude to the State and the message of Jesus can here be brought out. Paul, too, is no pious citizen who sees it as his task solemnly to insist on giving full value to our duties to worldly authorities alongside of our duties to God. For him also the world and its ordinances are provisional, transient powers; and his essential message, which can save men in time only for eternity, deals with wholly different matters. Yet we are not to conclude from this that believers, the saved, the citizens of the coming Kingdom, are to launch an attack against this world order and so accord it an importance that it no longer really has. In turning away from the Pharisaic question about the tribute, Jesus had already left this tribute and with it the imperial law its status as earthly law. So also Paul now sees himself compelled by the situation expressly to emphasise the same law, to combine with it additional civil duties, and to enjoin respect of the authorities as a moral necessity, as a divine imperative and institution. The Christian hope in a coming Kingdom of God does not mean that Christians are entitled to ignore present realities and in an exalted mood to omit existing duties in the realm of this world. They are, it is true, free from the dictation of the world in matters of conscience; they reckon with higher standards and are no longer blindly at the mercy of the world and its aims. But their redemption in this sense is not yet the final separation from and dissolution of the world order as such, which it is rather for the Last Day to bring about. After as before, all that Christians can do is to await with eager expectation the Kingdom of God, the future prepared for them by Christ. Thus for Paul, too, faith does not mean a reorientation towards new political goals in time, and for that very reason Christians are to be in earnest about their political duties to the temporal State power and to carry them out as well as other people.[2]

[1] I Cor. 6.1-4.

[2] In criticism of the recently attempted interpretation of the *Exousiai* of Rom. 13 as angelic powers, cf. my essay in the *Bertholet Festschrift* (1949), *Zur Auslegung von Röm* 13: *die dämonistische Deutung des Exousiai Begriffs*. I go no further here into this attempt, which in my estimation cannot be maintained.

In viewing the total relationship to the world and therewith to the secular authority, there is no essential difference between Paul and Jesus himself. But in the passage from Romans just examined, in order to guard against a new danger, he emphasises particularly the first, and, so to say, more lightly stressed, half of the famous saying of Jesus more strongly than had yet been done. But that is only the one side of the total relationship to the State in primitive Christianity. We have also in the New Testament a book which, on the other hand, lays the whole emphasis on the opposite insight into the offending—indeed, demonic—character of political power; that is the Revelation of John. This is not the place for a detailed commentary on it.[1] The reason for the transfer of emphasis lies in the outbreak of bloody public persecutions which the civil authorities in Asia Minor have set on foot. The main thing now is to encourage the assaulted churches to endurance amid the persecutions, to faithfulness even unto death, and to present the assaults coming from the political sphere as temptations of the devil, as a final trial which requires nothing but resistance and again resistance, until the Lord comes and puts an end to all distress, suffering and lamentation. Total enmity to God, every form of apotheosis of the 'unrighteous' world is, for the Christian seer, concentrated at the point where humanity reveals its most resolute purpose, its loftiest pride and its most extravagant pomp in the power of the State, in Babylon, the giant city, enthroned on seven hills which throughout the whole world has shed the blood of the martyrs.[2] Rome, which demands Caesar-worship and persecutes Christians, has for this end received power from Satan.[3] It is the last world power, the beast from the abyss adorned with the weird symbols of world dominion and earthly omnipotence. From its presence the Church of Christ flees 'into the wilderness', till the measure of the times is fulfilled and the Avenger and Saviour appears on the clouds of heaven. Naturally, the Seer of Revelation also preaches no violent resistance nor revolution, but only the 'patience and faith of the saints'.[4] But in vain do we strain our ears to catch from this record of martyrdom the slightest whisper stressing civil loyalty

[1] That holds especially for the difficult question how much there is in occasional specific contemporary references to political forces, which Emperor is meant, and so on. With the great majority of scholars I assume as proved that the Apocalypse cannot be understood in complete isolation from all concrete political connections.

[2] Rev. 17.9ff., 18.24. [3] Rev. 13. [4] Rev. 13.10, 14.12.

and political submission. Such points of view have no longer any part to play in the final conflict which seems now to have begun. The last book of the Bible that has so much to say about the Emperor, the State and the powers of this world does not consider them as secular political forces at all, but as religious and demonic, and so qualified, does not recognise, but rejects them.

From this point it is not difficult to see what the practical theological problem of the State for the succeeding period will be. The question is how to teach and carry out at the same time two different lines of conduct—Paul's unhesitating demand for civil obedience to the political power as a source of order[1] and the Seer John's passionate demand for religious resistance to the same power as the instrument of demonic presumption. Under the pressure of the killing time, the old saying of Jesus has acquired a new meaning in which the juxtaposition and simultaneous validity of the two halves seem to be the solution and the decisively new element: 'We ought to obey God rather than men.'[2] But Christians recognise at the same time a duty of prayer for the hostile, persecuting power; and obedience to it is rendered in all cases where it is possible without denying the Faith.[3] To draw the line correctly between the two is in practice not always an easy matter, but here or there it must be drawn. In making this choice, the Christian lives in a different way from a man of the ancient world, in two realms at the same time, to both of which by God's commandment and 'for conscience' sake' he must belong, in a realm of outward order and submission and in a realm of faith and free and confident confession—in medieval terms, under Emperor and Pope, in the Church and in the State. It is a unique relationship of tension that at once burdens political life and stirs it to its depth, and in this sense has become the starting point for the whole development of the western idea of freedom.

This is not the place to follow out this development. One

[1] Just because of this unhesitating recognition of State authority, the passage from Romans does not play the part one might have expected during the centuries of persecution; cf. Walter Bauer, *Jedermann sei Untertan der Obrigkeit* (1930), 3ff.

[2] Acts 5.29; on the application of this word in the ancient Church, cf. Herm. Dorries, '*Gottesgehorsam u. Menschengehorsam bei Luther*', *Archiv f. Ref. Gesch.*, 39. (1942), 47ff.

[3] I Tim. 2.1-4; Tit. 3.1; I Clem. 61; Polyc. Phil. 12.3. Intercession for pagan authorities corresponds also to Jewish tradition.

thing above all, however, is as a matter of principle not to be overlooked if we take the New Testament as our standard. A judgment on the State can only be called Christian in the real sense of that word so long and in so far as it keeps a firm hold on the peculiar, eschatological outlook of primitive Christianity, i.e. so long as the two realms in question are not regarded simply as two orders coexisting in timeless juxtaposition, to be weighed in the balance together in respect of their due—in which case it would not make much difference whether the one side or the other was more emphasised and more highly valued. Such a judgment is rather only then Christian when the proclamation of the coming Kingdom of God brings each person to perform in his own life the inward act of turning from the transient and for ever provisional structure of this world, and with it of the political world, to the coming, new and freely given order and reality of God, which Christ has brought and in the proclamation and realisation of which he himself was nailed to the Cross. The proper political message of the Church is not simply that Christians should recognise the divine ordinance of government, carry out their obligations as citizens, and for the rest seek to foster their religious life in peace. Its main points are rather that Christians are to lay hold of another Kingdom whose coming is the only source of all their hopes (or fears!). A real ordering of life on the basis of the potentialities in man and the current means and methods of politics cannot be achieved at all; and all politics that attempt this realisation and openly or tacitly claim the power to do so—and what politics do not?—are robbing God of his glory. But Christians who carry out their political duties with entire seriousness according to the will of God, for that very reason do not in any sense base their hopes on the power of the State or a conception of it or on any form of social or political order at all, but solely on the new possibilities promised by Christ, which the world neither knows nor recognises.

In the New Testament the First Epistle of Peter already reveals in an outstanding way this unique coexistence of provisional affirmation and eschatological rejection of the State, with the historical tensions it brings. This letter, too, is written under the shadow of approaching persecutions[1] and sees judgment already beginning with the house of God.[2] There are to be found

[1] I Pet. 5.9. [2] I Pet. 4.17.

in it not even the faintest illusions about the strength of the swiftly approaching opposition: the letter is issued as written from 'Babylon',[1] i.e. from Rome as the scene of the demonic enmity against God and his Church.[2] The situation of Christians is seen in basically the same light as in the Apocalypse, which is somewhat later in date, and, like John, the author of our missive, issued in the name of Peter, tries to exhort the churches to firmness and to arm them against the temptations of a persecuting time. But in contrast to John, 'Peter' has, for all that, not forgotten the Pauline exhortation to civil and political obedience and does not fail to stress the point that in spite of appearances the State has a divine vocation to maintain order. 'Be subject for the Lord's sake to every human institution, whether it be to the emperor as supreme, or to governors as sent by him to punish those who do wrong and to praise those who do right. For it is God's will that by doing right you should put to silence the ignorance of foolish men.' Such must be the expression of that freedom which is the mark of God's servants.[4] Accordingly, the important question is not alone the anxiety lest Christians should weaken in confessing their faith, regard as unheard of and unendurable the inevitable, and in a manner of speaking natural, enmity which they have to face and be ashamed at being outlawed by society.[5] Rather there is also sounded all the time the note of a second warning to remain really blameless in the sight of the secular tribunals and to give no justification for the widespread calumnies about the Christian walk and conduct of life.[6] No Christian is to suffer as a murderer, thief or riotous person, but only as a Christian,[7] and although Christians also 'fear' only God, they must none the less 'honour' the king, indeed everyone,[8] and be subject not only to kind

[1] I Pet. 5.13.

[2] On this meaning of the notion, cf. especially Hans Lietzmann, '*Petrus römischer Märtyrer*' (*Sitzungsber. preuss. Akad. phil. hist. Kl.*, 1936, XXIX, 11f.), according to which the otherwise so loyal Epistle of Peter shows here that it is a fundamental perversion of the facts to divide the development of early Christianity into two separate tendencies, one apocalyptic and hostile to the State, and one in supposed contradiction 'well disposed' to it. The case is rather that 'in reality in Christendom of old, just as in later centuries, the attitude of correct loyalty to the State found in the catechism was able to live alongside the enthusiastic hope in the end of the kingdoms of this world'.

[3] On the many attempts at interpretation which the idea of *Ktisis* has undergone here, cf. Horst Teichert, '*I Pet. 2.13—Eine crux interpretum?*', *Theol. Lit. Zeit.*, 74 (1949), 303f.

[4] I Pet. 2.13-16. [5] I Pet. 4.12-16. [6] I Pet. 2.11f. [7] I Pet. 4.15. [8] I Pet. 2.17f.

masters but also to the froward. These are not just a lot of rules of virtue and faith to be proclaimed as general principles, but in fact many ways in which Christians fulfil the particular vocation to which they are called in this present age: in the midst of a godless and perverse generation to bear testimony to a new, meek and quiet spirit and to realise an existence of a totally different kind from anything else that is to be found in the world.[1] 'For the end of all things is at hand.'[2] By not rewarding evil with evil, reproach with reproach, by not being swept away into the stream of licentiousness round about, Christians indeed excite surprise and hatred, but by the issue that they *now* raise in this way compel the nations to face up now to a vital decision and the final reckoning—in the presence of him who is coming to judge the quick and the dead.[3]

As may be seen, the early stages of Christian political thought are wholly characterised by the distinction between, or rather confrontation of God's people with, the peoples of this world. Faith in God's Kingdom has made of the Christians on the earth strangers and pilgrims[4] having their true citizenship in heaven.[5] It is already a great concession if on occasion mention is made of the value of a public state of law and order for Christians also.[6] There is no interest in political and social problems as such, i.e. beyond the bounds of the Christian Church, and the reality of the State is principally experienced in persecutions. Yet the result was not hostility to the State, but a criticism of it that was gradually to lose its purely negative character the longer it

[1] I Pet. 3.7-10. [2] I Pet. 4.7. [3] I Pet. 4.4f.

[4] Jas. 1.1; I Pet. 1.1; Heb. 11.13. On this subject see K. L. Schmidt, '*Israels Stellung zu den Fremdlingen und Beisassen und Israels Wissen um seine Fremdlings-und Beisassenschaft*', *Judaica* 1 (1945), 269-96.

[5] Phil. 3.20; Heb. 13.14; cf. K.L. Schmidt, *Die Polis in Kirche und Welt. Eine lexikogr. und exeget. Studie* (1939), especially pp. 21ff.; for the earlier and later history, cf. also Ant. Causse, '*De la Jérusalem terrestre à la Jérusalem celeste*', *Rev. d'Hist. et de Philos. relig.* 27 (1947), 12-36, and W. Bieder, *Ekklesia und Polis im Neuen Testament und in der alten Kirche*; also a discussion of Erik Peterson's idea of the Church (*Diss. Theol. Basel*, 1931).

[6] I Tim. 2.2. The idea itself is old and often witnessed since Jer. 29.7 and in Judaism. It links up with the later interpretation of I Thess. 2.6f. as referring to the Roman Empire, which restrains the Antichrist from breaking loose (*vide supra*, p. 299, note 2). Luke's Acts of the Apostles shows already a definite emphasis on the loyalty of Christians as something to be acknowledged by a just authority in spite of all misinterpretations (Acts 17.7f.); cf. especially the light in which Paul's conflicts with the public authorities appear: Acts 16.35ff., 22.25ff., 25.7ff., 18ff., 26.31ff., 28.18f.

continued. From the time of Justin onwards, Christians are conscious, not only of their religious, but also of their political, responsibilities in the world. By degrees they begin to open their minds to new questions in this quarter, which are at first raised for them by the complaints and accusations of pagans. Thereby a new chapter in the development is begun. The Church could not shut itself off from the new political and social tasks because new tasks were what it was called to undertake; but still less could it lose its identity among them because the New Testament remained as a safeguard, preventing it from finding the meaning of its existence in the kingdoms of the world instead of in the Kingdom of God.

5

NATION AND RACE

SURJIT SINGH

I *Introductory remarks*

If we try to discover what the Bible has to say about the modern problems of nation and race, our first observation must be that today these problems present themselves in quite a different form from anything which the Bible says on similar questions. It would not be helpful to try to apply Biblical passages direct to our present situation. Our first task is to state the difference between the two (or more) conceptions as clearly as possible.

After we have done so very briefly and tentatively, we must define the Biblical conception of our problem more in detail. This implies not only examining some outstanding passages in their proper context, but also—and this is, in fact, the most important task of the present study—seeing the question in the light of the whole Bible, the centre of which is the message of God's acts in Jesus Christ, our Lord. One could easily compile a lengthy document about the race problem at the different levels of Old Testament literature; for our purposes the result would be meagre, since it would not be relevant to our situation as Christians in the world today. Thus we are forced to take the Bible right from the beginning as a unit, which for us Christians it is. The writer of this paper finds himself in this respect in full accord with the statement of the Wadham College Conference, Oxford, 1949: 'that the unity of the Old and the New Testaments is not to be found in any naturalistic development, nor in any static identity, but in the ongoing redemptive activity of God in the history of one people, reaching its fulfilment in Christ. Accordingly it is of decisive importance for hermeneutical method to interpret the Old Testament in the light of the total revelation in the person of Jesus Christ, the Incarnate Word of God, from which arises the full Trinitarian faith of the Church' (*Guiding Principles for the Interpretation of the Bible*, Wadham College, Oxford, 1949, see p. 240ff., *supra*.).

If we are able to discover how the problem of nation and race is regarded in the Bible as a whole, we may, at the same time, recognise what solutions are offered within the context of Biblical thinking and terminology. And it is only after we have reached that stage of interpretation that we may try to formulate some suggestions as to the relevance of those answers to our modern problems in this field.

II *Differing aspects of our problem*

When we speak today about the problem of nation and race, we refer to the fact that many nations in our modern world have become aware of their particular character as distinct from that of other nations. When meeting people from other countries or continents (as a consequence of modern world communications), we immediately observe differences of language, race and colour. It is noteworthy that these are the things that strike us first. We do not start by noticing that other people whom we happen to meet have another *God*. It is, however, precisely this point which is central whenever these problems arise in the Bible. This difference in approach has many consequences, as we shall see.

In modern terminology nation and race are two entities which are closely interrelated. At first sight it may seem that the Bible was well acquainted with this problem. Was it not religious and racial nationalism that was introduced into Palestine after the Exile by Nehemiah and Ezra? Jews had married women from the surrounding peoples and Nehemiah forbids such marriages (Neh. 13.23, 27). Evidently not satisfied with this measure, Ezra took stronger action to enforce the divorce of foreign women and to cast off their children. He also instructed the community to separate themselves from foreigners (Ezra 10). But why were these rules established? Both statesmen did so because they believed this to be the only means of safeguarding the integrity of the Jewish religion. The main emphasis is laid on this religious aspect, whereas modern adherents of racialism think primarily in terms of biology. Many modern men believe that a 'pure race' is biologically stronger and that for that reason intermarriage should be forbidden. The Book of Ruth, on the other hand, indicates clearly that the marriage of a Moabite woman with the Israelite Boaz was not considered a danger, since she had said: 'Thy people shall be my people and thy God my God.'

Two conclusions are to be drawn from these observations: (*a*) the race problem, like the national question, is for the Bible primarily a religious question, and (*b*) though we have, in modern terminology, to make a distinction between nation and race, this is not necessary in regard to the Biblical terminology, since the biological aspect, which calls for such a distinction today, plays no real rôle in the Bible.

But one aspect of our theme has not yet received adequate consideration; we are confronted today not only with the problem of the difference between nations, but more particularly with *nationalism*. This means more than the mere recognition of differences between nations. It implies a certain admiration, if not adoration, of the qualities of one's own nation. Although love and admiration of one's own nation are only natural and may politically be justified to some extent, as long as an oppressed nation has to fight for its freedom (this being the origin of modern nationalism in all parts of the world), the exploitation of one nation by others can never be justified by pointing to any so-called superiority of one nation. In addition a nationalistic spirit between independent nations may endanger international co-operation or even result in wars between them.

But that is not all. For many of our fellow-men, nationalism has become a substitute for religion. As soon as such tendencies become apparent, the Christian is faced with serious questions. They are religious questions, like those in the Bible, and yet the context is very different, and so are the conclusions to be drawn. It is at this point that we have to begin our biblical research, properly speaking.

III *Nation and race as a religious problem in the Bible*

In the *Nunc dimittis* we give thanks with Simeon that Christ has come 'to be a light to lighten the Gentiles, and the glory of thy people Israel' (Luke 2.32), a phrase of which we find the source in the Old Testament (Isa. 42.6, 49.6). This passage contains, if read in the context of the whole Bible, the most important answer to our problem. It points to three facts: (*a*) there is, apparently, a difference between Gentiles and the people of Israel; (*b*) the latter are, in a special sense, called 'Thy [i.e. God's] people'; and (*c*) Christ came not only to be the light and the glory of God's chosen people, but also to lighten the Gentiles. In a sense, in him, the difference between the Gentiles and the people of Israel is overcome.

The difference between Israel and the Gentiles is recognised throughout the Bible by using different terms for them: there are few exceptions to the rule that the Greek word λαός refers to the people of Israel and is, consequently, normally used in the singular, whereas the Gentiles are τὰ ἔθνη—normally spoken of in the plural. This indicates that for the Biblical writers this distinction must have had great significance; it was understood to be more important than the differences between the other nations, though these are not overlooked.

What the New Testament thinks about the Gentiles is most typically expressed in a passage like Acts 14.16: God has 'in the generations gone by suffered all the nations to walk in their own ways'. God could have done something special with them—but he did not, though he is Creator of heaven and earth. But he selected one of the nations; this one he did not allow to go its own way. As it is put in Deut. 4.19f.: God allowed 'all the people under the whole heaven' to worship 'the sun, the moon and the stars, even all the host of heaven'. But to the people of Israel it was said: 'Yahweh has taken you, and brought you forth out of the iron furnace, out of Egypt, to be unto him a people of inheritance.'

That is the core of the matter for the Bible; there was this one nation, the people of Israel, whom the Almighty had chosen to be his own people. He had delivered them from Egypt. As the result of the experience of the Exodus, Israel became a nation. They were not chosen because they had any special characteristics which made them precious for him, but 'because he would keep the oath which he sware' unto their fathers (Deut. 7.8f.). In other words, God had chosen them of his own free will. That is why the question of nationalism and race for the people of Israel was a religious question in every respect. Since their very constitution as a nation was based upon a fundamentally religious experience, any dissension or compromise of their religion was bound to have a serious effect on their identity as a nation. This is borne out by their subsequent history.

This danger had already become apparent in the conquest and settlement of Canaan. The Israelites had much to learn from the inhabitants of the land. They were not yet acquainted with agricultural methods, nor with the arts and crafts of the town-dwellers. But the most important question was, for them, a religious one: the Baals of Canaan were the givers of natural gifts, including the fertility of the soil (Hos. 2.8; Deut. 12.2; I Kings 14.23). This secret the Israelites wanted to learn. There were two ways of learning. They could either add Baal-worship as a supplementary cult to Yahweh-worship, or they could add certain rites of Baal-worship to the worship of Yahweh. At the popular level, the result seems to have been that the Israelites paid homage to Baal and meant Yahweh. And gradually a religion of a largely Canaanite complexion became prevalent throughout the mixed population which constituted Israel during the period of the Monarchy. It was against this blurring of the lines between Yahweh-worship and Baal-worship that the prophets of the eighth and seventh centuries protested.

The Exile was another landmark in the life of Israel, and with it vanished the political independence of the Israelites. The Temple was in ruins and the political State was no more. But what happened to their religion? The people of the Northern Kingdom did not show any religious vitality, but the Babylonian exiles refused to be merged into the life of their neighbours of different religion and social *ethos*. The choice was a crucial one: either to be merged or to hold apart. They decided upon the latter course and thus became the custodians of the religion of Yahweh. It was in Babylon, among the exiles, that religious nationalism was born again. It was the exclusiveness and particularism of these exiles which saved Yahweh-worship from destruction and started a new life for it in Palestine. It was through this inspiration that the religious and moral rehabilitation of 'the people of the Land' took place.

We have already referred to the return from captivity as the next landmark in the chequered history of Israel, and especially to the 'racial laws' of Nehemiah and Ezra (see above, p. 311). And we have suggested that the main aspect here, too, was not racial hostility but the anxiety to preserve the religious inheritance of Israel. As Christians who are actually heirs to this inheritance, we should be able to appreciate even these measures in the right spirit: in the context of God's special promises to this nation—promises which have been fulfilled in Christ—they were justified. But this does not justify similar measures by other nations or modern governments.

Jesus was the Messiah of Israel. He was doubtless a member of this one chosen race. But he came not only to be the glory of this people, but also to be a light 'to lighten the Gentiles'. The New Testament clearly sets forth both aspects of his life and his significance for mankind. Jesus recognised the fact that he was a Jew and that he was descended from the house of David. But, as he points out very sharply, the decisive thing was not this earthly descent, but the fact that he was the Son of God, and as such was bound by the will of his Father during his sojourn in this world. When people came and told him that his relations had come to see him, he at once replied that his relatives are those who do the will of God (Matt. 12.46ff.). This does not mean that Jesus despised his earthly ties. But for him kith and kin were not the most important thing.

In one of the chapters which precede this story, it is recorded that 'he called unto him his twelve disciples . . .'; this is generally understood as the selection of the twelve representatives of the New Israel, the people which would acknowledge him as their Messiah (Matt. 10.1). The decisive question which had to be answered now was: Would this New Israel be confined to members of the old chosen people? John the Baptist had warned them: 'Begin not to say: we have Abraham to our father: for I say unto you, that God is able of these stones to raise up children unto Abraham' (Luke 3.8). In spite of this, we read in the so-called 'mission charge' that Jesus sent out his twelve disciples with instructions not to 'go into any way of the Gentiles' nor into the towns of the Samaritans. They were only to go 'to the lost sheep of the house of Israel' (Matt. 10.6). This saying seems to be in sharp contrast to other reports in the gospel which indicate the universal character of the Christian message.[1] Some scholars

[1] It is this observation which has led some scholars to the assumption that these words could not have been spoken by our Lord. Others have, however, pointed out that this would make it all the more difficult to explain who may have added these

explain this apparent contradiction by referring to the phrase in Isa. 49.6 indicated above as one of the Old Testament sources of Luke 2.32. Here it was assumed that the first task of the Messiah would be to 'raise up the tribe of Jacob'. It may well be that Jesus thought that Israel had to be converted first, before he could begin his work among the Gentiles.

The example of the Syro-Phoenician woman, however, serves as a connecting link and a transition point from the narrow to the universal application of the Gospel (Mark 7.25-29; see also Luke 4.23ff.). This healing of a Gentile in the midst of a special ministry to the Israelites is the exception which proves the rule: that the ministry is universal. This event provides the positive basis for the universal application of the message of salvation. This basis is faith, which is not the prerogative of any particular ethnic community.

The story of the Centurion (Matt. 8.5-13) and the parable of the Feast (Matt. 22.4-14; Luke 14.16-24) are both indications of another interpretation of Isa. 49.6. Since it is said there that 'it is too light a thing' for the servant of Yahweh 'to raise the tribes of the house of Israel' and that *therefore* he should be 'a light to the Gentiles', the implication which the early Church may have deduced from these words may have been that the Messiah would *not* succeed in converting the house of Israel, and that consequently the door was open to invite members of other nations to the table of the Lord. The account given in Acts of the preaching of the early missionaries, especially St. Paul, shows clearly that they followed the same practice, always preaching first in the synagogue and only afterwards to the 'heathen'.

Generally speaking, there can be no doubt that Jesus and his apostles very soon applied the many passages of the Old Testament to their situation, in which it is said that the Gentiles shall seek the Messiah (Isa. 11.10) to be ruled by him (Gen. 49.10; see also Isa. 62.12) and that the nations shall be 'gathered' unto Jerusalem (Jer. 3.17; see also Isa. 2.2-4; Mic. 4.1-3; Isa. 25.6f., 51.4f. and other passages). The New Testament shows, however, that the apostles at the beginning were not of one mind as to what the fulfilment of these promises would actually imply.

words to the gospel, since the early Christians very soon began to preach in Samaria (Acts 8) and other countries. The very difficulties which these words create for the exegete are an indication that in all probability they are authentic.

We need not repeat here the story of the struggle between Peter and Paul on the implications of this (Gal. 2 and Acts 15). We only note that here again the point was always a religious one (see Acts 10.14) and not racialism in the modern sense of the term. After the issue had been settled, Paul could say with authority that the Gentile Christians, who had been 'alienated from the commonwealth of Israel' are now 'made nigh in the blood of Christ. For he is our peace, who made both one, and brake down the middle wall of partition,' and that now they are 'no more strangers and sojourners, but fellow-citizens with the saints' (Eph. 2.11f., 19). And the same Christians are called 'an elect race, a royal priesthood, a holy nation, a people for God's own possession' (I Pet. 2.9)—all quotations from the Old Testament applied to those who believe in Christ, regardless of their ethnic origin. Here the 'racial' tension is definitely overcome. But now the question remains: what is the significance of this for the existing differences between nations and races on this earth?

V *God's chosen people and the variety of nations*

There can be no doubt that both the Old and the New Testaments recognise the differences which exist between the nations. The Old Testament presents a list of nations (Gen. 10) even before the story of the Tower of Babel is told (Gen. 11); the underlying assumption of the compiler must have been that this variety did exist even before the universal human language had been destroyed. The punishment which follows the erection of the tower consisted in the fact that from now on members of different nations could no longer understand each other. It is not the variety of nations as such which the Old Testament regards as a consequence of human sin. In any case, this seems to have been the view of those who preserved these old mythical stories in the Bible.

This is in harmony with Deut. 32.8 where it is stated that 'the Most High gave the nations their inheritance, when he separated the children of men' and 'set the bounds of the peoples'. This reflects already the view of the prophets and more especially of Deutero-Isaiah, for whom Yahweh is not only the God of Israel but also the Creator of heaven and earth (Isa. 40.25ff.); consequently, they say that God rules all the nations (Jer. 10.7). Their gods are nothing (Jer. 16.19f.) and the nations themselves are instruments of God's wrath (Hos. 10.10).

In the New Testament, the variety of nations is equally recognised. It may suffice to mention, in addition to Acts 14.16 quoted above, Acts 2.9f. which in fact contains a list of nations as they were known to the writer of this book, and Acts 17.26ff.: God has 'made of one every nation of men to dwell on all the face of the earth, having determined their appointed seasons, and the bounds of their habitation'. It does not matter, whether the 'one' referred to here is Adam or rather Noah: in any case both the existing variety and the common origin of all the nations is stated. Whatever interpretation may be placed on Rom. 5.12ff., here, too, the solidarity of mankind is an established fact. This assumption plays a considerable rôle in Paul's preaching, as the Epistle to the Romans clearly indicates. The Jews may have some advantage over the Gentiles, but in the last analysis both of them are sinners. All have sinned and fallen short of the glory of God. The works of law cannot help anybody. It is through faith in the Lord Jesus Christ that both Jews and Gentiles can be saved.

And yet the New Testament, like the Old, sticks to the basic difference between these nations and God's chosen people, though, as we have seen, the latter are no longer confined to the people of Israel 'according to the flesh'. To put it as sharply as possible: the Church could not claim to be the heir of Israel of old, it could not preach that Jesus was the Messiah of Israel and of the Gentiles, unless first of all it recognised the differences which exist between them. Through Christ sin is conquered and the wall of estrangement which separates man from God and from his fellow men is destroyed. Then is born the New Creation (II Cor. 5.17), the new race. But this was possible only as the fulfilment of God's promises to this one nation which he had chosen. The former distinction is now overcome, but that does not mean that God's promises have ceased to apply to the people of Israel. Paul, who more than any other apostle emphasises the missionary obligation towards the Gentiles, could say in equally strong terms: 'I could pray to be myself accursed from Christ for the sake of my brethren, my natural kinsfolk, who are Israelites, to whom belong the adoption by God, his glorious Presence, the Covenants, the giving of the Law, the Temple service, and the Promises. To them the patriarchs belong, and from them in respect of his human lineage came the Christ' (Rom 9.3-5). And though the Israelites are now 'enemies' of the

Gospel, 'the gifts and the calling of God are not repented of'. 'For God hath shut up all unto disobedience, that he might have mercy upon all' (Rom. 11.28-32).

From this we have to draw two conclusions. First, that the tension between Israel and the Gentiles is now overcome in the Church, the body of Christ: 'There can be neither Jew nor Greek, there can be neither bond nor free, there can be no male and female; for ye all are one man in Christ Jesus. And if ye are Christ's, then are ye Abraham's seed, heirs according to promise' (Gal. 3.28-29). In Christ, man is established in the original status of a person. He becomes the *imago Dei*. This is a fact already, here and now, during the earthly pilgrimage of the Church.

But to this we must immediately add our second conclusion: that these existing tensions and differences between Israel and the other nations will not ultimately be eliminated until the new age. Then the Israelites, who are now separated from the Church, will recognise Jesus Christ as their Messiah and will glorify his name, together with the Christian Gentiles. This is apparently the view of the New Testament or—we may say—the way in which the early Church understood the promises given in the Old Testament to God's chosen people.

According to this view, then, we may say that the Church represents, in regard to the racial question, the ἀρραβών (the 'earnest', II Cor. 1.22) of something which will find its ultimate fulfilment only in the *Eschaton*, in the age to come. This does not diminish the fact that these tensions are already overcome in the Church in a real way. It is by no means only a 'spiritual' unity which becomes manifest here, but rather something visible like Communion at the Lord's table and other manifestations of the life of the Church. But in so far as Christians are members of the existing world, the distinction between nations and races are not yet overcome, just as the distinction between 'male and female' still plays a real rôle in our lives. These distinctions do not wither away, but they are now seen in a new aspect. Their validity is limited. It is at this stage that we should try to discover the relevance of the Bible to the problems of nation and race in our time.

But before doing so, we may note that we have in all this not put the main emphasis on the fact that the Bible speaks of the common *origin* of all mankind. This we have stated as something taken for granted in both the Old and the New Testaments. There are certainly some important conclusions to be drawn from this idea, such as the doctrine of the *imago Dei* which is to be respected in every human being regardless of his race, colour or language. The Bible believes in this common origin of mankind. The parable of the Good Samaritan and the example of Jesus himself clearly show how we, as Christians, are to behave towards members of other families of the human race. We have reason not to overlook these aspects of the Bible's message.

These observations, however, do not lead us to the basic solution of our problem as seen in the Bible. The Bible affirms the solidarity of mankind in *sin*—not only in their common origin nor in any positive values which man certainly has as the image of God. This solidarity in sin overshadows, so to speak, the other solidarity which is not denied, but which, for this reason, can no longer provide an adequate solution. Fortunately, however, the Bible does not end with this negative aspect. It goes further: this very solidarity in sin provides at the same time the common possibility of being saved through Christ. This is the real eschatological solution of our problem, as promised in the Bible.

V *The relevance of this Biblical outlook to our modern problems*

We may now try to deduce from the above brief study some guiding principles for our contemporary Christian teaching.

We have been led to recognise the right of the people of Israel to stand for their national and racial integrity, since they were God's chosen people. This religious justification is the only one which can claim any validity—and even that is not the last word for us as Christians.[1] Consequently, it would be utterly senseless for any Christian to quote some passages of the Old Testament in order to justify similar measures in our own time for the protection of other races. This was the error of the 'German Christians', the Nazi Party in the German Churches after 1933. The events which followed (the introduction of the 'Aryan paragraph' into the Church, etc.) clearly indicate what serious consequences the wrong application of Biblical texts may have for the Church. Nowhere does the Bible subscribe to

[1] Space does not permit us to treat here the modern 'Jewish' problem as such; this would call for an extensive study on the relation between Israel and the Church.

the myth of the 'pure race' which was, and still is, in the minds of some people in our century.

If we want to consider this problem in a Biblical way, we must start from the opposite angle. Since the gods of the nations are 'no gods' (Jer. 16.20), the nations have no religious justification for any racial discrimination; it can result in nothing but estrangement from the chosen people, which is now the New Israel, the Church. Christians cannot, therefore, support any active policy along these lines. At this point the relevance of the Biblical message stands out rather clearly: though modern nationalism is in a sense secular (not being closely related to the gods of different national religions), it is nevertheless a religious phenomenon in that for many people it is a substitute for religion. It should not be difficult for Christians in the twentieth century to expose this religious aspect of modern nationalism, as the prophets did in Israel.

The second reason for our refusal to join the ranks of nationalism is that Christ is the end of the Law (Rom. 10.4). It is significant that Paul says this when discussing the racial problem as he had to face it. This means that we, as Christians in the twentieth century, are unable to support anything which, from our point of view, is a reversion to a pre-Christian attitude.

So much had to be said against misapplication of the Biblical doctrine to our modern problems. But what can we say on the positive side? We try to answer this question by arranging our material according to the 'Trinitarian faith of the Church' (see above, p. 311).

The Biblical belief in God, the Creator of heaven and earth, leads us to recognise the common origin of all men. In every man we have to honour the image of God. We have constantly to oppose in ourselves, and wherever we meet it, that human pride and that false sense of superiority which prevent us from loving our fellow men as children of God.

The same belief leads us also to recognise the God-given variety between members of different race and colour. We should not be ashamed of these differences, but should thank God for making us as we are. Let us enjoy the gifts he has given and use them in the best possible way, for the benefit of mankind, to which each nation can make its special contribution.

The Biblical faith in Jesus Christ, however, leads us further than that: here we have to manifest a fellowship which really transcends all these barriers. It is absolutely impossible for the Church to recognise within its fellowship any discrimination between members of different races.[1] Through the gift of God, we have a foretaste of that reality here and now. But when we look at the world of today, the ideal of the new race seems to be far off, and it is our solemn Christian duty so to live in the situation in which God has placed us that the false superiority and pride of race and national origin may be burnt out like dross from our own lives and from the nations of this world, so that exploitation of man by man shall remain no more. This means that we have to act here and now in the light of eternity. Our endeavours may not always bear visible fruit, but, if God is with us, we can never be defeated in the long perspective of history.

This attitude is made possible for Christians because we believe, in the words of the third article of the creed, in the life everlasting. There the differences between nations and races will no longer exist. This conviction has two consequences, as we have already stated: first, we are free to face in a realistic way the difficulties of this world, and in this case especially the tensions which constantly arise between nations. They have their root in the abuse of God's gifts. We must do our utmost to overcome them, and in doing so we take part in Christ's work of reconciliation. We know at the same time that the ultimate victory will not be ours, but God's alone. We are looking forward to the day when 'a great multitude, which no man can number, out of every nation and all tribes and peoples and tongues' will stand 'before the throne and before the Lamb' to praise him (Rev. 7.9)—God the Father, the Son and the Holy Ghost.

[1] In a comment which the author received from South Africa, it was pointed out that there distinctions are made between the phrases 'discrimination between' (= seeing and acknowledging the differences between persons and groups) and 'discrimination against' (= including a detrimental attitude towards a person or group). If this terminology were commonly accepted, the above sentence should read: '. . . discrimination against . . .'. It seems, however, that in most parts of the world the term 'discrimination' has always a detrimental connotation.

6

CIVILISATION

by

STEPHEN NEILL

It would be possible to answer the question implied in the title by a simple negative: the Bible has no doctrine of civilisation. It is true that the whole Biblical revelation moves *sub specie aeternitatis*, and that its essential concern is with man as the object of God's grace, and of the redemption in Christ that is foreshadowed in the Old Testament and accomplished in the New. It is not surprising therefore that terms such as *civilisation* and its correlatives are nowhere to be found in the text of Scripture.

But such a negative solution would be hasty and ill-founded. Though the Bible deals with man's life in the ample perspectives of eternity, it still does deal with man's life on this earth, in great detail and particularity, just because the eternal reference gives such significance to the events and the actions of time. The life of man is lived in societies—the family, the clan, the tribe, the nation. The Bible recognises that these are part of God's providential ordering of the life of man, and that he himself takes the initiative in the institution of them. The general Biblical view is briefly and poetically set forth in Ps. 107.35:

He turneth a wilderness into a pool of water,
  And a dry land into watersprings.
And there he maketh the hungry to dwell,
  That they may prepare a city of habitation;
And sow fields and plant vineyards,
  And get them fruits of increase.

This is a theme in support of which it would be otiose to quote a large number of references.

It has to be observed that the word *civilisation* can be used in two distinct senses, and for the sake of clarity it is essential to keep these clearly separate. The word may refer to the material basis of human life, the means by which man keeps himself in existence, that mastery of man over nature by which the human race is sustained, but which differs in method and versatility rather than generically from the similar methods by which the animal kingdom keeps itself alive. On the other hand, civilisation is more ordinarily and correctly used of the organisation of man in society. Civilised man is by definition *civis*, a citizen of no mean city, or of a country which claims his pride and his allegiance. Into it enter such ethical elements as justice, co-operation, mutual respect, responsibility, the subordination of the interests of the individual to those of the whole, and so forth. Though there are faint foreshadowings of these in the animal kingdom, on their higher and conscious level they are generally reckoned as distinctively human, and on the development of them as against the animal instincts, which remain extremely strong in man, depends the growth of societies which are designated as civilised, in contrast to those savage orders of existence, in which man has not far outgrown the law of the herd or the pack.

There is yet a third aspect of civilisation, for which it would be convenient if the word *culture* could be exclusively reserved. Civilisation is concerned with the ordering of man's life, culture with its adornment. The archaeological revelation of the ancient world has made plain to us the astonishing rapidity with which man, once he has begun to become civilised, develops skills in the attainment of comfort and the production of beauty. Art, music, learning—these things add grace to life; and man's life falls short of its highest unless it is characterised by both strength and grace, order and beauty. Each one of the higher civilisations has in a measure been marked by both. It may be maintained that when a civilisation begins to aim too much at one of these at the expense of the other, the beginning of its period of downfall has been reached.

On civilisation, in the first of these senses, the Bible has a good deal to say. The first chapter of Genesis is not by any means the earliest of the written Scriptures; but its place at the beginning of the Canon in both the Hebrew and the Greek Scriptures corresponds to its importance as the key to the significance of the

Biblical revelation. No other Old Testament passage can compare with it in the depth and range of its influence on the New Testament. Here the purpose of God's creation of man is set forth as follows (verse 28): 'And God blessed them; and God said unto them, Be fruitful and multiply and replenish the earth, and subdue it; and have dominion over the fish of the sea, and the fowl of the air, and over every living thing that moveth upon the earth.' To the Biblical writer, man is unquestionably the crown of Creation, the last and highest of created things, made mysteriously in the image of God. In the more primitive account of Creation in Gen. 2, we read (verse 15): 'And the Lord God took the man, and put him into the garden of Eden to keep it and to dress it.' This doctrine of the supremacy of man over all other created things is uncompromisingly repeated in a document which, unfortunately, we have no means of dating with any precision, Ps. 8: 'Thou madest him to have dominion over the works of thy hands; thou hast put all things under his feet. All sheep and oxen, yea, and the beasts of the field; the fowl of the air and the fishes of the sea, whatsoever passeth through the paths of the seas' (verses 6-8). The writer to the Hebrews, in his inspired comment on this passage (2.5-18), starting, as he always does, with the assumption that every divine promise must sooner or later have its fulfilment, sees the fulfilment of this promise in Christ the firstborn, in whom for the first time the sovereignty of man over the Creation is realised, and in whom alone mankind can find the perfection of its divinely-appointed destiny.

But this sovereignty is not unconditional. It is always subject to the absolute overlordship of God, to whom in the end Christ himself will hand over the Kingdom, that God may be all in all (I Cor. 15.24-28). Man is put into the garden to tend it and to keep it, in obedience to the specific command of God, neither to destroy it, nor to exploit it selfishly for his own ends. There seems to be an echo of this sense of responsibility in the remarkable saying of Job: 'If my land cry out against me, and the furrows thereof weep together. . . . Let thistles grow instead of wheat, and cockle instead of barley' (31.38-40).[1]

When we turn to civilisation in its other sense, the life of man

[1] It is possible that the reference here is to the unjust acquisition of land by oppression, and not to the wrong use of land legitimately owned; this passage, therefore, can be quoted only with a certain measure of reserve.

in ordered societies, we shall do best to begin at the end of the Biblical revelation and to look backward. The theme of the Apocalypse is the conflict between two cities, Jerusalem and Babylon. It is clear that the heavenly Jerusalem, though fulfilling that which the earthly Jerusalem was intended to signify, is not simply a city, in the ordinary sense of the term. Its descent out of heaven from God is a divine consummation; it is to be the centre of the whole life of humanity, into which the kings bring their glory, 'and they shall bring the glory and the honour of the nations into it' (21.24, 26). Here are found again the tree of life, the living streams, the perennial fertility of the garden of Eden. But there is no regression to the state of primitive innocence; the city represents the ordered and developed life of man, as God intends it to be and as lived in the perpetual presence of God.

Babylon is portrayed in such a way as to make it almost certain that the seer of the Apocalypse identified the Babylon of his day with imperial and persecuting Rome, and that his readers could scarcely have understood his meaning in any other way. But it is equally true that the significance of this great Babylon, the fall of which ushers in the final consummation of the judgments of God and the marriage of the Lamb, cannot be exhausted by any one human city. What the seer is depicting with prophetic power is the whole wickedness of man, arrayed in rebellion against God and against the company of his saints. All Old Testament prophecy is summed up in this final manifestation of prophetic inspiration. To the prophets of old, one city after another, Nineveh, Babylon, Tyre, had presented itself as the incarnation of rebellion. Echoes of all these denunciations, and especially of those in Ezekiel, are found in the Apocalypse. The seer adds a new and unexpected note by adding to the list the city of David itself, the earthly Jerusalem, the great city 'which spiritually is called Sodom and Egypt, where also their Lord was crucified' (11.8). This identification warns us that we must proceed cautiously when we attempt to interpret the writer's meaning.

Looking back to the Old Testament, we shall find not one view of civilisation and of the purpose of God in it, but a continuing tension between differing views, one of which gradually establishes itself as dominant.

There is first the nostalgic view, which looks back to the

period before Israel entered Canaan as the golden age of divine revelation and of fellowship between God and his people. Here is heard again the perpetual conflict between the desert and the sown. The desert is the place of stark simplicity, where man is face to face, without shelter and without defence, with his Creator. Here are no cities, with their extreme inequalities of wealth and poverty, with their corruptions, and with that veil of obscurity between man and the Word of God by which he is to live.

Hosea, Micah and Jeremiah all at times express this attitude: 'I remember for thee the love of thine espousals; how thou wentest after me in the wilderness, in a land that was not sown. Israel was holiness unto the Lord, the first fruits of his increase' (Jer. 2.2, 3). The faithfulness that God has sought in vain in Israel is found in the Rechabites, that nomad tribe that, within the limits of the Holy Land, had kept to the old ways from which Israel had departed: 'Rechab our father commanded us, saying, 'Ye shall drink no wine, neither ye nor your sons for ever; neither shall ye build house, nor sow seed, nor plant vineyard, nor have any; but all your days ye shall dwell in tents; that ye may live many days in the land wherein ye sojourn. And we have obeyed the voice of Jonadab the son of Rechab our father in all that he charged us, to drink no wine all our days, we, our wives, our sons, nor our daughters, nor to build houses for us to dwell in: neither have we vineyard nor field nor seed: but we have dwelt in tents, and have obeyed and done according to all that Jonadab our father commanded us' (35.6-10).

The prophets do not suggest that Israel should literally return to the conditions of desert life. Hosea the farmer recognises that corn and wine and oil, the typical gifts of the sown land, come from God, and not as Israel wantonly supposed from the Baalim. Yet even in Hosea the recovery of Israel is even here spoken of in terms of return to the wilderness, the place of betrothal and espousal, of the direct meeting of man with God: 'I will allure her, and bring her into the wilderness, and speak comfortably unto her. . . . I will even betroth thee unto me in faithfulness: and thou shalt know the Lord' (2.14, 20). The same theme is taken up, centuries later, in words so closely resembling those of Hosea as to suggest direct quotation, by Ezekiel: 'And I will bring you into the wilderness of the peoples, and there will I plead with you face to face. Like as I pleaded with your fathers in the wilderness of the land of Egypt, so will I plead with you, saith the Lord God' (20.35, 36).

There is a strain in the early narratives of Genesis, identified by some as a separate source, in which every development of human civilisation seems to be viewed under the pessimistic conviction that 'cultural progress is accompanied by increased wickedness and unhappiness' (R. H. Pfeiffer, *Introduction to the Old Testament*, p. 163, quoted by Reinhold Niebuhr, *Faith and History*, p. 123). Even if this cannot be sustained in detail, it is scarcely possible to miss the significance of 4.16-24. Here the discovery of musical instruments is attributed to the Cainite tradition of rebellion against God. This is followed by the discovery of metal working (the mention of iron, to which, in the age of transition between the bronze and iron ages a very strong taboo attached, is specially to be noted), and this in turn is followed by an outbreak of lawless violence, and the gleeful song of vengeance of the Cainite murderer. Wine is not here the gift of God, 'wine that maketh glad the heart of man', but a baleful discovery that results in the shameful fall of Noah. And finally the building of cities, again a Cainite discovery, initiated by the great rebel Nimrod, leads to the culminating rebellion against God, the building of the tower of Babel, and the consequent dispersion of the human race.

This pessimistic attitude towards human culture and development is to be noted in many contexts in the Bible. It seems as though every attempt of man to raise himself above primitive poverty, or to depart from the pastoral stage of development, is condemned as in itself sinful and rebellious. But this pessimistic attitude is rightly judged in relation to the Canaanite culture in which, and in its baleful influence on Israel, the earlier prophets discovered the great enemy of the faith. We may anticipate here a later conclusion, that the developed Biblical view is that all these things, while they may be an occasion for rebellion against God, and create the possibility of new and hitherto unimagined sin, are yet part of the purpose of God for man. Man by art and craft and discovery is fulfilling his destiny of sovereignty over the created works of God.

At the other extreme stands the narrative of the reign of Solomon. In his time, the Kingdom of Judah reached its apogee of splendour. The compiler of the Books of Kings, using earlier

Solomonic sources, lets himself go in panegyric upon the unsurpassed magnificence of the great king in all his glory. It was not only that Solomon made silver to be in Jerusalem as stones. In the story of the visit of the Queen of Sheba, the language rises to the hieratic pitch of hymnody; this is a genuinely messianic picture; the king is the divine king, sitting in the state appropriate to the anointed of God himself. And when, at the dedication of the Temple, Solomon turns and blesses the people, we have at least a hint of reversion to that earlier time in which king and priest were one (as they may have been even in the time of David: II Sam. 8.18) and a foreshadowing of the much later messianic passage, in which Zechariah sees the man who 'shall be a priest upon his throne' (Zech. 6.13).

It is clear that to this particular writer the reign of Solomon is the golden age. But this is not the only, or in the end the specific, Biblical judgment on the situation. It is remarkable that outside the Books of Kings and Chronicles, Solomon is hardly ever referred to again in the Hebrew Scriptures. A notable exception is the title of the 72nd Psalm, an unauthoritative note of uncertain date. Our Lord's two references, 'I say unto you that Solomon in all his glory was not arrayed like one of these' and 'a greater than Solomon is here', are hardly complimentary. The compiler of the Books of Kings, with characteristic Biblical honesty, shows us the reason for this later silence. The reign of Solomon was, in fact, the moment of greatest peril in the whole history of Israel. To finance his great works and to support his extravagant court, Solomon was in process of introducing a heavy burden of taxation, the *corvée*, forced labour, and all the other practices of the great ethnic civilisations which built the pyramids and destroyed the souls of men. The obstinacy of Rehoboam and the democratic revolt of Jeroboam brought the experiment to an end.[1]

The Solomonic tyranny was marked by three features which could not but bring upon it the condemnation of the prophetic writer: idolatry, profligacy and heartlessness. It is very remarkable that these three correspond exactly to the stages in the process of

[1] The democratic revolt resulted only in a temporary amelioration of the situation. No other King attained to the glory of Solomon, but many of them, notably such strong monarchs as Jeroboam II, did their best to reintroduce the evil features of his administration. This was the source of many of the charges of the prophets against them. (See Jer. 13-19.)

human demoralisation, when man turns away from God, as they are analysed by St. Paul in his description of the heathen world in Rom. 1. This is not a description of primitive man, but of civilised man, when in his arrogance he believes himself to be wise and turns to his own conceits. Idolatry, whether literal or the mammon-worship of a professedly Christian civilisation, disturbs the relationship of man with God. This brings about at once a disturbance in the relationship of man with himself; the resulting disharmony brings into gross and excessive prominence the sexual elements: so beautiful in their due proportion and in their proper use, so ghastly in the manifold perversions which man has succeeded in inventing for himself. And, finally, man at war with himself turns to war with his neighbours; the bases of true society in pity, trustworthiness and honour are broken down, and mankind becomes what Thomas Hobbes in his bitterness also imagined it to be—a wilderness of wild animals, in which only a limited self-interest prevents the mutual extermination of all by all.

Paul is summing up the gravamen of all the charges made by the prophets against the non-Jewish civilisations, and against the people of Israel and Judah, whenever they refused 'the waters of Shiloah that go softly, and cast longing looks on the waters of the River, strong and many' (Isa. 8.6, 7).

The most remarkable expression of this Biblical condemnation of civilisation gone astray is the judgment on Tyre in Ezek. 26-28. This unsurpassed piece of noble rhetoric must be read as a whole, and no quotation can give any idea of the total effect on the mind of the reader of the whole long passage. Certain features only can be mentioned here. The lament over Tyre is cast in terms of that pre-cosmic fall of which faint hints are heard elsewhere in the Old Testament. Tyre, the representative of the wisdom, the brilliance and the wealth of man, is seen first in the glory which God gave him, and which God intended him to have. 'Thou wast in Eden the garden of God; every precious stone was thy covering . . . the workmanship of thy tabrets and of thy pipes was in thee; in the day that thou wast created they were prepared.' Here music and ornament are not part of sinful man's aggression upon the world; they are seen as splendour given by God and decreed for his favourite in the Creation. Then comes the fall: 'Thou hast said, I am a god, I sit in the seat of God in the midst of the seas. . . . Because thou hast set thine heart as the heart of God. . . . Wilt thou yet say before him that slayeth thee, I am God? but thou art man and not God, in the hand of him that woundeth thee.' The rhetoric of this passage supplies much of the material for the corresponding dirge over Jerusalem in the Apocalypse.

What we are considering here is a remarkable doctrine of the fall of civilisation. Civilisation itself is not sinful, any more than Adam was sinful before he sinned. But like Adam, civilisation was tempted, sinned, and was cast out of the garden of Eden. In each case, the nature of the temptation and of the fall was the same, the desire to be as God, to be independent of God and free from his control. So man comes to worship himself. And, because they worshipped and served the creature rather than the Creator, who is blessed for ever (Rom. 1.25), civilisation, that power which makes man free from the peril of nature and the jungle, and sets him up on the pinnacle of sovereignty over the world, becomes instead the poison of Nessus raging through his veins, and driving him forward in a fury of self-destruction, in which God has no need to let loose the avenger, since man himself, as we see him today, and the more civilised he becomes in rebellion against God, will do all that could be needed in the way of clearing the earth of the burden of himself.

In the Bible, we are confronted with the remarkable phenomenon of the fall of civilisations. Each in turn is so strong that its dominion seems to be permanently assured; yet each in turn goes down rather by reason of its own inner weakness than of the strength of its adversary. The prophetic judgment suggests that it is just the illusion of permanence that makes destruction inevitable. The virgin daughter of Babylon claims that 'I shall be a lady for ever: so that thou didst not lay these things to thy heart, neither didst remember the latter end thereof' (Isa. 47.7). The sense of unshaken security makes impossible self-criticism and repentance; and since what needs to be done is not done in time, the unrepentant civilisation is swept away.

It is just this impermanence of all human institutions that gives the reason for the separateness of the people of God. They become a nation among the nations, but they are never to be a nation like the other nations. This theme is heard, for example, in the prophecy of Balaam: 'Lo, it is a people that dwell alone, and shall not be reckoned among the nations' (Num. 23.9). The vocation of Israel is to trust in the Most High; but such trust excludes that false security which is its own undoing. If Israel, old or new, allows itself to become identified with a human civilisation and to share its illusions, it too will accomplish its own destruction. If it is faithful to its God, then, by not seeking the false permanence of human power, it alone will abide until the end of time, when all other nations and civilisations are destroyed.

We turn to the third Biblical approach. As against the Solomonic, we have the Davidic kingdom.

Here again, our definitive Biblical picture emerges only gradually. There were in fact three traditions in Israel concerning the kingship. One was that the kingship was from the start a mistake, and constituted a permanent act of rebellion against Jehovah. The second was that the kingship was divinely ordained, but that Saul was the true king, and David merely a usurper. The third, which so strongly prevailed as to overlay the others, was that David was the chosen of the Lord. 'I have found David the son of Jesse, a man after my heart, who shall do all my will' (Acts 13.22). But the later has not concealed all traces of the earlier tradition, such as the intriguing note in II Sam. 21.19 that it was not really David who slew Goliath of Gath, but Elhanan, the son of Jaare-oregim the Beth-lehemite.

Later Israelite tradition, looking back, no doubt greatly idealised the figure of David. There was much in his character that was far from admirable;[1] and the tragic decline of his later years takes away from the grandeur of the earlier. But it is not difficult to see why the people dwelt with such affection on the memory of the shepherd boy who became a king, the successful leader in war and peace, the sweet-singer of Israel, the man who on the whole gave peace and justice and prosperity.

It is only by working through the references with a concordance that one becomes aware of the extent to which the Davidic picture has imposed itself on the whole subsequent history and on the writings of the prophets. Whenever the present is dark, men look forward to the return of the Davidic era. Sometimes it is the restoration of the Davidic kingdom that is

[1] Is not Queen Victoria alleged to have remarked on one occasion: 'King David is not a person with whom I should wish to associate'?

the object of hope; sometimes, it is David himself who is mysteriously to appear. 'And I will set up one shepherd over them, and he shall feed them, even my servant David; he shall feed them and shall be their shepherd. And I the Lord will be their God, and my servant David prince among them; I the Lord have spoken it' (Ezek. 34.23-24). 'He that is feeble among them at that day shall be as David; and the house of David shall be as God, as the angel of the Lord before them' (Zech. 12.8ff.).

It is difficult to exhaust the significance of the Davidic idea in Biblical theology. A few leading ideas only can be drawn out here.

In the first place, the reign of David finally constituted the people of Israel as a nation. It is notoriously difficult to define the word nation. Yet it appears in Scripture from Genesis to Revelation as expressing part of God's providential ordering of the history of men. Israel is primarily a people, the people of God. But in order that Israel may accomplish its destiny among the nations, it must itself become one of them, it must as it were become incarnate in the world of nations.

The constant use of the word *shepherd* demands notice, especially because of its messianic significance in the New Testament. God is the shepherd of his people. The king is also the shepherd, but only in so far as he is consciously under the rule of God, and himself exercising authority as God exercises it, and with a constant sense of his accountability to God. The evil king is an evil (or as Zechariah remarkably has it) an idol shepherd. When Jesus claims that he is the good shepherd, the picture in the mind of his hearers would not be that of the stained glass window, of a kindly gentleman with a beard, carrying a lamb, and leading a small collection of miscellaneous quadrupeds. They would see David, the great shepherd under God. They could not mistake the immense messianic significance of the claim. The use of the term in its Davidic connection makes clear the nature of authority as Biblically conceived. The task of the shepherd is to care for the sheep, personally, watchfully, and without regard to the cost to himself, to gather together that which was scattered in the cloudy and dark day. His business is to combine justice with mercy, to give security from outside enemies and to be the focus of that inner loyalty, which makes men dwell at peace with their neighbours. It can hardly be denied that such authority, however exercised, provided that it be exercised under the guiding hand of God, is the condition and the guarantee for any civilisation worthy of the name.

The Davidic ideal is not one of golden splendour. It can do without the six hundred three score and six talents of gold, which came annually into the revenues of Solomon, and the significance of which must leap immediately to the eye of the typologist. The Davidic pattern is not that of regression to the primitive, or contentment with the nomad life of the wilderness. It looks to the quiet, steady prosperity of a people settled on their own land. When the tabernacle of David that is fallen is raised up, Israel 'shall plant vineyards and drink the wine thereof; they shall also make gardens and eat the fruit of them' (Amos. 9.11-15). 'Ye shall call every man his neighbour under the vine and under the fig tree' (Zech. 3.10). In such a society, there are no extremes of wealth and poverty. Every man has a stake, though it may be a small one, in the welfare of the whole. There is a sense of the dignity of each man, and of brotherliness within the unity of the nation.

It is time to turn back from the Old Testament to the New. We shall not expect to find much on our subject either in the Gospels or the Epistles, partly because of the special subjects with which they deal, partly because of the political conditions under which the Jews and the Early Christians lived.

The Roman domination had made impossible the political development of the subject peoples. The great outburst of literary production which had accompanied the rise and fall of the Hebrew monarchies had spent itself, and died away in feverish apocalypse or tedious scribal annotation. Jesus and the apostles were not concerned with the problems of culture, as these were later to be faced by the Christian Fathers in Alexandria and Rome and the other great centres of dying classical antiquity. There is no indication that Paul in Athens was concerned with anything but his own specifically religious message.

But to say that civilisation and culture are not in the first rank of New Testament interests is not to say that nothing can be learned here of the Biblical judgment on them.

Our Lord grew up at a meeting point of cultures. Galilee was in the main a country of peasant proprietors, of villages and small towns, freer in its religious practices than Jerusalem and more affected by Gentile infiltration. But nearby were Tiberias and the other Greek cities of the plain. There were to be seen the characteristic monuments of Hellenic genius, and the characteristic forms of Hellenic life, now past their first greatness and rendered a little febrile by the excitable atmosphere of the Levant. There is no evidence that Jesus ever entered any of these cities, but it is scarcely possible that he can have been unaware of the type of civilisation represented in them. The number of his visits to Jerusalem is still a matter of controversy; many scholars would now give greater weight than was till recently customary to the Johannine tradition of a number of visits. If so, there was yet a third world of civilisation in which Jesus was at home.

In the Gospels, all the ordinary processes of civilised life are referred to and taken for granted; we meet the merchant, the banker, the rich ruler, the judge, the tax-collector, no less than the farmer, the fisherman and the housewife. There is no suggestion that any of these avocations is to be condemned in itself. Each is recognised as an occupation having its opportunities and its perils, and the vices of men no less than their virtues are taken as the occasion for the parabolic teaching.

There are two points, however, at which the teaching of Jesus does stand in conflict with the ordinary run of human thought.

First, there is a steady and radical condemnation of materialism. Materialism does not mean the use of material things. Jesus himself had been a carpenter. It does mean a distortion of the divinely appointed order of things in which the material is always the servant of the true purposes of man as a child of God. The rich man is condemned, not because he is rich, but because it is so hard for him to manifest that single-hearted trust in God without which one cannot enter into the Kingdom of God. The whole teaching can be summed up in one saying: 'A man's life consisteth not in the abundance of that which he possesseth.'

Secondly, the narrative moves throughout in the dimension of eschatological tension. This is manifest, whatever school of eschatological interpretation is followed. Hence the intense concentration on the religious issue. The important thing is that the Kingdom of God is here, revealed in the person of Jesus, and everything turns on the attitude men take to him. Everything else is secondary. All these other things pass away, but on a decision taken in time rest consequences in the eternal sphere.

All human orderings and civilisations will pass away, and therefore, whatever their importance in their own sphere, they pass on to the second plane of interest, when the eschatological plane, the descent of the eternal on time, is apprehended.

This eschatological tension is present throughout the New Testament, and has left its mark on the Petrine and Johannine writings no less than on the Pauline, though the emphasis is more marked in some of the Pauline epistles. If the *Parousia* may happen at any moment, and the reign of God take the place of the futile and self-contradictory sovereignties of men, who can take over-seriously the affairs of this world, who will sell his soul to abuse the world, instead of using it as God intended?

But this eschatological attitude must not be exaggerated. Christians understood very well that, until the *Parousia*, they must stand upon their watch, and fulfil their ordinary duty as colonies of heaven in an earthly country. One of the most fascinating subjects of speculation is the finances of the early Church. How was it that Paul was always able to take passage by ship, sometimes with a number of companions, as the conditions of the Church needed? Who supplied the necessary money? Presumably, Lydia and others like her. Paul never hesitated to use the circumstances of rapid and easy travel provided by the Roman Empire. He took the responsibility for the collection and transmission of a large sum of money in coin of the realm, for the relief of the poor saints at Jerusalem.

But never is the New Testament Christian allowed to forget that these are at best interim arrangements, which will all perish in the using.

This eschatological tension is the perfect safeguard against the characteristic vice of civilisations, the belief in their own eternity and perfection. From this comes the pride that breeds blindness and inadaptability, and through these God works out his own sentence of judgment on each in turn. To the Christian, each civilisation can be no more than the concretion of a number of human ideas and purposes, permitted by God to exist as a framework for the working out of his purposes on earth, but dependent on him at every moment for its continuance, and doomed to disappearance as soon as it has fulfilled its providentially appointed work.

But the recognition of the *interim* character of civilisation, the failure of each, even of Israel, to *be* the Kingdom of God, must not lead us too far in a negative direction. To say that a civilisation cannot be the expression of the justice of God is not at all the same as to say that it cannot be the expression of justice at all. There is a wide distance between man's justice and the justice of God. But there is also a wide distance between man's justice and the injustice of man. There is no ground in the New Testament on which to maintain the most pessimistic of the Old Testament traditions, that every form of human progress is in itself sin against God. The New Testament has its own pessimism; it recognises the certainty of ever-renewed rebellion of man against God. But it leaves a place for the reality of human achievement as not only the occasion of rebellion, but also as the means by which the purposes of God can be fulfilled. The Roman Emperor, like the king of Assyria of old, has his power and authority from God, and bears responsibility under him, even though he himself may not know the source from which his authority comes.

We may now sum up our results:

1. There is no Biblical doctrine of civilisation as such.

2. But the main stream of Biblical tradition recognises man as the crown of creation, and that dominion over nature, of which civilisation is the expression, as part of the purpose of God for him.

3. But the Biblical ideal for man is social; it is that of fellowship in a society which resembles a flock under a shepherd, where justice is tempered by mercy, and man lives in neighbourliness with others of his kind. The city of David, the prototype of the new Jerusalem, is the Biblical expression of this type of society.

4. Every advance in civilisation may be the occasion of sin, when it turns to self-confidence instead of dependence on God; the marks of this pride are idolatry, sensuality and heartlessness.

5. Every civilisation which yields to these temptations repeats the fall of Adam, and brings about its own destruction.

6. This will be repeated until the end, when the final judgment of God, set forth symbolically in the judgment on Babylon in the Apocalypse, will be fulfilled, followed by the bringing in of his Kingdom.

7. The eschatological tension is heightened in the New Testament. All civilisation is seen, in the light of the *Parousia*, as no more than a temporary adjustment.

8. Christians in this world are always to live in a state of eschatological tension, remembering that their citizenship is in heaven; but this does not debar them from loyalty to their temporary home in an earthly State, nor from carrying on the ordinary avocations of civilised society, since these too have their place in the purpose of God, and point forward to the divine fulfilment.

9. But they are called on always to beware of the sin of avarice, the love of mammon, which makes the service of God impossible, and blinds the eyes of man to his true nature and destiny as the child of God and the heir of an eternal redemption.

INDEXES

A. PROPER NAMES

Addleshaw, G. W. O., 123
Alt, A., 237n.
Ambrose, St., 19
Aquinas, St. Thomas, 118, 279
Augustine, St., 23, 121, 165, 171, 175f., 279

Barth, K., 88, 148, 150ff.
Bartsch, H. W., 135
Baur, F. C., 133
Bieder, W., 308n.
Bonhoeffer, D., 152
Bultmann, R., 146f., 300n.

Calvin, J., 31, 92, 96, 113, 188n., 279, 287, 289n.
Causse, A., 308n.
Chillingworth, W., 113
Clement, St. (Alex.), 298n.
Cosin, J., 113
Cullmann, O., 149, 299n.

Dante, 284
David, 332ff.
Dibelius, M., 294n., 297n., 299n.
Dodd, C. H., 46, 145, 148, 191, 195

Eck, O., 294n.
Eichrodt, W., 136
Ellul, J., 290n.

Forsyth, P. T., 149

Gandhi, M., 62n., 75
Grant, R., 237n.

Hilary, St., 163
Hooker, R., 113f., 117, 120
Hoskyns, Sir E., 133f.

Irenaeus, St., 20, 297n., 298n.

Justin Martyr, St., 177, 297f., 308

Kaehler, M., 149
Kierkegaard, S., 149
Kittel, G., 208, 300n.
Koch, H., 294n.
Kümmel, W. G., 295n.

Laud, W., 115, 119
Lietzmann, H., 307n.
Locke, J., 124
Luther, M., 102, 105, 108, 113, 226, 279, 286

Marcion, 137, 194
More, P. E., 121
Moses, 135

Nygren, A., 153f.

Origen, 18, 211, 298n.

Peterson, E., 308n.
Pfeiffer, R. H., 328

Quervain, A. de, 85, 152, 288n.

Radhakrishnan, S., 64
Rowley, H. H., 144

Salin, E., 295n.
Sarma, D. S., 66, 68
Schlatter, A., 149
Schmidt, K. L., 308n.
Schniewind, J., 149
Schweitzer, A., 132, 297n.
Schweitzer, W., 294n., 300n.
Solomon, 328ff.
Stauffer, E., 294n., 296n., 299n.

Tertullian, 164, 299n., 301n.

Whitgift, J., 117
Wilder, A., 137
Williams, A. T. P., 114f.
Windisch, H., 295n.

B. SUBJECTS

ALLEGORISM, 137, 175, 227
Anglican divines, 112ff.
Authority, 31ff., 56, 59, 70f., 77, 82, 89, 101ff., 160, etc.

BAPTISM, 189f.
Bhagavad-gita, 64
Bhakti, 68
Biblicism, 110f., 141f., 149. See also Fundamentalism, Scripturism.
Bossey, Conference at, 10, 150f., 153, 197, 230
Buddhism, 60

CHURCH AND BIBLE, 17ff., 89ff., 138ff., 157, 163f., 177, 216f., 278
Commandments, Ten. See Decalogue.
Covenant, 135f., 157ff., 164, 166ff., 176f., 202ff., 259f.
Creation, 100ff., 120. See also Orders.
Criticism, Biblical, 131ff.

DECALOGUE, 27, 135, 158, 178, 237, 287ff.
Deism, 109
Democracy, 109
Dialectical theology, 147f.

ELECTION, 92, 135, 151f., 166f., 201, 313
Entmythologisierung, 146f., 223ff.
Eschatology, 41f., 132, 145, 179f., 201, 306, 319f., 335f.

Eucharist, 159, 191, 206
Existentialism, 146f., 214, 223ff.

FUNDAMENTALISM, 141, 149, 178, 279. See also Biblicism, Scripturism.

GOSPEL AND LAW, 92ff., 105ff., 152f., 207

Heilsgeschichte, 19, 83, 136, 145, 159ff., 206, 242, 258
Hinduism, 59ff.
Historicism, 149
History, 65, 69f., 144ff., 161f., 165f., 192ff., 198, 220ff.
Humanism, 73, 120f.
Humanitarianism, 271

Imago Dei, 120, 319f., 325
Incarnation, 66, 122, 166
Inspiration, 71, 141, 172
Intercession, 253

JAINISM, 60
Justice, 78, 275ff.
Justification, 282f.

KARMA, 65ff., 75
Kerygma, 133, 135, 142, 146f., 158

LAW. See Decalogue, Gospel, Moral law, Natural law.

Lex Talionis, 261
Liberalism, 122, 132, 142ff., 223, 277

Man, Doctrine of, 260ff.
Marriage, 230ff.
Moral law, 103ff., 116ff.
Myth, 146f., 223ff.

Nation, 179, 310ff., 333
Nationalism, 312, 321
Natural law, 29, 36f., 46f., 67, 88f., 108ff., 116, 120, 161, 238, 281
Natural theology, 18, 25, 73, 88, 100ff.
Noachic Covenant, 122, 161, 248, 290

Obedience, 47f., 124f., 300ff.
Orders (of Creation), 86f.
Orthodoxy, 17ff.

Paganism, 107
Pelagianism, 121
Preaching, 249, 252f.
Property, 257ff.
Puritans, 114, 117ff.

Race, 310ff.
Reason, 87f., 103ff., 116f., 120
Revelation, 17ff., 68ff., 98ff.
Roman Catholicism, 11, 138f.

Sabbath, 288
Sabbatarianism, 118
Science, 48, 87, 98, 110
Scripturism, 117. See Fundamentalism.
Secularism, 73, 107, 124ff.
Sermon on the Mount, 26f.
Shepherd, 333f.
Spirit. See *Testimonium Spiritus*.
State, 87, 92, 107ff., 116, 293ff.
Syncretism, 61

Testimonium Spiritus, 21, 38ff., 57f., 89ff., 108ff., 119, 160, 169f., 212, 220
Time, 168, 192ff., 198f., 224f.
Toleration, 62, 115
Tradition, 20ff., 37f., 55ff., 108ff., 118, 140, 221
Trinitarian interpretation, 228
Trinity, The, 83
Typology, 136, 146, 168, 175f., 179, 227

Unity of Bible, 198ff.
Upanishads, 60ff.
Usury, 265

Vedas, 59ff.

Wadham Conference, Oxford, 10, 151, 240ff.
World (*Kosmos*), 247ff.
Witness of the Spirit, see *Testimonium Spiritus*.

Zetten, Conference at, 10

C. SCRIPTURAL REFERENCES

Gen.
1–11...200
1.1...165
1.27...231
1.28...325
2.15...325
2.24...231
4.16–24...328
6.1–8...206
10...317
11...317
12.1–3...200
12.3...255
15.6...210
49.10...316

Exod.
2.23–25...261
19.3–6...200
20–23...260
20.1–17...215
20.14...121
21.2ff....263
21.18–19...237
21.24...35
21.20...264
21.26ff....264
22.18...121
22.20–23...262
22.25...265
23.4...35
23.4–5...235
23.11...264
23.6...262
34.26...35

Lev.
19...235
19.17–18...235
19.34...235
19.36...195
24.19f....261
25...255
25.23...264
25.36f....265
25.47ff....263

Num.
11.23...192
23.9...332
24.17...185

Deut.
1–11...264
1.9, 16, 18...193
2.34...193
3.4, 8, 12, 18, 21, 23...
193
4.14...193
4.19f....313
5.5...193
6.4...237
7.8f....313
9.19...193
10.1, 8...193
10.12–13...237
10.19...235
12.2...314
15.4...28
15.7–11...53
15,12ff....263
17.17...231
18.22...188
19.21...261
21.15–17...230
22.1–4...53
23.16f....264
23.20...265
23.25...286
24.1...35
24.1–4...231
24.10–13...53
24.17–18...53
30.15...186
31.10...264
32.8...317

Judg.
8.22–23...203

I Sam.
8.4–9...203
13.8–14...255

II Sam.
8.18...329
21.19...332

I Kings
14.23...314
22.23...41

II Chron.
26.16–21...255

Job
31...215
31.38–40...325

Ezra
10...311

Neh.
13.23, 27...311

Ps.
8.6-8...325
69.14...192
72...329
82.1–5...215

Ps.—cont.
99.4...283
107.35...323
130...202

Prov.
25.21...235

Isa.
1.27...215
2.2–4...316
5.1–8...209
6.5...203
8.6, 7...330
8.16–18...202
9.6–7...203
10...255
10.1–4...267
11.1f....189
11.10...316
18.7...194
25.6f....316
28.9–13...217
40.10...204
40.18...225
40.25ff....317
40.28–31...202
42.6...312
44.26f....192
47.7...331
49.6...312, 316
49.8...192
51.4f....316
55.3–5...202
56.1...215
62.12...316

Jer.
1.4...194
2.2, 3...327
3.17...316
5.4–5...215
7.1–15...240
8.8...267
10.7...317
11...239
13–19...329
16.19...317
16.20...321
22...270
22.3...215
22.15f....121
28...39
29.7...308
31.31–34...202, 206
35.6–10...327

Ezek.
20.35, 36...328
26–28...330
34.23–24...333

Hos.
2.8...314
2.12–23...202
2.14, 20...327
6.6...215, 270
10.10...317

Joel
2.11ff....187

Amos
1–2...50
3.2...215
3.7...159
5.14–15...237
5.21–24...270
5.24...215
9.11–15...334

Mic.
3.1, 5, 6...215
4.1–3...316
6.8...88, 215, 237

Hab.
2.1ff....202

Zech.
3.10...334
6.13...329
12.8...333
14.20...256

Mal.
2.14–15...231

Matt.
1.1...168
3.2...295
3.15...286
4.4...85
4.17...295
5...26
5.13–16...91
5.14–16...250
5.16...252
5.17ff....286
5.17–19...283
5.17–48...25
5.22...285, 286
5.32...232, 285
5.34ff....285, 286
5.38...35
5.39ff....34
5.46, 47...47
6.14–34...54
6.19...285
6.33...85
7.12...89
7.21...25
7.24...25, 27
8.4...286
8.15–13...316
10.1...315
10.6...315
11.13...174
11.27...83
12.1ff....286
12.46ff....315
15.6...286
17.24f....285, 286
17.24–27...298
18.10...285, 286
18.15ff....285
19.6, 9...285
19.9....232
19.18ff....286
22.4–14...316
22.15–22...296
22.21...28, 285
22.39...251

Matt.—cont.
22.40...27, 89
25...96
25.10...286
25.31ff....96
25.32...161
25.35f....25, 285, 286
26.55ff....286
27.11ff....286
28.18–20...83
28.19...249
28.20...27

Mark
1.15...182, 205, 295
1.21...286
7.25–29...316
10...232
10.2–9...231
10.2–12...230
10.5–9...35
10.17–31...103
10.25...34
12.13–17...296
12.31...234, 236
13.10...253
16.15...249

Luke
2.32...312, 316
2.51...286
3.8...315
4.21...82, 184, 189
4.23ff....316
6.15...295
6.20...34
6.35...34
9.31...189
10.16...91, 249
10.25–37...103, 289
10.21...17
12.13ff....298
12.33ff....285
12.50...190
12.57...161
13.1f....298
13.16...48
13.28–30...234
14.16–24...316
17.10...27
18.31...82
20.20–26...296
22.20...202
22.38...295
24.25–27...82
24.27...181
44...82

John
1.1–14...182, 206
1.4...252
1.17...168
1.9...167
1.11ff....187
1.14...66, 170
1.17...168, 206
1.18...83, 166
3.8...160
3.16...186, 248
3.20...251
4.22...167
5.39...82, 181
5.46...82
7.39...160
9.3...17
13.[illegible]...183
13.34...27
14.1[illegible], 21...27
14.17...247
14.21[illegible]...284
15.10, 12...27
15.18ff...247
15.24...247
15.26...[illegible]3
16.13...21, 39, 91
16.14...83
16.33...247, 254
17.14...247
17.21...252
18.29–19.16...299
18.36...234
19.11...285
20.30–31...164
20.31...181

Acts
1.8...91
1.13...295
2.9f....318
2.32...169
2.36...188
2.38...187
4...286
4.19...254
4.34...28
5...286
5.1–11...54
5.29...254
7...286
8...316
8.35...184
10.14...317
10.35f....89
10.43...82
13.3...253
13.22...332
14.16...313, 318
14.15–17...102
14.17...18, 37
15...317
16.27ff....286
16.35ff....308
16.37...254
17.4ff....286
17.7f....308
17.22–23...102
17.24...18
17.26ff....318
17.27...30
20.17ff....286
21.27ff....286
22.25ff....308
22.26...286
22.38...295
25.7ff., 18ff....308
25.11...254
26.31ff....308
28.18f....308

Rom.
1...330
1.18–2.16...102
1.19...17

Rom.—cont.
1.19–20...99
1.20...18, 102
1.21...99
1.25...331
2.14...18, 29
2.14ff....89, 121
2.14–16...102
2.15...37
3.2...164
3.3...163
3.21...17
3.28...283
3.31...283
5.12ff....318
5.19...182
6.5ff....190
8...40
8.2...27
8.19ff....202
8.38ff....255
9.3–5...318
10.4...321
11.28–32...319
12.2...27, 109, 248
12.7–21...285
13.1...29
13.1ff....28, 285
13.1–7...102, 253, 299, 302
13.8...234
13.10...27
16.25...17
16.26...184

I Cor.
1.21...18
2.10...17
2.16...143
3.21...37
3.23...37
5.11...285
6.1...285
6.1–4...303
6.12...302
6.15...230
7.10...285
7.20f....285
7.21–24...42
7.25...285
7.31...96, 248
10.23...302
11.3f....285
11.25...202
12.3...83, 170
13.12...19
14.8...44
14.24–25...252
15.3ff....133, 181, 184
15.3–4...82
15.24–28...95, 325
15.41...24
15.51...42

II Cor.
1.20...191
1.22...319
3.4–9...202
3.6...21, 52
3.12–16...202
3.14...206
4...206
4.6...206
4.7...21
5.10...96
5.17...96, 318

Gal.
1.16...17
2...317
3.8-9...200
3.22–4.7...106
3.24...26, 286
3.28...42
3.28–29...319
4.3...255
4.4...166, 182
4.4–10...102
4.9...255
4.24...175
5.6...24
5.14...234, 236
5.19f....285
6.2...27
6.10...251
6.14...248

Eph.
2.11f....317
2.14...200
2.19...317
3.8...254
4.32...195
5, 6...251, 286
5.8–14...250
5.13...251
5.22–33...230
6.17...95
6.18f....253

Phil.
2.8...182
2.15...248, 249
3.20...308
4.8...103

Col.
1.15...83
1.19...19
2.8...255
2.9...83, 169
2.15ff....255
2.20...248, 255
3, 4...251
3.8f....286
3.11...200
4.3...253

I Thess.
2.6f....308
4.9–12...103
4.11...302
5.12f....302
5.14...302
5.17ff....97

II Thess.
2.6f....299
3.1...253
3.11...302

I Tim.
2.1ff....96
2.1–4...305
2.2...28, 308

I Tim.—cont.
2.2–4...248, 253
2.8f....285
3.15...171
3.16...133
6.1...286
6.16...167

II Tim.
3.15...184
3.16...24

Tit.
2...286
3.1...305

Heb.
1.1...18, 19, 165, 187
1.1ff....82
1.1–3...206
1.3...194
2.5–18...325
2.8f....83
6.5...96
8.8–12...202
9.15...202
10.16–18...202
11.1...170
11.7...251
11.13...308
13...286
13.14...308

Jas.
1.1...308
1.18...248
22.20...165
1.25...27
1.27...248
2.8...27, 236
4.4...248
5.1–8...42

I Pet.
1.1...308
1.11...252
1.14...248
1.20...183
2...286
2.5...201
2.9...249, 317
2.11f....307
2.11–17...253
2.12...47, 250, 252
2.13–16...307
2.13f....43
2.17f....307
2.18...286
2.21–25...133
3.7–10...308
3.13ff....307
3.15...252, 253
4.1–3...248
4.4f....308
4.7...308
4.11...43
4.12...307
4.15...307
4.16...307
4.17...306
5.5...286
5.9...306
5.13...307

II Pet.
3.8...42
3.9...96, 253
21–25...133

I John
1.3...169
2.15...247
2.17...96
3...169
3.2...42
4.2f....83
5.3...27
5.4f....247
5.19...96

II John
5, 6...27

Rev.
3.2...289
5.9...201
7.9...322
7.13–17...254
11.8...326
13...304
13.10...304
14.12...304
14.13...25
17.9ff....304
18.24...304
19.6–9...191
20.13...25
21.5...168
21.22...255
21.24, 26...326
22.4–5...19
22.14...25